LEMOX BOOK COMPANY
1305 N. 9th Ave.
Phone 433-8283
and 1012 Underwood
Behind PJC Student Center

Name ....
Subject No. ....
Subject ....
Price 1260

A Study Guide to THE MONEY PUZZLE: The World of Macroeconomics

A Study Guide to THE MONEY PUZZLE: The World of Macroeconomics

Joanna S. Cruse
Associate Professor of Economics

Miami-Dade Community College

HARPER & ROW, PUBLISHERS, New York
Cambridge, Philadelphia, San Francisco,
London, Mexico City, São Paulo, Sydney

Author:	Joanna S. Cruse
	Miami-Dade Community College
Sponsoring Editor:	John Greenman
	Harper & Row, Publishers, Inc.
Project Editor:	Virginia Gentle/Richard Janaro
	Miami-Dade Community College
Development Editor:	Tom Cunningham/Steven Ullmann
	Miami-Dade Community College/
	University of Miami
Project Consultant:	Roger L. Miller
	University of Miami
Designer:	Cynthia Elliott
	Miami-Dade Community College
Compositor:	TriStar Graphics
Printer and Binder:	The Murray Printing Company
Cover:	Concept and Design by Infield
	D'Astolfo Associates, Direction by
	Lorraine Mullaney, Harper & Row,
	Publishers, Inc.

A Study Guide to THE MONEY PUZZLE: The World of Macroeconomics

Copyright © 1983 by Miami-Dade Community College

All rights reserved. Printed in the United States of America.
No part of this book may be used or reproduced in any manner
whatsoever without written permission, except in the case of
brief quotations embodied in critical articles and reviews.
For information address Harper & Row, Publishers, Inc.,
10 East 53rd Street, New York, NY 10022.

ISBN 0-06-43273-X

CONTENTS

PUTTING THE PUZZLE TOGETHER .... *vii*
    FOREWORD .... *ix*
    INTRODUCTION: ECONOMICS AND YOU .... *xi*
    USING YOUR STUDY GUIDE .... *xiii*
    HOW TO SUCCEED IN THIS COURSE .... *xxi*
    FINAL WORDS OF ADVICE .... *xxiii*
    PLAYBILL: THE MONEY PUZZLE .... *xxv*
    CHART OF VIDEO PROGRAMS/TEXTBOOK CHAPTER .... *xxviii*

UNIT I   THE MONEY PUZZLE: AN INTRODUCTION 1
    PART ONE 5
    PART TWO 16

UNIT II   HOW OUR AMERICAN ECONOMY WORKS 33
    PART ONE 36
    PART TWO 51

UNIT III   GOVERNMENT: HOW IT SPENDS 77
    PART ONE 80
    PART TWO 95

UNIT IV   GOVERNMENT: HOW IT TAXES 101
    PART ONE AND PART TWO 105

UNIT V   BUSINESS ORGANIZATONS AND FLUCTUATIONS 125
    PART ONE 128
    PART TWO 150

UNIT VI   THE CIRCULAR FLOW AND NATIONAL INCOME ACCOUNTING 161
    PART ONE 165
    PART TWO 182

UNIT VII   ANALYZING THE MACROECONOMY 203
    PART ONE 206
    PART TWO 226

UNIT VIII	**INCOME AND EMPLOYMENT DETERMINATION**	255
	PART ONE	258
	PART TWO	264
UNIT IX	**GOVERNMENT FISCAL POLICY**	289
	PART ONE AND PART TWO	292
UNIT X	**INFLATION**	307
	PART ONE AND PART TWO	310
UNIT XI	**MONEY AND BANKING**	335
	PART ONE	338
	PART TWO	355
UNIT XII	**THE DILEMMA AND POLICIES OF STABILIZATION**	391
	PART ONE	394
	PART TWO	408
UNIT XIII	**GROWTH AND DEVELOPMENT**	429
	PART ONE	432
	PART TWO	448
UNIT XIV	**INTERNATIONAL TRADE**	467
	PART ONE AND PART TWO	470
UNIT XV	**INTERNATIONAL FINANCES**	495
	PART ONE AND PART TWO	499
	OPTIONAL	517
WHAT BUSINESSPERSONS READ		535

PUTTING THE PUZZLE TOGETHER

FOREWORD

A TV course in economics! A set of televised lectures about economics? No. Rather, a set of 30-minute situation dramas that explore the present and revisit the past world of economics. They will touch on issues and pose problems about real, live, everyday concerns while some of the major questions in economics will be addressed.

All right, you've signed up for the economics course on TV. You've bought your books, checked the times of the video airing and I hope, have committed blocks of your time for study in the next few months. If you're like most of us, you're looking forward to the semester a little excited and, possibly, a little worried too. However, to assist you, in addition to the two video programs each week, a textbook and your *Study Guide* will help serve as your mentors.

This *Study Guide* is an organizer. It structures your studying and attempts to bring cohesion to what will sometimes be confusing. The *Guide* tells you what to do, how to do it, which points to take seriously and which points can be lightly touched on. In short, it serves some of the functions of a "best friend"—someone who is sympathetic and also isn't afraid to nudge you when it's necessary.

The video touches on the central ideas. The suggested textbook, *Economics Today: The Macro View,* 4th edition, by Roger L. Miller, goes deeply into the issues, and the *Study Guide* ties the video and text concepts together. Most of us need a pacesetter; the *Guide* sets the pace. How much it helps you depends on what you make of it.

Students learn in different ways. What works for one doesn't work for all. Not everyone learns most efficiently by listening to lectures. A video course gives considerable excitement and flavor to the economic concepts and issues, and the video portion of this course does just that; it provides you glimpses into human situations that will set you thinking. It will not be and is not meant to be a set of filmed lectures. Because it isn't, you're going to be on your own much more than you would be in a conventional college lecture course.

Before and after you view the television programs, you should study the text and work on the *Study Guide* questions.

If you do, you will find the television component meaningful as well as entertaining. When you look back through the assigned text and *Study Guide* material in the light of the video, you will discover new methods of thinking that will stay with you from now on.

You are both a student and teacher. The *Study Guide* tells you how much to teach yourself. Although you have a television set instead of a professor's formal lectures, you are not alone. In addition to your text, this *Guide* will help you, prompt you, cajole you and keep you current with the course material. If it is friendly, it is at the same time rigorous. The *Guide* is meant to be fun as well as a mentor. I enjoyed writing it and believe you will enjoy working with it.

Many thanks to the many people who helped; you know who you are. Special thanks to Tom, Stan, Cindy, John, Dave, Julie, Steve, Barbara C., Barbara D., Gloria, Doug, Sam, Roland, Laura, Virginia, Meg, Jeanne, and Lyn.

Joanna S. Cruse
Miami, Florida
October, 1982

INTRODUCTION

ECONOMICS AND YOU

Despite the fact that it too can be fun, economics is demanding. Don't underestimate the concentration and time that will be required. Games and lighthearted talk are sometimes part of the *Study Guide* package, but that is because economics can be fun as well as exciting, not because it is simple.

Economists sometimes use familiar terms in new ways. Economists use their terms and concepts to create models of how the parts of the economy fit together, move and respond to change. Economists look at the amount of unemployment, or consumer spending, or government spending. They measure these variables and track how they behave in their models of the economy. Economists consider the effect of policies such as higher taxes or less government spending. They suggest the benefits and also the costs of decisions involving these policies.

Why bother to learn about economics? Where are you in the picture? Read the following collection of definitions of economics. Look closely: you are in every definition.

- Economics is the study of how to use what is available in order to get what we want.

- Economics is the study of scarcity and choice, showing how available resources can be used to attain desired goals.

- Economics is the study of how society chooses, and the consequences of choice.

- Economics is the study of the allocation of scarce resources among alternative and competing ends.

We all have to choose. Governments, groups, firms and individuals all make choices. The modern social science of economics results from the need for choice. Whenever we have the opportunity to make a choice between alternatives, we have economics. In some definitions of economics the concept of choice appears, but economics goes beyond just the study of choice. It also looks into the way the economy is structured, the framework it is built on.

Economics inquires into the *need* for choices, the effects on those who choose and the consequences for everyone else in the society. You are, thus, always in the picture. You are affected by national economic policy decision. And since, ultimately, the policy decisions are made by your own senators and congresspersons, you are involved. You are in this economy, right along with the economists who are studying it. Short of opting out into a life of go-it-alone solitude, there is no way you cannot be in the picture. You are part of the whole set of processes you will be studying this semester.

So let's take some hard looks at the way our economic world works. Maybe the more you understand the workings, the better you can make it work for you. But let's not worry about the world for awhile. Let's look at the way this *Study Guide* works. The rest of this section will be used to explain the structure of the *Study Guide,* give instructions for its use and include a few hints on studying.

USING YOUR STUDY GUIDE

Your *Study Guide* is divided into 15 basic units and each unit covers two video programs. The units are divided into two parts to correspond to the two video programs. Each unit will direct you to which of the textbook chapters must be studied for each program and provides you with viewing preparation and follow-up. Each has the number and title of the video program so that it will be easy to keep track of where you should be. A grid corresponding the video programs and textbook chapters is at the end of this unit.

There are some variations in the structure of the units, but all are organized in a similar fashion. First, there is a list of the sections and then some explanations.

UNIT IN A NUTSHELL

UNIT OBJECTIVES

UNIT ASSIGNMENTS FOR PARTS ONE AND TWO

FILM SUMMARY

NEW TERMS USED

CHAPTER HIGHLIGHTS

FILL-IN REVIEW

PROBLEMS, PROBLEMS, PROBLEMS . . .

    TRUE-FALSE

    MATCH-UP

    MULTIPLE CHOICE

ABOVE AND BEYOND

SPECIAL INSTRUCTIONS, REMINDER, HINT

ECONOWORD PUZZLE

UNIT IN A NUTSHELL

This is meant to be an overview of the unit. It will describe briefly, in a paragraph or two, the subject of the unit. As the name implies, this section is short and sweet.

UNIT OBJECTIVES

An objective is a specific performance that is expected of you when you complete each section. "Unit Objectives" lists the objectives on which you will be tested and tells you which text chapter to use in studying for them. You should be pretty clear about them before working the "Problems, Problems, Problems..." section.

UNIT ASSIGNMENTS FOR PARTS ONE AND TWO

Units are divided into two parts, corresponding to two video programs. This section reminds you what to study for each part of the unit.

FILM SUMMARY

You should scan this section before and read it carefully after each program. Many of the programs are stories behind which economic principles are at work. These segments highlight principles for you. Keep in mind that you may have the chance to view the program only once at home. You will benefit more from your viewing if you are prepared to recognize some of what you see. Actually, a lot will be quite confusing at first. This is a new method for thinking about issues; and old ways must be disturbed before new methods can be learned, hence the confusion. Being open to new learning isn't easy, but it is part of the process of getting a worthwhile education.

NEW TERMS USED

In the first few video programs, there are a number of new terms introduced. These have been defined when it has been appropriate to do so. In the later programs, there are no new terms for which identifications have been given. In the "Chapter Highlights" of the *Study Guide* many of the text terms will be defined.

CHAPTER HIGHLIGHTS

This is a step-by-step outline of the text material. This useful tool for organizing your study offers a good way to prepare yourself for the exams.

FILL-IN REVIEW

This is a narrative review of the text material you have studied, with the spaces left for you to test and clarify your understanding. The "Fill-In Review" can be a self-teaching summary that is useful to reinforce what you have already learned and alert you to what you may still need to study. The correct answers to the fill-ins are printed beside the narrative. Use a file card or folded piece of paper to cover the answer until you have completed your own. You may find it helpful to write the fill-ins on another sheet of paper instead of in your *Guide*.

PROBLEMS, PROBLEMS, PROBLEMS...

Within this section there are three sets of typical exam-like questions, True-False, Match-Up, and Multiple Choice. The answers are given at the end of each unit.

ABOVE AND BEYOND

These are projects that are above and beyond the call of duty but which can prove to be fun as well as enlightening. They have been selected to provide you with practice in using common concepts in everyday life. Some chapters will include "Above and Beyond" and some won't.

HINT, SPECIAL INSTRUCTIONS, REMINDER

These hints can appear anywhere. They offer the kind of advice your classroom professor might give.

HINT

When you are completing the study questions, write your answers on a separate piece of paper rather than in the *Guide*. After you answer each one, you can check immediately whether you are correct; or you can go through an entire set and then compare your answers with the correct ones. In either case, the whole point of the exercise is lost if you don't work them out yourself. No one is judging how you do; since you are competing against yourself, you can't lose. You can win understanding, and that is the name of the game. You are using a modern teaching device that really works.

If you have written your answers on a separate page, you will be able to use the *Guide* again to review for exams. It is probably a good idea to do this even in the Fill-In-Review section, which has spaces provided for your answers. You are learning a method of analysis that is necessary to understand issues confronted in this course, a method that will also be applicable to political, economic, and personal situations.

You will want to learn the method and way of thinking, not to memorize a set of answers. You aren't expected to "know everything"; you need to learn fundamentals and then apply them to analyzing problems. In this way you will acquire your own tools for understanding many of the real issues that underlie much political and economic discussion.

ECONOWORD PUZZLE

Occasionally, puzzles appear at the end of units and you may enjoy trying to solve them. The puzzles are built from terms in the section. The words in the Econoword Puzzle in this unit are filled in; however, you will have an opportunity to test your skills for all of the other puzzles appearing in the *Guide*. For each of the others, answers are at the end of that unit.

ECONOWORD PUZZLE SAMPLE

The one on the facing page is all worked out for you. All of the others you will do yourself. This one is to remind you of the ways to succeed in an economics course; the words for the others will come straight out of the lesson. Have fun with the puzzles; they were fun to make.

CLUES ACROSS

2. remove the top layer
4. apply your mind to acquire knowledge
6. to be sure of
7. originate something new
10. labor
11. understand printed matter
12. accomplish
16. commit to memory
17. choose
19. to work toward a goal
21. dispute
22. keep account of time units spent
23. carry on a disagreement

CLUES DOWN

1. mix your thoughts up a little, like mixing up a stew
2. put parts together to make up a whole
3. dig down to get out the valuable material below
5. have fun
8. work without interruption
9. sum things up
13. put things together in order
14. look ahead briefly
15. move ahead
18. urge on, or push
20. modern, "cool" expression for enjoy (travel)

HOW TO SUCCEED IN THIS COURSE

When all is said and done, your immediate question is probably: "What is going to happen to me, and how difficult is it all going to be?" Remember, I haven't promised you that economics is always easy to grasp. However, thousands and thousands of students all over the world manage to succeed in economics courses, and those who do, study.

First, your attitude toward the subject is vital. Convince yourself that economics is worth the time you devote to it. People with a working understanding of the macroeconomy find themselves hearing more when they listen, seeing more when they read the daily news, and understanding more of what is happening or likely to happen. Economics is an important way of interpreting what goes on.

Second, remind yourself often that this is a telecourse, and that you must watch video programs twice a week for thirty minutes each time. You need to be faithful to the viewing requirements. The 30 programs which make up the course are not televised lectures restating what is in the text. It is assumed that you can and will keep up with the reading and studying. The programs are quite different. Described as "situation drama," they tell stories of real people in human situations who are affected by the economic problems of our complex, changing society.

A number of your exam questions will be based on these 30 programs. You are responsible for a knowledge of the general story line and what it has to do with the subject studied during that week. This guide will give you important tips and pave the way for a successful, in-depth viewing of each program.

Third, you must be extremely faithful to the text reading assignments. Study them as they come, preferably more than once. The ideal approach is to do the assignment once over lightly before you watch the television program and then go back to the studying with more insight.

Complete the "Problems, Problems, Problems..." sections of your *Study Guide.* Allow yourself plenty of time, since many of the concepts are difficult at first. You'll find that completing the text will become your base support as you go through the course, because it is always there and can always be consulted.

Fourth, this *Guide* will help you not only as you view but as you read. It will help to distill and, in some cases, simplify the material; as well as offer examples to help you understand the concepts as they appear in the text.

FINAL WORDS OF ADVICE

Everyone is possessed of knowledge. What I have done here is to share with you what has proved useful for other students studying economics for the first time.

1. Try out new concepts or terms in your everyday conversation. That's how we all learn, by trying things out. Not expertly at first; no one is expert at anything at first. So everyone present doesn't understand the words you are using? That's O.K., *you* will. The more you use them, the more you will understand.

2. Keep up. Forge ahead a little. Don't wait to study until you get a lovely, long stretch of time with nothing else pressing to fill it. Finding this much time almost never happens; and if it did, you probably would rather go to the beach or clean out a closet. Study whenever you can. Frequent, rather short, concentrated periods of study can result in more understanding than long, tiring hours.

3. Enjoy as much as possible. Play with the words a little. Talk back to the video or this *Study Guide* ... disagree or agree: there may be controversial material.

4. Just hang in there. Plan to organize some of your thinking around new concepts that may seem strange, at first. Plan to work hard at this new way of thinking and be prepared to tolerate quite a bit of confusion. Set yourself the goal of successfully completing the course.

Let's get started.

PLAYBILL: THE MONEY PUZZLE

by Richard P. Janaro

ABOUT THE TELEVISION SERIES

The Money Puzzle: The World of Macroeconomics is unlike other telecourse in that, instead of learning the subject from a series of filmed lectures or documentaries, you will be learning from thirty episodes in the lives of Thomas and Karen Weldon; you will be learning from a story. But then again, why not? If economics is to be meaningful and relevant, we should be able to embody the principles and issues in situations with which we can identify. Television programs that merely restate what is already in your textbook is not the purpose. Television education can offer a dimension to each subject that explains it in a different and more interesting way.

ABOUT THE MAIN CHARACTERS

THOMAS WELDON is a 35-year-old junior executive with the Dynamics Corporation, a large conglomerate with many subsidiaries. Thomas performs a variety of functions for the company, but mainly he is an investment counselor. In order to advance, he is taking courses in economics at the local university. Thus, he is learning the subject along with you, but because of his job, he has an opportunity to apply what he is learning almost immediately. Sometimes, however, Thomas becomes confused about the money puzzle, falling into certain misunderstandings. When this happens, the misunderstanding is cleared up before the end of the program.

KAREN WELDON, Thomas's wife, works as the producer of a public service television program. Like her husband, Karen is concerned about the money puzzle, because whatever happens to the economy can affect her home and her job. A contemporary woman, Karen sometimes has to remind Thomas about the equality of the sexes. (But he's learning *that* as well as economics!)

LARRY DUTWEILER is the President of the Dynamics Corporation, having inherited the position from his father. Some of the teaching in the series comes as a consequence of Larry's points of view, especially his explanations of the role played by business in our economy. But since there is an ongoing debate over the degree of government intervention used in the economy, there are different viewpoints expressed. When Larry advocates limited government intervention, he is not speaking for the course, but rather expressing opinions of some members of society.

ELYSE MERCADO, a receptionist for the Dynamics Corporation, is also enrolled in economics courses, hoping to advance in the company. As Thomas's classmate, she exchanges ideas with him about the meaning of this or that concept, and on occasion even disputes his interpretation. Their debates play an important part in the series.

VERNON STERLING is President of the Arbordale Savings and Loan Association and brings to the series a knowledge of banking as a major factor in our economy. Sterling, in fact, is knowledgeable about almost every phase, is Thomas's friend and mentor, and serves as a voice of economic experience.

DR. HENRY BECK is a professor of economics at the university where Thomas is studying, teaches one of Thomas's courses, and also serves as a source of economic authority. In certain matters of controversy, however, such as the debate between the Keynesians and the monetarists, Dr. Beck tends to support the Keynesian viewpoint.

DR. STEPHANIE TEAL, a colleague of Henry Beck in the university's economics department, is another voice of authority. Her position is that of a monetarist, who believe that the quantity of money in the economy is of major importance.

WALTER BILLINGS, a stockbroker, is another friend and advisor of Thomas Weldon. Billings demonstrates a firm grasp of how the economy works.

ELEANOR THACKERAY is Karen's best friend and in one program her business partner. Eleanor expresses certain economic misconceptions, yet seems to understand quickly and, by the end of the series, has grown in economic insight.

MOTHER WELDON is Thomas's mother, a woman of great energy and determination. Her involvements in certain economic and political activities provide a setting within which Thomas and Karen come to be a better understanding of macroeconomic principles.

This chart correlates video programs and units with the respective chapters from Roger Miller's textbook, **Economics Today: The Macro View**.

VIDEO PROGRAMS	TEXTBOOK CHAPTERS
UNIT I. PUTTING THE PUZZLE TOGETHER	
PART ONE "The Pieces of the Puzzle"	PART ONE No Assignment
PART TWO "The Choice is Yours"	PART TWO Chapter 1—"What Economics is All About"
UNIT II. HOW OUR AMERICAN ECONOMY WORKS	
PART ONE "The Invisible Hand"	PART ONE Chapter 2—"Capitalism and the American Economy"
PART TWO "You Can't Always Get What You Want"	PART TWO Chapter 3—"Demand and Supply"
UNIT III. GOVERNMENT: HOW IT SPENDS	
PART ONE "The Free Rider"	PARTS ONE and TWO
PART TWO "Blowing the Whistle"	Chapter 6—"The Role and Size of Government"
UNIT IV. GOVERNMENT: HOW IT TAXES	
PART ONE "Familiar Fallacies"	PARTS ONE and TWO
PART TWO "Loopholes"	Chapter 7—"Government Spending, Taxation, and Debt"
UNIT V. BUSINESS ORGANIZATIONS AND FLUCTUATIONS	
PART ONE "Karen's Magic Flute"	PART ONE Chapter 4—"The Price System" Chapter 5—"Private Business Organizations and Financing"
PART TWO "The Economic Roller Coaster"	PART TWO Chapter 8—"Business Fluctuations, Unemployment, and Inflation"
UNIT VI. THE CIRCULAR FLOW AND NATIONAL INCOME ACCOUNTING	
PART ONE "Go With the Flow"	PART ONE Chapter 9—"The Circular Flow of Income and Product"
PART TWO "Measuring My Success"	PART TWO Chapter 10—"Measuring the Economy's Performance"
UNIT VII. ANALYZING THE MACROECONOMY	
PART ONE "Getting and Spending"	PART ONE Chapter 11—"Consumption, Saving, and Investment"
PART TWO "Withdrawal Symptoms"	PART TWO Chapter 12—"Income and Employment Determination"

VIDEO PROGRAMS	TEXTBOOK CHAPTERS
UNIT VIII. INCOME AND EMPLOYMENT DETERMINATION	
PART ONE "Income, Go Forth and Multiply" PART TWO "Balancing Act"	PART ONE Chapter 12—"Income and Employment Determination" PART TWO Chapter 13—"Fiscal Policy"
UNIT IX. GOVERNMENT FISCAL POLICY	
PART ONE "Thomas and the Fiscal Fighters" PART TWO "The Inspectors"	PARTS ONE AND TWO Chapter 13—"Fiscal Policy"
UNIT X. INFLATION	
PART ONE "The Shrinking Dollar" PART TWO "Fast Food Economics"	PARTS ONE AND TWO Chapter 8—"Business Fluctuations, Unemployment, and Inflation"
UNIT XI. MONEY AND BANKING	
PART ONE "All That Glitters is Gold" PART TWO "A Run for Your Money"	PART ONE Chapter 14—"Money and the Banking System" PART TWO Chapter 15—"The Process of Money Creation" Chapter 16—"The Federal Reserve, Monetary Policy, and the Multiplier"
UNIT XII. THE DILEMMA AND POLICIES OF STABILIZATION	
PART ONE "Karen Goes Political" PART TWO "All of the People, All of the Time"	PART ONE Chapter 17—"Another View of Money's Role" PART TWO Chapter 18—"Stagflation, Supply-Side Economics, and Stabilization"
UNIT XIII. GROWTH AND DEVELOPMENT	
PART ONE "Slippin' Away" PART TWO "A Steep and Thorny Path"	PART ONE Chapter 19—"Economic Growth" PART TWO Chapter 20—"The Economics of Developing Countries"
UNIT XIV. INTERNATIONAL TRADE	
PART ONE "Don't Let Them Take My Job Away" PART TWO "The Man Who Needed Nobody"	PARTS ONE and TWO Chapter 21—"Comparative Advantage and International Trade"
UNIT XV. INTERNATIONAL FINANCES	
PART ONE "The Tightrope Walkers" PART TWO "The Investors"	PARTS ONE and TWO Chapter 22—"The Balance of Payments and Exchange Rates"

THE MONEY PUZZLE: AN INTRODUCTION

UNIT IN A NUTSHELL

PART ONE
Film: "The Pieces of the Puzzle"

Text: General overview of text

PART TWO
Film: "The Choice Is Yours"

Text: Chapter 1

We begin the study of macroeconomics with the most basic of concepts: scarcity is the start of it all. To an economist, scarcity simply means that amounts of most things are limited; that is, they are not unlimited. Since the things that we want aren't unlimited, we must choose between alternatives. When we use something in one way, we can't use it in another, so the choices we make are important. The economic problems of what goods to produce, how these will get produced, and who will receive them when they are produced are basically problems of choosing.

Every society has a resource base of land, labor and capital equipment. The ways it chooses to use its resources to get the things it wants determines its economic system. No society (and no individual) can escape paying opportunity costs—which is defined in terms of what it must give up for each choice it makes.

Economics surrounds us and shapes our surroundings in obvious and subtle ways. Economic principles are tools that can be used to make sense of some of the puzzling questions in the economy as a whole and in our own lives in particular.

Economics is now topical. What is it all about?

Journalists, who keep us informed of the economy, seem to delight in scaring us with catchy phrases such as "spiraling inflation," "chronic unemployment," "tax revolt" and "the demise of the dollar." What after all, *is* inflation? Is everyone hurt by it? Why is there unemployment? What makes the dollar "strong" or "weak"? Why does the economy speed up or slow down? How does it all fit together? How does the economy work? Stay with us. You may be glad you did.

WHAT IS MACROECONOMICS?

Macroeconomics (macro: large) is the study of the economy as a whole, beginning with aggregate concepts. Some of these are inflation, government influence, unemployment, national income, national product and economic growth or decline. The study of macroeconomics involves getting a larger view: it studies the forests rather than the trees.

Microeconomics, (micro: small) also studies the entire economy but begins with the study of individual decisions: microeconomics looks specifically at the trees. Macroeconomics developed because it is so hard to see the forest through the trees. For this course, our topic is macroeconomics—everything put together and looked at "in the aggregate."

UNIT OBJECTIVES

Objectives 1 and 2 can be met by studying the information in this unit, and viewing "The Pieces of the Puzzle." After completing Part One, the student should be able to:

1. Be acquainted with your text and your *Study Guide*.

2. Have a bird's eye view in this "Get Acquainted" lesson of the rather extensive territory your macroeconomics course will cover.

Objectives 3–8 can be met by studying Chapter 1 "What Economics Is All About" and viewing "The Choice Is Yours." After completing Part Two, the student should be able to:

3. Define scarcity and opportunity cost.

4. List and define the factors of production.

5. Define "economic good" and "free good."

6. Represent opportunity cost graphically with a production possibilities curve.

7. Explain how economic models are used.

8. Contrast positive economics with normative economics.

PART ONE

UNIT I ASSIGNMENT: PART ONE

SKIM: The textbook, *Economics Today: The Macro View*, Miller, Roger L., and the study guide, *A Study Guide to The Money Puzzle: The World of Macroeconomics*, Cruse, Joanna S.

STUDY: Film Summary: "The Pieces of the Puzzle," *Study Guide*

VIEW: "The Pieces of the Puzzle"

COMPLETE: Fill-in Review *and* Problems, Problems, Problems . . . , *and* Econoword Puzzle, *Study Guide*

FILM SUMMARY: "The Pieces of the Puzzle"

Thomas Weldon will be your host for our filmed macroeconomics course. In the series, he will register for a night course in economics while working during the day at Dynamics Corporation. In this first program, he and his wife Karen show you bits and pieces of the dramas that are forthcoming. The dramas unfold Thomas's and Karen's efforts to solve the puzzle of how the parts of the economy fit together. The search is called *The Money Puzzle*.

Many times in the series Thomas's introduction to parts of the puzzle are through individuals who hold strong opinions and biases. Everyone knows a little bit about the economy. But a little knowledge can be troublesome since it includes prejudices and emotions and may ignore facts and objective analysis.

Thomas Weldon begins his look at the Money Puzzle—the Macroeconomy—and begins to fit together some of the pieces and to recognize some of the problems. The parts of the puzzle include government (with its spending and its taxes), national product, employment and unemployment, inflation, the value of money, the banking system, gold, international trade, depressions and periods of growth. Thomas notices government mostly through the taxes he pays—too many taxes he feels. He comes to appreciate that his feeling is shared by a large number of people who have inspired "tax revolts." (An example is "Proposition 13" by which California voters amended their state constitution, cutting their property taxes by 57%.)

That 1978 California initiative may be the most publicized current example, but the so-called "tax revolt" bubbles up constantly in a number of local and state governments. Thomas hears about some of the less direct (and incidently, illegal) ways of rebelling against taxation. When an employee is paid "under-the-counter," his employer is avoiding withholding taxes on wages paid while the worker avoids income tax on wages received in this "cash economy" transaction. To avoid taxation, many services are traded without any money changing hands. For example, when a dentist fixes a painter's teeth in exchange for having his house painted, there is no money payment. No income is reported to the Internal Revenue Service, and so no income taxes are paid. The aggregate of this bartering process is commonly called the "subterranean economy" or "underground economy."

Such tax evasion limits the ability of government to collect tax. Either government must lower the total amounts it spends, or the burden of the escaped taxes shifts to the taxpayers who do not evade them. Thus, there will likely be an argument about the inequity of taxes.

The U.S. hasn't done too well in following Colbert's maxim "the fine art of taxation is to pluck a goose to get the most feathers and least hiss." Actually, the U.S. tax system was designed by our founding fathers to maximize "the hiss." The original philoshpy was to keep taxation obvious so that citizens would be very much aware of what was happening.

Taxation may be painful, but taxes pay for schools, courts, roads, harbor and airport maintenance, protection of private property rights necessary for our markets and thousands of public goods that the private sector does not produce for itself. In many cases government spending allows the private sector to provide us with goods and services more economically. There will be more about both sides of this issue in upcoming Units.

In the video program, Thomas encounters another strong bias during discussions of imports. This is the kind of nationalism that inspires otherwise sensible people to insist that our problems would be solved if we just produce everything Americans need here in the U.S. and refuse to buy any more "cheap imports." This bias says, "Every dollar paid for an import could go into the pocket of an American worker." Economic analysis clears up a lot of the confusion about international trade and the importance of exports (what we produce and sell abroad) and imports (what we buy from abroad).

There is no international currency. In order to buy from other countries (crude oil, bananas, French perfume, Scotch whisky, aluminum, pepper), we must sell our products abroad. To be able to buy from us, other countries must sell their products to us. "Going it alone" would be very expensive indeed, in terms of what we would have to give up. The value of our dollar is tied to our sales abroad. In short, international trade is part of macroeconomics.

What about the international value of the dollar? In recent years it has been declining. It costs us more to buy from other countries; travel is more expensive for Americans abroad. Many people who once invested in U.S. dollars, now prefer to invest in gold. Why? Is there really an intrinsic value in gold, as the gold bug in the program insists? Not really. Intrinsic may be defined as the value of something not being dependent on external circumstances. But the value of gold depends almost entirely on "external circumstances." You can't eat gold, clothe yourself in gold, use it to keep warm, or keep off the rain with it. The value of gold is dependent on people's belief in it. Gold is inconvenient: heavy, hard to store and divide up—a poor choice for a modern currency. Money then, the various kinds of money, and the control of money by the banking system are all parts of macroeconomics.

With talk about money comes a subject that interests most Americans—inflation, which can be defined as a continued rise in the average price level. The analysis of inflation, recession (which are periods of greater than usual unemployment) and "booms" (periods of high employment and expansion) are major parts of macroeconomics.

Like everything else the value of money is determined by how much of it people want (demand) and how much of it there is around (supply). When something is in relative abundance, its value falls. When something is scarce, its value rises.

The price level represents the value of money: that is, just how many things you can buy with it. We have inflation when the value of a currency decreases continuously over a period of time. In the U.S., we have experienced inflation for the last several years.

As a later program will point out, our inflation has been relatively mild compared to that of many European and South American countries. There are historical examples of inflation that have devastated economies. During the American Revolution, so many "Continentals" were printed that they became worthless. The currency of the Confederacy during the American Civil War met the same fate. By far the worst inflation in recent history was in Germany in the 1920s following World War I. Housewives went to the factory each day to collect and immediately to spend their husbands' wages before the money's value fell. A suitcase full of money bought a sausage.

This program should have left you with a lot of questions. It was meant to do that. There are many weeks in the course, and you will come to know more intimately all the subjects you have met today—as you begin to work the Money Puzzle.

SPECIAL INSTRUCTIONS

This is an introductory lesson without the specific text chapter reading, and without the Chapter Highlights. For this lesson you scan the entire text and concentrate on the section of this *Study Guide* to get a light overview of some of the topics of the course.

Now is a perfect time to reread "Putting the Puzzle Together" and scan "What Business Persons Read." You are not required to learn this material for exams; it is part of the *Guide* designed to help you get the best possible start.

However, this lesson is an exception, corresponding a little bit to the first lecture in which professors introduce themselves, the course, and share clues on "How to Survive Happily and Prosper in Your Macroeconomics Course." (The living happily ever after is up to you.)

NEW TERMS USED

Aggregate: When used as an adjective, means total or overall.

Analysis: Examination of the various parts of a problem to discover how they fit together as a whole.

"Boom": Slang term for a period of unusually high employment.

Currency: In economics, coins and paper money.

Exchange rate: The rate at which the money of one nation exchanges with the money of another nation. For example, the number of U.S. dollars that can be bought with a British pound sterling and vice versa.

Exports: Sale of goods to another country.

Imports: Goods purchased from another country.

Inflation: A continued rise in the average price level.

Intrinsic: Belonging to the real nature of a thing; not dependent on external circumstances.

Objective: When used as an adjective, means without bias or prejudice.

Private sector: The business and consumer part of the economy.

Public sector: Government part of the economy where decisions of a public nature predominate.

Recession: Period of greater than usual unemployment.

Tax evasion: Not reporting income of transactions that are taxable.

10 UNIT I: PART ONE

FILL-IN REVIEW

Select between the choices underlined or fill in the blank. Cover the answers until you have provided your own.

HINT

This is a self-teaching device just for you. You don't hand it in as an assignment.

Cover the answers at the side of the page until you have completed your own. You may need to check back through the text or other parts of the unit. In any case, be sure not to look until you have written your own answer (preferably on another sheet of paper so that you can use the Fill-In Reviews again to prepare for exams). Some students clip a folded paper to the answer column and slide it down as they finish one or more fill-ins.

Often two words mean nearly the same thing. In Fill-In Reviews maybe the word you choose is close enough to the answer word given. Possible alternatives will sometimes be included. In general, it is usually important to be exact, since any discipline is built on its vocabulary.

overview	This lesson provides a general _____ of the subject. It is a "get acquainted" session to introduce you to the subject, the *Study*
Guide text	_____, the video, and the ____. The textbook
Economics Today: The	for this course is _____ _____: ___
Macro View Miller	_____ _____ written by _____.
Terms Summary	Each chapter finishes with a "Definition of _____," a Chapter _____, Study

FILL-IN REVIEW

_____ and on page _____ the text contains an appendix on graphs. At the end of the textbook there is an Index of _____, an Index of _____ _____, and an Index of _____.   *Questions   twenty-one*

Names

Glossary Terms

Subjects

Your *Study* _____ for this television course includes Chapter _____, Fill-In _____, and Problems, Problems, _____ ... sections. For each video program there is a Film _____. The entire *Study Guide* ties together the video units to the textbook. Each unit is designed as a self-_____ package.   *Guide*

Highlights

Review   Problems

Summary

teaching

Macroeconomics is a study of the economy as a _____, or in the _____. Parts of _____economics include employment and unemployment, the value of _____, the banking system, _____ trade, _____ (with its spending and its taxes), periods of growth and periods of _____. Although everyone has opinions about the economy, economic analysis does not include prejudice or _____ about one part or another. We call unbiased examination of various parts of the economy to consider how they fit together as a whole _____ _____.   *whole   aggregate*

macro

money

international

government

recession

biases

objective

analysis

UNIT I: PART ONE

tax revolt	A recent unwillingness to submit to government's authority in taxation has been called the ___ _____. "Proposition 13," a state constitutional amendment, represents an
limit	attempt to *extend/limit* government's ability to collect taxes. To avoid taxation many
under-ground economy/subterranean economy	Americans participate in the _____-_____ _____/_____ _____ (either)
cash	by paying for goods or services in ____ or by trading services.
public goods	Taxation provides _____ _____ that the
private	_____ sector does not provide for itself.
international	Trade between nations, called _____
exports	trade, involves selling our _____ to foreign
imports	nations in exchange for _____. To be able
sell	to ___ U.S.-made products, other nations
sell	must be able to ___ their products to us. The international value of our dollar is *independent of/dependent on* our sales abroad. Some
dependent on	
intrinsic	people believe gold has an _____ value. To economists, the value of gold has to do with
belief	people's _____ in it.

PROBLEMS, PROBLEMS, PROBLEMS . . .

Answers are at the end of this unit.

TRUE-FALSE

Circle either "T" or "F" for each statement.

(T) F   1. To be objective is to be without bias or prejudice.

T (F)   2. Exports to other countries just lower our own ability to have goods for ourselves.

T (F)   3. "Proposition 13" has allowed the California state government to collect a greater amount of taxes.

(T) F   4. When some people avoid taxes, others must pay more, unless the size of government is made smaller.

T (F)   5. Other countries can buy our products even though we do not buy products from abroad.

(T) F   6. Bias can be defined as prejudice.

T (F)   7. Macroeconomics is the study of individual markets in the economy; it makes no attempt to analyze the total economy.

T (F)   8. A continued rise in the average price level is called a recession.

(T) F   9. An intrinsic quality of something is not dependent on external circumstances.

(T) F   10. Unemployment and national production are part of the study of macroeconomics.

MATCH-UP

Match each item in the first column with a term in the second column. Use no term more than once.

__c__ 1. Without bias or prejudice

__f__ 2. A mental leaning or partiality; prejudice

__d__ 3. "The art of taxation consists of plucking a goose to get the most feathers with the least amount of hiss."

__j__ 4. Products and services we sell to other countries

__g__ 5. Belonging to the real nature of a thing; not dependent on external circumstances

__h__ 6. Periods of greater than usual unemployment

__e__ 7. A continued rise in the average price level

__i__ 8. Business and consumer part of the economy

__k__ 9. Government part of the economy

__a__ 10. Coins and paper money

__b__ 11. The study of the economy as a whole

a. currency
b. macroeconomics
c. objective
d. Colbert
e. inflation
f. bias
g. intrinsic
h. recession
i. private sector
j. exports
k. public sector

ECONOWORD PUZZLE—PART ONE

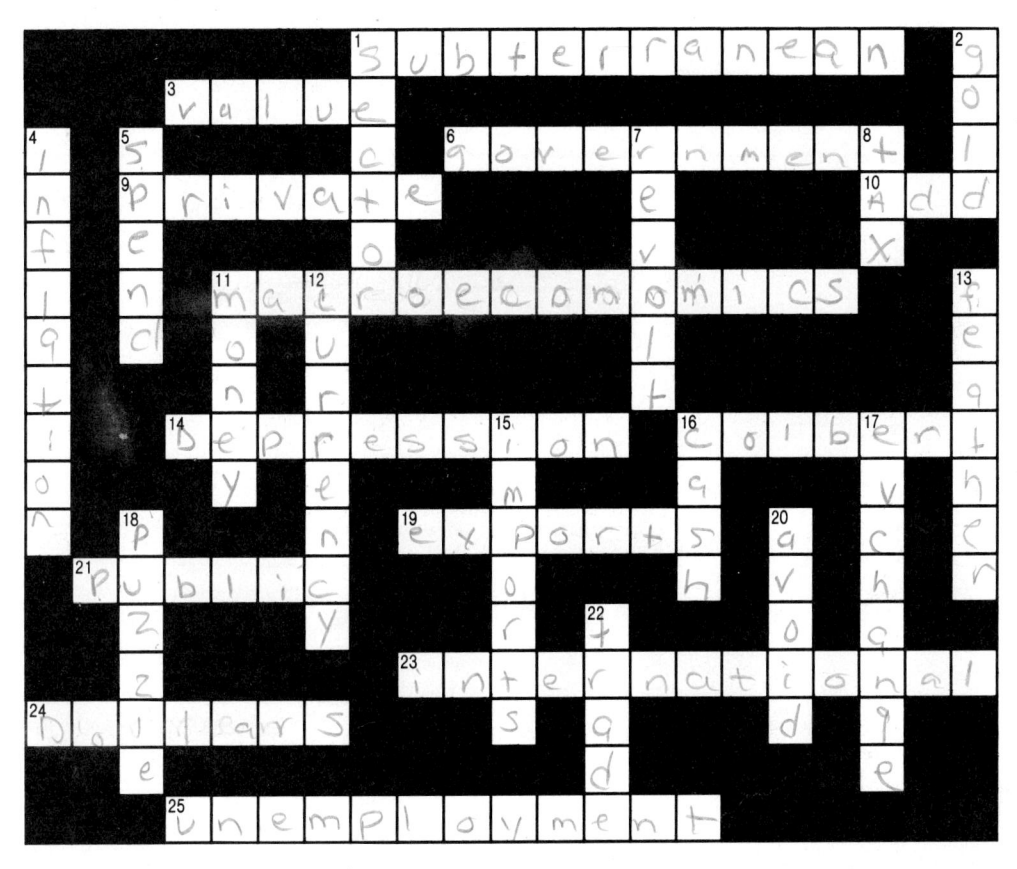

CLUES ACROSS

1. A name for the cash economy; literally, it means under the earth's surface.
3. The worth of something
6. Taxes are collected by _____.
9. The opposite of public
10. To sum
11. The study of large groupings in the economy
14. A long period of larger than usual employment
16. Louis XIV's finance minister who had defined taxation as plucking a goose
19. Goods and services produced by the U.S. economy and sold abroad
21. Opposite of private
23. Trade between nations is _____ trade.
24. U.S. units of money
25. The opposite of employment

CLUES DOWN

1. Large portion of the economy, divided by its characteristics, as in private _____ or public _____
2. "All that glitters is not _____."
4. A sustained rise in the general price level
5. To buy
7. A refusal to submit to authority as in "tax _____."
8. A percentage of transactions or income appropriated by government
11. Dollars, coins, checks
12. Coins and paper money
13. Fluffy part of bird that helps it to fly and keep warm
15. Goods and services bought from abroad
16. Payment with this means there is no record of the transaction for the IRS to find
17. To trade
18. Something you figure out by the shapes and colors of its pieces
20. To try to stay away from
22. To exchange

PART TWO

UNIT I ASSIGNMENT: PART TWO

STUDY: Chapter 1, "What Economics is All About," *Economics Today*

STUDY: Film Summary: "The Choice is Yours," *Study Guide*

VIEW: "The Choice is Yours"

REVIEW: Chapter 1 Highlights, *Study Guide*

COMPLETE: Fill-in Review *and* Problems, Problems, Problems ..., *Study Guide*

FILM SUMMARY: "The Choice is Yours"

For most good things, more is better than less. There are few of us who would not enjoy more of the good things that money buys, but as individuals and as society we are constrained by our resources. As individuals, income is our constraint, while societies' production possibilities are limited by the resources and the state of the technology. We can't have more of everything at the same time; as Dr. Beck says, "An economy's resources available to produce what is wanted are limited. They are scarce. Because of scarcity, to get more of some things means we have to have less of others. We must choose between the alternatives." As Thomas Weldon says, "We do without this, so that we can have that; instead of children, my education!"

In addition to what we own, our resources are time, talents, and skills that we can combine to get what we want from life. The choices a nation must make requires a process similar to the one individuals use in their lives. Thomas Weldon's boss, Mr. Dutweiler tells him "... You have to make hard choices, that's what economics is all about... hard choices." The Weldons already know about the need to choose. They know that their resources are limited and that to achieve their goals they must choose among alternative uses of their time and money. They must choose between Thomas's education or beginning a family. As long as there is a limit on time or any resource, everyone must choose. There is no way to avoid it.

Decisions are sometimes obvious and easy to make; others are really difficult. We all go through a thought-process something like Dr. Beck describes, "This rather than that, here rather than there." We think out loud, "If I do that, this will happen, and if I do the other thing, that is bound to follow." When we do this, we are analyzing the opportunity costs of the trade-off between alternatives. Haven't you ever considered the choice of whether to get up in the morning? What is the opportunity cost of just not bothering to go to work?

Economics is about how to make decision-making less painful. A layman's definition of the efficient use of resources might be, "How to use what we have to make scarcity hurt least." Simply stated, it means choosing the best possible use of scarce resources to produce what we want most. There is no such thing as a "free lunch." Economic analysis involves consideration of how, when, and by whom the bill for what is chosen will be paid. Economics deals with a comparison of costs and benefits of an alternative course of action in a world of scarcity, a world of limited resources.

Cost is not just a money cost, but is the benefit that could have been had from the best alternative choice. When we choose, the value of what we did not take is the "opportunity cost." Elyse Mercado, the office worker who is taking macroeconomics with Thomas tells of her choice of a job over the future advantages of attending college. She says, "If I had gone to college, I would have had no income for four years." The opportunity cost of going to college had been too high for her. Professor Beck traded the chance to be an artist to study economics. He calculates that the opportunity cost of college was $40,000. This amount represents the money he could have earned working instead of going to college four years.

Thomas and Karen notice the many trade-offs we all make. Karen resents the results of some of the choices large corporations make that she believes will affect her. She also worries about the future and wonders whether anyone is really concerned about it. Who, for instance, is taking care of the trees? In desperation she asks, "There's no way to plant more oil?"

We can ask if trees should be cut, and, if so, how much should *they* cost? Is the opportunity cost in cutting down a forest (the pleasures lost picnicking or camping) worth it? More generally, is the future change in the environment an opportunity cost we are willing to pay for technological development? What do you think?

We live in a "market system"; how does a market respond to scarcity? As things become relatively more abundant, their prices fall. As things are relatively scarcer, their prices rise. Prices reflect the opportunity cost of something in a market society. As an illustration of this, when trees become scarce their cost goes up. You already know about the price of oil.

Response to market price directs many of our choices. Prices help us decide just how much we want something. Do we want cleaner air or water? As prices of some products go up because we decide to clean up the environment, it is possible to decide how much clean environment we want on the basis of its price, or its opportunity cost. In sum, choice is an unavoidable part of our lives, and it is the heart of economics.

HINT

Here is your first and simplest look at an "economics" vocabulary. Most terms are old standby words. They are simple enough, but just wait. There are complicated words coming up. The gradual process of acquiring economic understanding will be easier and more fun if you accept new meanings for some terms and consistently use them hereafter in this course. For example, from now on land means, generally, natural resources. Capital is not money; capital is things that make other things like tools and machines.

NEW TERMS USED

Efficiency: A broad term for describing how well an economy uses its resources for attaining its goals.

Macroeconomics: See "Putting the Puzzle Together" in this *Study Guide*.

Resources: The basic inputs in an economy, also called factors of production; they are land, labor, capital, entrepreneurial ability.

Scarcity: All of economics is based upon the fact that resources are limited, or scarce, so that a price has to be paid for them.

Subsidiary: A firm that is owned by another firm.

CHAPTER 1 HIGHLIGHTS

Defined words are underlined.

I. SCARCITY IS THE REASON ALL INDIVIDUALS AND NATIONS FACE ECONOMIC PROBLEMS.

Scarcity: More of a good is wanted than is available. A scarce good is something that is limited; most things are scarce in this sense.

  A. Resources are scarce. *Resources:* Ingredients used in producing things; also called factors of production or inputs to production. Resources are loosely classified into:

   1. *Land:* In economics, land stands for all natural resources.

   2. *Labor:* Human resources.

   3. *Capital:* Machines, buildings and tools, manufactured resources.

   4. *Entrepreneurship:* Risk-taking, decision-making, innovation and initiative in forming and maintaining business organizations.

  B. *Economic Goods:* Goods produced from scarce resources.

  C. *Free Goods:* Goods freely available at zero price. A free good is not scarce. (Example: fresh air.)

II. CHOICE AND OPPORTUNITY COST: CHOOSING ONE THING REQUIRES GIVING UP SOMETHING ELSE.

  A. *Opportunity Cost:* The value of the next-best alternative choice; the opportunity foregone.

   1. Graphing examples (Text exhibits 1-2, 1-3, 1-4, 1-5) show the costs or trade-offs of choices. Economists call this illustration of opportunity cost a production possibilities curve.

2. Text exhibit 1-2 shows the trade-off between study hours for economics and accounting. If a student only has ten hours to study, the opportunity cost (or trade-off) of an hour of economics study is an hour of accounting study. This is a one-to-one trade-off.

B. *Production Possibilities Curve:* All possible combinations of the maximum amount of any two goods and services that an economy can produce from using all resources fully.

1. Text exhibit 1-3 is a graphic representation of society's trade-off between military and civilian goods.

2. Assumptions of the production possibilities curve:

   a. Output is represented per period of time (a year, for example).

   b. Resources are fixed and do not change during the time period.

3. Positions on the production possibilities curve

   a. Any point on the curve itself (called the frontier) shows the combination of goods that can be achieved using all of society's resources.

   b. Any point beyond the curve is impossible to achieve.

HINT

Turn now to the text appendix on graphing following Chapter One. Spend sufficient time working through the appendix to be able to understand clearly what graphs represent, how graphs are made, and to construct your own graphs.

c. Any point inside the curve means that resources are unused due to unemployment or inefficiency.

4. The production possibilities curve bows outward because the trade-off terms are not fixed, they vary.

a. *The Law of Increased Relative Costs:* The opportunity cost of producing more and more units of one good goes up at an increasing rate, since some resources are better suited to certain types of production than others.

b. In Text exhibit 1-2, the production possibilities curve for grades is a straight line (linear), since the opportunity cost of changing the combination of study hours is a one-to-one trade-off. (One study hour can be traded from economics to accounting at any point.) The production possibilities curve bows-outward in the military and civilian goods example. (The trade-offs are not one-to-one, but instead show increasing relative costs rather than constant costs of transferring resources.)

c. *Specialization:* Concentration on one type of activity or production: producing only one good rather than dividing resources up into the production of many goods. The benefits of specialization are that

1. higher output is produced from similar inputs.

2. each factor is utilized to do what it does best.

d. *Comparative Advantage:* A country or person has a comparative advantage when its production of a good is more efficient, in terms of opportunity cost, than production of the same good by another country or person. (A Central American country has a comparative advantage in producing bananas over Canada, for example.)

e. *Division of Labor:* The subdivision of tasks into simplest parts; the special organization of taxes so as to increase the amount of output from fixed resources available.

FILL-IN REVIEW 23

III. ECONOMICS AS A SOCIAL SCIENCE

A. *Economic Models:* Simplifications of the economy to include only essential relationships under consideration; Economic models

1. are based on a set of assumptions;

2. exclude details.

B. The function of a model is to clarify or predict real world economic events.

1. Economic models relate to how people act, not think.

2. Evidence is collected to test usefulness of the model.

C. *Positive Economics:* Relates to the "value free" nature of the analysis. This kind of economic analysis is sometimes referred to as "what is."

D. *Normative Economics:* Includes value judgements in the analysis, sometimes referred to as "what should be," and sometimes used by economists to recommend changes in economics policy.

FILL-IN REVIEW

Select between the choices underlined or fill in the blank. Cover the answers until you have provided your own.

We can't get everything we want from nature because of __scarcity__. Economics is the study of how we __choose__ among __alternative__ uses of scarce __resources__ to produce goods and services. Resources are also called __factors__ of production. Resources categories are __land__, __labor__, __capital__, and __entrepreneurship__. A	scarcity choose alternative resources factors land labor capital entrepreneurship

24 UNIT I: PART TWO

good produced from scarce resources is an *economic* good. Since it is not scarce, fresh air in the mountains is used as a *free* good.

Whenever you use a limited resource in one way, you *can use it*/*cannot use it* another way. When you sleep late, you can't get to work on time; when you read a novel during an afternoon, you can't study economics. Being late to work is the *opportunity* cost of sleeping late. Studying economics is the opportunity *cost* of reading the novel. The benefit that could have been derived from the best alternative choice is the _____ ____. Opportunity costs are shown graphically with a production _____ curve. This curve shows the _____ amount of any ____ goods that can be produced from a *limited*/*unlimited* amount of resources. In a production possibilities graph, any point beyond the curve is *simple*/*impossible* to achieve. A _____-___ exists whenever the choice of taking one action prohibits taking an _____ action. This trade-off is the _____ ____ of the choice. If production is inside the production possibilities curve, resources are *being fully used*/*not being fully used*. Because resources are not en-

economic
free

cannot use it

opportunity

cost

opportunity
cost
possibilities
maximum
two   limited

impossible
trade-off

alternative
opportunity cost

not being fully used

tirely adaptable to alternate uses, the production of any good is subject to the law of increasing _____. The _____-out shape of the _____ _____ _____ is caused by increasing relative costs.

*costs   bowed
production possibilities curve*

HINT

The production possibilities curve is used to show the economic implications of limited resources. It is an illustrative device showing the concept of upper limits of production. Of course, no economy produces only two goods. Learn the concepts of scarcity and efficiency from this simplified diagram, but don't expect real world complexity from it.

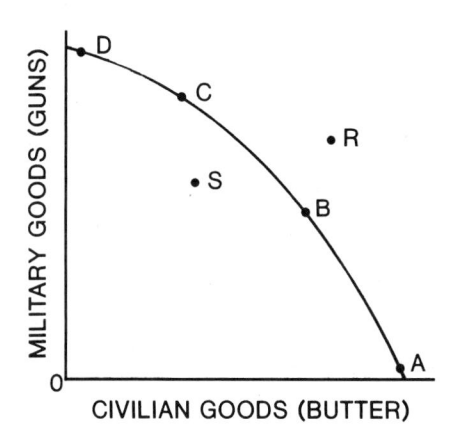

This production possibilities graph shows all the possible combinations of military goods (guns) and civilian goods per year (butter). At point S, factors of production are _____. If the economy moves from point C to point B in

unused

butter	its production, more *butter/guns* will be produced, and less *butter/guns*. If the economy
guns	
less	moves from point B to point C in production *less/more* butter will be produced. The opportunity cost of producing more guns is less butter. To be able to produce at point R the
grow productive	economy must _____, (or be more _____). An economy producing at point A is using all of its resources to specialize in producing
butter	_____.
advantage	A person has a comparative _____ in the kind of activity or work which has the lowest opportunity cost.
economic	To build an _____ model an economist will simplify the economy to include only
essential	_____ relationships based on a set of
assumptions	_____. The function of a model is to
predict explain	_____, and _____ economic events in the real world. "During 1980, the unemployment rate in some parts of the U.S. was 10%," is an
positive	example of a statement of _____ economics. "The unemployment rate should not be 12%; the government should use tax incentives to raise employment" is a statement of
normative	_____ economics.

PROBLEMS, PROBLEMS, PROBLEMS...

Answers are at the end of this unit.

TRUE-FALSE

Circle either "T" or "F" for each statement.

(T) F 1. The law of increasing costs accounts for the bowed-out shape of the production possibilities curve.

T (F) 2. A point beyond (outside) the production possibilities curve represents unemployment.

T (F) 3. A statement that makes a value judgment about the economy is a positive economic statement.

(T) (F) 4. Modern technology has produced such surpluses that the term scarcity no longer has any meaning.

(T) F 5. In the economics classification of resources, the oil underneath the ground in Texas can be termed "land."

(T) F 6. What you have to give up to get something else can be called its opportunity cost.

T (F) 7. Really wealthy people do not have an opportunity cost when they choose among alternatives.

(T) F 8. Air is an economic good when it comes through an operating air conditioner.

(T) (F) 9. A curved production possibilities curve reflects constant opportunity cost.

(T) F 10. The existence of scarcity means there are not enough available resources to meet all our desires.

28 UNIT I: PART TWO

(T) F 11. A production possibilities curve is an illustrative device which can be used to show scarcity and increasing costs.

(T) F 12. A basic reason for using an economic model is real-world complexity.

T (F) 13. Scarcity need not be of concern to us and can be avoided if we produce fast enough.

MATCH-UP

Match each item in the first column with a term in the second column. Use no term more than once.

__e__ 1. Without this, we would live in a world of total abundance.

__d__ 2. Explains the bowed-out production possibility curve

__f__ 3. Goods produced from scarce resources

__h__ 4. A statement that makes value judgments

__c__ 5. A statement that does not make value judgments

__i__ 6. A graph showing different maximum combinations of two goods that can be produced in an economy using all of its resources.

__b__ 7. Equipment, machines and tools used to produce goods

__g__ 8. The choice of taking one action prohibits taking another.

__a__ 9. A simplified version of how reality works

a. model
b. capital
c. positive economic statement
d. law of increasing cost
e. scarcity
f. economic good
g. opportunity cost
h. normative economic statement
i. production possibilities curve

MULTIPLE CHOICE

For each of the following statements, choose the one best alternative.

1. An economy that is producing its production possibility curve
    a. is experiencing underemployment.
    b. could produce more of everything at the current time.
    c. is not using all of its resources in their best way.
    d. cannot produce more of one good without giving up some of another good.

2. The basic problem for an economy is
    a. how to best use plentiful resources for society's limited wants.
    b. how to best use scarce resources for society's limited wants.
    c. how to best use scarce resources for society's unlimited wants.
    d. how to keep people from wanting what they can't have.

3. Capital goods are
    a. gold and silver, stocks and bonds.
    b. goods that households buy and use.
    c. manufactured goods used to produce other goods.
    d. free goods.

4. Which of the following best describes opportunity cost?
    a. You can't have your cake and eat it too.
    b. We all pay the piper eventually.
    c. The chance given up to have one thing by choosing an alternative.
    d. all of the above.

5. All of the following are factors of production, *except*
   a. capital.
   b. frontier.
   c. labor.
   d. land.

ABOVE AND BEYOND

1. Someone defined scarcity by saying "it's when there's not enough to go around." Elaborate on this statement and write a brief essay on the importance of the concept of scarcity in economics.

2. A production possibilities graph is an illustrative device, not an accurate picture of an economy. Comment on this statement. Include in your answer why it is necessary to simplify complex reality in studying basic economics.

ANSWERS TO STUDY QUESTIONS

PART ONE

TRUE-FALSE

1. T **2.** F **3.** F **4.** T **5.** F **6.** T **7.** F **8.** F **9.** T **10.** T

MATCH-UP

1. c **2.** f **3.** d **4.** j **5.** g **6.** h **7.** e **8.** i **9.** k **10.** a **11.** b

COMPLETED ECONOWORD PUZZLE

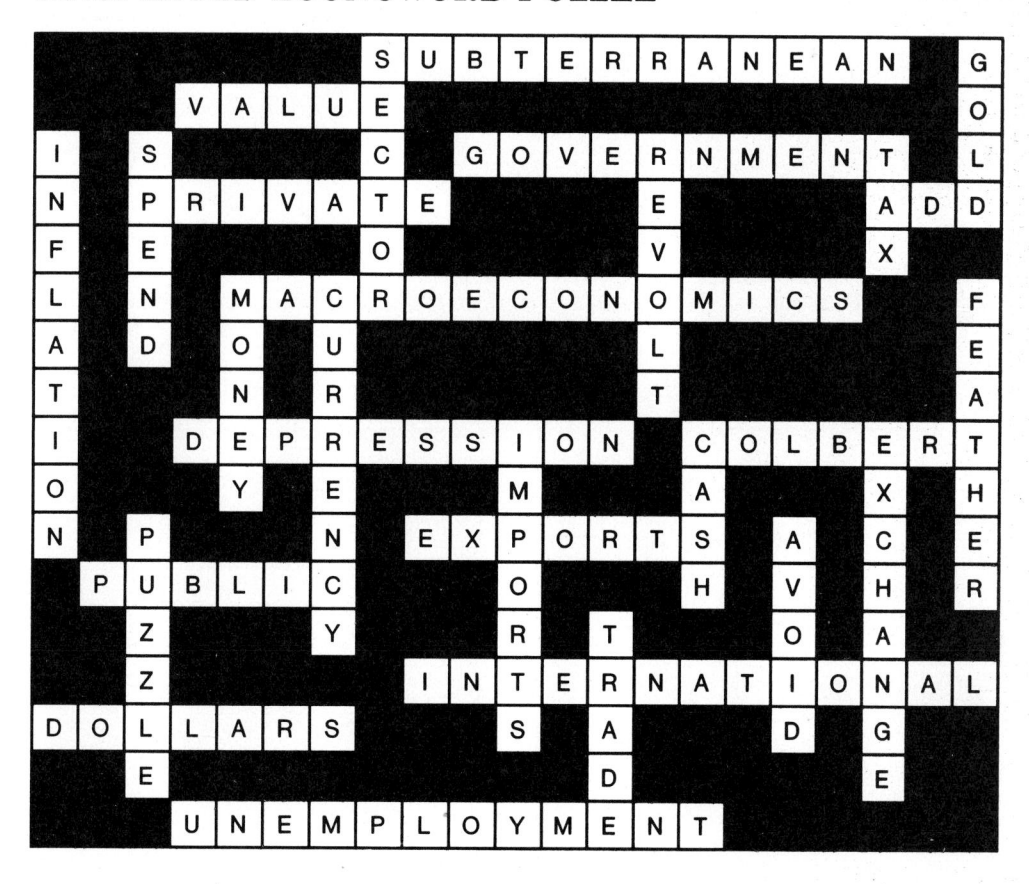

						S	U	B	T	E	R	R	A	N	E	A	N		G
			V	A	L	U	E												O
	I					C		G	O	V	E	R	N	M	E	N	T		L
	N		P	R	I	V	A	T	E				E			A	D	D
	F		E			O							V			X		
	L		N	M	A	C	R	O	E	C	O	N	O	M	I	C	S		F
	A		D	O	U								L						E
	T			N	R								T						A
	I		D	E	P	R	E	S	S	I	O	N		C	O	L	B	E	R	T
	O			Y	E		M			A				X		H
	N		P		N	E	X	P	O	R	T	S		A		C		E
		P	U	B	L	I	C		O		H		V		H		R
		Z			Y		R		T			O		A
		Z				I	N	T	E	R	N	A	T	I	O	N	A	L
	D	O	L	L	A	R	S		S		A			D		G
		E							D						E
		U	N	E	M	P	L	O	Y	M	E	N	T

PART TWO

TRUE-FALSE

1. T 2. F 3. F 4. F 5. T 6. T 7. F 8. T 9. F 10. T
11. T 12. T 13. F

MATCH-UP

1. e 2. d 3. f 4. h 5. c 6. i 7. b 8. g 9. a

MULTIPLE CHOICE

1. d 2. c 3. c 4. c 5. b

HOW OUR AMERICAN ECONOMY WORKS

UNIT II

UNIT IN A NUTSHELL

PART ONE

Film: "The Invisible Hand"

Text: Chapter 2

PART TWO

Film: "You Can't Always Get What You Want"

Text: Chapter 3

Capitalism runs on an automatic pilot, called the market. Individuals pursue their own self-interest by doing what seems best to them and in so doing cause the market's "invisible hand" to direct activity toward producing goods that satisfy the wants of the whole society. Thus, in a well-functioning market economy individuals serve the public interest by furthering their own self-interest. No one tells people what to produce; no central planner tells people where to work or what job must be taken, and yet the economy keeps functioning.

In a competitive economy, the two forces of supply and of demand constantly shift and pull prices up and down across all markets. These forces act to release resources from a depressed market and pull resources into a booming market. Although our economy is not a pure market economy, and contains considerable government influence as well as market forces, supply and demand are actively at work in many areas.

UNIT OBJECTIVES

Objectives 1-5 can be met by studying Chapter 2 and viewing "The Invisible Hand." After completing Part One, the student should be able to:

1. Define a market economy.

2. Understand what is meant by "economic system," and capitalism as an economic system.

3. Be acquainted with the role of private property in a capitalist system.

4. Explain Adam Smith's concept of the invisible hand.

5. Be acquainted with the simplest model of circular flow.

Objectives 6-9 can be met by studying Chapter 3 and reading Chapter 4 and viewing "You Can't Always Get What You Want" After completing Part Two, the student should be able to:

6. Define the concept of demand and supply and be able to show these concepts in graphical form.

7. Know the difference between a change in demand (supply) and changes in quantity demanded (supplied).

8. Define and show graphically the equilibrium price and quantity using supply and demand schedules.

9. Explain the concept of market equilibrium and how competition in the economy causes markets to move toward equilibrium.

PART ONE

UNIT II ASSIGNMENT: PART ONE

STUDY: Chapter 2, "Capitalism and the American Economy," *Economics Today*

STUDY: Film Summary: "The Invisible Hand," *Study Guide*

VIEW: "The Invisible Hand"

REVIEW: Chapter 2 Highlights, *Study Guide*

COMPLETE: Fill-in Review *and* Problems, Problems, Problems . . . , *and* Econoword Puzzle *Study Guide*

FILM SUMMARY: "The Invisible Hand"

We can't get along without each other in our modern economy. No one can do it "all by herself." Even if Thomas had managed to produce an edible loaf of bread, it wouldn't have been "all by himself." The flour alone in the loaf of bread represents the labor of farmers, millers, truckers, bakers, grocers, and hundreds of others, each acting in her or his own self-interest.

By specializing in a particular economic activity, an individual can demand a higher price for his services than the jack-of-all-trades. But the more specialized people become, the more they rely on each other. This is known as interdependence. The problem of every society is to organize this interdependence in an efficient and equitable way. We call the organization developed by society for this purpose an "economic system."

FILM SUMMARY: "THE INVISIBLE HAND"

The economic system is a collection of all the processes that the people in a society employ to determine what resources will be used to satisfy their wants. Market economies and centrally planned economies are the two basic types of economic systems.

In a capitalistic system, individuals are free to own productive resources and to use them as they see fit, subject to legal restrictions. In a centrally planned economy, factors of production are collectively owned and their use planned by a central authority which decides what goods are produced, which resources will be used to produce them, and what production processes will be used. There is little central direction in the pure market economy where supply and demand in markets establish prices and allocate resources to their highest paying use. In this same pure market economy, it is every man for himself; each individual follows his or her own interest and is only constrained by the competition of others.

The production and distribution choices must be made in every economy. In a market system, they are made by the free interaction of the forces of supply and demand in the market. The market is a concept, it includes all the producers and all the consumers of a particular product. We can talk of the structure of a market by talking about the number and the relative sizes of the buyers and sellers in the market. If there are many small independent buyers and sellers, the market is competitive; if there is only one seller of a product, the market structure is a monopoly.

Markets spring up where people have things to exchange. In the film, the prisoner-of-war camp is an example of the free-market system at work. In free markets, money is used as a medium of exchange. Actually, anything that people will generally accept in payment can be called money. In the closed "mini-economy" of a prison, cigarettes often become money. In the film, the prisoner wanted to get as many cigarettes as possible for his Red Cross package. In trading, he confronts other prisoners who plan to give up as few cigarettes as they can for the same goods. How many cigarettes will the trader charge? If he charges too high a price, he loses the trade to someone else. A competitive economy with unregulated markets requires participants to be on their own to figure out what will work best. As long as there are many buyers and sellers, the potential for competition exists; no one seller can have a monopoly.

In a competitive pure-market economy, businesses are free to enter and leave the market. When firms are making high profits, new businesses are attracted into the market to compete for some of that profit. In a completely competitive economy, no new producer can be kept out. The opposite is also true. Any producer can fail and shut the business down if it cannot earn sufficient profit to stay afloat. The interaction of self-interest and competition means that: 1) only those goods demanded on the market will be produced, and 2) these goods will be produced at prices and in quantities acceptable to both buyers and sellers. The result of this competitive process is that prices are forced down to cost of production so that the consumer is able to buy at the lowest price possible.

The role of prices and profits is crucial to the competitive process. The "invisible hand" that makes the market work is the price mechanism that sends signals of market conditions to buyers and sellers. A firm cannot charge a price higher than the market price without losing part of its share of the market. A laborer cannot demand a wage above the market wage without losing his job to someone who will work for less. There is a constant search for substitutes for high priced inputs. In a pure market economy, prices represent the allocative decisions of the market that all economic actors must accept. Prices decide what resources will be used, and how and by whom.

Thomas Weldon asks, "Who's directing the play?" Think of his question. Who does direct it all? Who decides what is produced? Who produces it? Who receives the profit? Does a committee in Washington D.C.? Sometimes!! In a pure market economy, prices and profits determine most of the economic activity; however, in the U.S., as in most advanced societies, we have a mixed economy of both market forces and government participation. Government often enters the picture to change some of the results of a market system. Through the political process, government directs some economic choices, but it is not these choices which is of most concern to us yet. At this time, our emphasis is on the study of the market and the market process.

NEW TERMS USED

Allocation: The division or apportionment of resources among different uses.

Glut: A surplus on the market so that there are more goods supplied than demanded.

Market Economy (Market System): An economy in which the basic economical decisions are answered freely in the market place, rather than by government direction.

Medium: A go-between.

Medium of Exchange: Something (such as money) that facilitates transfer of a good or service from one person to another.

Mixed Economy: A system in which both the government and the private sector make decisions concerning allocation of resources.

Model: Simplified representation of the real world.

CHAPTER 2 HIGHLIGHTS

Defined words are underlined.

I. ECONOMIC SYSTEM: INSTITUTIONAL MEANS THROUGH WHICH NATIONAL RESOURCES ARE USED TO SATISFY HUMAN WANTS.

    A. Every economic system must answer:

        1. Who is permitted to own what?

        2. What incentives induce people to produce?

        3. What determines benefits people get from producing?

        4. What activities are permitted; which are forbidden?

        5. What are individuals allowed to do with proceeds of these permitted activities?

II. INSTITUTIONS AND ASSUMPTIONS OF CAPITALIST IDEOLOGY

    A. *Private Property:* Individuals' rights to own property are protected by law; people are free to use their property as they will, as long as the use does not infringe upon others' property rights.

B. *Free Enterprise* and *Free Choice:* Firms can obtain resources, organize them, and sell finished products any way they choose; members of society are free to choose how they want to consume and produce.

   1. With consumer sovereignty, every consumer is free to choose the goods desired.

   2. Consumers' desires determine what will be produced in a purely competitive economy.

C. Self-interest and the "Invisible Hand"

   1. Adam Smith, a Scottish economist (1723–1790) and author of *The Wealth of Nations,* described a system where individuals pursue their own self-interest and where there is a limited role for government. Fundamental economic questions are answered without deliberate decision, as if an invisible hand directs production.

   2. Self-interest motivates the economic activity of individuals into the most efficient utilization of society's resources.

      a. For a business person, self-interest is maximizing profit or minimizing losses.

      b. For an individual, self-interest means maximizing satisfaction in spending income.

D. Competition and unrestricted markets lead to rivalry among sellers. Competition imposes limits on self-interest and requires

   1. large numbers of independent buyers and sellers, diffusing power among many.

   2. easy exit or entry into or from industry by buyers and sellers.

E. *Market System:* In a pure market system, buyers and sellers express opinions by how much they will pay for goods and services. Also, called the "price system," the market system is a major organizing force in our economy.

F. A limited role for government: government supports the system of property rights, and provides national defense.

G. *Capitalism:* An economic system in which people privately own productive resources, and have the right to use them as they choose.

   1. Capital is different from capitalism. Capital (capital goods) refers to manufactured productive resources. Capital goods are machines, tools and equipment that transform materials into products.

   2. If we include land in the definition of capital, all economic systems have capital.

III. THE U.S. ECONOMY IS A MIXED ECONOMY

   A. A mixed economy has an expanded role for government along with the private sector. In the U.S.,

      1. the government sector is greatly expanded and controls an important share of total income.

      2. government affects private economic dealings through taxes or subsidies to industries.

      3. through its agencies, government exerts control on transportation, communication, energy policy and education.

   B. American workers have large numbers of capital goods to work with. Capital goods are those consumed indirectly, since capital goods are machinery and tools used to produce other things.

      1. To build capital goods, some present consumption must be given up. *Consumption Good:* Goods we consume directly.

      2. The growth of an economy depends on past accumulation of capital goods.

   C. *Specialization:* Individuals and regions engage in activities for which they have comparative advantage.

1. The U.S. has regional specialization in production.

2. The cost of specialization increases interdependence and risk-taking.

D. *Money:* A generally accepted medium of exchange that facilitates specialization and exchange. *Barter:* The exchange of goods for goods without money. Barter can be called a model of "real" flow of goods.

IV. SIMPLE MODEL OF ECONOMY: THE CIRCULAR FLOW

A. The assumptions of the very simplest:

1. In the very simplest circular flow, households and businesses are shown in a barter economy without money or government.

2. Households own all land, labor and capital, and provide them to businesses.

3. Businesses use land, labor and capital to produce goods.

HINT

We have begun with the simplest of models. The next step toward reality is the introduction of money, for households must have a constantly replenished flow of money income to be consumers of business products; and for businesses to be able to produce goods and services they have the same income requirements. The mutual dependency of these two sectors of the economy becomes obvious.

B. With the use of money, the circular flow model becomes a monetary economy where

   1. money flows in one direction,

   2. real goods flow in the other direction.

FILL-IN REVIEW

Select between the choices underlined or fill in the blank. Cover the answers until you have provided our own.

Capitalism as an economic system is characterized by *private*/*state* ownership of _____ __ _____ and limited _____ control. Two basic freedoms found in _____ are free _____ and free _____. Free enterprise exists when private businesses choose ____ they will produce and ____ they will produce and sell output without interference. Free choice includes the ability of a firm to do what it wishes and the ability of all people in the economy to work where they wish and buy what they want. Self-interest means all individuals and groups in the economy do what is best for _____. This self-interest is prevented from working to the disadvantage of the society by other individuals pursuing their own ____-_____. In short, competition regulates	*private factors of production (or inputs, resources) government* *capitalism enterprise* *choice* *what* *how* *themselves* *self-interest*

44 UNIT II: PART ONE

Smith

hand

sellers

price

enter

go out of

market

consumer

model
capitalism
mixed   free
market   government

capital
consumer
goods

capital goods

and constrains the economy. It was the insight of Adam _____ in his book, *The Wealth of Nations,* that behind this mad scramble, an "invisible _____" works to make the market a finely tuned efficient allocative mechanism. Competition requires many _____ of a good so that no one can arbitrarily affect the price. Anyone charging a higher _____ will lose business to competing firms. If one seller tries to restrict output in the industry, others will *enter/leave* the market. Firms producing goods which are no longer desired *go out of/remain in* business. Thus, competition is at the heart of the _____ economic system. Ideally, consumers, by buying or not buying, decide what will be produced. This is often called _____ sovereignty.

Pure capitalism is a theoretical _____. The U.S. does not have pure _____; rather, ours is a _____ system, with a _____ _____ system plus _____ control in many areas. Our economy has huge amounts of _____ goods to work with. Those goods we consume directly are called _____ _____. Those goods we consume indirectly, which are machinery and tools used to produce other things, are called _____ _____.

FILL-IN REVIEW

The existence of this capital means that in the past we gave up considerable _____. This past consumption foregone has resulted in _____ of our ability to produce and accounts for our *low/high* national income.

consumption

growth

high

The cost of specialization is _____ as individuals share the benefits of specialization through _____. Money is a medium of _____ which facilitates this trade. In the simple circular flow model, households sell their ____, _____, and _____ to businesses who pay ____, _____, and _____ in return. In the simpler circular flow diagram, _____ is ignored.

interdependence

trade

exchange

land   labor   capital

rent   wages   profit

government

PROBLEMS, PROBLEMS, PROBLEMS . . .

Answers are at the end of this unit.

TRUE-FALSE

Circle either "T" or "F" for each statement.

T F 1. The relative scarcity of resources and products is shown by prices of goods and services.

T F 2. Although every man pursues his self-interest in a pure market economy, according to Adam Smith, an "invisible hand" leads to an efficient allocation of goods and resources.

T **F** 3. The price mechanism is the "invisible hand" that makes the economy work.

T F 4. In a market economy, high profits in an industry will attract new products into the industry.

T **F** 5. The market economy is characterized by a central planner who decides what, when, how, and for whom goods will be produced.

T F 6. An economic system is the set of institutions, laws and customs developed by a society to allocate scarce resources.

T **F** 7. If we produce only consumer goods now and no capital goods, our capacity to produce consumer goods in the future will decrease.

T **F** 8. Only the U.S. mixed economy uses capital goods.

T F 9. Competition is characterized by a large number of buyers and sellers and ease of entry into the market.

MATCH-UP

Match each item in the first column with a term in the second column. Use no term more than once.

_b_ 1. An economy with private ownership of the means of production and minimal government intervention

_a_ 2. An economy in which goods are exchanged for goods and no money is used

_h_ 3. A generally accepted medium of exchange

_f_ 4. Author of *The Wealth of Nations*

_c_ 5. The set of institutions, laws and customs developed by a society to allocate scarce resources

_g_ 6. Has an expanded role for government along with the private sector

_e_ 7. Goods we consume directly

_d_ 8. Goods we consume indirectly

a. barter
b. capitalism
c. economic system
d. capital
e. consumer
f. Adam Smith
g. a mixed economy
h. money

MULTIPLE CHOICE

For each of the following statements, choose the one best alternative.

1. The U.S. economy
    a. is an example of a pure market economy.
    b. is a mixed economy with an expanded government role and a private sector.
    c. is entirely directed by the central government.
    d. All the above are correct.

2. Competition requires
    a. government intervention.
    b. monopoly control.
    c. a large number of buyers and sellers.
    d. freedom of entry and exit.
    e. Both c and d are correct.

3. Capital goods are
    a. used to transform other things.
    b. tools and machinery.
    c. used to produce consumer goods.
    d. consumed indirectly.
    e. All the above are correct.

4. Which of the following is *not* a characteristic of the capitalist ideology?
    a. government control of capital
    b. self-interest
    c. private enterprise
    d. a price system
    e. freely operating markets

MULTIPLE CHOICE

5. Specialization leads to

   a. increased interdependence.

   b. increased productivity.

   c. increased ability to trade.

   d. All the above are correct.

   e. None of the above are correct.

6. All of the following are true of the simple circular flow model *except* one. Choose that one.

   a. Government directs the flow.

   b. Only barter is used.

   c. Only household and business sectors are included.

   d. Businesses use land, labor and capital to produce goods.

   e. Households own all land, labor and capital and provide them to business in return for rent, wages and profit.

ECONOWORD PUZZLE — PART ONE

CLUES ACROSS

1. The set of institutions, laws, and customs developed by a society to allocate scarce resources is its economic _____.
7. Adam Smith said it was invisible but so powerful it made the whole system work efficiently.
8. The one who ultimately buys the national product. You and I qualify.
10. When there is only one producer of a good in a market this producer has a _____.
12. The opposite of public
14. The freedom to participate as you wish in the economy is sometimes referred to as free _____.
16. The chapter names two kinds of this; choice and enterprise.
17. We all respond to this; it helps us make our choices; it reflects opportunity cost.
18. In an economy characterized by this, there can be no monopoly.

CLUES DOWN

2. Set of institutions, laws and customs developed by a society to allocate scarce resources is its _____ system.
3. Any means or arrangement where individuals exchange with one another.
4. In a pure market economy, prices and profits decide _____ will be produced.
5. The price mechanism is the _____ hand which makes the market work.
6. The opposite of private; this sector makes decisions that affect everyone.
9. When we describe the authorities who decide on our national money supply, we refer to them as having _____ authority.
11. Form of economic system characterized by private ownership of the means of production and limited government.
12. The existence of this provides a signal in a market economy for more producers to enter a market.
13. Our economy has elements of both extensive private ownership and extensive government regulation; it is a _____ economic system.
15. In a purely competitive economy, there is a _____ to government intervention.

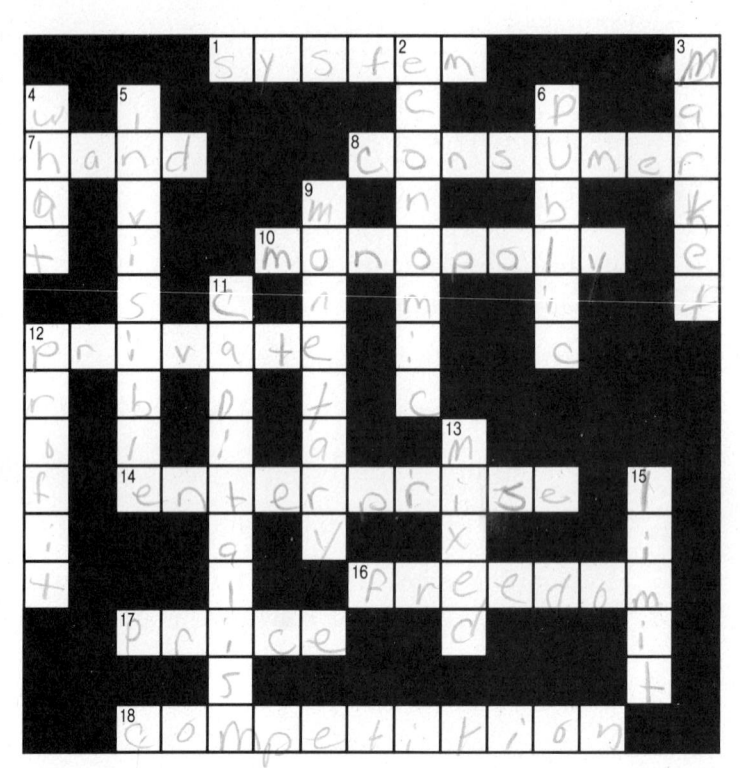

PART TWO

UNIT II ASSIGNMENT: PART TWO

STUDY: Chapter 3, "Demand and Supply", *Economics Today*

STUDY: Film Summary: "You Can't Always Get What You Want," *Study Guide*

VIEW: "You Can't Always Get What You Want"

REVIEW: Chapter 3 Highlights, *Study Guide*

COMPLETE: Fill-in Review *and* Problems, Problems, Problems *... and* Econoword Puzzle, *Study Guide*

FILM SUMMARY: "You Can't Always Get What You Want"

Through Thomas's mother's experience in the operation of her own retail shop, we glimpse the workings of the market mechanism. Her gift shop sells porcelain deer figurines and other gift treasures and she initially is swamped by eager customers. Her daughter-in-law, Karen, immediately recognizes that the gift prices are too low. To convince Mother Weldon that she must raise her prices, Karen explains how supply and demand interact. In her explanation, Karen rightly begins with the concept of consumer behavior demand.

Demand refers to the desire, ability and willingness of consumers to buy a good. The different amounts of a good consumers are willing and able to buy at different prices establish their demand curve. When the price for a certain good is high, consumers will buy smaller amounts. Naturally, when the price is low, consumers buy more. For example, consider your own demand for something like shoes; when the price is very high (keeping everything but price out of our consideration), the number of pairs you buy (quantity demanded) is low, whereas, at a lower price, you will buy more pairs.

Your demand for shoes gives the total picture of how you will respond to different prices. In a graphical illustration, the demand curve depicts the functional relationship between prices and quantities people will buy at those prices. The demand relationship is inverse, and is shown as a downward sloping line on a graph, which has price on the vertical axis and quantity on the horizontal axis.

The demand curve shows the willingness to buy, given certain prices. Since it shows responses to price, this demand curve itself doesn't move when prices change. The demand/price relationship is described as people buying less when prices rise. This is true, but be careful to avoid saying that demand changes in response to price changes. What happens, is that when price goes up, people buy less, or when price goes down, people buy more. One way to be careful of this distinction is to refer to the quantity people buy as the quantity demanded. Demand only changes when one of its background conditions is altered. Important to the understanding of why demand changes are background conditions or determinants of demand.

The demand curve stays the same unless the background conditions of demand change. Incomes, tastes and preferences, prices of related goods, population changes and expectations of changes in future prices are the five background conditions of demand. Thomas and Karen discuss these determinants of demand; the change of any one can cause a shift of the whole curve. Thomas lists them beginning with income. When income goes up you are able to buy more of the goods you prefer. Tastes and preferences are also important non-price determinants of demand. Advertisers develop advertising campaigns to influence your preferences in order to encourage you to buy their products. What they are doing, in effect, is trying to influence your demand.

Prices of related goods is another of the important non-price determinants. Generally, instead of buying the good we usually purchase, we will buy a close substitute good if its price drops.

Notice how this lowers our demand for the good we had been buying and increases the quantity demanded of the good whose price has fallen. When the use of a good is closely linked to another good, the change in price of one will influence the demand for the other. Gas and cars are an excellent example. As the price of gasoline goes up, the demand for heavy, gas-guzzling cars goes down. Population changes and expectations of future changes in price also influence demand itself.

All of these five background conditions of demand, singly or in combination, can change or shift the entire demand for a good. A shift or change in demand results when people are willing to buy more, or less, than before, at any price.

Price has an important rationing effect on goods in a market place. The two functions of price which help explain how the market functions are: 1) to direct resources into areas of production of the goods people want, and, 2) to conserve things which are scarce. You sometimes hear the worried comment, "We will use up every bit of our resource until there is no more." In order to consider this statement we need to look at the other side of the market, the supply side.

What is supply and what determines supply? Supply is quite analogous to demand. It refers to quantities producers offer in the market place in response to various prices. The relationship between price and quantity supplied is a positive one and produces an upward sloping graph line, showing that, as price goes up the quantity of a good supplied also goes up. The reason is a simple one: when the price goes up, producers offer more to take advantage of the opportunity to earn greater profits. Failing to understand this phenomenon leads to some confusion on Mother Weldon's part. But an even more serious error of hers, at least in the beginning, is that she fails to include in the price of her gift items the cost of both buying her inventory and operating her store.

Mother Weldon is not, at least initially, typical of those who supply the market with goods. Producers of market goods base quantity supplied on costs of production and on a search for profits. At low prices thus, small amounts of a goods are usually supplied in the market. When prices go up, the amount supplied also increases. This positive relationship has been called the law of supply.

Mother Weldon's operating costs and the prices that she pays for her inputs (gifts) give us a simple example of the way a supply curve reflects the producer's costs of production. As an input becomes more scarce and thus more difficult and costly to supply to the market, its price will rise. The higher the price of something, the less of it is used. Businesses in their search for profits, produce as efficiently as possible, using fewer of the more expensive inputs and more of the less expensive.

A corresponding law of demand describes the inverse or negative relationship of price to quantity demanded. As price goes down, quantity demanded goes up. In our film, Mother Weldon's customers are following the "law of demand" (which is less of a law but more of a way of describing a predictable relationship), while Mrs. Weldon is ignoring the law of supply and is, finally, unable to continue to supply a retail market for gifts.

Thus, when supply and demand for a good are considered together, their interaction produce the forces of the market place which result in an equilibrium price. In the discussion of equilibrium price which follows, we talk about an ever-present tendency of the market process for price to *approach* equilibrium: an amount where the quantity offered for sale (quantity supplied) at equilibrium price is entirely sold, and is equal to the amount (quantity demanded) people are willing and able to buy at that price. Thus, equilibrium price is a market-clearing price, with no surpluses and no shortages. When Mother Weldon offers her gifts for sale at prices that are much lower than for comparable goods, the quantity demanded is indeed high. Had her shop stayed open, she would have quickly sold her available supply, and even experienced shortages, as customers tried to buy more.

Yet, when Karen is able to help her to calculate her actual cost of supplying her gifts, she finds that her price does not cover her costs.

Now that we have looked at demand and supply and equilibrium price, we are better able to deal with the concern about using up all of a resource. When an input to production, such as oil, for example, becomes scarce, its supply lowers. The result is that equilibrium price becomes higher and higher. The high price of the scarce good rations its use, through the working of the price mechanism. Goods that become scarce are high priced inputs. Through the law of demand, less and less quantity of a good is demanded as its price rises. No one conserves a free good, but a high-priced economic good is used carefully indeed. As the price of a resource rises, there is a search for a low-priced substitute; the market mechanism itself prevents us from exhausting a resource if its price reflects its scarcity.

In our discussion of the price mechanism, we can infer that the strength of consumer demand results, ultimately, in consumer sovereignty. Consumer demand affects market prices, and in so doing directs the economy. In a completely competitive economy, it is consumers' demands for something they want which creates a temporary shortage in the market and causes the market price to rise. At the higher price, a signal of available profit is received by possible producers of the good, who enter the profitable, expanding industry. The reverse process takes place when consumers decide they want less of a good, leaving surpluses on the market: sellers then lower price in order to get rid of the surplus. Sellers lose money at the lower price and some will leave the industry. This is the way the "automatic pilot" of a true market economy functions—in response to the ways consumers choose to spend their money: it functions to produce goods at their lowest possible price, and rations scarce resources.

HINT

This unit contains a lot of hints because the material covered is considered difficult. Therefore, extra directions and help are included.

A helpful way to deal with the most basic concepts in economics is with graphs. You need to know how they are constructed and how to read them. You must be able to:

1. Identify what two variables are being measured.
2. Understand the relationship of the variables being measured.

Understanding the graphical relationships boils down to being able to answer these questions. As one variable gets larger/smaller, what happens to the other one? Does the other one get larger/smaller, too? If you are not secure about answering these questions for each graph, turn now to the graphing Appendix in your text.

CHAPTER 3 HIGHLIGHTS

Defined words are underlined.

I. DEMAND FOR A GOOD

  A. *Law of Demand:* At higher relative prices, a smaller quantity will be demanded, other things being equal; or at lower relative prices, a higher quantity will be demanded, other things being equal.

  1. *Inverse Relationship:* When one variable moves up in value, the other variable moves down in value. In the law of demand, price and quantity demanded are inversely related; as price rises, quantity demanded falls.

  2. *Relative Price:* The price of any item relative to the price of other goods.

  3. *Absolute Price:* The price paid in dollars and cents for any good at any time.

  4. *Other Things Equal:* All other things that affect the variable under consideration are held constant.

  B. Reasons for the law of demand are:

  1. *Substitution Effect:* When the price of a good rises (falls), consumers will substitute another good for it (substitute it for another good).

  2. *Income Effect:* If price of a good you normally buy goes up (down), your ability to buy goes down (up).

  C. *The Demand Schedule:* Table of alternative quantities demanded at different prices, per time period.

  1. *Constant Quality Units:* Convenient groupings of similar products with assumption that all are the same quality.

2. *Demand Curve:* Picture of the inverse relationship between price and quantity with price on the vertical number-line (axis) and quantity on the horizontal number-line (axis).

D. Determinants of demand: demand for a good depends upon

1. incomes of consumers,

2. tastes and preferences of consumers,

3. prices of related goods,

4. changes in expectations about prices,

5. population.

E. Distinguishing between change in demand and change in quantity demanded

1. *Change in Demand:* Shift in entire demand curve so that there is a change in quantity demanded at each and every price (caused by a change in a determinant of demand).

2. *Change in Quantity Demanded:* Consumer response to relative price change; a movement along a given demand curve.

II. SUPPLY OF A GOOD

Supply Schedule: Table of prices and quantity supplied at each price.
Supply Curve: Picture of the positive relationship between price and quantity.

A. *Law of Supply:* At higher relative prices, a larger quantity will be supplied, other things being equal; at lower relative prices, a smaller quantity will be supplied, all other things being equal.

1. *Direct or Positive Relationship:* When one variable moves up in value, the other variable being measured will also increase.

2. Producers are willing to supply more at higher prices.

B. Determinants of supply. The supply of a good depends upon

1. input prices,

2. technology,

3. taxes and subsidies,

4. price expectations.

C. Distinguishing between change in supply and change in quantity supplied

1. *Change in Supply:* Shift in entire supply curve so that there is a change in quantity supplied at each and every price (caused by a change in a determinant of supply).

2. *Change in Quantity Supplied:* Supplier response to a change in relative price; a movement along a supply curve.

III. DEMAND AND SUPPLY TOGETHER

Equilibrium: Market-clearing price where quantity supplied equals quantity demanded.

1. *Shortage:* Occurs when price is below equilibrium.

2. *Surplus:* Occurs when price is above equilibrium.

HINT

This chapter forms the basis for understanding how markets determine prices of goods, services and resources. It is presented in "Chapter Highlights" in much the same detail as it is found in your text. In microeconomics, you will study the chapter in complete detail.

For your macroeconomics course, it is recommended that you work intensively on selected portions: supply, demand, the laws for both, equilibrium, surplus and shortage.

Test your understanding so far. Answer the questions and then score them yourself.

FILL-IN REVIEW

Select between the choices underlined or fill in the blank. Cover the answers until you have provided your own.

A system of markets in a competitive economy ties together all the individual decisions that are made in buying and selling goods and services. Basic cornerstones in analyzing how it all works are _____ and _____. The law of demand states that at higher prices a _____ quantity will be demanded, other things being _____. Stated the other way, at lower prices a _____ quantity will be demanded. A demand schedule is all the different amounts of a good consumers are willing and able to ____ at all possible _____. When consumers demand less of a good, the price will tend to ____, giving producers a reason to supply ____ of that good on the market. This relationship produces a line with a _____ slope when graphed. We can use a schedule of prices and quantities demanded to draw a demand _____. The demand schedule is defined with all other things _____. This means that we hold the determinants of demand the same. These determinants are _____, _____, and _____; prices

supply   demand
smaller
equal
higher
buy   prices
fall
less
negative
curve
constant (or equal)
income   tastes preferences

goods	of related _____; and changes in expectations. To hold determinants of demand constant means that we *will/will not* consider them changing as we consider the demand for a good. If the demand of a consumer for a product goes up when the price of a related good goes down, the two products are _____ goods. If the demand for a product decreases when the price of a related product increases, the two products are _____ goods.
will not	
complementary	
substitute	
movement along	A change in quantity demanded means a *movement along/shift in* the demand curve. A change in demand means a *movement along/shift in* the demand curve itself.
shift in	
shift	An increase in demand is a _____ to the _____ of the demand curve. An increase in demand means that buyers will buy *larger/smaller* amounts at every price or will pay *more/less* for the same amount.
right	
larger	
more	
with	If a good is a complement, it is used *in place of/with* another good. If a good is a substitute, it is used *in place of/with* another good.
in place of	
	The price that we pay in dollars and cents for any good at a particular time is called the

FILL-IN REVIEW

_____ price. This is different from the price of a good relative to other goods. It is the price of a good _____ to all other prices that determines the relationship between the price and _____ demanded.

Supply is the schedule of a quantity of a good that will be *offered for sale/sold* at different _____ of the good. Supply curves have _____ slopes indicating a _____ relationship. This is the *same as/opposite of* the demand relationship. For supply, as the price rises the quantity supplied also _____. This relationship is called the law of _____. When the price of a good goes up, there is an incentive for sellers to increase the *supply/quantity supplied*. The determinants of supply are _____ _____/_____ and _____/_____/_____ _____. Changes in any of these determinants of supply are likely to cause changes in *quantity supplied/supply*. A movement along a supply curve that is a response to a price change is a change in *supply/quantity supplied*.

An increase in the input costs of producing a good is likely to _____ the supply of that good; the same effect can be produced by a ___ on that good.

absolute

relative

quantity

offered for sale
prices
positive   direct
opposite of

rises
supply

quantity supplied
input prices/taxes
subsidies/technology/
price expectations

supply

quantity supplied

lower

tax

equilibrium	The only price at which the market is cleared is the _____ price. At equilibrium, quantity _____ equals _____
supplied *quantity*	
demanded	
exceeds	_____. If the price of a good is above equilibrium, the quantity supplied *exceeds*/*is less than* quantity demanded. If the price is below equilibrium, quantity supplied *exceeds*/*is less than* quantity demanded. If the price exceeds equilibrium, there is a _____ and the price in a competitive market will ___. If the price is less than equilibrium, there is a _____ and the price in a competitive market will ___.
is less than	
surplus	
fall	
shortage	
rise	
rationing	One of the functions of price in a market economy is to ration scarce resources in an economy. When there are no surpluses or shortages in a market, this _____ function is operating correctly.

FILL-IN REVIEW

Here are some fill-in review problems related to graphs. Cover the answers until you have provided your own.

1. Label the vertical axis on this graph "price" of hamburgers. Label the horizontal axis "quantity" of hamburgers per month. Use the demand schedule below to plot the demand curve. Label the demand curve D1.

TABLE 3.1
DEMAND SCHEDULE (1)

PRICE	DEMAND QUANTITY
4.00	2
3.75	3
3.50	4
3.25	5
3.00	6
2.75	7
2.50	8

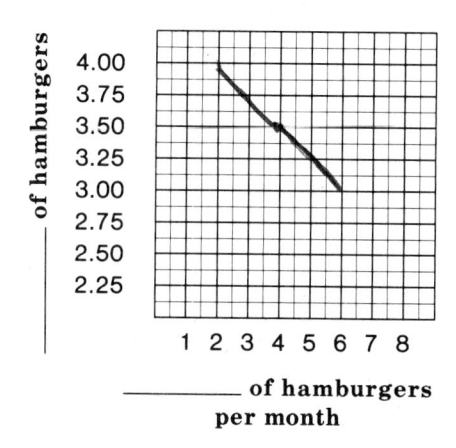

2. If price is initially $3.50, the quantity demanded is _. If price falls to $3.00, the new quantity demanded is _. This movement along the demand curve is called _____ __ _____ _____.

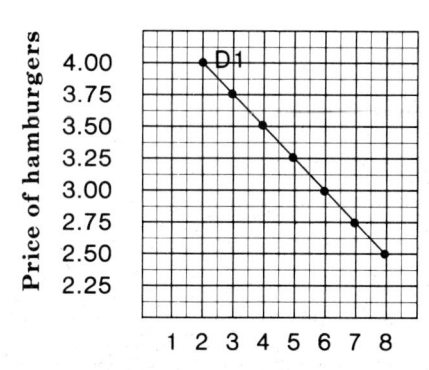

4

6

change in

quantity demanded

64   UNIT II: PART TWO

3. Now suppose consumer tastes change in such a way that at every price consumers will buy fewer hamburgers. In other words, the demand schedule becomes the following:

TABLE 3.2
DEMAND SCHEDULE (2)

PRICE	DEMAND QUANTITY
4.00	0
3.75	1
3.50	2
3.25	3
3.00	4
2.75	5
2.50	6

Plot the new demand curve on the same graph as before. Label the curve D2. (The completed graph from question 1 is repeated below.)

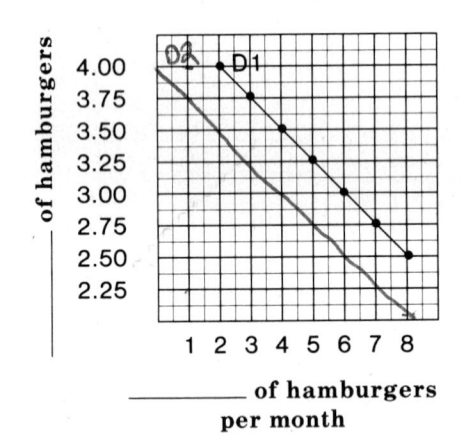

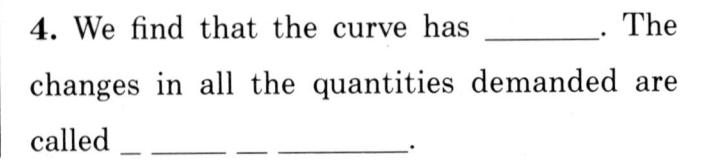

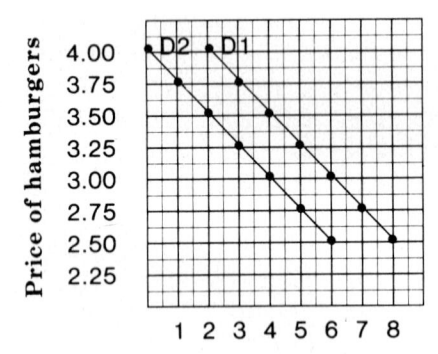

shifted

a shift in demand

4. We find that the curve has _____. The changes in all the quantities demanded are called __ ____ __ _____.

FILL-IN REVIEW

5. Table 3.3 shows a supply schedule for hamburgers (obviously very simplified). Label the vertical and horizontal axes as before. Draw in the supply curve. Label the curve "S" for supply. The relationship between the price and quantity demanded is _____. As price goes up, quantity _____ also goes up.

positive

supplied

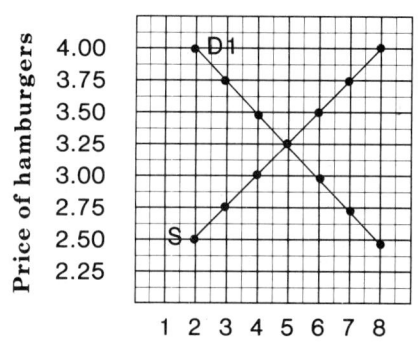

TABLE 3.3
SUPPLY SCHEDULE (3)

PRICE	SUPPLY QUANTITY
4.00	8
3.75	7
3.50	6
3.25	5
3.00	4
2.75	3
2.50	2

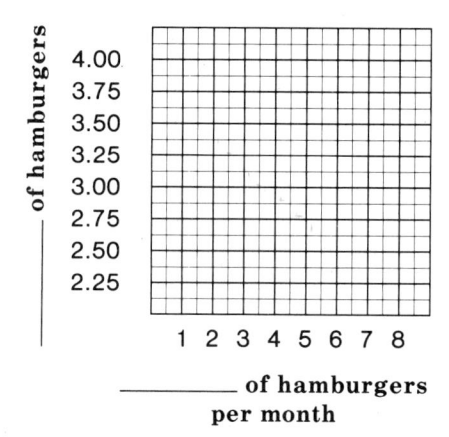

6. On the new graph (above) plot the demand curve D1 from Table 3.1 with the supply curve from Table 3.3. The equilibrium price is _____.

$3.25

66 UNIT II: PART TWO

7

3   above

surplus

7. If the price is $3.75, the quantity supplied is _. At that price, the quantity demanded is _. This price is *above/below* equilibrium, and there is a *shortage/surplus*.

8. Now, plot the demand curve from the demand Table 3.2 along with the supply curve from Table 3.3. Label the new demand curve D2.

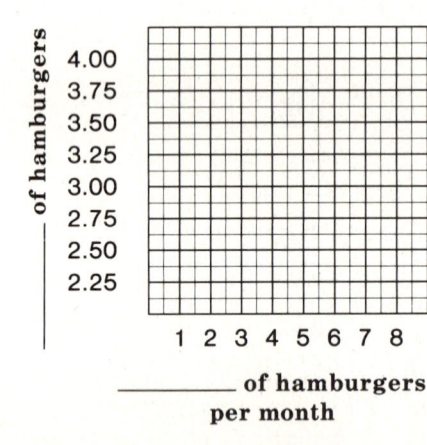

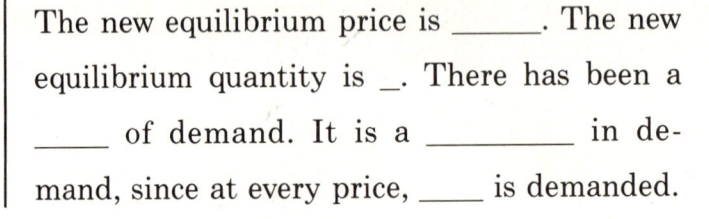

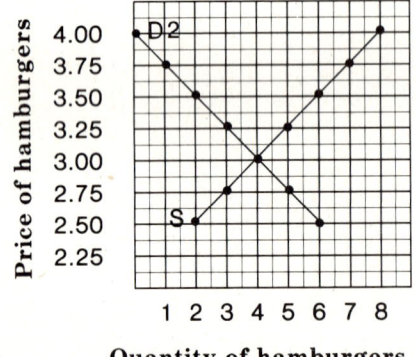

$3.00

4

shift   decrease

less

The new equilibrium price is _____. The new equilibrium quantity is _. There has been a ____ of demand. It is a _____ in demand, since at every price, ____ is demanded.

PROBLEMS, PROBLEMS, PROBLEMS...

Answers are at the end of this unit.

TRUE-FALSE

Circle either "T" or "F" for each statement.

T **F** 1. The law of demand states that the quantity of any good demanded tends to decrease as the price decreases.

T F 2. When the term "change in demand" is used, it refers to a movement of the whole demand curve.

T F 3. When the term "change in quantity demanded" is used, it refers to a response of quantity demanded to a change in price.

T F 4. A change in equilibrium price results from the shift of a demand curve.

T F 5. Bread and margarine generally are complementary goods.

T F 6. One of the basic determinants of supply is the cost of inputs to production.

T **F** 7. The law of supply states that the quantity of any good supplied tends to decrease as the price increases.

T F 8. Changes in supply are represented by shifts of the entire supply schedule.

T F 9. On a demand and supply graph, the intersection of the two indicates market equilibrium.

T F 10. To have a surplus of a good, in the economic sense, means price is above market equilibrium.

T F 11. At an equilibrium price, all buyers and sellers who want to buy or sell at that price can do so.

T **F** 12. A change in demand and a change in the quantity demanded are the same thing.

MATCH-UP

Match each item in the first column with a term in the second column. Use no term more than once.

__d__ 1. A schedule of prices and amounts that consumers will buy at each of these prices

__e__ 2. Consumers' incomes, tastes and preferences, and expectations of price changes, and prices of other related goods

__g__ 3. The result of a change in the price of a good

__f__ 4. Input costs, technology, taxes and subsidies

__h__ 5. If a determinant of demand for a good changes, the whole schedule will _____.

__j__ 6. When consumers' incomes go down, their demand for a (normal) good will _____.

__c__ 7. A schedule of prices and amounts of a good producers will offer on the market at each of these prices

__b__ 8. Where quantity demanded equals quantity supplied, and the market is cleared

__a__ 9. The prices we pay in dollars and cents for any good at a particular time

__i__ 10. When there is a surplus of a good in a competitive market, price will _____.

a. absolute price
b. equilibrium
c. supply
d. demand
e. determinants of demand
f. determinants of supply
g. change in quantity demanded
h. shift
i. fall
j. shift down

MULTIPLE CHOICE

For each of the following statements, choose the one best alternative. (Starred questions may be considered by some professors more suitable for a microeconomics course.)

1. The law of demand states that
    a. there is a direct relationship between price and quantity.
    b. at high prices, a smaller quantity will be demanded than at lower prices.
    c. at high prices, a larger quantity will be demanded than at lower prices.
    d. people are not influenced by advertising.

2. A demand curve
    a. slopes downward and to the right.
    b. is created from a demand schedule.
    c. demonstrates an inverse relationship between price and quantity.
    d. all of the above

3. For the laws of supply and demand to be valid
    a. price and quantity supplied must be inversely related while price and quantity demanded must show a positive relationship.
    b. price and quantity supplied must be inversely related and price and quantity demanded must also be inversely related.
    c. price and quantity supplied must show a positive relationship while price and quantity demanded must be inversely related.
    d. price and quantity supplied must show a positive relationship and price and quantity demanded must also show a positive relationship.

4. An increase in demand is represented by

   a. a shift of the demand curve to the left.

   b. a movement up along the existing curve.

   c. a shift of the demand curve to the right.

   d. a movement down the existing curve.

*5. As a person's income increases, the demand for potatoes decreases. This is an example of a/an

   a. normal good.

   b. free good.

   c. utility good.

   d. inferior good.

*6. If the quantity demanded for goods complementary to good A goes up, we can conclude

   a. the demand for good A decreases.

   b. the demand for good A increases.

   c. the demand for good A is constant.

   d. the relative price of the complementary good has risen.

*7. If the price of a substitute to A increases, then the demand for A

   a. will decrease.

   b. will shift down.

   c. will increase.

   d. will not change; there will only be a change in the quantity demanded.

*8. A drop in birth rates in the U.S. would cause which of the following (assuming all other things remain the same):

   a. the supply curve for baby food to shift to the right

   b. the demand curve for baby food to shift to the right

   c. a decrease in the quantity demanded for baby food

   d. the demand curve for baby food to shift to the left

9. Which of the following would cause supply of a good to shift?

   a. a change in the price of the good

   b. a change in the number of consumers who were willing and able to buy the good

   c. a change in demand for the good

   d. an increase in the number and the output of the producers of the good

10. The law of supply states that

   a. at higher prices, less is supplied.

   b. at lower prices, more is supplied.

   c. there is an inverse relationship between quantity supplied and relative price.

   d. there is a positive relationship between quantity supplied and relative price.

11. The intersection of a supply curve and a demand curve on a graph

   a. determines equilibrium price and quantity.

   b. determines the market-clearing price.

   c. is the point at which quantity demanded equals quantity supplied.

   d. all of the above

12. A shortage will occur at a price where

    a. quantity demanded equals quantity supplied.

    (b.) quantity demanded exceeds quantity supplied.

    c. quantity supplied exceeds quantity demanded.

    d. government sets a price above equilibrium.

13. A surplus will occur at a price

    a. where quantity demanded equals quantity supplied.

    b. where quantity demanded exceeds quantity supplied.

    (c.) where quantity supplied exceeds quantity demanded.

    d. where government sets a price below equilibrium.

x • *14. If supply increases and demand decreases, then

    a. relative price rises, quantity falls.

    b. relative price rises, quantity rises.

    c. relative price falls, quantity can go up or down.

    d. relative price can go up or down, quantity falls.

ECONOWORD PUZZLE—PART TWO

CLUES ACROSS

1. Schedule of quantities of a good that will be demanded at different prices (at some time period and with other things equal)
4. Schedule of amounts of a good that will be offered for sale at different prices of the good (at some period of time and with other things equal)
6. The movement of an entire schedule of either supply or demand
8. Goods which are relatively interchangeable with one another
9. The negative relationship between price and quantity in demand
10. Too much of a good supplied on the market because price is below equilibrium, also called surplus
11. The supply and demand curves are this at equilibrium.

CLUES DOWN

2. Here quantity demanded and quantity supplied are equal.
3. Demand is a schedule of the _____ of a good that will be demanded at different prices.
5. The direct relationship between price and quantity supplied.
7. Demand and supply curves will _____ at equilibrium.
8. When price is below equilibrium, there will be a _____ of that good (also called deficit).

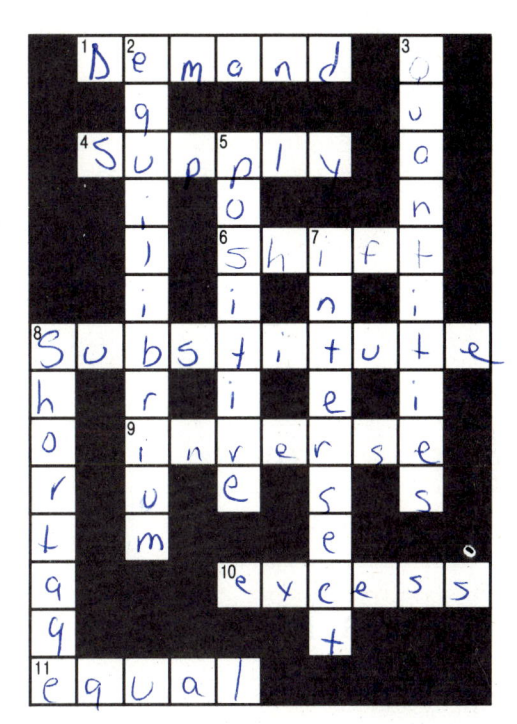

ANSWERS TO STUDY QUESTIONS

PART ONE

TRUE-FALSE

1. T 2. T 3. F 4. T 5. F 6. T 7. F 8. F 9. T

MATCH-UP

1. b 2. a 3. h 4. f 5. c 6. g 7. e 8. d

MULTIPLE CHOICE

1. b 2. e 3. e 4. a 5. d 6. a

COMPLETED ECONOWORD PUZZLE

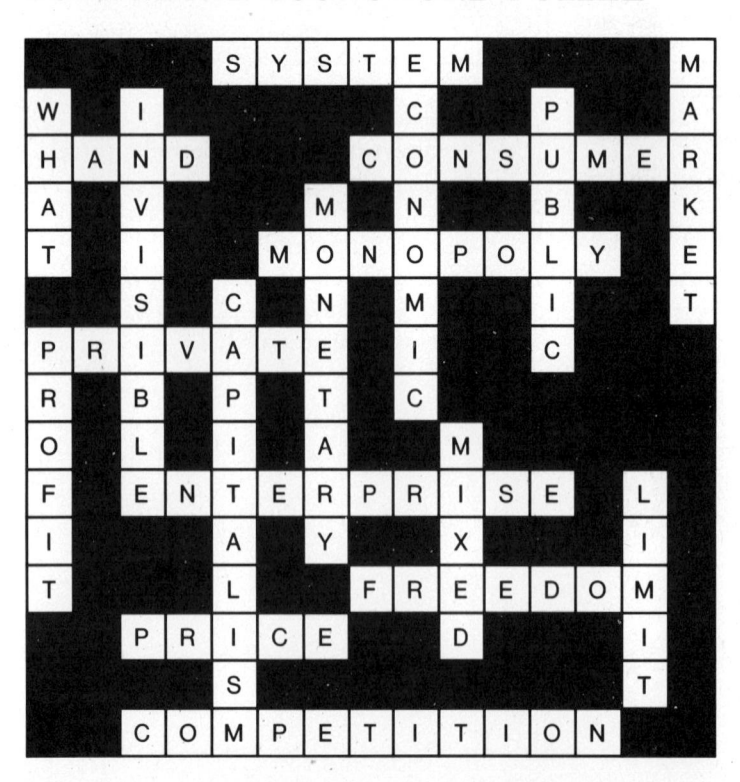

			S	Y	S	T	E	M			M
W		I				C		P			A
H	A	N	D		C	O	N	S	U	M	R
A		V				M		B			K
T		I		M	O	N	O	P	O	L	Y	E
S		S		C		N		M		I		T
P	R	I	V	A	T	E		I		C	
	R		B		P		T		C		
O	L		I		A			M			
F		E	N	T	E	R	P	R	I	S	E	L
I			A		Y		X				L	I
T			L			F	R	E	E	D	O	M
			P	R	I	C	E		D			I
				S								T
			C	O	M	P	E	T	I	T	I	O	N

ANSWERS TO STUDY QUESTIONS

PART TWO

TRUE-FALSE

1. F **2.** T **3.** T **4.** T **5.** T **6.** T **7.** F **8.** T **9.** T **10.** T
11. T **12.** F

MATCH-UP

1. d **2.** e **3.** g **4.** f **5.** h **6.** j **7.** c **8.** b **9.** a **10.** i

MULTIPLE CHOICE

1. b **2.** d **3.** c **4.** c **5.** d **6.** a **7.** c **8.** d **9.** d **10.** d
11. d **12.** b **13.** c **14.** c

COMPLETED ECONOWORD PUZZLE

	D	E	M	A	N	D		Q	
		Q						U	
	S	U	P	P	L	Y		A	
		I		O				N	
		L		S	H	I	F	T	
		I		I		N		I	
S	U	B	S	T	I	T	U	T	E
H		R		I		E		I	
O		I	N	V	E	R	S	E	
R		U		E		S		S	
T		M				E			
A			E	X	C	E	S	S	
G						T			
E	Q	U	A	L					

GOVERNMENT: HOW IT SPENDS

UNIT III

UNIT IN A NUTSHELL

PART ONE

Film: "The Free Rider"

Text: Chapter 6

PART TWO

Film: "Blowing the Whistle"

Text: Chapter 6

In our complex economy, there are millions of households and businesses numbering in the hundreds of thousands. Yet all these independent business and household units fit together to form an interlocked and interdependent society. We work together as an economic society partly through the way markets operate, and partly by the rule-making and rule-keeping functions of government.

Government is an important non-market force in our economy. The government sector has special characteristics that distinguish it from the household and business sectors: decisions are made collectively and government is able to use force in the regulation of both political and economic affairs. Through government, we provide our population with social goods and services. Through government, we also maintain courts and legislatures to enforce the rules that keep our economic system working, and to adapt the rules to changing conditions.

UNIT OBJECTIVES

Objectives 1-6 can be met by studying Chapter 6 and viewing "The Free Rider." After completing Part One, the student should be able to:

1. List both economic and political functions of government.

2. Define a public good and list its characteristics.

3. State some common examples of public goods.

4. Define externality (spillover).

5. Distinguish between positive and negative externalities.

6. List different actions government undertakes to correct externalities.

Objectives 7-9 can be met by studying Chapter 6 and viewing "Blowing the Whistle." After completing Part Two, the student should be able to:

7. List the tools used by government to attempt to redistribute income.

8. Be aware of the size of the government sector of the economy relative to the total national output.

9. List the special characteristics of governments that distinguish them from businesses and individuals.

PART ONE

UNIT III ASSIGNMENT: PART ONE

STUDY: Chapter 6, "The Role and Size of Government," *Economics Today*

STUDY: Film Summary: "The Free Rider," *Study Guide*

VIEW: "The Free Rider"

REVIEW: Chapter 6 Highlights, *Study Guide*

COMPLETE: (Note: Activities in Part One and Part Two overlap.) Begin Fill-in Review *and* Problems, Problems, Problems..., *Study Guide*

FILM SUMMARY: "The Free Rider"

In this program, Thomas is worried about the encroachment of the government into the economy, and we watch a controversy develop between Thomas and his boss, Larry Dutweiler, regarding their views about government's role in the economy. As government has grown in size and power over the past decades, its effects on our mixed economy have also increased. Government has a number of purely economic functions: 1) it provides a legal system to protect the rights of private property; 2) it attempts to correct economic externalities (situations where costs of production spill-over to third parties); 3) it acts to protect the competitive system; 4) provides public goods; and 5) it attempts to regulate the ups and downs of economic activity.

Larry Dutweiler resents paying for government. He doesn't want to be taxed to provide public goods and believes that the economy should rely on the private sector for most everything. In his repudiation of the role of government as a major participant in the economy, Larry even uses government-imposed, high corporate taxes as a reason for denying Thomas a raise. Thomas, however, should have been more alert to Larry's faulty reasoning. A corporation pays taxes only on profits, not on income.

To find taxable business profit, all legitimate business expenses are deducted from business income. These deductions include salaries of executives as well as wages paid to employees. It is true, however, that the tax on corporate profits is progressive; that is, as profits go up, the percentage of tax on additional amounts of profit also goes up. When Larry Dutweiler complains, "Dynamics Corporation is getting hit with high taxes," we recognize that this also means Dyanmics' profits are high.

Stronger reasons for Dutweiler's complaints could be that increasing tax rates lower incentives to make additional profit, or that the business costs of complying with governmental rules and regulations raise prices. Preparing reports for the government and following complicated regulations also increase costs and don't add a thing to productivity.

Government would have few functions in Dutweiler's ideal world, however, he doesn't say which of those he would leave to government. The question could be asked: what would happen if the government withdrew from as many areas of support and regulation as Larry Dutweiler wishes?

The film depicts Thomas's fantasies of life, and in this whimsical drama, public goods such as police protection and national defense are provided by the private sector instead of by government. When "volunteers" don't show up, we have an example of the "free rider" problem: many people will ride free if they can avoid paying. People are willing to benefit, but few are willing to contribute their manpower for volunteer neighborhood safety, and few contribute directly to national defense. Who is eager to pay for something that can be obtained without cost? Government solves the free-rider problem by taxing everybody in order to provide public goods such as police, lighthouses, roads, a national defense, airport safety, weather reports, agricultural research, health products testing, and on and on.

Susan makes the assertion that the government shouldn't do what the private economy can do. She does not then go on to explain. What does she mean? If she means public goods, which goods presently provided by government can the private economy supply more efficiently, when *all* costs are considered? The film gives examples which are easy enough to make fun of, but it is clear that neighborhood protection, maintaining lighthouses, and national defense are services that are beyond the scope of the private economy.

When government does intervene in the market, all costs of goods and services must be taken into account. Consideration must also be given as to whether the government is doing something that the private economy can do at a lower cost. At times, when government enters into the economy, it does not always accomplish what it intended. Sometimes it disturbs market forces and it frequently changes incentives as a result of its intervention.

Keep in mind, also, that government services are not free. What may appear to be free to you or me as individuals, is surely not free to the society—of which we are a part—that provided it. When resources are allocated to public goods, they have opportunity costs—just like everything else. All of these factors must be taken into consideration when evaluating government action in the economy.

As Dr. Beck points out, the market would not work well in providing public goods. Consider the characteristics of public goods. They can't be produced in small units; they can be used by large numbers of people at no extra cost without depriving others of their use, and it is difficult to charge for them on the basis of the quantity used. Providing public goods collectively costs the economy fewer resources.

Let's consider, again, Susan's assertion that government shouldn't do what the private economy can do. In some of its functions, the government attempts to *undo* what has happened in the private economy. In the village scene, for example, when the fishermen who monopolized the market are stopped by government, we are reminded of government's role in protecting the competitive system. Government defines illegal market activities and has the power to enforce its decisions regarding market competition.

As an attempt to correct market failure, government may require both producers and consumers to pay to third parties the spillover costs caused by certain types of manufacturing. The terms "spillover" or "externality" are used to identify the production costs to society that aren't taken care of in the marketplace. When a product is sold, its price is assumed to cover all the costs associated with making the product, but we know this is not always the case. The air in some cities imposes a health cost on citizens. The water in some lakes, streams or bays may no longer support aquatic life. In some areas, industrial or traffic noises are so loud that schools must close windows and use air conditioning. These are examples of externalities or spillovers from productive processes that are costly to society in terms either of the lowered quality of life, or in the presentation of health hazards.

Externalities, however, need not always be negative. We can locate positive examples of externalities if we look around. When a company includes beautiful landscaping and a picnic area near its plant, a benefit is created and received by people who do not necessarily buy the company's products. Government may pay companies for beneficial spillovers and tax or regulate producers of harmful spillovers. Thus, by its subsidizing or taxing of externalities, government acts to both account for, and control some of, the less obvious social costs associated with industrial production.

The film briefly touches on three of the purely economic functions of government: provision of public goods, protection of the competitive system, and correction of externalities. The next three films that relate to government in the economy will return to some of the subjects mentioned in this program and also continue to develop the themes of government taxation.

HINT

"The Free Rider," and the next three films, "Blowing the Whistle," "Familiar Falacies" and "Loopholes," all relate to government. To successfully complete these units, you should study the Chapter Highlights for text Chapters 6 and 7 of *Economics Today*. These chapters are descriptive, rather than analytic, and will not be difficult. After you have studied the Highlights, complete the exercises for each, then move ahead to preview upcoming text chapters and *Study Guide* sections. The real core of macroeconomics begins with Chapter 9, "The Circular Flow of Income and Product" and continues through Chapter 12, "Income and Employment Determination." Much of the core material is abstract and theoretical, and will require careful study and concentration. You should begin to preview Chapters 9 through 12.

CHAPTER 6 HIGHLIGHTS

Defined words are underlined.

I. PURELY ECONOMIC FUNCTIONS OF GOVERNMENT THAT AFFECT EXCHANGE

   A. Government provides the legal/judiciary system. To maintain rights upon which our system is based, the courts

      1. enforce legal contracts,

      2. protect rights of private property.

   B. As a protector of the competitive system, government

      1. defines illegal activities that prevent competition: *e.g.*, antitrust legislation to control monopoly power,

      2. maintains regulatory agencies to require competitive-like results from government-created monopolies. (Government regulates prices and services.)

   C. Correction of spillovers (which are also called externalities). <u>*Externalities:*</u> Effects of a decision not taken into account when that decision was made. Externalities can be either positive (a benefit) or negative (a cost).

      1. Examples of spillovers (externalities):

         a. A dam built only for flood control creates a lake that provides boating, swimming, and fishing. Recreational opportunities are "external" to the decision to build the dam; a *positive* externality is created.

         b. Wastes poured into a stream destroys the stream's other uses. This social cost is not included in the costs faced by the firm creating the wastes; a *negative* externality is created.

2. Externalities can be corrected to reflect their costs or benefits to society by

   a. regulation,

   b. taxation (in the case of negative externalities),

   c. subsidies (in the case of positive externalities).

D. Public goods are provided by government.

   1. Public goods have certain characteristics.

      a. They are usually indivisible, and cannot be produced in small units.

      b. They are used by increasing numbers of users at no additional cost.

      c. Additional users do not deprive others of the good's services.

      d. Users can rarely be charged on the basis of the quantity used.

   2. Public goods make it possible for people to be "free riders"; public goods can be used without a user payment.

   3. If we relied on the private sector to provide public-type goods, there wouldn't be enough produced.

E. Economy-wide stabilization is attempted by the federal government to smooth out the ups and downs of overall business activity. A study of stabilization is the central issue in macroeconomics.

II. THE POLITICAL FUNCTIONS OF GOVERNMENT

A. Government provides merit goods and attempts to discourage production of demerit goods.

1. *Merit Goods:* Goods that the political process decides are socially desirable.

2. *Demerit Goods:* Goods that the political process has deemed as socially undesirable.

B. Government redistributes income through transfer payments.

1. *Income Redistribution:* Through progressive taxes and transfer payments, government takes income from some groups and gives it to others.

2. *Transfer Payments:* Payments made by government to individuals for which no services or goods are rendered in exchange: Social Security benefits, unemployment compensation and welfare payments.

C. A trade-off between equity and efficiency is involved in choosing government policies.

1. *Efficiency:* A situation in which resources are used with a minimum of waste, expense, and effort.

2. *Equity:* The fairness of how the goods provided by society are divided.

3. Government's attempts to achieve equity often clash with efficiency considerations.

III. THE SPECIAL CHARACTERISTICS OF GOVERNMENTS DISTINGUISH THEM FROM BUSINESSES AND INDIVIDUALS.

A. Government provides zero-priced social goods. Generally, there is no user-charge system; society pays by means of taxes.

B. Governments can legally use force in the regulation of economic affairs.

C. The "general interest" is the basis for government decision-making.

IV. GOVERNMENTS TODAY ACCOUNT FOR 40 PERCENT OF TOTAL NATIONAL OUTPUT.

　A. The 40 percent is divided among the federal, state and local governments.

　B. Since the mid-1940s, state and local government outlays have increased at nearly two times the rate of federal government outlays.

FILL-IN REVIEW

Select from the choices underlined or fill in the blank. Cover the answers until you have provided your own.

We do not live in a purely market world. There are other non-market forces at work that affect the allocation of resources. One of the most important of these non-market forces is the _____. The government	*government*
provides many purely _____ functions.	*economic*
These have to do with the way _____ is carried out in the economy.	*exchange*
One of the most important functions of government is to provide and maintain _____ institutions (courts and police) to govern exchanges. The legal/_____ system defines	*legal*
	judiciary
and enforces the legal status of business and private ownership _____. It also provides a	*rights*
system for enforcement of _____. Private ownership and property rights are the basis of	*contracts*

market	the _____ system. The rules of the game necessary for the market to function are established and enforced by _____.
government	
competitive	Another important function of government is to protect the _____ system. In this role, government defines _____ activities that prevent competition. ____-____ legislation is intended to restrict activities that lower competition. Government also sets up _____ agencies which place restrictions on certain business activities the government believes are not in society's interest.
illegal	
Anti-trust	
regulatory	
externalities	Another function of government is to correct spillovers, called _____. Externalities are the effects arising from production that are not included in the _____ _____ of the goods being produced. Externalities can be useful or harmful; in other words, they can be positive or _____. Government may correct negative externalities by special _____ or through _____. Both actions by government will shift the producer's supply curve so that the private cost also reflects the cost or benefit of the externality to the society.
market price	
negative	
taxes	
legislation	

Another function of government is to provide public goods (sometimes called collective goods) which are used by many at the same time. These _____ goods are _____ and can be used by increasing numbers of people at *high/no* additional cost. Public goods users *do/do not* deprive others of the goods' services, and these goods are not easily adapted to _____ charges on the basis of quantity used. The primary source of money for providing public goods is *taxes/user charges*. If goods with the characteristics of social goods are provided privately, it is difficult to force people to pay their share and to prevent people from taking a free ride on what is provided by others. A case for government financing by taxes of social goods is based on this _____-_____ problem. A final but very important economic function of government is to provide economy-wide _____ to smooth out the ups and downs of overall business activity.

public   indivisible

no

do not

user

taxes

free-rider

stabilization

The political functions of government include provision and regulation of merit and demerit goods and income redistribution. A good that the political process has deemed as socially desirable is a _____ _____, while one deemed undesirable is termed a _____ _____. Government also works to accomplish a

merit good

demerit good

UNIT III: PART ONE

redistribution *taxation*	change in the relative shares of income of individuals in the economy. This income _____ is attempted by using progressive _____ to transfer income from those who have more to those who have less. A payment to individuals, for which no good or service is rendered at the time, is called a
transfer payment *Social* *Security unemployment compensation* *welfare*	_____ _____. Important types of money transfer payments are _____ _____, _____ _____, and _____.
equity *efficiency* *resources*	In choosing government policies, there is often a trade-off between _____ and _____. Government's attempts to achieve equity may clash with an efficient use of _____.
increasing *40*	Government's outlays account for an *increasing/decreasing* share of national output. The total of all government spending as a percentage of gross national product was 25 percent in 1950 and __ percent in 1980.

PROBLEMS, PROBLEMS, PROBLEMS...

Answers are at the end of this unit.

TRUE-FALSE

Circle either "T" or "F" for each statement.

T **(F)** 1. Protecting the competitive system cannot be a function of government.

(T) F 2. Private ownership and property rights are the basis of the market system.

T **(F)** 3. Since government goods are usually provided at zero cost, the cost to the society of those goods is zero.

T **(F)** 4. As more and more people use a social good, the additional cost to the consumer goes up.

(T) F 5. Some production creates spillovers or externalities in the form of uncompensated benefits or costs.

(T) F 6. Transfer payments are payments for goods or services not currently rendered in exchange.

T **(F)** 7. Transfer payments are salaries to individuals who work for the government.

(T) F 8. Government has economic functions in addition to political functions.

(T) F 9. Economy-wide stabilization is attempted by the federal government to smooth out the ups and downs of business activity.

(T) F 10. State and local governments account for the major share of total government pending.

MATCH-UP

Match each item in the first column with a term in the second column. Use no term more than once.

h 1. Beneficial or harmful effects arising from production which affect third parties

g 2. Payments by governments to individuals for which no services or goods are rendered in exchange

d 3. Those who will use goods without paying for them

e 4. Provision of merit and demerit goods, and income redistribution

a 5. Legal/judicial system, protection of competitive system, correction of externalities, economy-wide stabilization

b 6. Indivisible, used by increasing numbers of people at no extra cost, difficult to charge users

c 7. Through transfer payments and taxes, government takes income from some and gives it to others.

f 8. Expenditures that have increased at nearly two times the speed of federal government outlays

a. economic functions of government
b. public goods
c. income redistribution
d. free riders
e. political functions of government
f. state and local government expenditure
g. transfer payments
h. externalities

MULTIPLE CHOICE

For each of the following statements, choose the one best alternative.

1. To provide a legal system, promote competition, correct externalities, produce public goods, stabilize the economy are all the

    a. international functions of government.

    b. international regulation by government.

    c. economic functions of government.

    d. political regulations by government.

2. Anti-trust legislation has been passed by Congress to reduce the

    a. competition of small firms.

    b. power of monopolies.

    c. competition of international trade.

    d. power of government.

3. A payment by government to an individual, for which no service or good is rendered in exchange defines

    a. an externality payment.

    b. a free rider payment.

    c. a demerit good payment.

    d. a transfer payment.

4. When production is providing important positive externalities, the government may choose to

    a. subsidize their production.

    b. tax their production.

    c. forbid their production.

    d. limit their production.

5. Pure public goods
    a. are usually indivisible.
    b. can be used by additional people at no extra cost.
    c. can be used by additional people without depriving other users.
    d. are all of the above, a and b and c.

6. There are characteristics that distinguish governments from businesses. Which of the following is *not* one of those characteristics?
    a. Government produces goods for the market.
    b. Government provides social goods.
    c. Government may use force in economic regulation.
    d. Government considers the general interest in decision-making.

PART TWO

UNIT III ASSIGNMENT: PART TWO

STUDY: Review Chapter 6, "The Role and Size of Government," *Economics Today*

STUDY: Film Summary: "Blowing the Whistle," *Study Guide*

VIEW: "Blowing the Whistle"

COMPLETE: Fill-in Review *and* Problems, Problems, Problems . . . from Part One, *Study Guide*

COMPLETE: Above and Beyond *and* Econoword Puzzle, *Study Guide*

FILM SUMMARY: "Blowing The Whistle"

The role of the government in the economy and the sources of its revenue are the themes of the film, "Blowing the Whistle." In it, Thomas is portrayed as a man of unpredictable moods whose present concern is that of the all-consuming role of government in our lives. The building of one of a large number of government buildings by Dynamics Corporation's subsidiary is the spark which helps to bring out all of his biases and misinformed beliefs about government and its role in present day society's complex economic life.

Thomas, however, serves our purpose admirably; his prejudices and wrong-headed obstinancy are useful for us as a teaching tool in trying to convey economic principles, concepts, and eventually the building of important economic models. We are left to conclude that the government is less than the monster Thomas believes it to be; and although its role is not always appreciated, it is crucial and an understanding of it is necessary if we are to be made aware of how the entire economy functions.

In a dream sequence, Thomas becomes a candidate for public office because he wants to take a more active part in doing something to limit the size of government. He is successful and quickly becomes a part of the government bureaucracy he is attempting to limit! At each step up his spectacular political career (in which he serves at all levels of government) he is confronted by the problems resulting from severely restricted revenues.

As a successful politician—if only in his dreams—Thomas holds office at the local, state and, finally, the federal levels of government. In so doing, he learns of the source of revenue and the types of expenditures for each governmental level: property taxes provide local governments with their largest source of revenue, the sales tax is the biggest source for state governments and individual income tax is the main source of funds for the federal level.

In Thomas's dream, as part of his platform, a tax-cut proposition is passed. Now deprived of 75 percent of their income, local governments must drastically scale down their expenditures. Since state and local governments support education, public assistance, hospitals, clinics and highway systems, large tax cuts will force curtailment of these services. National defense and transfer payments (cash benefits to veterans, to the aged, unemployed, the poor and disabled), which together amount to over 60 percent of the federal budget, will also be drastically cut after a national "Proposition Weldon" goes into effect.

The question now has to be asked, which of the thousands of programs (meaning, in effect, "jobs") that depend on government revenues will be supported? Thomas's dilemma, although presented in a whimsical fashion, is a real one.

Thomas Weldon proposes an education voucher system that calls for tax revenues to subsidize the students, so that they will then be able to attend whatever schools they choose. This voucher system might have the effect of reducing taxes. However, the economic effect of such a system would be to reduce government tax support for education, since it would change the group which receives funds directly from government.

Our present tax support of education funnels income to those who direct our public education apparatus; namely, teachers and administrators. Students under our present system must attend the area school in which they reside. Under Thomas's plan (actually, a form of 1976 Nobel prize-winning economist Milton Friedman's proposal), students are free to choose any school, and will pay some or all of the fees with a government voucher redeemable at the school chosen. Thomas's (and Dr. Friedman's) belief is that competitive capitalism can do most anything governments can do, and do it more efficiently.

Thomas's voucher proposal is another indication of his belief that government is too large and intrusive, and attempts to accomplish social aims through economic policy. While Thomas's dreams of holding high elective office are little more than personal fantasies and may not be taken seriously, the role he envisions for government and the policies he would like government to pursue and implement should, indeed, be of concern to us. In effect, his views are meant to prod us into considering what is to be the role of government in our modern, mixed economy; and, specifically, what kinds of problems we want government to tackle and try to solve.

ABOVE AND BEYOND

Most of us receive some kind of government subsidy in one way or another, at one time or another in our lives. A subsidy can be called a negative tax. A better definition of subsidy is government economic help to private individual consumers or producers at the expense of others in the economy. The subsidy has the effect of changing the cost of a good or service to the recipient.

1. As an exercise for yourself, make a list of ways in which you receive government outlays or subsidies. To help you make your list, answer "yes" or "no" for the following questions:

    Do you attend a state-supported college? Do you receive a tuition waiver? Have you participated in a government-supported training program or seminar? Do you buy groceries on a military base? Have you sold farm goods to the government loan at interest rates below the market rate? Do you deduct the cost of interest paid on your home mortgage when you pay your income tax? Do you deduct a percentage of your medical costs from your income tax?

2. For each item on your list, could you be considered a part of a special interest group?

/ # ECONOWORD PUZZLE

ECONOWORD PUZZLE

CLUES ACROSS

1. One of the purely economic functions of government is to provide a legal/_____ system to maintain the rights upon which our system is based.
4. Provision of merit and discouragement of demerit goods are two _____ functions of government.
6. The opposite of private
9. When goods with the characteristics of social goods are provided privately it is difficult to force people to pay their share. This is called the _____ rider problem.
11. Everything produced by the economy is termed either a _____ or a service.
12. A situation in which there is a minimum amount of waste, expense and effort
13. A payment levied by the government
16. The legal/judicial system protects the rights of private _____.
17. The month in which the federal government collects income taxes
21. A payment made by government for which no goods or services are rendered in exchange
22. In April, the federal government collects _____ taxes.
23. A negative tax (For this clue check the ABOVE AND BEYOND section.)
24. Legislation defining illegal monopolistic activities that attempt to lower competition and restrain trade

CLUES DOWN

2. In its role in the protection of competition, government defines _____ activities that prevent competition.
3. Your text defines purely _____ functions of government that affect exchange.
4. Externalities are the effects arising from production that are not included in the market _____ of the goods being produced.
5. One of the purely economic functions of government is enforcement of _____ contracts.
7. A fee for use of public goods is termed a _____ charge.
8. One of the purely economic functions of government is enforcement of a legal _____.
10. When goods with the characteristics of social goods are provided privately, it's difficult to force people to pay their share. This is called the free _____ problem.
12. The effect arising from production that is not included in the market price of the goods being produced; it can be useful or harmful.
14. The opposite of public
15. Another name for externality - describing the overflow of effects of production
18. Goods the political process decides are socially desirable
19. The "fairness" of the division of the goods society produces
20. In a market system, the market price of a good fully covers its total _____.

ANSWERS TO STUDY QUESTIONS

TRUE-FALSE

1. F 2. T 3. F 4. F 5. T 6. T 7. F 8. T 9. T 10. T

MATCH-UP

1. h 2. g 3. d 4. e 5. a 6. b 7. c 8. f

MULTIPLE CHOICE

1. c 2. b 3. d 4. a 5. d 6. a

COMPLETED ECONOWORD PUZZLE

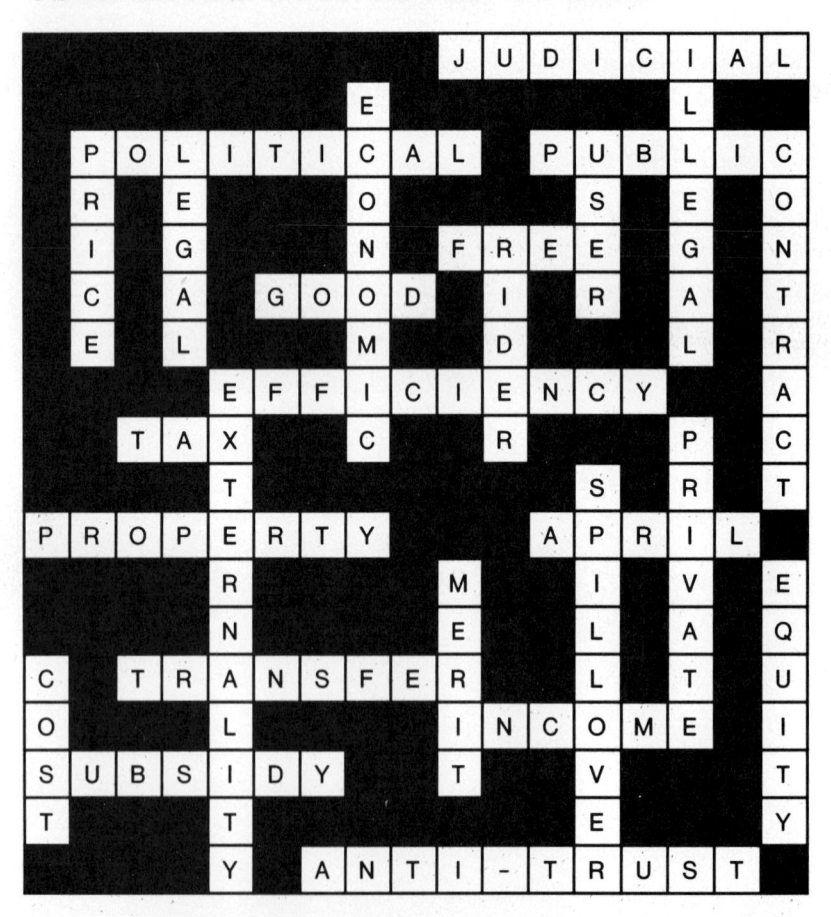

GOVERNMENT: HOW IT TAXES

UNIT IV

UNIT IN A NUTSHELL

PART ONE
Film: "Familiar Fallacies"

Text: Chapter 7

PART TWO
Film: "Loopholes"

Text: Chapter 7

Taxation and politics are each subjects guaranteed to provoke controversy from almost any group. In this and the preceding unit, government's spending, taxation and the resulting national debt are explosive topics on the films, but rather more calmly discussed here and in your text.

The understanding of the taxation policies and spending patterns of each level of government is vital to your later grasp of the modern controversies around supply-side economics.

Government diverts to itself a share of our national output by taxation, by selling bonds and by printing money. The system of taxation used by each level of government (to raise funds and stabilize the economy) can be viewed as a system of incentives.

UNIT OBJECTIVES

The following objectives can be met by studying Chapter 7 and viewing "Familiar Fallacies" and "Loopholes." After completing this unit, the student should be able to:

1. State how each level of government obtains its revenues and the types of goods and services that are obtained with these revenues.

2. Define progressive, proportional and regressive types of taxation systems, and be able to identify each type.

3. Distinguish between marginal and average tax rates.

4. Define "effective tax rate."

5. Be able to identify tax loopholes and comment on their effects on the U.S. tax system.

6. Understand what is meant by the national debt, or the public debt.

7. State why the national government cannot go bankrupt.

SPECIAL INSTRUCTIONS

Part One and Two have been combined in this Unit. You have been assigned but one chapter, Chapter 7, in the text. The content of the two films for this Unit, "Loopholes" and "Familiar Fallacies," have been combined in a single film summary, and are a continuation of material concerned with government spending, taxation and debt, introduced in text Chapter 6.

Take the time now to preview the important material beginning in Unit VI and continued in Units VII and VIII. These units are central to an understanding of macroeconomics, and are best studied by proceeding in short, easy stages. Concentrate first on the concepts, then go on to memorize the definitions and the ways spending affects the economy. Begin now so that when the material is assigned in its regular sequence, the terms and concepts will be familiar to you.

PART ONE AND PART TWO

UNIT IV ASSIGNMENT: PARTS ONE AND TWO

STUDY: Chapter 7, "Government Spending, Taxation, and Debt," *Economics Today*

STUDY: Film Summary: "Familiar Fallacies" and "Loopholes," *Study Guide*

VIEW: "Familiar Fallacies"

VIEW: "Loopholes"

REVIEW: Chapter 7 Highlights, *Study Guide*

COMPLETE: Fill-in Review *and* Problems, Problems, Problems *... and* Econoword Puzzle, *Study Guide*

FILM SUMMARY: "Familiar Fallacies" and "Loopholes"

In these two programs, Thomas first becomes interested in taxation systems and then, with much nervousness and apprehension, grapples with the subject of the national debt. Clearly, government uses tax policy to change the level of national income. Right now, we are dealing with how government *can* tax, not *why* it taxes. The reasons for government taxation will be discussed fully in a later Unit.

Let's look first at the three types of taxation systems: progressive, proportional and regressive. They are quite straightforward. The personal income tax is a *progressive tax,* one in which the fraction of income paid in tax goes up as income increases. The fraction of each additional dollar of income that must be paid in tax is called the marginal tax rate. Don't be confused between marginal tax and average tax as taxpayers sometimes are. The average tax rate is the fraction of *entire* income that is paid in taxes, and marginal tax rate refers to tax on *additional* units of income. When someone is said to be in the "50s" tax bracket, that person pays 50 percent tax only on the last dollars of income. The average tax, or the tax as a percentage of the entire income, will be lower.

The *progressive* tax rate is considered to be a way of promoting equality of income. In theory, the rich pay a higher percentage of their incomes in tax than the poor. However, the belief in the progressive tax's having an equalizing effect may not be fully justified. If a tax has an equalizing impact, incomes after the tax is paid are more equal for everyone than before the tax. In fact, the equalizing effect of our progressive tax is fairly modest, and, in the face of increasing proportional tax rates, high income groups seek ways to avoid the high tax. Those with lower incomes, to some extent, do the same.

Looking out for your best interests (which means, in effect, lowering your tax liability) may take the form of convincing the company you work for to grant job fringe benefits instead of paying larger incomes. It may also involve working fewer days: the time off has the effect of buying leisure. Those with low incomes also take precaution to pay as little tax as possible. Welfare programs may lead recipients to work fewer days, so as to earn less taxable income.

Tax avoidance is not sinful, it represents realistic response to incentives and is legal. All sorts of ways to avoid tax are written into the tax law. Simply, such loopholes are legal methods to reduce taxes owed to government.

A *proportional tax* is one in which the fraction of income paid as tax is the same at every income level. In other words, if the proportional rate is 20 percent, every individual income earner pays a flat 20 percent, no matter what the income. If income tax were proportional, with no loopholes, incentives to find ways to shelter income from taxes would be reduced.

It is possible to think of any taxation system as one which provides incentives to either spend or save. Congress has granted lower tax liability with certain kinds of purchases and investments. Consider what kinds of expenditures are undertaken in order to capture these tax benefits. For example, the ability to deduct mortgage and car loan interest payments from income tax increases the incentive to buy houses and cars. Certain types of spending or saving are further promoted when the government provides tax advantages for medical expenditures, energy-saving home improvements, and business related outlays such as travel and expensive business conference lunches.

These tax benefits and incentives are powerful levers of economic and political clout for legislators in our country. Individually, or working as a congressional body, they exert a great deal of influence in proposing and granting certain types of incomes exempt from taxation. This is now the case under our progressive tax system. Should there by an attempt to change the present methods of taxation to, say, a proportional system, with loopholes eliminated would mean upsetting and altering many long established practices and sources of political power.

A *regressive* tax is one in which the average tax rate declines as income rises. It is a tax which takes a larger fraction of income from low income people than from those with higher incomes. Most taxes other than income taxes are typically regressive in their impact, such as sales taxes, Social Security payments, etc.

Since the film "Familiar Fallacies" deals with Thomas's worry about the national debt, it is important here to briefly describe *why* we have a national debt. It can be asked why the government sometimes chooses to spend more than it collects in taxes. One of the answers may lie in the fact that money is used for all sorts of job-creating programs to raise national income during a recession. In the past, this deficit spending has made both economic and political good sense.

As you continue to study macroeconomics, you will learn that the economy is divided, for purposes of analysis, into the private sectors of households and businesses, and the public sector, government. We will develop a model that will analyze the level of the total income in the economy as a result of the spending of the sectors.

First, we will construct the model with only the spending of private sectors. Then we will add government as a stabilizer which may choose to increase its own expenditures when the country's income is low, and withdraw spending when inflation becomes a problem. It is in performing this stabilizing function that government may choose to spend more than it receives in taxes. And many of our modern-day governments have increased their own spending ability by deficit spending, thereby creating, along the way, a large national debt.

The national debt results from government borrowing. For its spending, the government borrows from the private sector by selling bonds. We will deal later with the specifics of why this is done when the Keynesian model of the economy is discussed. Right now, we are only interested in the *mechanics* of how the national debt is created. Simply, when government spends more than it has, it is using deficit spending, and government finances what it borrows by selling bonds. The total amount of these bonds outstanding is the national debt.

In the film "Familiar Fallacies," Thomas reacts emotionally to several issues involving government. He refers to government as a "monster," and here, as in several other parts of the film series, he sees little middle ground: for him the world is either perfect, or about to end. Be aware that we are using Thomas's worries, exuberances and wrong-headed obstinancy, as well as his ability to learn some things rapidly as learning tools. He and his wife, Karen, later become enmeshed in economic problems. These crises range from concerns about their jobs, to their struggle to understand models of the economy. These situation dramas are vehicles to teach economics.

The particular film program plays to a commonly held fear. Thomas calls Danny and Celia "innocent lambs," stuck with paying the debts of earlier generations. Is Thomas really gullible enough to believe this? If he, or anybody else, agrees that this is the case, then each must believe that the increasing public debt will become a crushing burden on generations not yet born. Let's consider this fear.

What about the costs of wars or of other kinds of deficit spending? Are we paying for the wars of the past? Not really. Recall the production possibilities graph from Chapter 1. It shows that, at full employment, of all of the nation's resources available to us, we *choose* to produce only certain combinations of goods. For example, in a war we choose to give up cars to produce tanks and choose to give up nylon stockings to produce parachutes. The war-time society *itself* pays the opportunity cost of giving up these goods. The government has diverted productive resources for military use. As a result, society gives up a certain amount of consumer goods. The burden of the war falls on that society which does without consumer goods *at the time* of the war.

Another important fact cannot be overlooked. In building war goods, the opportunity to produce more capital equipment is also given up. Therefore, the total amount of capital goods we have now as an industrial base for production is lower than it would have been without the war. That burden—a reduced industrial base of production—we still bear today.

What about the public debt that results from government bond sales? Interest payments on this debt are financed by taxpayers and are collected by the people who hold the bonds. This means that government debt, as any debt, transfers money from one group at this time to another group at this time. It does not involve a transfer of money from a group in one time, to a group in another time.

There are costs to the debt but they, in general, do not involve burdening future generations. These costs involve both redistribution of income from those who pay the taxes to those who hold the bonds; and the creation of incentives for people to change their buying behavior that results in tax avoidance. (This behavior may distort the use of resources and lower the overall efficiency of the economy.) And, perhaps most importantly, the creation of inflation by not collecting *taxes* to pay the debt but by increasing the deficit through selling even more bonds.

Before the use of federal government deficit spending, the argument was advanced that the government was like a household and, accordingly, could not keep on running a budget deficit without eventually bankrupting itself. At first, it seemed obvious: an individual household had a life-time span and the debt would have to be paid back within that life-time, or through an estate after death. But government can be viewed as everyone, collectively, over time. As individuals we live and then die, but as a society we live on. Government has almost perpetual life and doesn't have to be sure to pay off its debt within a life span. It may only need to issue new bonds and pay the currently due debt with those funds.

Will the federal government "go broke" because of its ever-increasing debt? No, government has the power, through its Federal Reserve central bank, to create new money by selling bonds to pay off its debts. Although this causes some inflation, as long as the debt does not increase at a faster rate than the Gross National Product, or faster than the ability to pay it back, there is every likelihood the government will survive. When the debt falls due, and *if* it is paid off (retired), it is worth a payment exactly like the interest payment—from one group now (taxpayers) to another group now (bondholders). In fact, debt is rarely reduced; government merely sells new bonds to pay off the old ones.

REMINDER

Again, a reminder that both parts of Unit IV are combined. Chapter Highlights, Fill-in Review and Problems, Problems, Problems . . . for text Chapter 7, and the Film Summary, comprise the entire Unit.

CHAPTER 7 HIGHLIGHTS

Defined words are underlined.

I. MAKEUP OF GOVERNMENT EXPENDITURES

A. *Federal Budget:* A statement showing planned federal expenditures. Major categories of the budget are:

1. defense (includes military outlays, space programs and foreign affairs),

2. cash income maintenance (transfer payments, Social Security benefits, unemployment compensation, public assistance to the poor and aged),

3. helping people buy the essentials,

4. aid for social programs,

5. investment in the physical environment,

6. revenue sharing,

7. direct subsidies to producers,

8. net interest on the federal debt,

9. federal loan guarantees.

B. Until 1981, changes in the composition of federal budget outlays had been away from military expenditures and toward social and income redistribution programs.

C. Education is the largest category in state and local government expenditure.

II. TAXES ARE THE MAIN SOURCES OF REVENUE FOR ALL LEVELS OF GOVERNMENT.

A. The federal government derives most of its revenue from income taxes. (Other are Social Security, corporate income taxes, taxes on imported goods, and special-source excise taxes.)

B. Property tax is the largest source of state and local receipts.

III. TAXATION SYSTEMS

A. There are three classifications of taxation.

1. *Proportional Taxation:* The tax rate remains the same, regardless of income size.

2. *Progressive Taxation:* The tax rate increases as income increases.

3. *Regressive Taxation:* The tax rate declines as income increases.

B. The legislated tax rate may differ from the effective tax rate.

1. *Effective Tax Rate:* Is found by dividing the tax bill by total income.

2. If the effective rate rises as income rises, the tax is progressive; if the effective rate is constant, the tax is proportional; if the effective rate falls, the tax is regressive.

IV. IS THERE A BEST TAX? TAXES DIFFER IN IMPACT.

A. Popular "normative taxation" theories are:

1. *Ability-To-Pay Principle:* Individuals should pay taxes according to their ability to pay, with higher incomes taxed at higher rates.

2. *Benefits-Received Principle:* Taxes should be collected in proportion to benefits received.

3. *Productivity-Ethics Principle:* Individuals who are more productive than average should have more spendable after-tax income than the average person.

B. The federal, personal income tax (a progressive tax) accounts for 44 percent of federal revenues.

C. Corporate income taxes account for 15 percent of federal, and over 8 percent of all state and local taxes collected.

1. Corporations are taxed on profits.

2. Corporations' after-tax profits are taxed again when stockholders are taxed on dividends received, or on realized capital gains.

3. Who actually pays corporate tax? One or more of the following pay:

   a. owners,

   b. consumers of the corporate-produced products,

   c. corporation employees.

4. To the extent that taxes are passed on to consumers in higher-priced products, the tax is regressive.

D. Other taxes are:

1. taxes on wealth (property and estate taxes),

2. sales and excise taxes hidden in the price of a product. Sales taxes are levied by states on final sales of goods and services while excise taxes are special federal or state taxes on specific items.

V. *Tax Loopholes:* LEGAL METHODS TO REDUCE TAXES OWED TO GOVERNMENT.

Effective Rates Of Taxation: Can also be defined as tax rates after loopholes are accounted for.

A. *Tax Exempt Bonds:* Interest income from bonds (issued by state and local governments) is not reported on income tax returns.

1. Prices of these bonds are therefore bid up to reflect tax savings.

2. Local governments pay less to borrow.

3. Bonds provide tax shelters for high-income earners.

B. *Capital Gains (losses):* The difference between the buying and selling price of an asset; a long-term capital gain is given favorable tax treatment.

VI. GOVERNMENT CONTROLS 40 PERCENT OF THE TOTAL OUTPUT OF OUR ECONOMY AND FINANCES OUTLAYS BY:

A. taxation,

B. borrowing from the private sector. *Budget Deficit:* Whenever government outlays exceed its revenues.

1. Sales of government bonds to the private sector finance the deficit.

2. Borrowing from the private sector transfers purchasing power to the government.

C. money creation. Only the Federal government is able to create new money to purchase output from the private sector.

VII. *Government Debt:* WHEN GOVERNMENT BORROWS FROM THE PRIVATE SECTOR BY SELLING BONDS, WHAT IT OWES IS CALLED THE PUBLIC (OR NATIONAL) DEBT.

A. The more federal government bonds in the hands of the public, the larger the public debt.

B. The interest payments on the national debt

1. have been between one and two percent of Gross National Product for the last 45 years.

2. go to Americans when the government borrows from Americans.

FILL-IN REVIEW

Select between the choices underlined or fill in the blank. Cover the answers until you have provided your own.

A statement showing planned federal expenditures is the federal _____. Until the 1980s the change in composition of this _____ budget had been away from *military programs*/*social programs* and toward *military programs*/*social programs*. In state and local government expenditure, the largest budget category is _____. The main source of revenue of all levels of government are _____. For the federal government, the largest source of revenue is the individual _____ _____. The largest source of state and local receipts is the _____ tax.

When taxpayers of all income levels pay the same percentage of their income in taxes, that tax is called a _____ tax. When the marginal tax rate increases as income goes up, that tax is a _____ tax. A _____ tax takes away a smaller and smaller percentage of additional income as income rises. The effective tax rate can be found by dividing the tax bill by total _____; if the effective rate rises as income rises, the tax

budget
federal
military programs

social programs

education
taxes

income tax

property

proportional

progressive
regressive

income

progressive	is _____; if the effective rate stays the
proportional	same, the tax is _____; and if the ef-
regressive	fective rate falls, the tax is _____.
	There are a number of popular "normative"
Ability-to-pay	theories of taxation. ____-__-____ principle
	states that people should pay more taxes as
	their income rises. The principle that calls for
	taxes to be distributed according to the use
	they receive from government services is
benefits-received	called the _____-_____ principle.
	Our federal personal income tax is a
progressive	_____ tax. A corporate income tax is
	paid by owners or employees of the
corporation consumers	_____ or _____ of the product.
a legal	A tax loophole is <u>an illegal/a legal</u> method to
	reduce taxes owed to government.
	If the price of an asset rises, the differ-
	ences between the original and the present
capital gain	price is called a _____ ____ if it is a posi-
capital loss	tive difference, and a _____ ____ if it is a
	negative difference. When government bor-
	rows from the private sector by selling bonds,
public	what it owes is called the _____ (or
national) debt	_____) ____.

PROBLEMS, PROBLEMS, PROBLEMS . . .

Answers are at the end of this unit.

TRUE-FALSE

Circle either "T" or "F" for each statement.

T (F) 1. The largest source of receipts for the federal government is the corporate income tax.

(T) F 2. The largest category of state and local expenditures is education.

T (F) 3. A regressive tax takes away a larger and larger percentage of additional income as income rises.

(T) F 4. The effective tax rate can be calculated by dividing the total tax bill by total income.

T (F) 5. A tax loophole is an illegal means by which people avoid paying income taxes.

T (F) 6. The ability-to-pay principle of taxation states that the more one earns, the fewer taxes one should pay.

(T) F 7. Borrowing from the private sector is one of the methods by which the government finances its expenditures.

(T) F 8. The Social Security tax is an example of a regressive tax.

MATCH-UP

Match each item in the first column with a term in the second column. Use no term more than once.

_f_ 1. The rate declines as income increases.

_d_ 2. The rate remains the same regardless of income size.

_e_ 3. The marginal tax increases as income increases.

_b_ 4. The total amount of government bonds owned by the public

_c_ 5. Government outlays exceed its revenues.

_i_ 6. Legal opportunities to reduce taxes owed to government

_a_ 7. Methods of financing government expenditures

_g_ 8. A statement showing planned federal expenditures

_h_ 9. The difference between the initial and the present price of an asset

a. taxation, borrowing and money creation
b. national debt (or public debt)
c. budget deficit
d. proportional taxation
e. progressive taxation
f. regressive taxation
g. federal budget
h. capital gain or loss
i. loopholes

MULTIPLE CHOICE

For each of the following statements, choose the one best alternative.

1. If a tax of $400 is paid on an income of $4,000, $600 on an income of $6,000 and $800 on an income of $8,000, then the tax is

    a. progressive.

    b. proportional.

    c. regressive.

    d. none of the above

2. If a tax of $400 is paid on an income of $4,000, $660 on an income of $6,000 and $960 on an income of $8,000, then the tax is

    a. progressive.

    b. proportional.

    c. regressive.

    d. none of the above

3. The federal government finances its expenditures in three ways. Choose which of the following is *not* one of these ways.

    a. sale of stock

    b. sale of bonds

    c. taxation

    d. money creation

4. The ability-to-pay principle of taxation suggests that taxes should be

    a. progressive.

    b. proportional.

    c. regressive.

    d. All the above are correct.

5. Tax loopholes are legal methods to reduce taxes owed to government. Which of the following is *not* a tax loophole?

   a. purchase of tax-exempt bonds

   b. capital gains

   c. purchase of tax-exempt certificates of deposit

   d. not filing an income tax return

6. The largest source of revenue for local governments is the

   a. property tax.

   b. income tax.

   c. sales tax.

   d. excise tax.

7. The largest source of tax receipts of the federal government is

   a. inheritance tax.

   b. excise tax.

   c. personal income tax.

   d. corporate income tax.

8. The corporate income tax is paid by

   a. the corporation owners.

   b. consumers in higher product price.

   c. corporation employees.

   d. All the above are correct.

MULTIPLE CHOICE

9a. Using information from the first two columns, calculate the next two and fill in your answers. Use the completed table to answer questions 9b and 10.

INCOME OF TAXPAYER	TAX BILL	AVERAGE TAX RATE	MARGINAL TAX RATE
$100	$10	10 %	10 %
200	21	10.5 %	11 %
300	33	11 %	12
400	47	11.75 %	14

9b. Since the marginal tax rate for a specific level of income is the increase in the tax bill divided by the increase in income, the marginal tax rate of the taxpayer at the $200 income level illustrated above is

(a) 11%.

b. 10.5%.

c. 10%.

d. 20%.

10. Over the income range illustrated above, the tax structure is

a. regressive.

b. proportional.

(c) progressive.

d. regressive to $200, then progressive.

ECONOWORD PUZZLE

CLUES ACROSS

1. The economy can be said to have both a public and a _____ sector.
4. The average tax rate is the fraction of _____ income that is paid in taxes.
8. Personal income tax is a _____ tax.
9. Main source of revenues for all levels of government
10. Internal revenue service
11. Critics of high marginal tax rates argue that high taxes result in _____ incentives to earn extra income.
14. Progressive, proportional, regressive, each is a _____ of taxation.
15. The body of government which imposes federal taxes
16. Different taxes are levied by each _____ of government.
19. Results of economic decision making by government
21. Not _____ income is subject to the same marginal rates of taxation.
22. Opposite of high taxes are _____ taxes.
24. When a person is in the 50% tax _____, he/she does *not* pay 50% tax in his/her entire income.
25. Tax loopholes are perfectly legal methods to _____ paying tax.
27. Labor
28. When we analyze who actually pays a

ANSWERS TO STUDY QUESTIONS

TRUE-FALSE

1. F 2. T 3. F 4. T 5. F 6. F 7. T 8. T

MATCH-UP

1. f 2. d 3. e 4. b 5. c 6. i 7. a 8. g 9. h

MULTIPLE-CHOICE

1. a 2. a 3. a 4. a 5. d 6. a 7. c 8. d

9a.

INCOME OF TAXPAYER	TAX BILL	AVERAGE TAX RATE	MARGINAL TAX RATE
$100	$10	10 %	10%
200	21	10.5	11
300	33	11	12
400	47	11.75	14

9b. a **10.** c

---

tax and is not able to shift it to another, we say that person bears the _____ of the tax.
30. Some types of income provide a haven or _____ from tax.
31. The income government receives from its taxes is the tax _____.

CLUES DOWN

2. As income goes up, the percentage paid in tax goes down; sales tax is this form of tax.
3. The opposite of liability
5. The influences of a tax
6. Fraction of entire income that is paid in taxes is _____ tax rate.
7. When we detail the types of taxation levied by each level of government we are describing our tax _____.
8. Government is the _____ sector.
12. A legal method to reduce taxes owed to government
13. Allowed by government
17. When government spends more than it collects
18. A tax rate which goes up as income goes up is a _____ tax rate.
20. Average tax calculated as the fraction of _____ paid in tax
23. In the film "Familiar Fallacies," Thomas is concerned about the _____ in size of government.
26. A proportional tax _____ collects the same percentage of all income in taxes.
29. In April, the IRS reminds you that your income taxes are _____.

COMPLETED ECONOWORD PUZZLE

BUSINESS ORGANIZATIONS AND FLUCTUATIONS

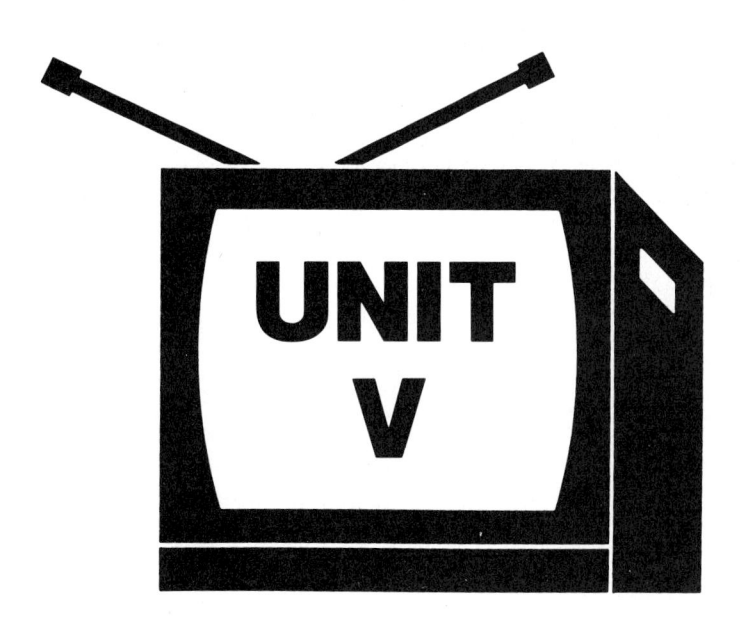

UNIT V

UNIT IN A NUTSHELL

PART ONE
Film: "Karen's Magic Flute"

Text: Chapter 4, Chapter 5

PART TWO
Film: "The Economic Roller Coaster"

Text: Chapter 8

The economy is constantly moving: like a huge, complex, living being, it adjusts and responds to what it encounters. The aggregates—unemployment, prices, output and income—of the whole grand mechanism we call the economy are always moving up or down. When all happen to move at once in the same direction, we are in a recession—or an expansion. We often pretend that conditions are stable in order to analyze one part or another; but we are constantly in the *business cycle,* and few of us are exempted from its effects.

We are all linked together by mutual interdependence, although the business cycle may affect individuals or parts of the economy in different ways. The manufacturers of small, non-durable products may escape a downturn that throws much of the construction industry out of work. New, small businesses may not survive an economic downturn. Producers of capital goods and durable equipment are especially vulnerable to recessions but may, as well, be stimulated by upturns. These industries generally respond to changes in demand by curtailing or expanding production, not by changing their prices. Consequently, it is employment which changes.

UNIT OBJECTIVES

Objectives 1-6 can be met by studying Chapters 4 and 5 and viewing "Karen's Magic Flute." After completing Part One, the student should be able to:

1. Define market.

2. Explain how the market system allocates scarce resources among competing uses.

3. Explain how profits provide an incentive to move resources to alternative uses.

4. Define plant, firm and industry.

5. List and describe the three principal forms of business enterprise, including the advantages and disadvantages of each.

6. Define stock and bond and state the difference between the two.

Objectives 7-9 can be met by reading Chapter 8 and viewing "The Economic Roller Coaster" and studying the Film Summary. After completing Part Two, the student should be able to:

7. Define both recession and expansion as parts of a business cycle (or fluctuation).

8. List and briefly describe several theories of the business cycle.

9. Define full employment, then define structural, cyclical and frictional unemployment.

PART ONE

UNIT V ASSIGNMENT: PART ONE

STUDY: Chapter 4, "The Price System," *Economics Today*

STUDY: Chapter 5, "Private Business Organizations and Financing," *Economics Today*

STUDY: Film Summary: "Karen's Magic Flute," *Study Guide*

VIEW: "Karen's Magic Flute"

REVIEW: Chapter 4 Highlights, *Study Guide*

COMPLETE: Fill-in Review *and* Problems, Problems, Problems ... for Chapter 4, *Study Guide*

REVIEW: Chapter 5 Highlights, *Study Guide*

COMPLETE: Fill-in Review *and* Problems, Problems, Problems ... for Chapter 5, *Study Guide*

SPECIAL INSTRUCTIONS

For this Unit you will read three chapters, 4, 5, and 8, that all relate to the business economy. First, an overview on the price system itself, then a chapter on how businesses are organized and lastly, one on the business cycle. For the first two of these chapters, 4 and 5, this *Study Guide* unit contains complete self-help sections of Chapter Highlights, Fill-in Review, etc.

To complete Unit V, you will answer several questions based on the Film Summary: "The Economic Roller Coaster." For Chapter 8, you will simply read the text chapter and wait until Unit X to work the self-help section.

FILM SUMMARY: "Karen's Magic Flute"

For many, the American dream includes the chance to run one's own business. Many of us only dream; some of us, like Karen, go ahead and work to make the dream come true. When she begins her own business, manufacturing plastic flutes, her experience is not unlike that of thousands of others who try their hand at capitalism. Karen begins as a sole proprietor. Although a sole proprietorship is the commonest form of business enterprise, the odds are strongly against a proprietorship surviving for more than a few years.

Karen's need for working capital demonstrates one of the problems of beginning a business. It is one of the three major reasons for the failure of sole proprietorships; the other two are financial responsibility for all losses, and unlimited liability for all debts. There are, of course, many other reasons why proprietorships fail. These may include: producing a product that is not competitive in a market dominated by well-established businesses; lack of managerial or accounting skills that may be required; or selection of an inaccessible, unattractive or otherwise inappropriate location for a retail business. Some of the other reasons accounting for failure are the lack of funds to pay the advertising costs that may be necessary to develop a market for an unknown product; attempting to sell a product for which there is no developed market; or the inability to survive a downturn of the business cycle.

In our examples of different forms of business enterprises, we will limit ourselves to considerations of the entrepreneur who, like Karen, is immediately successful and able to sell her product in a receptive market. Such an enterprise usually requires a continuing flow of operating financial capital beyond the initial venture money, and Karen's is no exception. A business isn't paid in advance for what it sells, so that the claims of the business creditors for raw materials and services, and salary payments for workers occur before payments are received for the finished product.

The first few years of an unproven business are difficult for business owners who do not have large financial assets to draw upon. As Karen discovers, banks are not set up to provide the kind of help needed. All the profits of a proprietorship can be kept by the owner, but *all* the bills, responsibilities and losses are the owner's because of unlimited liability. Most of the personal assets of the owner can be forfeited for debts of the company if costs and debts outstrip profits.

In the partnership form of business enterprise, there is more than one owner to share the liabilities, and each partner is ultimately liable for all of the debts of the business. A persistent problem for the growing, successful business, even for the partnership, is the need for financial capital. When Eleanor is admitted as a partner to Karen's company, she brings in additional financial capital and, even though the business is a success and experiences growth, still more capital is needed.

More ownership capital could have been added by finding new partners, since there is no limitation to the number of partners a firm can admit. But, each time this happens the partnership must be reformed. Recall, however, that each partner is liable for all of the debts of the partnership and under some circumstances, even to the full extent of each one's personal assets. This unlimited liability is a major disadvantage of the partnership form of business enterprise.

Another problem is that partners must agree on business decisions, and although Thomas and Karen tease about a partnership resembling a marriage—there *are* similarities. The difficulty of achieving agreement on business decisions is potentially an important drawback for the partnership form of business enterprise. As the film program shows, the friendship of Eleanor and Karen appears to be as shaky as the verbal agreements of their partnership.

Ultimately, they agree that new owners must be brought into the business. Karen and Eleanor (with Vernon Stirling's advice) decide to incorporate "Karen's Magic Flute." As the partners discover, it is simple enough to form the corporation. An attorney draws up the papers of incorporation, writing into the charter the powers needed. Then Karen and Eleanor go through a simple procedure to sell shares, having them marketed through a local investment banking firm which keeps a small percentage of the shares' purchase price for its profit. In "going public," Karen and Eleanor now share with others all of the risks and profits of the firm. As a corporation, the business now has limited liability for debts, so that an individual stockowner risks only the value of the stock bought. The risks of business activity are now shared by many—who stand to gain or lose according to the profitability of the corporation.

Two major advantages to this dominant business form are: 1) the ability to raise capital, and 2) limited liability for debts. The names of individuals who own stock in the corporation are of little importance to the managers of a corporation. There is no need to reform the corporation when stock ownership changes. A corporation is defined as a fictitious, legal person created by the state which has its own identity. The corporation itself can sue and be sued; individual stock owners cannot be sued for debts. Also, corporate decisions are made on the basis of stock ownership, one share of stock equalling one vote.

A major disadvantage of the corporate form is that the federal government taxes corporate profits. This tax is levied in addition to personal income tax the owners pay on dividends.

In the film, Karen and Eleanor hardly have time to adjust to their new status as corporate managers when they are bought out by Musitron, a large corporation which produces its own plastic flute. Karen recognizes how much personal satisfaction she has obtained from forming her own business, and is deeply disappointed at the thought of the experience's being over. But, like most who own their own businesses, Karen and Eleanor have worked long, hard hours for relatively low pay. The experience has been thrilling in some ways, tiring in others. After the initial shock of losing her independence, Karen is indeed relieved to go back to her job at the TV station, where she can leave work at the end of the day, and not have to worry about it until the following day.

CHAPTER 4 HIGHLIGHTS

Defined words are underlined.

I. EVERY ECONOMIC SYSTEM PROVIDES A METHOD OF RESOURCE ALLOCATION. IN THE MARKET SYSTEM, CHANGES IN PRICE ANSWER BASIC ECONOMIC QUESTIONS.

  A. What will be produced? What combination of what goods is produced?

  B. How will it be produced? What materials and processes will be used?

  C. For whom will it be produced?

II. EXCHANGE TAKES PLACE IN MARKETS

  Market: A general term that refers to any arrangement that brings buyers and sellers of a product together for exchange. The study of how goods get produced and exchanged in the market process is a major part of economics.

  A. Exchange is entered into because it makes both parties better off. It is voluntary.

  B. *Terms of Exchange:* The price paid which is determined by the market forces of supply and demand.

  C. Markets reduce transaction costs. *Transaction Costs:* The costs of buying and selling, and of being informed about the qualities of a product.

   1. Reduction in transaction cost is an important measure of efficiency of the market process.

   2. The less organized the market, the higher the transaction costs.

3. Relative prices convey information in the market, giving buyers the method for choosing. *Relative Price:* In a broad sense, the other goods a consumer must give up to buy a particular good.

   a. Sellers can see an increase in relative price as a chance to increase profits.

   b. Buyers can see an increase in relative price as an indication of scarcity.

III. PRODUCTION IN AN ECONOMY DEPENDS ON THE INCENTIVES IN THE SYSTEM. PROFITS ARE THE INCENTIVES IN THE MARKET SYSTEM.

   A. Profits determine what is produced. *Profit:* The difference between the cost of producing a good and its market price.

   1. Profits provide a signal to producers to produce more of a good.

   2. Profits signal would-be producers to move into a market.

   3. The search for profits moves resources from lower to higher-valued uses.

   B. In a pure market system, consumers ultimately decide what is produced. This is often referred to as *consumer sovereignty*.

IV. IN A MARKET SYSTEM, EFFICIENCY DETERMINES THE "HOW," "WHAT," AND "FOR WHOM" OF PRODUCTION.

   A. *Technical Efficiency:* The use of the lowest-cost production methods; determines "how" goods are produced. (Firms choose production methods and inputs for maximum output per dollar of expenditure, the least-cost combination.)

   B. *Economic Efficiency:* The requirement that the goods produced are those goods society most values; determines "what" goods are produced.

C. The distribution of total output determines "for whom" goods are produced. People's money income depends on qualities, types and quantities of human resources (skill, talent, training) and the other non-human resources (capital, land) that they own.

V. EVALUATING THE PRICE SYSTEM, MAKING NORMATIVE JUDGMENTS

A. The case "for" the price system is based on

1. freedom of choice and enterprise,

2. technical and economic efficiency,

3. competition—which insures that the least-cost production methods are used.

B. The case "against" the price system: that the market doesn't always work (market failure) or, when it does work, it produces unsatisfactory results.

1. Market failure criticism concerns externalities produced by the market, and the lack of social goods.

   a. *Externality:* The costs and benefits from production not reflected in the price of a good, e.g. air and water pollution.

   b. *Public Goods:* Goods that can be used only by a large part of society; examples are national defense and flood control.

2. Some market critics claim that unequal income distribution (resulting from economic efficiency) is unsatisfactory and unfair. Perfect economic efficiency might allow certain members of society to starve.

FILL-IN REVIEW

Select between the choices underlined or fill in the blank. Cover the answers until you have provided your own.

Four major questions must be answered by every economic system. They are: _____ will be produced? _____ will it be produced? _____ will produce it, and _____ _____ will it be produced? These questions are answered in a capitalist economy by competition in the market. Any arrangement buyers and sellers of a product have for exchange is called the _____. The study of how goods get produced and exchanged in the market process is a <u>minor</u>/<u>major</u> part of economics. The market system (or price system) solves the problems of resource allocation.	*What* *How* *Who* *for whom* *market* *major*
In a pure market system, efficiency determines much of the "how," "what" and "for whom" of production. The use of the least-cost production method is termed _____ efficiency and this efficiency determines _____ goods are produced. The production of those goods that society values most is termed _____ efficiency. This economic efficiency determines _____ goods are produced. Change in relative prices is the mechanism	 *technical* *how* *economic* *what*

through which "what," "how," "who," and "for whom" resource allocation questions are answered.

In a market system, relative prices reflect relative _____. What is produced in an economic system depends on the incentives in the system. An important incentive in a market system is _____, which is defined as the difference between the cost of producing a good and its _____. The existence of high profit signals for *more/less* producers to move into an industry. Losses cause businesses to *leave/stay* in an industry. Competition assures both technical and economic efficiency.

The case against the price system argues that the market *always works perfectly/does not always work,* or that, when it does work, it produces unequal distribution of _____. Costs or benefits that spillover from production to affect unplanned areas of the economy are called _____. The cost of externalities *are/are not* included in the price system. Goods that can be used only on a social or group basis are called _____ _____.

scarcities

profit

price
more

leave

does not always work
income

externalities
are not

social goods

PROBLEMS, PROBLEMS, PROBLEMS...

Answers are at the end of this unit.

TRUE-FALSE

Circle either "T" or "F" for each statement.

T **(F)** 1. The United States has a pure market economy.

(T) F 2. All economic systems must answer the basic economic questions of "what," "how," and "for whom" goods are produced.

T **(F)** 3. The study of how goods get produced and exchanged in the market process is a minor part of economics.

T **(F)** 4. What is produced in a market system depends in a large measure on directions from a central authority.

(T) F 5. The use of least-cost production methods is called technical efficiency.

(T) F 6. In a pure market economy, many producers are able to earn large profits using inefficient methods.

MATCH-UP

Match each item in the first column with a term in the second column. Use no term more than once.

d 1. The costs of buying and selling and being informed about products

e 2. Use of the least-cost production methods

b 3. The incentives in a market system; the difference between cost of production and market price of a good

g 4. In a pure market system, consumers ultimately decide what is produced.

a 5. Production of the combination of goods that society values the highest

f 6. A term referring to any arrangement that brings buyers and sellers of a product together for exchange

c 7. In a broad sense, the other goods a customer must give up to buy a particular product

a. economic efficiency
b. profit
c. relative price
d. transaction costs
e. technical efficiency
f. market
g. consumer sovereignty

MULTIPLE CHOICE

For each of the following statements, choose the one best alternative.

1. All of the following are basic questions every economy must answer *except* one. Choose that one.

    a. For whom will goods be produced?

    (b.) Why will goods be produced?

    c. What goods will be produced?

    d. How will goods be produced?

2. All of the following are ways a market system answers the basic economic questions *except* one. Choose that one.

    a. by supply and demand in the market

    b. by changes in relative market prices

    c. by government market production planning

    (d.) by the signals of profits in markets

3. Goods that can be more efficiently produced by government than by the market are called

    a. allocative goods.

    b. external goods.

    (c.) public goods.

    d. economic goods.

4. In a market system, relative prices reflect

    a. incentives.

    b. profits.

    c. efficiency.

    (d.) scarcity.

5. The production of those goods society values most is called

   a. profitable efficiency.

   b. social efficiency.

   c. economic efficiency.

   d. technical efficiency.

REMINDER

To complete Part I of this Unit, go directly on to Chapter 5 Highlights which follow.

CHAPTER 5 HIGHLIGHTS

Defined words are underlined.

I. DISTINCTIONS AMONG PLANT, FIRM AND INDUSTRY

   A. *Plant:* A physical establishment (usually buildings) where manufacturing or distribution takes place.

   B. *Business Firm:* An enterprise which owns and operates one or more plants.

   C. *Industry:* A group of firms producing similar products.

II. A BRIEF HISTORY OF AMERICAN INDUSTRY

   A. Originally, industry was almost 100 percent agriculture.

   B. By 1900, manufacturing accounted for 53 percent of U.S. output.

C. At present, the service sector (medical care, legal work, repairs, etc.) is the fastest growing sector.

III. THREE FORMS OF BUSINESS ORGANIZATION

A. *Sole Proprietorship:* A business owned by one person; the oldest and most common form.

1. Advantages of a sole proprietorship are

   a. proprietor keeps all profits,

   b. starting a business is not difficult,

   c. pride of ownership,

   d. absence of corporate income taxes.

2. Disadvantages of a sole proprietorship are

   a. responsibility for all losses,

   b. limited access to financial capital,

   c. unlimited liability for all debts.

B. *Partnership:* Any business two or more individuals own and operate.

1. Advantages of a partnership are

   a. more financial capital,

   b. greater efficiency.

2. Disadvantages of a partnership are

   a. unlimited liability for debts created by any partner,

   b. shared profits,

        c. possible disagreements,

        d. potential death of a partner.

    C. *Corporation:* A form of business legally separate from persons who own or control it.

        1. To start a corporation and sell stock, a board of directors must be chosen and a charter registered with the state.

        2. Advantages of a corporation are

            a. greater access to financial capital through the sale of bonds or stocks,

            b. stockholders' financial liability is limited to their shares of stock,

            c. unlimited lifetime of the corporation,

            d. ability to have professional management.

        3. Disadvantages of the corporate form are

            a. the federal government levies a corporate profits tax,

            b. increased government control.

        4. The corporation is the dominant business form in the U.S.

IV. THE SALE OF SECURITIES IS AN IMPORTANT SOURCE OF FINANCING FOR CORPORATIONS.

    Security: A certificate of investment in a business firm or in the government. (Stocks and bonds are the major types of securities.)

    A. The earnings of a corporation are either retained in the business (called *retained earnings*), or paid out in cash dividends to stock shareholders.

Stock: A legal document giving the owner a claim on a portion of the profits of the issuing company. (Most stock is common stock.)

1. Common stockholders received earning residuals after those with earlier claims (suppliers, managers, bondholders, preferred stockholders).

2. Each share of stock grants the investor one vote in the decisions which are made by stockholders.

3. Owners of preferred stock receive periodic dividend payments and have no voting rights.

B. *Bond:* A promissory note of debt by government or a corporation to the bondholder. The holder of the bond receives periodic interest payments plus repayment of the loan at a specified time.

1. *Bond Indenture:* A lending agreement that describes the terms of a bond issue, specifying maturity date and interest payments.

2. *Corporate Trustee:* The party which oversees the terms of a bond issue (usually the commercial bank trust department).

C. The use of stocks vs. bonds to finance business

1. Common stock has the lowest risk for corporations because there is no legal requirement to pay dividends.

2. Long-term bonds may be the cheapest corporate financing method because of tax advantages.

FILL-IN REVIEW

Select between the choices underlined or fill in the blank. Cover the answers until you have provided your own.

plant	A structure where manufacturing or distribution is carried on is called a _____. A business
firm	_____ owns and operates one or more plants. A group of firms producing similar products is
industry	termed an _____. The major industry in the early history of the U.S. was
agriculture *manufacturing*	_____. By 1900 _____ accounted for over 50 percent of U.S. output.
service	Currently, the _____ sector is a rapidly growing component of U.S. output.
sole proprietorship	A business owned and operated by one person is a _____ _____. The advantages of this form of business organization are:
profits	1) the proprietor keeps all _____; 2) starting
not difficult	a business is <u>difficult</u>/<u>not difficult</u>; 3) there's the psychological benefit of pride of
ownership *corporate profit*	_____; 4) absence of _____ _____ tax. The disadvantages of the sole proprietor-
losses	ship are: 1) responsibility for all _____; 2)
financial capital	limited _____ _____; 3) unlimited
liability	_____.

FILL-IN REVIEW

A business that two or more individuals own is a _____. The advantages of a partnership are: 1) more _____ _____; 2) greater _____. | *partnership*
financial capital
efficiency

The corporation is the *dominant/least important* business enterprise. Corporations are financed by the sale of securities. A certificate of investment in a business firm or government is a _____. The major types of securities are _____ and _____. The security that gives its owner a claim on a portion of the profits of the issuing company is a _____. Each share of stock grants the investor one ____ in ownership decisions. Owners of _____ stock receive periodic dividends and have *double/no* voting rights in the corporation. A promissory note of debt by a corporation or government to the holder is a _____. | *dominant*

security
stocks   bonds

stock

vote

preferred
no

bond

Among the advantages of the corporate form of business organizations are: 1) greater access to _____ _____ through the sale of _____ or _____; 2) limited financial _____; 3) unlimited ___; 4) ability to hire professional _____. | *financial capital*
bonds   stocks
liability   life
management

PROBLEMS, PROBLEMS, PROBLEMS...

Answers are at the end of this unit.

TRUE-FALSE

Circle either "T" or "F" for each statement.

T (F) 1. Historically, in the U.S., the service sector was originally the most important sector.

T (F) 2. An advantage of a sole proprietorship is the ability to issue stock.

(T) F 3. To form a corporation, a charter must be registered with the state and a board of directors chosen.

(T) F 4. Limited liability and greater access to money capital are important advantages of the corporate form of business.

T (F) 5. Presently, over 50% of U.S. industry is agriculture.

(T) F 6. Each share of common stock grants the investor one vote in decisions made by the shareholders.

(T) F 7. The corporation is now the dominant form of business enterprise in the U.S.

MATCH-UP

Match each item in the first column with a term in the second column. Use no term more than once.

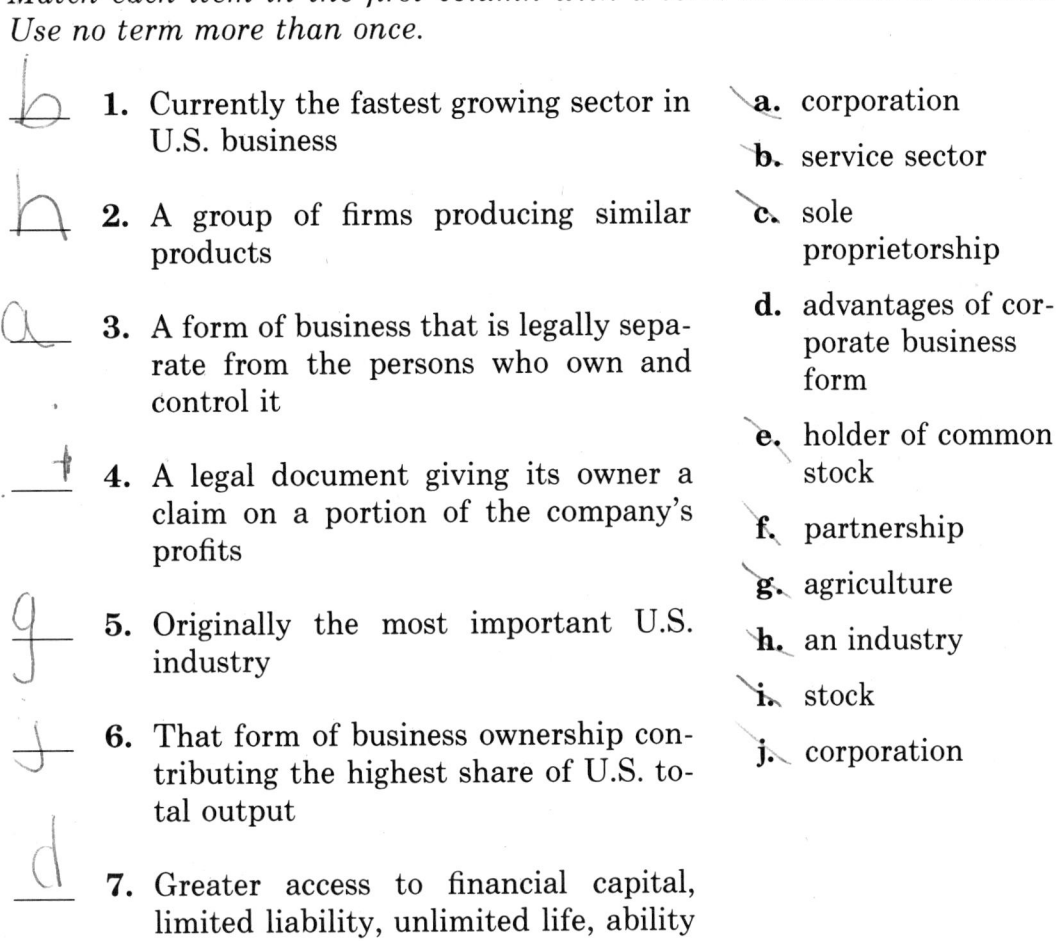

b 1. Currently the fastest growing sector in U.S. business

h 2. A group of firms producing similar products

a 3. A form of business that is legally separate from the persons who own and control it

i 4. A legal document giving its owner a claim on a portion of the company's profits

g 5. Originally the most important U.S. industry

j 6. That form of business ownership contributing the highest share of U.S. total output

d 7. Greater access to financial capital, limited liability, unlimited life, ability to hire professional management

f 8. Any unincorporated business that two or more persons own

c 9. A business owned and operated by one person

e 10. Receives the residuals of earnings after those who have earlier claims.

a. corporation
b. service sector
c. sole proprietorship
d. advantages of corporate business form
e. holder of common stock
f. partnership
g. agriculture
h. an industry
i. stock
j. corporation

148 UNIT V: PART ONE

MULTIPLE CHOICE

For each of the following statements, choose the one best alternative.

1. In terms of total sales, one form of business ownership is the most dominant. Choose that one.

    a. partnership

    (b.) corporation

    c. cooperative

    d. sole proprietorship

2. American industry has changed over time

    a. from early dominance of manufacturing to current importance of agriculture.

    b. from early dominance of the service sector to current importance of agriculture.

    (c.) from early dominance of agriculture to current importance of manufacturing and the service sector.

    d. The direction of the change is not clear.

3. Choose the form of business enterprise the following list of advantages describes: the owner keeps all the profits, psychological pride of ownership, freedom from business income taxes.

    a. partnership

    b. corporation

    c. cooperative

    (d.) sole proprietorship

4. Which of the following is correct regarding the distinctions among plant, firm, or industry?

    a. A plant is a group of firms which produces similar products.

    b. A firm is a physical establishment where manufacturing or distribution is done.

c. An industry can be loosely defined as a group of firms producing similar products.

d. None of the above are correct.

5. Choose the form of business enterprise the following list of advantages describes: greater access to financial capital, limited liability, unlimited lifetime, ability to hire professional management.

   a. corporation

   b. sole proprietorship

   c. cooperative

   d. partnership

6. A promissory note of debt by government or by a corporation to the holder is a definition of

   a. a corporate charter.

   b. a bond.

   c. a stock.

   d. a partnership agreement.

PART TWO

UNIT V ASSIGNMENT: PART TWO

STUDY: Read Chapter 8, "Business Fluctuations, Unemployment, and Inflation," *Economics Today* (*Note:* Chapter 8 will be studied in more detail in Unit X.)

STUDY: Film Summary: "The Economic Roller Coaster," *Study Guide*

VIEW: "The Economic Roller Coaster"

COMPLETE: Problems, Problems, Problems . . . *and* Econoword Puzzle, *Study Guide*

FILM SUMMARY: "The Economic Roller Coaster"

In this program, Karen and Thomas become interested in business cycles (fluctuations) when they consider spending their savings for stocks in a new energy-producing company. Business cycles (or fluctuations) is the term given to the periodic speeding up and slowing down of economic activity over time. The fluctuations affect output, employment, income and prices, so that, if the phases of a cycle can be identified and their movements predicted, the cycle may be modified by actions of the government. Later, when you study government stabilization policy, you will recognize that the intended use of its policy is to moderate unemployment and inflation that accompany business cycles.

Business fluctuations can be seen as one part of the economic problem of achieving a high employment and level of income in the economy while maintaining relatively stable prices. Variations in employment are part of the up and down fluctuations of production in the economy. In a business slump, unemployment climbs, while during an expansion, unemployment falls. (The rate of unemployment can be defined as the number of unemployed divided by the total civilian labor force.)

Measuring employment is not a simple matter of counting how many are out of work and how many have jobs. Statistics sometimes include persons in categories that overlap, as well as understate or overstate actual employment rates. In spite of the difficulties in computing accurate rates, unemployment figures for the economy are closely monitored by policy makers.

There are three major types of unemployment. Those who are *structurally* unemployed cannot find a job that fits their skills; the system has passed these workers by. If the structurally unemployed do not retain or move to where their skills are employable, they remain unemployed. The *cyclically* unemployed are without work because of depressed business conditions. The cyclically unemployed are the major focus of policy makers since this type of unemployment is related to the business cycle. A third type of unemployment includes those people changing jobs. *Frictional* unemployment, as it is called, is the size of the flow of persons changing jobs. (If we had no frictional unemployment, we would no longer have freedom of movement from job to job.)

In determining full employment, it is important to know the size of the labor force who are categorized as being frictionally unemployed. Full employment, in fact, is defined by subtracting frictional unemployment from 100 percent of the work force. If a figure of, say, 6 percent is assigned to that part of the work force changing jobs, or the frictional unemployed, then full employment is defined as 94 percent of the work force having jobs.

The long-term trend in the economy has been upward, but short-run business activity has varied in a jagged, up-and-down cycle. We can identify phases of the cycle as both expansion and recession. Specifically, the expansion phase of a cycle is a time when output, employment and national income are rising, and the recession phase is a time of slowdown in business activity that results in unemployment and loss of income. The business cycle can even be linked to areas not considered as economic, such as levels of malnutrition, marriage and suicide rates. Most of us are aware that economic events and politics are closely related: political officeholders are likely to be swept out of office during recessions.

Forecasts of future business trends are needed by businesses in order to decide how much production and investment will be undertaken. If businesses expect a high inflation rate, they may decide to pay *now* for new capital equipment, or new buildings and even stockpile goods in advance of the forecasted price increases. On the other hand, if businesses expect a recession they may attempt to lower inventories quickly. Concern about the direction of the economy is shared also by those who want to speculate on the stock and bond markets. Forecasts are used by government policy makers, as well, in order to plan the kinds of spending or taxation changes they believe will remedy unemployment and national income problems.

There are indicators of business activity which either lead, coincide with or lag behind any fluctuation. Leading indicators often turn up or down several months in advance of a cycle, but not always. Coincidental indicators change along with the ups and downs of a cycle, while lagging indicators move after the cycle's changes.

Economists, businesses and government policy makers interested in predicting business activity may use leading indicators in their forecasts. When forecasts are made predicting unemployment, price levels, and consumer and business spending, sophisticated econometric techniques are used employing theories (or models) of how income is actually determined. These forecasting techniques that use models of the economy involve both collecting relevant data and feeding that data into a computer. The data are then analyzed on the basis of a particular economic theory. (The Keynes theory of income determination is an example of one that might be used. A more thorough examination of this particular Keynesian model will be studied in the next Unit.) Until then, let us consider some of the earlier business cycle theories mentioned in the film program.

One early theory blamed sun spots for business fluctuations. These theorists believed storms on the sun change weather patterns, which in turn influence output. If an economy depends on agriculture for much of its output (a characteristic of less-developed economies), expansions or recessions can be influenced this way.

Psychological reactions of businesses to social and political change may influence business fluctuations. Optimism regarding the future may help a company decide to undertake new investment according to this theory. Conversely, pessimism about what is currently happening will deter investment.

The innovation theory explains fluctuations in terms of new scientific discoveries and inventions. A new wave of the business cycle is set off by the successful adaptation of a new invention to production: the telephone, plastics and computers are examples of inventions which have generated investment and increased national income.

Although cycles are not regular, many economists believe that an expansion followed by a recession cycle runs its course over a period of about eight to ten years. In the United States, it is the construction industry which is closely linked with extended periods of expansion and recession. The construction industry is associated with every other one of these eight-to-ten-year cycle periods of long slumps and booms. Its growth is crucial during these alternate periods of expansion, and, conversely, when the building industry slumps, the recession which accompanies it is long and deep. (These longer cycles that coincide with building booms and slumps are called Kuznets cycles.) Factors such as changes in immigration, population growth and money supply changes may also affect these economic ups and downs.

Government can itself cause wide changes (or fluctuations) in business activity. Taxation policies can, for example, initiate or deepen a cycle if they are not used carefully. In its attempts to stabilize business conditions, government can overcompensate for changes in the private sector, and instead of providing the stabilization it had intended, create the opposite: destabilization.

PROBLEMS, PROBLEMS, PROBLEMS...

Answers are at the end of this unit.

TRUE-FALSE

Circle either "T" or "F" for each statement.

(T) F 1. The energy source for the economy is spending.

T (F) 2. Government policies to cool down the economy are more effective than is policies to get the economy moving again.

(T) F 3. Higher incomes mean more spending.

T (F) 4. Economists can predict with certainty the time and speed of an upswing in the economy.

T (F) 5. Prices always fall when the economy slows down.

(T) F 6. For the most part, economists use theories of business cycles to account for fluctuations in the economy.

T (F) 7. It matters little to an economist which kind of worker is out of a job: a job is a job.

(T) F 8. When there is a slow-down in one part of the economy, it can affect other parts of the economy.

T (F) 9. Business fluctuations have nothing to do with business cycles.

MULTIPLE CHOICE

For each of the following statements, choose the one best alternative.

1. Which of the following would *not* likely happen if an inexpensive new energy source were found?
    a. increased investment
    b. business expansion
    c. unsold inventories overflow
    d. more optimism about the future
    e. more jobs available

2. When incomes rise and more spending takes place, the circular flow
    a. gets smaller.
    b. gets larger.
    c. generally stays the same.
    d. is unaffected.
    e. none of the above

3. The economy cannot always keep on accelerating because
    a. it is a circular flow phenomenon.
    b. it is dynamic and unpredictable.
    c. it is always in motion.
    d. its motion is not guaranteed to be a steady one.
    e. all of the above

4. Which of the following types of unemployment is of most concern to government and political leaders?
    a. structural
    b. cyclical
    c. seasonal
    d. technical
    e. frictional

5. In calculating full employment figures, the most important kind of unemployment considered is

   a. structural.

   b. cyclical.

   c. seasonal.

   d. technical.

   (e.) frictional.

6. Which of the following is tied most directly to the sale of non-durable goods?

   (a.) national income

   b. durable goods

   c. capital equipment

   d. average prime interest rates

   e. net business formation

7. Two of the most important aspects of business fluctuations are: (a) changes in unemployment; (b) manufacturers' inventories; (c) consumer debt; (d) sunspots.

   a. a and c

   b. b and d

   c. a and d

   (d.) a and b

   e. b and c

8. Since the 1950s, the total labor force in the United States has continuously increased. In addition,

   a. the male labor participation rate has risen.

   b. unemployment has increased.

   c. the female labor participation rate has risen.

   d. a and c only

   (e.) b and c only

ECONOWORD PUZZLE

CLUES ACROSS

1. Business farming sector
3. Any unincorporated business that two or more individuals own and operate
6. The form of business that is legally separate from the persons who own and control it
7. Corporations are subject to profits taxed by the _____ government.
8. A bond is a promissory note of _____ by government or corporation.
11. The business sector which is growing rapidly
13. The physical establishment where manufacturing is done
15. Corporations are subject to tax on this.
16. A legal document giving its owner a claim on a portion of the profits of the issuing company
18. A certificate of investment in business firm or government
19. There are three _____ of business organization.

CLUES DOWN

2. A bond pays _____ to its holder.
4. A stock gives its owner one vote per _____ of stock.
5. A business owned by one person is called a sole _____.
10. Literally, a division. Economists speak of the private _____ or the public _____.
12. A share of stock gives its owner one _____ per share.
14. A bond is a form of _____ to business or government.
17. A business _____ owns and operates one or more plants.

ANSWERS TO STUDY QUESTIONS

PART ONE

(Related to Chapter 4)

TRUE-FALSE

1. F 2. T 3. F 4. F 5. T 6. F

MATCH-UP

1. d 2. e 3. b 4. g 5. a 6. f 7. c

MULTIPLE CHOICE

1. b 2. c 3. c 4. d 5. c

(Related to Chapter 5)

TRUE-FALSE

1. F 2. F 3. T 4. T 5. F 6. T 7. T

MATCH-UP

1. b 2. h 3. a 4. i 5. g 6. a 7. d 8. f 9. c 10. e

MULTIPLE CHOICE

1. b 2. c 3. d 4. c 5. a 6. b

PART TWO

TRUE-FALSE

1. T 2. F 3. T 4. F 5. F 6. T 7. F 8. T 9. F

MULTIPLE CHOICE

1. c 2. b 3. e 4. b 5. e 6. a 7. d 8. e

COMPLETED ECONOWORD PUZZLE

		A	G	R	I	C	U	L	T	U	R	E	
				N									
		P	A	R	T	N	E	R	S	H	I	P	
				E				H				R	
		C	O	R	P	O	R	A	T	I	O	N	
				E				R				P	
				S		F	E	D	E	R	A	L	
	D	E	B	T		S			I				
			O		S	E	R	V	I	C	E		V
P	L	A	N	T		C			T				O
	O		D			T		P	R	O	F	I	T
	A			S	T	O	C	K		R			E
	N		F		R				S				
			I						H				
			R		S	E	C	U	R	I	T	Y	
F	O	R	M	S					P				

THE CIRCULAR FLOW AND NATIONAL INCOME ACCOUNTING

UNIT VI

UNIT IN A NUTSHELL

PART ONE

Film: "Go With the Flow"

Text: Chapter 9

PART TWO

Film: "Measuring My Success"

Text: Chapter 10

With this unit, the study of macroeconomics really begins. Since we cannot study the economy in all its detail, we make simplified models of how it all works. With models we analyze the process of how an economy provides goods and services for itself. What we see is that all the different parts are locked together in continuous repeats of "getting and spending." They are so dependent on each other that what happens in one sector ultimately affects the rest of the economy. And *what* affects the whole economy? Spending does.

This Unit introduces the central concepts of macroeconomics: the circular flow of income and product, and the measurement of the elements of that flow. Here we develop the foundation for understanding the models that explain how our national income is determined. This will allow us to see clearly that, in producing its output, the economy generates its own flow of income.

UNIT OBJECTIVES

Objectives 1-7 can be met by studying Chapter 9 and viewing "Go With the Flow." After completing Part One, the student should be able to:

1. Describe the simplest model of the circular flow of income and product.

2. Define national income and national product and state why they are the same.

3. Define product market and factor market. (How does each function in the circular flow?)

4. Define savings, investment and credit market.

5. Define equilibrium national income and describe why we cannot be sure of a stable equilibrium level when we add savings and investment to the model.

6. Define the differences between planned savings and actual savings and between planned investment and actual investment.

7. Explain why planned savings must equal planned investment for a stable equilibrium national income.

Objectives 8-11 can be met by studying Chapter 10 and viewing "Measuring My Success." After completing Part Two, the student should be able to:

8. State the purposes and uses of national income accounting as a measurement of the economy's performance.

9. Define GNP and know what productive transactions are included and why purely financial transactions and transfers are excluded.

10. Differentiate between the expenditure approach and income approach in calculating GNP.

11. Indicate how to use a price index on economic measurements to measure the impact of inflation.

PART ONE

UNIT VI ASSIGNMENT: PART ONE

STUDY: Chapter 9, "The Circular Flow of Income and Product," *Economics Today*

STUDY: Film Summary: "Go With the Flow," *Study Guide*

VIEW: "Go With the Flow"

REVIEW: Chapter 9 Highlights, *Study Guide*

COMPLETE: Fill-in Review *and* Problems, Problems, Problems . . . , *Study Guide*.

FILM SUMMARY: "Go With the Flow"

In this program, Thomas and Elyse build a simple circular flow model of the economy. The circular flow of income and product shows how the different sectors of our economy are tied together, and how spending determines the size of the national income and national product. This important theoretical tool illustrates the interaction of the basic elements in our system that produces goods and services. That is what our economic system is organized to do: produce the goods and services we want.

Thomas's and Elyse's two-sector model is simplicity itself. (It is important to first understand this simplest model thoroughly. The next model is much easier to understand if this one is clear.) So far there are only households that consume and businesses that produce consumer goods. There is no government and no rest-of-the-world. Let's agree that, in this model, households own all the factors of production and that businesses use these factors to produce all the goods and services in the economy. Initially, we focus on the interaction between these two sectors, households and businesses.

Earlier, you learned how supply and demand in markets determine what goods will be produced, what their prices will be, and what combination of factors are used in their production. Now we will use that understanding of how markets function. The exchanges of both factors and goods for money occur in the factor market as well as the product market.

First, remember that the "factor market" is a concept. It is *all* the exchanges of the factors of production—land, labor and capital equipment—for money. If you're a land owner, factor markets establish the rent you receive; when you labor, the same is true of your salary. Second, the "product market" is a concept which describes all the exchanges of goods and services for money. When you go to the drugstore, get a haircut, or have your car's brakes fixed, you're in the product market.

So, now, we have a simple two-sector model. We can look into the flow at any point to see it operating in the following manner. Businesses buy factors from households and pay rent, wages or interest for their use. (Profit is what businesses have left over after wages, rent and interest have been paid.) The money-income households receive for the use of their factors is entirely spent in the product market for the goods and services businesses produce; household expenditures are equal to their incomes. Payment for the goods and services becomes the income of business. If it sounds rather circular, it is. This production and exchange process goes round and round, with money providing the medium of exchange in the markets.

Let's identify the flows.

The flow of goods, services and the factors of production is a "real" flow. The flow in return payment for the goods and services and factors is a money flow. The size of the two is the same. The dollar value of the goods-and-services flow is our *national product;* the dollar value of the factor flow is the *national income* we earn from making the product.

As the next step in our model building, let's add saving. Saving is defined as "not spending" out of income. Some of national income is not used directly for consumption spending, but is saved for future spending, "leaking" out of the spending system into credit markets. When *all* savings are borrowed by businesses, they flow right through the banking credit markets as investment expenditures back into the circular flow. Now we have a new flow and a new market: a savings/investment flow and a credit market. When the savings and investment flows are the same, national income is in equilibrium. Total planned expenditures by businesses and households equal national product; what businesses plan to invest equals what households plan to save. But, when available savings are not entirely used up for business investment, the economy slows down.

Why does it slow down? Let's look into the process. Business investment means expenditures on plant and equipment, plus any inventory changes. Businesses produce for the market, but can't ever be sure of the exact amount of sales. If some of their product isn't sold, they are left with *unplanned* inventory investment. (This is different from the planned investment that happens when businesses decide to add new productive capacity.) What do they do then? Businesses cut down on production. (Why send more to market when there are existing surpluses?) As a result, some workers lose their jobs. The unemployed workers don't have as much income to buy goods and services as before, so that *more* businesses slow down production.

This same process of lowered production and higher unemployment continues. National income falls, and as it does, savings go down because people are not able to save what they intended to save. What is this called? A recession; and some people have to withdraw their savings just to make ends meet. To sum it up, when savings are greater than planned investment, the circular flow of both national product and national income (recall that the two are the same size) gets smaller.

Do you recall how this all started? Savings (withdrawals or "leakages" from the circular flow of income and product) were not used up and were not "reinjected" into the circular flow through business investment. Because savings hadn't been used for investment, national income and national product, it fell until people couldn't save anymore. The recession, the fall in national output and income, will stop only when the amount "leaking" into savings is balanced by the amount "reinjected" by investment. The important point of all this is that *savings must be invested to bring about long-run economic growth.* As long as investors do not divert the entire amount of savings, the economy will slow down. Conversely, the economy will speed up because of an opposite set of imbalances. With more and more spending, national product and income *rise*.

A final step in our model building: to the model of the circular flow now add government. Part of the flow of our national income is diverted by means of taxes to *government*. (Economists refer to this as a "leakage," also.) Purchasing power is thus transferred to government. The flow doesn't stop: government then spends the income for its own activities. (Economists refer to this introduction of spending as an "injection.")

We have now included the three major elements of the circular flow of the economy, without considering trade with the rest of the world. International trade will be introduced later.

NEW TERMS USED

Circular Flow Diagram: Shows graphically the flows of income and product within the economy.

Credit Market: The market where lenders and borrowers get together to exchange money for IOU's.

Equilibrium: A stable condition, when there is no tendency to change. Occurs in the circular flow model when the payments for the factors of production exactly equal the total expenditure in the economy.

Factor Markets: Markets where the factors of production are bought and sold.

Model: A simplified picture of reality. In economics, the purpose of the model is often to observe the possible effects from changes that are being considered. In economics, models are usually mathematical.

Product Markets: Markets where consumer goods and services are bought and sold.

Sector: A large portion of the economy, such as households, businesses and government.

CHAPTER 9 HIGHLIGHTS

Defined words are underlined.

NOTE: In this "Highlights," we begin with the very simplest of circular flow models, then add sectors one-by-one.

    I. THE CIRCULAR FLOW SHOWS HOW THE ENTIRE ECONOMY IS LINKED TOGETHER.

        A. Components of the circular flow:

            1. *Product Markets:* The concept that refers collectively to all markets where goods and services are bought and sold.

            2. *Factor Markets:* Where factor services (land, labor, capital, entrepreneurial activity) are exchanged. (When you look for a job you are participating in the factor market.)

                a. Payments to factors are considered business costs of production.

                b. Costs of production are rent, wages, interest and profit.

        B. There are two basic principles of the circular flow of income and product.

            1. For each economic exchange, the seller receives the amount of money the buyer spends.

            2. Goods and services flow in one direction; money payment for them flows in the other direction. (Thus, we are really talking about two circular flows.)

        C. The circular flows are equal to each other: the value of all goods and services (one flow) will add up to the payment for them (the other flow).

            1. *National Income:* The total money value of all payments to factors.

2. *National Product:* The total money value of all goods and services produced in the economy.

3. *National Income:* The income households receive in payment for producing the national product; so, national income is the same as national product.

4. If this is all there was to the economy, the two flows would always be equal to each other and national income would remain stable. However, there is more.

II. THE CIRCULAR FLOW MODEL WITH SAVINGS AND INVESTMENT ADDED

  A. Income that is not spent for consumption is saved. *Savings:* The difference between national income and payments made by households for goods and services.

  B. *Investment:* Expenditure by businesses to increase productive capacity. There are two types of investment components:

  1. *Fixed Investment:* The purchase of capital.

  2. *Inventory Investment:* Stocks of finished goods held by businesses for future sales.

  C. Credit markets are the link between household savings and business investment.

  1. In the simple model, household savings are the only source of investment funds.

  2. Households keep savings in banks in order to earn interest income.

  3. Banks (as credit markets) lend households' savings to businesses to invest.

III. **With Saving and Investment Included in the Circular Flow, We Are No Longer Sure of a Stable Equilibrium National Income.**

  A. *Equilibrium National Income* (usually referred to as equilibrium): Occurs when the total demand for goods and services is the same as the total supply of goods.

  B. *Disequilibrium* (out of equilibrium):

   1. Disequilibrium occurs when the demand for goods and services is not equal to the amount of goods and services being supplied.

   2. The economy is always moving from disequilibrium toward equilibrium.

  C. Why doesn't the economy stay at equilibrium national income? Because saving and investment is done by different groups, for different reasons.

   1. Households may plan to save more or less than businesses plan to use as investment.

   2. Businesses may plan to invest more or less than households plan to save.

  D. If savings are not equal to investment, then changes in the national income occur.

   1. Savings withdraw income from the circular flow. (The withdrawal is called a "leakage.")

   2. Investment injects income into the circular flow. (Investment spending is called an "injection.")

  E. When the economy is in disequilibrium, the level of income is changing.

   1. If savings are greater than the amount of investment, national income falls.

   2. If investment is greater than savings, national income rises.

IV. MAINTAINING THE CIRCULAR FLOW, EVEN IN DISEQUILIBRIUM—WHEN SPENDING IS NOT ENOUGH TO MAKE NATIONAL PRODUCT AND NATIONAL INCOME EQUAL, UNPLANNED CHANGES IN INVENTORY INVESTMENT MAKE THEM EQUAL. (*Note:* this is an accounting equality.)

   A. *Actual Investment:* Both planned and unplanned investment. Firms are unsure what the actual investment will be.

   B. *Actual Saving:* Both planned and unplanned saving. Saving depends on income level, and individuals are unsure what income will be.

      1. When savings increase, unsold goods are left in the market.

      2. Unsold goods become unplanned inventory adjustments. (Example: firm plans to invest $900 but is left with unsold inventories of $100 it cannot sell. The firm now has an actual investment of $1,000.)

      3. Actual investment increases to become equal to savings.

   C. Investment must equal saving. Do savings in the real economy actually equal investment?

      1. Not necessarily, if we only consider planned saving and planned investment.

      2. Yes, when we include actual amounts, then saving equals investment (S = I).

   D. When planned savings are not equal to planned investment, changes in inventories make actual investment equal to actual saving.

   E. The size of the circular flow shrinks or expands with spending changes.

      1. When planned investment is greater than planned savings, firms hire and use a greater amount of factors, causing increased production; national income rises.

CHAPTER 9 HIGHLIGHTS   173

    2. When planned savings are greater than planned investment, firms hire fewer factors, thus lowering production; national income falls.

V. CIRCULAR FLOW IN SYMBOLS

  A. The factor side of the circular flow is represented by Y (national income).

  B. The product side of the circular flow is represented by C + I (consumption plus investment).

  C. The equality of the product and factor sides of the circular flow means that Y = C + I.

  D. Income is only used for consumption (C) or savings (S).

    1. The equality of product and factor flows is also expressed as Y = C + S.

    2. Therefore, actual investment always equals actual savings I = S.

    3. Inventory changes always make I = S.

  E. When I is greater than S, Y goes up. When I is less than S, then Y goes down.

  F. When I = S, Y (national income) is in equilibrium.

VI. ADDING GOVERNMENT INTO THE CIRCULAR FLOW (a further and necessary complication of the model)

  A. Taxes flow from households to government; transfer payments and government spending flow from government to households.

  B. Government adds to total expenditure when it buys goods and services.

  C. Government sells bonds to finance its debts; it buys back its bonds when it has a surplus.

FILL-IN REVIEW

Select between the choices underlined or fill in the blank. Cover the answers until you have provided your own.

flow	The concept of the circular ____ illustrates
economy	how the different parts of the _____ are linked together.
	In economic theory, all labor, land, capital and entrepreneurship are regarded as
households	owned by _____ and are provided to
businesses (or firms)	_____. In exchange for the use of these
wages	factors, businesses pay, in return, _____,
rent interest	____ and _____. The total of these income payments to households (plus profit) is re-
national income	ferred to as _____ _____. The wages, rents, interests, and profit that businesses pay
costs	to households are considered ____ of production. The exchange of factors of production for money income is the first link between the
businesses (or firms)	households and _____ in the circular
flow	____ of the economy.
	When households have received their
income	money _____, they spend the major part for consumer goods and services. This expendi-
consumption	ture by households is called _____. The total monetary value of all final consumer

FILL-IN REVIEW

goods and services produced and sold is called
_____ _____. | *national product*

Because national income is the total of the receipts of income earned in producing the national product, the value of the two is the _____. This spending completes the cycle of the flow; goods and services flow in one direction, and money payments flow in the other _____. | *same*

direction

Income received by households that is not spent is _____. Savings provide the resources for business investment. Expenditures by _____ to increase productive capacity, plus inventory adjustment are called _____. Savings are made available to businesses for _____ through the banking systems' _____ markets. | *saved*

businesses

investment
investment
credit

In the simple model, the assumption is made that only households _____ and business firms _____. Therefore, savers and investors are *the same/different* groups, with *the same/different* motivations. For the circular flow of spending and product to stay the same size, planned investment must equal planned _____. | *save*
invest
different
different

saving

If firms receive back in expenditures ex-

| | actly what they paid out for the factors, they
exactly | will have produced _____ the amount of
            | goods demanded in the economy. This situa-
equals | tion, where the amount of production _____
            | the amount of expenditure is called
equilibrium | _____. There is no need for adjust-
equilibrium | ments in production decisions at _____.
            | However, if households withdraw more saving
            | from the spending stream than is used up by
investment | planned _____, businesses will not sell
            | all of their output, and unsold inventories will
            | accumulate. They will pile up in warehouses
            | and on the shelves of stores. We regard busi-
            | ness as investing in the unplanned inven-
            | tories, since part of our definition of invest-
inventory changes | ment is unplanned _____ _____.
investment | When this inventory _____ occurs the
equilibrium | economy will not be in _____. In sum-
            | mary, inventory adjustments happen when
less | the economy produces more or ____ than is
            | bought. These adjustments cause the economy
            | to change and the circular flow to get larger or
smaller | _____.

            | Total income in the economy is equal to
consumption | household spending for actual _____,
investment | plus business spending for actual _____.
Y   C | In symbols, _ (total income) = _ (consump-
     I | tion) plus _ (investment). Recall that national

FILL-IN REVIEW

income equals national product. If the planned __, plus the planned __ do not make national income equal to national _____, there will be _____ changes in _____ investment to bring them to equality.

C I

product

unplanned

inventory

Since income can only be spent or _____, total income must also equal __ plus savings (S). (In symbols: Y = C + I, Y = C + S, therefore I = S).

saved

C

A given level of income can be maintained only if planned _____ equal _____ _____. Firms can misjudge the demand for their products and, for example, produce $800 of goods while $900 of goods are demanded. In this case, actual _____ exceeds planned _____ and firms adjust their _____ by $100. As we will develop this model, this inventory adjustment causes changes in the size of the circular flow. Actual investment equals _____ investment plus _____ _____. Because inventory investment adjusts to fluctuations in demand, actual investment will always equal actual _____.

savings

planned investment

investment savings

inventories

planned

inventory investment

savings

PROBLEMS, PROBLEMS, PROBLEMS...

Answers are at the end of this unit.

TRUE-FALSE

Circle either "T" or "F" for each statement.

T (F) 1. Households consume factors of production in the factor market and supply goods and services in the product market.

(T) F 2. Firms consume factors of production in the factor market and supply goods and services in the product market.

T (F) 3. Households exchange money for purchases of goods and services in the capital market.

(T) F 4. In the circular flow model, goods and services and factors of production flow in one direction, while money payments for them flow in the other direction.

(T) F 5. Savings is defined as whatever is left from income after consumption.

(T) F 6. Equilibrium occurs when planned savings equals planned investment.

T (F) 7. If planned investment exceeds planned saving, inventory investment must increase.

(T) F 8. If planned saving exceeds planned investment, inventory investment must increase.

(T) F 9. Actual investment always equals actual saving.

MATCH-UP

Match each item in the first column with a term in the second column. Use no term more than once.

__j__ 1. A model that traces the circulation of goods and services and money through the economy

__a__ 2. Where households spend their incomes

__i__ 3. Labor, capital, land and entrepreneurship

__e__ 4. Undertaken by firms to increase productive capacity

__b__ 5. Where firms buy or hire labor, land and capital

__g__ 6. Always holds true in the circular flow model

__h__ 7. Only holds true in equilibrium

__c__ 8. Buy goods and services and supply factors of production

__f__ 9. Stocks of goods held by firms as a precaution against fluctuations in demand

__d__ 10. Whatever is not consumed out of income

a. goods and services market
b. factor market
c. households
d. saving
e. fixed investment
f. inventories
g. planned investment = planned savings
h. actual investment = actual savings
i. factors of production
j. circular flow

MULTIPLE CHOICE

For each of the following statements, choose the one best alternative.

1. The total of all the rent, wages, interest and profit that households receive is called

    a. national factors.

    b. national expenditure.

    c. national income.

    d. all of the above

2. In this simple model, households save and businesses invest. These two groups

    a. are identical in motivations.

    b. are different in motivations.

    c. may wish to save or invest different amounts.

    d. Both b and c are correct.

3. All of the below correctly complete the following statement *except* one. (Choose that one.) The circular flow of income and product is an economic concept that describes how the different parts of the economy

    a. function together.

    b. are linked.

    c. are independent.

    d. relate to one another.

4. Equilibrium national income is a basic concept in macroeconomics. Which of the following is *true* of equilibrium?

    a. There will be adjustments in production decisions.

    b. There will be no need for adjustment in production decisions.

    c. Savings are not equal to investment.

    d. There will be unplanned inventory adjustments.

MULTIPLE CHOICE

5. Households buy
   a. factors of production and sell goods and services.
   b. both goods and services and factors of production.
   c. neither goods and services nor factors of production.
   d. goods and services and sell factors of production.

6. Factors of production are
   a. land, labor, capital and entrepreneurship.
   b. rent, wages, interest and profits.
   c. consumption, investment and taxation.
   d. rent, wages, interest but not profits.

7. Business costs of production are
   a. land, labor, capital and entrepreneurship.
   b. rent, wages, interest and profits.
   c. consumption, investment and taxation.
   d. rent, wages, interest but not profits.

8. If planned investment exceeds planned saving,
   a. inventory investment will increase.
   b. inventory investment will not change.
   c. inventory investment will decrease.
   d. savings will increase.

PART TWO

UNIT VI ASSIGNMENT: PART TWO

STUDY: Chapter 10, "Measuring the Economy's Performance," *Economics Today*

STUDY: Film Summary: "Measuring My Success," *Study Guide*

VIEW: "Measuring My Success"

REVIEW: Chapter 10 Highlights, *Study Guide*

COMPLETE: Fill-in Review *and* Problems, Problems, Problems *...and* Econoword Puzzle, *Study Guide*

FILM SUMMARY: "Measuring My Success"

In this program, Thomas challenges Uncle Halvor Anderson's interpretation of the new GNP figures. Thomas is irritated by Halvor's belief that this single measurement of productivity stands for the well-being of the entire country.

Is Uncle Halvor correct? Actually, he is more right than wrong, since GNP is the single most reliable indicator we have of how well the economy is doing. But even though national income measurements are vital to economic policy making, forecasting and comparing standards of living are not, by any means, perfect measurements.

In Part One of this Unit, we said that, with the circular flow model, the real study of macroeconomics has begun. The well-being of the economy depends on what is happening to the size of the flow. The circular flow and the national income accounts that measure the elements of the flow provide the foundation for understanding models of national income determination. The national income accounts measure its elements. They attach numbers to the totals that are used in policy making; i.e., gross national product, net national product, national income, personal income and personal disposable income. The most used of the totals is gross national product, the total money value of all final goods and services produced during a year.

GNP can be measured in two ways. The first method adds all expenditures by consumers and government, plus investment by business and net exports. The second method adds up all the factor incomes derived from land, labor and capital. Recall the concept of the circular flow (in Part One of this Unit) mentioned that national product must equal national income. And remember that the national income accounts are measured as gross national product and gross national income.

Thomas is sure GNP is an imperfect measurement. Let's briefly consider some of Thomas's criticisms of the use of GNP for comparisons. GNP is a measurement of product, but much activity that involves productivity doesn't appear in the measurements. The "underground economy," where services are exchanged by barter to avoid income tax payment, is ignored; unpaid services of housewives and do-it-yourself activities involve a flow of goods and services, but no money flow. GNP does not show that people work shorter hours and enjoy increased leisure. GNP then undermeasures these economic activities. With our increased output we have also increased the amounts of various kinds of pollution. GNP accounts reflect expenditures on anti-pollution efforts which don't actually reflect increases in economic well-being. Finally, Thomas maintains that GNP figures do not take inflation into account.

In the program, Aunt Bettina learns how to make a simple, one-good price index. A price index is an important tool in adjusting the overstatement of economic activity made by GNP during periods of inflation. To compare the performance of the economy between two time periods, GNP must be adjusted to real GNP to account for price changes. To obtain real GNP, divide the GNP measured in current dollars by a price index. In this way, a comparison can be made that reflects changes in real buying power. So, Thomas is also right: there *are* biases in GNP figures.

CHAPTER 10 HIGHLIGHTS

Defined words are underlined.

I. GROSS NATIONAL PRODUCT (GNP) IS THE TOTAL MONEY VALUE OF THE NATION'S FINAL PRODUCT DURING A YEAR.

  A. GNP is a flow in a time period.

  B. To avoid double counting,

   1. only final output of the economy is counted, or,

   2. the value-added method can be used.

  C. Nonproductive transactions that are excluded are

   1. stocks and bond purchases (merely paper transfers of ownership),

   2. government transfer payments (They don't represent production),

   3. gifts and private transfer payments and used goods.

II. TWO METHODS OF MEASURING GNP

  A. There is the expenditure approach of GNP measurement, or the sum of all spending for goods and services. (This formula reads: GNP = C + I + G + EX.)

   1. (C) Consumption by households is measured at market prices.

   2. (I) Investment: The addition or replacement of business equipment adding to productive capacity.

   3. (G) Government expenditures on goods and services is measured at cost.

4. (EX) Net Exports: Total exports minus total imports.

B. The income approach of GNP measures gross national income as a sum of factor payments: wages, interest, rent, and profits.

III. TO ARRIVE AT OTHER CONCEPTS OF THE NATIONAL INCOME ACCOUNTS

A. From GNP, deduct depreciation (the "wear and tear" on existing capital stock) to get net national product (NNP).

B. From NNP, deduct indirect business taxes (excise, sales and property taxes) to get national income (in this case, the sum of payments to factor owners).

C. To national income, add government transfer payments, and subtract income earned but not received (such as undistributed corporate profits, Social Security contributions and corporate income taxes) to get personal income.

D. From personal income, subtract all personal income taxes to get disposable personal income (the income individuals actually have for consumption and savings).

IV. USES OF NATIONAL INCOME ACCOUNTING

A. to analyze the effects of economic policy;

B. to analyze the well-being of the economy. Different aggregates have different analytic uses. We use the concepts of

1. GNP, when referring to overall production.

2. NNP, in reference to production net of capital replacement.

3. national income to speak of income earned by the factors of production.

4. personal income to talk about the income received by households.

5. disposable personal income to refer to the actual amount households have available to save or spend.

V. USING GNP AS A MEASURE OF SOCIAL WELL-BEING

   A. Comparing GNP over time gives an inaccurate productivity measure unless price level changes are eliminated.

      1. Inflation overstates actual productivity.

      2. To distinguish between nominal and real or constant values,

         a. use a price index to translate nominal to real values.

            1) *Price Index:* Computed by making a comparison between prices of the same goods in a base year and a current year.

            2) *Nominal Values:* Income and product expressed in current dollars (uncorrected for price changes).

            3) *Real Values:* Nominal values deflated for changes in price. (Use of a price index allows us to compare buying power from one base year to the present.)

         b. use GNP divided by a price index to yield "real GNP."

   B. Per capita GNP is used to measure output per person. Per capita GNP: GNP divided by the total population.

   C. Many activities are outside the market and are not reported in GNP.

   D. Output may not equal satisfaction. GNP does not show

      1. income distribution,

      2. the value people may place on leisure.

FILL-IN REVIEW

Select between the choices underlined or fill in the blank. Cover the answers until you have provided your own.

In this chapter on national _____ accounting, we _____ the economy's performance by attaching numbers to the elements of the circular _____ of income and _____. We distinguish between the current or "face value" of a good (called its _____ value) and its real value. The value of something that has the effect of price level changes removed is called its ____ value.	*income* *measure* *flow product* *nominal* *real*
The total money value of the nation's final product for a year is called _____ _____ _____, or _____. The stress is on ____ output of the _____ (or _____) economy. If intermediate goods were included, the measure of GNP would be *too high/too low.* Since GNP is a measure of the economy's current productivity, ____-_____ transactions are *excluded/included.*	*Gross* *National Product GNP* *final entire whole* *too high* *non-productive* *excluded*
There are ____ methods of measuring GNP. One way is to add up all the spending for goods in the economy, called the _____ method of calculating GNP. In	*two* *expenditure*

188 UNIT VI: PART TWO

consumption — this method, all household _____ or (C), all expenditures of _____ or (G),
government
investment — all gross private domestic _____ or (I),
net exports — and _____ or (EX) are added.

The second method of measuring GNP is to add all the income payments to factor owners within the economy. In this approach,

wage   *interest* — _____ payments to labor, _____ payments
rent   *profits* — to capital, _____ payments to land and _____ to entrepreneurship are added. Both methods yield the same result, which is the sum of all productive activity within the economy.

OPTIONAL

The following extension of the fill-in review may prove useful for classes in which National Income Accounting is emphasized.

We can use the circular flow concept from Part One of this Unit to construct a combined flow diagram of resources and goods within the economy. In this way, we can illustrate the two methods of measuring GNP. (Note that here we are saying businesses and governments can be factor owners also.)

Figure VI.1

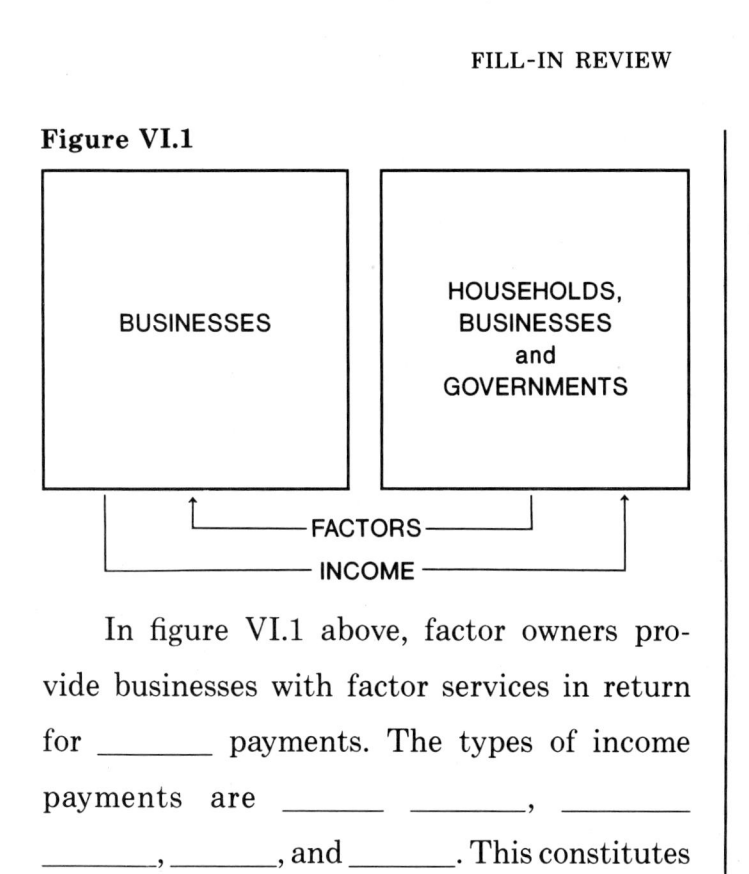

[Diagram: BUSINESSES ← FACTORS / INCOME → HOUSEHOLDS, BUSINESSES and GOVERNMENTS]

In figure VI.1 above, factor owners provide businesses with factor services in return for _____ payments. The types of income payments are _____ _____, _____ _____, _____, and _____. This constitutes a flow of factors from their owners to businesses and a return flow of _____ from businesses to factor owners.

income

rental income   interest income   wages   profits

income

To the diagram, add two overhead loops.

Figure VI.2

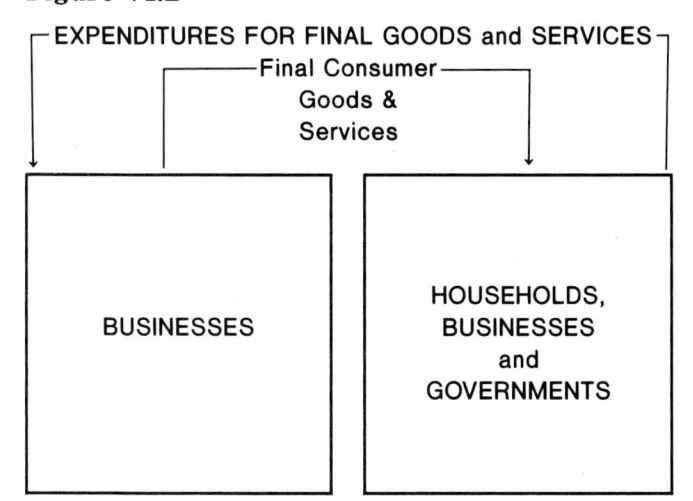

[Diagram: EXPENDITURES FOR FINAL GOODS and SERVICES / Final Consumer Goods & Services between BUSINESSES and HOUSEHOLDS, BUSINESSES and GOVERNMENTS]

190 UNIT VI: PART TWO

final

expenditures

These loops show the flow of _____ goods and services and the _____ for them.

When we combine the two diagrams, Fig. VI.1 and Fig. VI.2 we have the circular flow of income and product in a form that illustrates the two methods of calculating GNP.

Figure VI.3

EXPENDITURES FOR FINAL GOODS and SERVICES

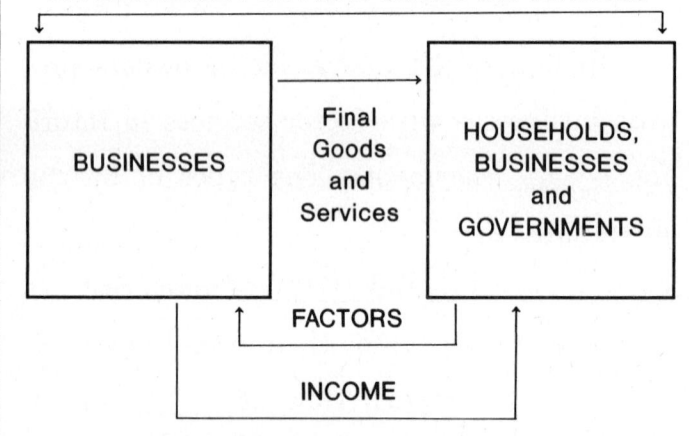

BUSINESSES → Final Goods and Services → HOUSEHOLDS, BUSINESSES and GOVERNMENTS

FACTORS INCOME

expenditures

income

As the total market value of final goods and services, GNP is equal to both total _____ for them by households, businesses and governments and total _____ earned by the owners of the factors.

Here are the two methods of calculating GNP for a hypothetical economy for one year.

EXPENDITURE METHOD

TYPE OF EXPENDITURE	AMOUNT OF EXPENDITURE
Consumption (C)	$ 89
Investment (I)	22
Government (G)	33
Net Exports (EX)	00
Total Expenditure (GNP)	$144

FILL-IN REVIEW

INCOME METHOD

TYPE OF INCOME	AMOUNT OF INCOME
Wages & Salaries	$ 86
Rents	3
Interest	4
Depreciation	12
Profits and Other Business Income	25
Indirect Business Taxes	14
Total Income (GNP)	$144

Both total expenditure and the total income measure the economy's _____, so that by either the expenditure method or the income method we can obtain the market value of the final output in this economy for one year. The two flows are _____. (In the real world, statistical error will keep them from being equal.)

GNP

equal

From Gross National Product, deduct depreciation to get ___ _____ _____. The replacement and repair of capital equipment is _____. From net national product, deduct indirect business taxes to get _____ _____. To national income, add government transfers, subtract income earned but not received to get _____ _____. From personal income, subtract all personal income taxes to get _____ _____ _____. (Personal disposable income is the amount individuals have available to either spend or save.)

Net National Product

depreciation

national income

personal income

personal disposable income

inaccurate *price index*	Comparing national income accounts over time without correcting for price changes will give an *accurate/inaccurate* picture of productivity. A _____ _____ must be used to change current (or nominal) dollars to constant dollars. Dollars deflated by a price index to show true buying power over time are
constant *real* *real GNP*	called _____ dollars. Values in constant dollars are _____ values. GNP divided by a price index shows _____ _____.

PROBLEMS, PROBLEMS, PROBLEMS...

Answers are at the end of this unit.

TRUE-FALSE

Circle either "T" or "F" for each statement.

T (F) 1. To obtain Personal Income, deduct depreciation from GNP.

T (F) 2. Stock and bond sales, intermediate sales and government transfer payments are included in GNP.

(T) F 3. GNP excludes the transfer of used/second-hand goods.

T (F) 4. In the expenditure approach of national income accounting, we add all final sales.

T (F) 5. GNP divided by population gives real GNP.

T (F) 6. The purchase of 100 shares of AT&T by a retired businessperson is considered by economists to be an investment.

(T) F 7. The piling up of inventories on a grocer's shelf is considered to be an investment.

(T) F 8. In Gross National Product, "gross" refers to the fact that we have not made a deduction for depreciation.

T (F) 9. If a man marries his paid housekeeper, then it is safe to say that GNP will go up.

MATCH-UP

Match each item in the first column with a term in the second column. Use no term more than once.

_h_ 1. Total money value of the nation's final product during a year

_f_ 2. Wear and tear of existing capital stock

_e_ 3. Stocks and bond purchases, transfer payments, gifts and sale of used goods

_d_ 4. Deduct indirect business taxes from Net National Product to get this.

_c_ 5. The expenditure approach and the income approach

_b_ 6. From personal income, subtract all personal income taxes to get this.

_a_ 7. Analyzes the effects of economic policy and analyzes the productivity and well-being of the economy

_i_ 8. A price index is used to translate nominal into this.

_g_ 9. GNP divided by a price index

a. uses of national income accounting
b. personal disposable income
c. two methods of measuring GNP
d. national income
e. nonproductive transactions excluded from GNP
f. depreciation
g. real GNP
h. gross national product
i. real values

MULTIPLE CHOICE

For each of the following statements, choose the one best alternative.

1. GNP that has been adjusted for price changes can be called
   a. money GNP.
   b. GNP in nominal dollars.
   c. GNP in current dollars.
   d. real GNP.

2. Which category is not included in the calculation of GNP by the expenditure approach?
   a. wages
   b. net exports
   c. consumption
   d. government
   e. investment

3. GNP is defined as
   a. the market value of all goods and services produced in the economy.
   b. the total market value (in current dollars) of all final goods and services produced in the economy during a year period.
   c. the market value (in real or constant dollars) of all goods and services produced in the economy during a year period.
   d. none of the above

4. Which of the following is included in determining GNP?
   a. a father's gift of stock to his son
   b. the purchase of a used automobile
   c. the purchase of a new automobile
   d. a welfare payment to a needy family

5. GNP excludes
   a. the buying and selling of securities.
   b. government transfer payments.
   c. private transfer payments.
   d. All of the above are correct, a and b and c.

6. You would be double counting if
   a. you didn't adjust GNP for price changes.
   b. you included intermediate goods in the calculation of GNP.
   c. you included in GNP the purchase price of a new sweater.
   d. you included in GNP the purchase price of a calculator.

7. NNP exceeds the national income by
   a. personal taxes.
   b. indirect business taxes.
   c. the capital consumption allowance.
   d. transfer payments.

8. Indirect taxes include
   a. excise taxes.
   b. sales taxes.
   c. property taxes.
   d. All of the above are correct, a and b and c.

9. If current dollar (or nominal) GNP in an economy is $600 billion, when the price index stands at 300 (percent), real GNP is
   a. $1,800 billion.
   b. $300 billion.
   c. $200 billion.
   d. $900 billion.

MULTIPLE CHOICE

10. | | |
|---|---:|
| Indirect Taxes | $ 20 |
| Imports | 15 |
| Interest income | 40 |
| Personal consumption expenditures | 200 |
| Exports | 20 |
| Personal income taxes | 10 |
| Gross private domestic investment | 75 |
| Depreciation | 20 |
| Government purchases | 100 |
| Rents | 40 |
| Employee compensation | 180 |

Given the expenditures (above), gross national product is

a. $380.
b. $360
c. $280.
d. $410.

11. In the hypothetical economy of question number 10, NNP is
a. $380.
b. $360.
c. $340.
d. $330.

12. In the hypothetical economy of question number 10, NI is
a. $380.
b. $360.
c. $340.
d. $330.

# ECONOWORD PUZZLE

CLUES ACROSS

1. Another name for spending
2. _____ sell their land, labor and shares of capital to businesses.
8. _____ produce goods and services to sell to households.
10. Savings withdrawal from the circular flow
11. Goods and services are exchanged in the _____ market.
14. GNP divided by a price index is _____ GNP.
15. _____ value is the face value of a good.
16. When it is time to pay a bill, we say it is _____.
17. Income that is not spent for consumption
19. Exchange takes place in a _____.
20. Government can sell _____ to pay for its expenditures.
23. Equilibrium occurs where savings and investment are the _____.
25. Planned investment may not be the same as _____ investment.
29. Payments for land, labor and capital are business _____.
30. When we measure national income, we are measuring the _____ of the circular flow.
31. National product is roughly equal to national _____.
33. To lower expenditures can be referred to as a _____ in spending.
34. To NNP add depreciation _____ obtain GNP.
36. GNP minus depreciation
37. Out of equilibrium
39. Inventory adjustment is frequently _____ investment.
41. If the amount households save is just equal to the amount investors _____.

42. GNP minus depreciation equals _____ national product.
43. The mere transfer of paper assets is _____ included in GNP.
44. The return on land is called _____.
45. Stocks of finished goods and goods in progress

CLUES DOWN

1. We read about unemployment statistics but don't often see statistics of those with jobs, or _____.
3. The circular flow is not actually as regular and _____ as it is shown in simple models.
4. If the amount of the circular flow is reduced, then national income will be _____.
5. The product market is where a good or _____ can be exchanged.
6. Those of us who hold jobs work for _____.
7. The wear and tear on existing capital stock
9. The income of the entire country is _____ income.
12. Expenditure by households
13. In symbols, I represents _____.
18. _____ is the total money value of the nation's final product during a year.
21. Use a price index to _____ prices.
22. Large economics
24. Investment spending is an _____.
26. When we measure GNP and NNP, we are using national income _____.
27. To deflate prices to compare those in a base year, you should _____ a price index.
28. When you look for a job, you are participating in the _____ market.

ECONOWORD PUZZLE

199

31. The payment for the use of capital is called _____.

32. A _____ flow of income and product shows how the different sectors of the economy are tied together.

35. At equilibrium, savings _____ investment.

38. In the circular flow, there is a real flow and a _____ flow.

40. A prefix meaning not.

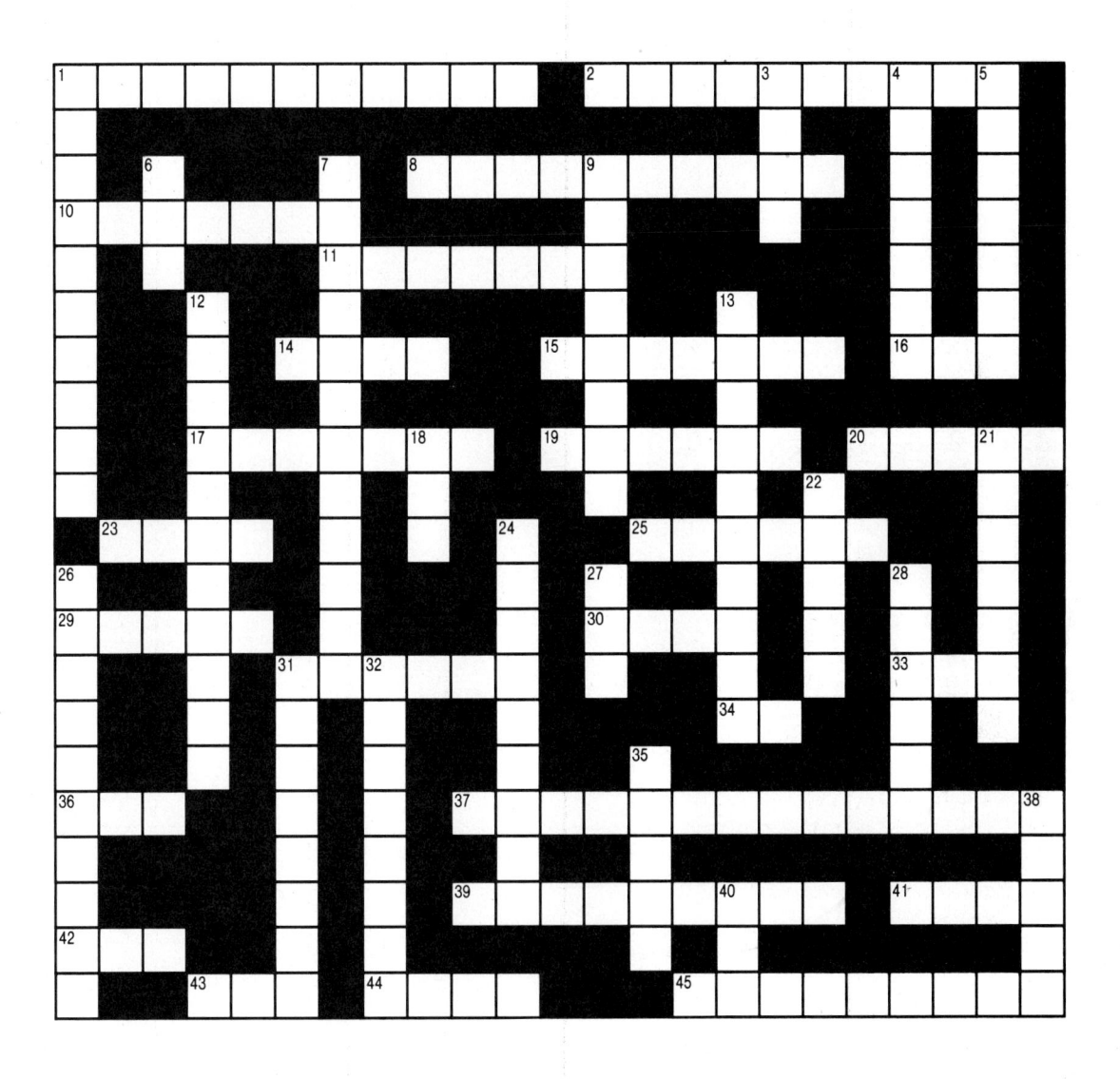

Answers to Study Questions

PART ONE

TRUE/FALSE

1. F 2. T 3. F 4. T 5. T 6. T 7. F 8. T 9. T

MATCH-UP

1. j 2. a 3. i 4. e 5. b 6. g 7. h 8. c 9. f 10. d

MULTIPLE CHOICE

1. c 2. d 3. c 4. b 5. d 6. a 7. b 8. c

PART TWO

TRUE/FALSE

1. F 2. F 3. T 4. F 5. F 6. F 7. T 8. T 9. F

MATCH-UP

1. h 2. f 3. e 4. d 5. c 6. b 7. a 8. i 9. g

MULTIPLE CHOICE

1. d 2. a 3. b 4. c 5. d 6. b 7. b 8. d 9. c 10. a 11. b 12. c

COMPLETED ECONOWORD PUZZLE

ANALYZING THE MACROECONOMY

UNIT VII

UNIT IN A NUTSHELL

PART ONE

Film: "Getting and Spending"

Text: Chapter 11

PART TWO

Film: "Withdrawal Symptoms"

Text: Chapter 12

In our macroeconomy, every economic unit is free to spend as it wishes; businesses may or may not choose to invest, and households act on their own reasons for consuming or saving. The spending flows of savings and investment are sensitive and changeable. Yet, we are all locked together in sharing the results of spending. Increased investment in one sector sends waves of re-spending throughout the economy. Also, when investment in one part of the economy is pinched, others feel the pressure. In effect, increased consumer and investment spending increases national income, while lowered spending reduces the national income. John Maynard Keynes concentrated on the total spending and its importance to the vigor of the economy. In this unit, the Keynesian income expenditures graph is introduced as we develop the theory of income analysis.

UNIT OBJECTIVES

Objectives 1-6 can be met by studying Chapter 11 and viewing "Getting and Spending." After completing Part One, the student should be able to:

1. Explain the basic hypothesis of the classical model, and those of the Keynesian model and then contrast the two models.

2. Define the consumption function, then explain how consumption, saving and income are related.

3. Define and give examples of MPC and MPS.

4. Explain the difference between a movement along the consumption function and a shift of the entire line.

5. Contrast the Keynes absolute income hypothesis with the permanent income hypothesis of Friedman.

6. Tell what determines planned investment.

Objectives 7 and 8 can be met by studying Chapter 12 and viewing "Withdrawal Symptoms." After completing Part Two, the student should be able to:

7. Define aggregate demand and aggregate supply and know when aggregate supply is equal to aggregate income.

8. Explain what happens when aggregate demand is not the same as aggregate supply.

    a) Define the multiplier and explain the multiplier effect.

    b) Know how a change in investment causes a change in equilibrium national income.

    c) Explain why the paradox of thrift describes a shift in the savings schedule.

PART ONE

UNIT VII ASSIGNMENT: PART ONE

STUDY: Chapter 11, "Consumption, Saving, and Investment," *Economics Today*

STUDY: Film Summary: "Getting and Spending," *Study Guide*

VIEW: "Getting and Spending"

REVIEW: Chapter 11 Highlights, *Study Guide*

COMPLETE: Fill-in Review *and* Problems, Problems, Problems . . . , *Study Guide*

FILM SUMMARY: "Getting and Spending"

The title tells the story. The theme of the program is spending: spending by households and spending by businesses. Thomas and Karen spend most of their bonus. How people spend extra income is of considerable interest to economists. (Remember that in our dramas we often use individuals' actions to develop economic concepts. We use the Weldons in this way.) But to generalize for the whole economy from a single example is dangerous in economics; confusing what is true of a *part* of something with that which is true of the *whole* is a "fallacy of composition." What may be true for all may be wrong for an individual and what is true for an individual may be false for the economy. Just keep in mind that the Weldons illustrate a statistically average household in their spending patterns.

In the last Unit, you learned that the two important kinds of spending, consumption by households and investment by businesses, determine much of our national income. An important function of investment is to offset leakages from the spending flow. Macroequilibrium has an unstable nature since the economy is only in equilibrium when planned saving equals planned investment.

We are beginning to construct the Keynesian theory of income determination. The model based on John Maynard Keynes' theory contrasts with the classical model. The classical economists believed that the economy had a built-in, self-regulating mechanism. They argued that enough income is generated in the economy to buy up all the goods and services produced. They held that this was accomplished by flexible prices that cleared markets and rapid adjustments in the interest rate that equated planned saving and planned investment. In this way the economy had the ability to keep itself at full-employment equilibrium.

Keynes disagreed. He pointed out what is shown in the program: households have different motivations for saving than businesses have for investing. Not only is a full-employment equilibrium not assured, but spending groups in the economy may not use the income they receive to buy the output of the economy, so that it is possible to become "stuck" at a low level of income with considerable unemployment.

Although Thomas and Karen save a little of their income, they spend most of it. Indeed, when Dr. Teal draws a graph of the consumption function, she illustrates the spending behavior which Thomas and Karen typify. The upward slope of the graph line shows the positive relationship of consumption spending to income; thus, as total income in the economy increases, so does total consumption, but by a smaller and smaller amount. This means that the higher the national income, the smaller the fraction spent on consumer goods.

Thomas grasps the concept of the consumption function when he recognizes that, to the left of the 45° line, income is low and the economy experiences planned dissaving. At the income where the consumption line crosses the 45° line, spending is exactly the same as the level of income. This is the break-even point, or equilibrium. At incomes above equilibrium, planned savings occur.

The consumption function concentrates on the way consumers are *trying* to use their incomes. When the consumption function is above the 45°

line, consumers are trying to buy more than is currently available; they buy up all the producers' shelf goods. Then, businesses produce and invest to keep up with the spending and the economy speeds up. When the consumption function is below the 45° line, people are trying to *save* more of their income. Consequently, the saving forces businesses to keep unplanned inventories (inventory investment) of their goods. Thus, the economy slows down. This process results in response to spending. It is only when spending and income are the same that equilibrium is stable.

In the program, the business investment undertaken by Satellites International creates new jobs in Arbordale. The new jobs create additional income; the increased incomes are spent, which results in even higher local incomes. Arbordale's prosperity illustrates the effects of increased spending on the entire economy. We see the income-multiplying effect on the economy resulting from the respending of extra income.

HINT

PART VII. 1

Before you attempt to read the consumption function graph, review the *text* explanation of graphs, Appendix A.

To read the consumption function graph, just pick out any level of income on the horizontal axis and go up to the consumption line to read the consumption amount at that level of income noted on the vertical axis. In other words, you will read *along* the consumption line for the changes in composition that relate to changes in income.

Each point on the consumption function line shows how much people would spend for consumer goods if national income was that amount on the income axis. Equally important, if the other determinants of consumption change (expectations, wealth), then the *whole curve* will *shift* up or down. The angle of the rise of the consumption function, the slope, shows how much of a *change* in income will be spent as consumption. This slope is the marginal propensity to consume (MPC). It gives the percentage of extra income that will be consumed. The percentage of extra income not consumed is the marginal propensity to save (MPS).

As Thomas and Karen spend their bonuses, they illustrate the concept of marginal propensity to consume. Thomas's and Karen's MPC (Marginal Propensity to Consume) is .80. This figure was calculated by determining how much of their extra income they used for extra consumption. Of the extra $3,000, they spent about $2,400, or about 80 percent or .80. (We will use the concepts of MPC and MPS in the next unit to show the way national income changes.)

In the program, the effect of the investment and additional production on Arbordale is dramatic. Just as dramatic are the economic consequences of the withdrawal of satellite dish production to the area's prosperity. Recall what was said earlier: spending is the key to the economy, and if investment spending slows down, everything slows down.

Remember, saving means *not* spending income on consumer products. Consequently, when there is saving for the entire economy, the effect is to *produce* goods but *not consume* them. When there is a general increase in saving, businesses may decide to use available savings for investment; but if the interest rate is high and there is pessimism about the future, business managers may decide not to invest. Planned business investment is undertaken because of the possibility of making a profit. Businesses consider the interest rate and the expected returns on the new investment. Costs of new capital goods and new technology are part of the decision of whether the extra revenue is worth the extra cost of investment.

There is another way of stating this concept. When households don't spend for consumer goods, factors of production are released which can produce capital goods such as machinery and equipment. These, in turn, can help produce growth for the economy. But are all planned household savings automatically used for planned business investment? Not at all. It must be kept in mind that, in an economy such as ours, any business or household is free to spend or not to spend. Their plans may not coincide at all.

John Maynard Keynes showed that there is an important difference between the attitudes of business about investments and the attitudes of households about saving. We saw that Thomas and Karen saved for a house. As individuals, we each save for purely personal reasons: some of us either save for future consumption or because we are worried about the future; some of us save when we think prices are presently too high and will soon fall. As far as businesses are concerned, the fact that people are saving more may not create an encouraging climate for new investment. But, if savings are not used for investment, then there is a failure to create buying power. Savings, therefore, "leak out" of the spending stream, and unused buying power leaves unsold goods on dealers' shelves or in producers' warehouses. In short, it becomes inventory investment. And you know what happens next.

This leakage cancels orders, eliminates some jobs, and lowers income people had planned on. People cannot save the amount they had planned to save, and the equilibrium national income falls. The foregoing progression of events is called "the paradox of thrift."

The relationship between injections and withdrawals (investment and savings) is vital in the economy. As we've said, businesses don't always plan to spend the exact amount households plan to save. But the forces within the system cause investment and savings to influence each other so that the *actual* amounts of both investment and saving turn out to be the same, although initially, this was (probably) not the plan. Thus, at equilibrium, actual savings are the same as actual investment.

NEW TERMS USED

Determinants of Investment: The amount of investment is directly related to the interest rate; the cost of buying and maintaining the capital goods, business taxes, expectations and new technology.

Investment Demand: Buying of capital goods. Demand for capital goods depends on the rate of profit businesses expect to be earned investment, minus the rate of interest paid for use of money.

Investment Demand Schedule: The inverse relationship between the interest rate and the level of investment spending.

Rate of Interest: The price paid for the use of money.

CHAPTER 11 HIGHLIGHTS

Defined words are underlined.

I. CHAPTER OVERVIEW

   A. A beginning model of the modern theory of income analysis

   1. Models are simplified and provide understanding.

   2. A variety of models are possible; we study only the simplest.

   3. We make a model by using simplifying assumptions.

   4. We pretend there are no taxes and no complicating business depreciation.

   5. With the simplifying assumptions, we will only consider consumption, saving, investment and income.

      a. *Consumptions (C)*: Household spending

      b. *Saving (S)*: Household current income not consumed

      c. *Income (Y)*: Savings plus consumption

      d. *Investment (I)*: Business capital goods spending

   B. Two models of economy are generally used: Classical and Keynesian.

   1. The classical theorists believed that interest rates equate saving and investment and that flexible prices always make the demand and the supply of goods equal.

   2. The classicists believed the economy always tends toward a full employment equilibrium.

   3. Keynesian theory disagreed: in Keynesian theory, disequilibrium between saving and investment is possible.

II. Classical Theory: Full Employment Equilibrium Is the Economy's Long-Run Natural Tendency

A. The classicists held that,

1. in producing goods for markets, sufficient income is created to buy up all the goods in the markets (supply creates its own demand).

2. long depressions are impossible since markets are self-regulating.

B. Classical theory implied that,

1. by interest rate adjustments, planned saving equals planned investment, resulting in full employment equilibrium in factor markets.

2. prices (including wages) are completely flexible and freely fall or rise with lower or higher demand, resulting in full employment equilibrium in product markets.

III. The Simple Keynesian Income-Expenditures Model

A. John Maynard Keynes attacked classical thought by arguing that

1. the market is not an automatic, self-regulating mechanism; prices are not downwardly flexible enough to always clear markets.

2. national income can fall and remain at a low level where high unemployment is a persistent problem.

3. savers are a different group from investors and each group has different motivations.

   a. The level of households' income determine saving; the interest rate is not of major importance.

   b. Expectation of profit is the most important reason for business investment, not the interest rate.

CHAPTER 11 HIGHLIGHTS

    c. The interest rate can change dramatically and saving and investment plans will be different.

B. Keynes defined the consumption function, relating spending to income.

    1. *The Consumption Function:* The relationship between household spending and current income. Consumption increases as incomes increase, but by smaller amounts.

        a. Example: Out of an additional $1,000 of income, consumption may only increase $750 or .75 of the extra $1,000.

        b. The percentage change in consumption as income changes is called marginal propensity to consume (MPC).

C. The saving function is the complement of the consumption function.

    1. Consumption plus saving equal disposable income.

    2. Income that is not consumed is saved.

D. Average propensity to consume and average propensity to save

    1. *Average Propensity to Consume (APC):* Spending out of entire income.

        a. Example: If all income is spent, APC is one; if 90 percent of income is spent, APC is .90.

        b. APC goes down as income goes up.

    2. *Average Propensity to Save (APS):* Saving out of entire income.

        a. Example: If 10 percent of income is saved, APS is .10.

        b. People save more out of entire income as income gets larger.

E. The three important propositions of the Keynes consumption function are

1. that consumption is related in a stable way to income; consumption is primarily determined by income, not by the interest rate.

2. as income goes up, consumption and saving both increase.

3. as income goes up, a greater and greater percentage is saved.

F. *Marginal Propensity to Consume (MPC):* The tendency to spend out of extra income.

1. MPC is a numerical measurement, the percentage of extra income spent on consumption rather than saved.

G. *Marginal Propensity to Save (MPS):* The tendency to save out of extra income.

1. $\text{MPS} = \dfrac{\text{change in planned savings}}{\text{change in disposable income}}$

2. MPS + MPC = 1. This is true because what is saved of extra income and what is spent together add up to all extra income, or 1.

H. There is a difference between a movement along the consumption function and a shift of the entire line to a new position.

1. The change of disposable income causes planned spending to change. This is shown graphically by a movement along (to another point on) the consumption function.

2. When people change spending behavior for reasons other than income, the entire function shifts. The curve moves upward for increased consumption, downward for lower consumption.

IV. **The Permanent Income Hypothesis of Milton Friedman: Consumption Spending Depends on Expected Average Earnings Over a Lifetime, Not Just Current Income.**

   A. Spending patterns are retained based on what individuals believe long-run income will be. Temporary variations in income are ignored; for example, extra income will be saved for periods of lowered income.

   B. There is no difference between MPC and APC if permanent, rather than current income, is examined.

   C. The rich do not save a greater percentage of income than the poor.

V. **Other Determinants of Consumption Besides Income Affect Consumption but not as Significantly as Income.**

   A. *Wealth:* When real wealth increases or decreases, the consumption function shifts.

   B. *Liquid Assets:* Assets that can easily and quickly be turned into money.

   C. Expectations about the future.

FILL-IN REVIEW

Select between the choices underlined or fill in the blank. Cover the answers until you have provided your own.

model	You are beginning to build a simple version of the income-expenditure _____ originally for-
J. M. Keynes	mulated by _ _ _____. In this model there are only two things households can do with after tax income; they can spend it or
save it	____ _. Household spending for goods and
consumption	services is called _____. Current in-
saving	come not consumed is termed _____. For brevity, consumption and saving are referred
C S	to respectively as _ and _. Consumption plus
income	saving equal _____. For brevity, income is
Y	referred to as _. Since government takes some income in the form of taxes, we refer to the after-tax income we have available to use as
disposable income	_____ _____.
	Business spending on goods is termed
investment	_____. For brevity, investment is re-
I	ferred to as _. When businesses buy capital goods, which they hope will yield income in
fixed investment	the future, we term it _____ _____. Changes in business inventories, in which the business in effect buys its own goods is called
inventory investment	_____ _____. To the economists,

stocks and bonds are only paper assets representing claims to ownership of capital and, therefore, *are/are not* considered capital.   *are not*

In the classical model, long-run full employment was believed to be assured by the existence of freely fluctuating _____ and/or   *prices*
_____ _____. According to this model, a   *interest rates*
surplus of goods on the product market would be temporary since _____ would fall until   *prices*
the market cleared. The prices of all goods and services were believed to be flexible, moving up or down in response to changing
_____. All savings were assumed to be   *demand*
automatically used for _____, with the   *investment*
interest rate varying to make the investment equal to the savings. Therefore, the classical model hypothesized that the market is a self-regulating mechanism that guarantees a full-employment equilibrium.

J. M. Keynes, challenging the classicists *agreed/denied* that the market as it exists in   *denied*
the modern world is a self-_____ mechanism. He pointed out that savings can leak   *regulating*
out of the _____ stream causing produc-   *spending*
tion and income to *rise/fall*. He said there is   *fall*
no guaranteed mechanism to bring saving leakages back into the economy as invest-

employment equilibrium	ment. Without a built-in mechanism that assures full _____ _____, income can stay at a low level where
unemployment	_____ is a persistent problem. In his attack on the classical theory, Keynes asserted that savers are different from
investors	_____, and respond to different
motivations	_____. In his view, even though savings accumulate, investors *may not/will always* use the entire amount for _____.
may not	
investment	He disagreed that savings and investment
interest	would be kept the same by the _____
rate	____.
	The relationship between household consumption and income is the _____
consumption	
function	_____. As income rises, consumption *falls/rises* but not at the same rate. The consumption function can indicate how much of additional income people will consume. The fraction which indicates this is the marginal propensity to consume. That is, the rate at which consumption changes with income is
rises	
marginal propensity	called the _____ _____ to
consume	_____ (MPC). MPC refers to the tendency of consumers to spend *all/extra* income. When graphing the relationship of spending to income, a helper line or reference line is
extra	

drawn at a __ degree angle to the axis. All along this line spending is equal to _____. This line can be called the aggregate supply line since it shows how much is produced in response to spending at each level of income.

45

income

The formula for obtaining MPC is

$$\text{MPC} = \frac{\text{change in planned consumption}}{\text{change in disposable income}}$$

When people get extra income, they can only save or _____ it. The tendency for consumers to save extra income is called _____ _____ to ____ (MPS). The formula for obtaining MPS is

spend

marginal

propensity   save

$$\text{MPS} = \frac{\text{change in planned spending}}{\text{change in disposable income}}$$

MPC and MPS are fractions which sum to _ (or percentages which sum to 100 percent). A movement along the consumption function is caused by a change in _____ income. A change in spending behavior for non-income reasons results in a ____ of the entire consumption function. The permanent income hypothesis of Milton _____, which challenges the Keynesian hypothesis, states that, as disposable income rises, people *spend/save* a greater percentage of it. The permanent income hypothesis says that instead, consumption depends on _____ _____ or the expected average income over a long period.

1

disposable

shift

Friedman

save

permanent income

PROBLEMS, PROBLEMS, PROBLEMS...

Answers are at the end of this unit.

TRUE-FALSE

Circle either "T" or "F" for each statement.

(T) F 1. The classical model predicted long-run full employment equilibrium.

(T) F 2. People usually consume more as their income increases.

(T) F 3. The amount of total income a person spends is the marginal propensity to consume.

T **(F)** 4. A person who spends $80 of a $100 raise in salary has a marginal propensity to consume of 0.60.

T **(F)** 5. If the marginal propensity to consume is 1, people will consume only part of an increase in income.

(T) F 6. If the average propensity to consume (APC) is 1, people spend their entire incomes.

T **(F)** 7. John Maynard Keynes was a classical economist who believed that the economy tends to long-run full employment.

T **(F)** 8. Keynes said savers the same motivations for saving as investors have for investing.

MATCH-UP

PART A

Put either a "C" for classical or a "K" for Keynesian in front of each statement to identify it as either Classical Theory or the Keynesian Income-Expenditure Theory.

C 1. In producing goods for markets, sufficient income is created to ensure that all goods created for the market are bought.

C 2. Long depressions are impossible since markets regulate themselves for changes in demand.

K 3. The market is not an automatic self-regulating mechanism.

K 4. National income can fall and stay at a low level, causing persistent unemployment.

C 5. Prices are completely flexible, resulting in equilibrium in product markets.

K 6. Savers are a different group from investors, each group has different motivations so that savings are not always used up by planned investment.

C 7. By interest rate adjustments, planned saving equals planned investment, resulting in equilibrium in factor markets.

PART B

Match each item in the first column with a term in the second column. Use no term more than once.

__f__ 8. A relationship between income and consumption

__e__ 9. All along this helper line consumption is equal to income.

__d__ 10. A numerical value which tells how much will be saved out of an increase of income

__c__ 11. This is the major determinant of consumption.

__b__ 12. Tendency to spend out of extra income

__a__ 13. Add up MPS and MPC to get this.

a. one
b. marginal propensity to consume
c. income
d. marginal propensity to save
e. 45 degree line
f. consumption function

MULTIPLE CHOICE

For each of the following statements, choose the one best alternative.

1. The economic term "saving" can be best described as
   a. money invested in real estate.
   b. consumption minus investment.
   c. money deposited in a savings account.
   d. income that is not spent.

2. The consumption function is
   a. the relationship between consumption and investment.
   b. the relationship between consumption and income.
   c. the relationship between savings and income.
   d. the relationship between two families' levels of consumption.

3. The major determinant of consumption is
   a. the stock of liquid assets.
   b. the level of taxation.
   c. the level of disposable income.
   d. expectation of the future.

4. Keynes believed that
   a. supply creates its own demand.
   b. the economy has no automatic mechanism to insure full employment.
   c. the economy would always tend automatically to full employment.
   d. prices and wages are flexible in general.

5. The MPC can be defined as
   a. the fraction of a change in income which is spent.
   b. the fraction of a change in income which is saved.

c. the fraction of income which is invested.

d. the fraction of total income which is spent.

6. One of the following would *not* have been accepted by the classical economists. Choose that one.

   a. Supply creates its own demand.

   b. Investment and saving are made equal by changes in the interest rates.

   c. All prices, including wages, are flexible, insuring full employment.

   d. The economy has no automatic mechanism to insure full employment.

7. If consumption demand is $750 when disposable income is $1,000, the average propensity to consume is

   a. .80

   b. .75

   c. .50

   d. None of the above is correct.

8. If MPC = 0.80 and someone earned an extra $100 of income, then

   a. saving would rise $100.

   b. saving would rise $80.

   c. consumption would rise by $100.

   d. consumption would rise by $80.

9. If the MPC is 0.80 and a person's disposable income suddenly goes from $18,000 to $20,000, consumption will increase by

   a. $2,000.

   b. $160.

   c. $1,600.

   d. $200.

MULTIPLE CHOICE

10. If a person with an income of $20,000 spends $20,000, the APC is

   a. 20,000.

   b. .20.

   c. 1.

   d. 0.

11. PROPENSITY TO CONSUME IN ALPHA

DISPOSABLE INCOME	CONSUMPTION SPENDING	SAVING	APC	APS	MPC	MPS
$50	$54	$ −4	108%	−8%	60%	40%
60	60	0	100%	—	60%	40%
70	66	4	94%	6%	60%	40%
80	72	8	90%	10%	60%	40%

Fill in the blanks in the above table representing hypothetical economy Alpha.

12. In the above hypothetical economy, the MPC in the $60–$70 range of DI is

   a. 40%.

   b. 60%.

   c. 80%.

   d. 94%.

13. In the above hypothetical economy, APC at the $80 level of DI is

   a. 40%.

   b. 60%.

   c. 90%.

   d. 94%.

PART TWO

UNIT VII ASSIGNMENT: PART TWO

STUDY: Chapter 12, "Income and Employment Determination," *Economics Today*

STUDY: Film Summary: "Withdrawal Symptoms," *Study Guide*

VIEW: "Withdrawal Symptoms"

REVIEW: Chapter 12 Highlights, *Study Guide*

COMPLETE: Fill-in Review *and* Problems, Problems, Problems ..., *and* Econoword Puzzle, *Study Guide*

FILM SUMMARY: "Withdrawal Symptoms"

The economic boom of new jobs and higher incomes enjoyed by Arbordale following the investment of Satellites International is in trouble.

Symptoms of spending withdrawal are obvious throughout the city. With the slowdown in production at Satellites International, workers are paid for fewer hours or are laid off. The smaller take-home pay means that there will be less spending in Arbordale, because here, as in the rest of the economy, when income goes down, consumption goes down.

Business investment spending is quickly affected. As Thomas says, when people stop spending, businesses stop growing or slow down. The prosperous times of big bonuses are gone. In fact, Thomas thinks twice as to what he can afford for lunch. Karen's public affairs program has been cut back to half an hour, and even Uncle Halvor is unhappy about his lowered income. Workers who have lost jobs in one part of the economy are seeking work in another. (These are some of the symptoms that show us that the slowdown is part of a national recession.)

In the last program, Dr. Teal described the consumption function and the vital role of new investment spending in changing national income. Now, Dr. Teal demonstrates that consumption and investment are two major parts of the nation's total spending. The total of all planned expenditures by all buyers in the economy is called aggregate demand, while aggregate supply is the total value of all goods and services sold by all firms in the economy. Dr. Teal demonstrates that a graph of aggregate demand is obtained by adding the consumption function to the investment function.

On the graph, the aggregate supply is the 45° line, and the point where the aggregate demand curve intersects this line is the equilibrium level of national income. At a given income level, if the aggregate demand is greater than aggregate supply, businesses will increase production by hiring more workers, thereby increasing national income. At an income level above equilibrium, unplanned increases in inventories will accumulate. Firms will then fire some workers and cut back production. As you now know, when this happens throughout the economy income falls toward equilibrium.

Equilibrium national income occurs when total planned expenditures equal total national product. The same equilibrium income is obtained when planned saving equals planned investment. This means that there are two methods for determining equilibrium national income: the aggregate supply-aggregate demand method and the leakages-injection method. They both yield the same result.

In the program, Uncle Halvor sends the couple a $5,000 gift check, and Karen's fear of the economy's future is reflected by her refusal to spend the extra income. Impulsive Thomas can think of many ways to spend the extra money, and when he insists that Karen should spend to help out the economy, his reasoning doesn't convince her at all. (Remember the explanation given earlier about "fallacy of composition"?) Karen answers that individuals are not responsible for how the economy works.

In refusing to be won over by Thomas's unconvincing assertion, Karen makes an important point. She is correct in her insistence that economic models are based on how large groups of people (aggregates) actually spend or save in different situations. (Macroeconomics concerns itself with identifying the behavior of aggregates, not in dictating how individuals should spend or save.) Karen recognizes that businesses or households do not act for the good of the economy; individual self-interest is an important basis of a freely competitive system.

As we discover the effects of a slowdown in economic activity in Arbordale, the question that is being considered by Larry Dutweiler at Dynamics Corporation is whether or not to invest in a large, new racing complex.

Dr. Teal is hired as a consultant to Dynamics Corporation and becomes involved in explaining the Keynesian model of income expenditures. She is not eager to advise on specific investment opportunities for Dynamics; her specialty is the analysis of how the economy works "in the aggregate." That is, she is able to describe the effects of spending of whole sectors (business investment, household consumption) on the national income.

This is a good place to remind you that macroeconomics deals with large aggregate measurements. When the economy is in recession and national product, income and employment are falling, can new investment also occur at the same time, as is illustrated with Raceways International? Yes, it can happen and regularly does happen. (You already know that investment is undertaken because of the possibility of profit.)

Consider applications of this investment determinant during periods of recession. When people are not buying *new* cars, those businesses which repair *existing* cars to keep them running and on the road will enjoy profits. Similarly, businesses helping people to overcome or forget the fears associated with a recession, such as producers of video games or escapist entertainment, are also likely to show profits for their business spending.

So far, we have traced the tendency of the economy to come to equilibrium, but have not related equilibrium national income to full employment. There is no guarantee that the economy will achieve full employment. Discussion will be continued in the next unit about the income-expenditures model and consideration of what happens when equilibrium national income does not coincide with full employment.

The next program, "Income, Go Forth and Multiply," also deals with the material found in Chapter 12 of the text: it will introduce the multiplier and examine its role in causing national income to change. As this is done, we will see the effects on the entire economy of the kinds of spending behavior that we have observed in Karen and Thomas Weldon.

NEW TERMS USED

Aggregate: Total or overall quantity for the economy. GNP is an aggregate, being the sum of figures for consumption and investment. (Government and net exports will be added as parts of aggregate as explained in later units.)

Aggregate Demand: The dollar total of planned expenditures for the economy on all final goods and services per year.

Aggregate Supply: The total dollar value of all final goods and services supplied by firms to the market economy per year.

CHAPTER 12 HIGHLIGHTS

Defined words are underlined.

I. CHAPTER OVERVIEW: CONTINUING TO BUILD THE SIMPLE MODEL OF INCOME AND EMPLOYMENT DETERMINATION: ANALYZING THE SOURCES OF SPENDING

   A. Model Summary

   1. The circular flow of income and product

      a. *Equilibrium:* When planned spending for output is equal to total output.

      b. At equilibrium, planned saving is equal to planned investment (S = I).

c. Inventory adjustments cause the circular flow to shrink or expand, which means national income and employment get smaller or larger.

B. Concepts explained in Chapter 11 are used to continue the development of the model.

1. The consumption function (the spending by households) and the savings investment function (spending by businesses)

2. MPC (the tendency to spend extra income) and MPS (the tendency to save extra income)

C. How national income and employment equilibrium is established will be shown by using two methods, each of which arrives at the same answer. The two methods are

1. consumption plus investment schedules for the economy.

2. leakages of savings equal to injections of investment.

II. SPENDING AND PRODUCTION: AGGREGATE CONCEPTS THAT REFER RESPECTIVELY TO ALL SPENDING AND ALL PRODUCTION THAT RESULTS FROM THAT SPENDING.

Aggregate Demand: Total of all planned spending in the economy.

Aggregate Supply: The total of all goods and services produced in the economy (national product).

A. Aggregate demand includes

1. planned consumption (C) by household.

a. One part is related to national income.

b. The other is autonomous consumption. *Autonomous Consumption:* Consumption independent of income.

CHAPTER 12 HIGHLIGHTS

2. planned investment (I) by businesses.

   a. All I in the simple model is assumed to be autonomous.

   b. *Autonomous Investment:* Investment stays the same at all levels of national income.

3. Graphed aggregate demand is a vertical sum of the C + I lines.

B. Aggregate Supply:

1. Businesses produce only what they expect to sell. The total is national product (aggregate supply).

2. Businesses pay for the factors used in production. The total is national income (aggregate income).

C. Firms only supply the quantity of output for which they expect to receive income to cover all their costs, so that aggregate supply equals aggregate income.

1. The values of goods and services. (National product is equal to national income.)

2. To graph aggregate supply, use a 45° helper line an equal distance from aggregate income on the horizontal axis and aggregate demand on the vertical axis.

3. Any point on the 45° aggregate supply line indicates equal amounts of aggregate spending and aggregate income.

HINT

PART VII. 2
What is said is graphed in your text, so let's be clear on what the graphs will show. Consider a graph with the vertical axis temporarily labeled "Spending" and the horizontal axis labeled "Income."

PART VII. 3
Now, a 45° line is drawn exactly half-way between the spending and income taxes.

PART VII. 4
Next, identical measuring scales are used for both axes. Any point on the 45° line measures the same amount of whatever is on each of the axes. This property of the graph is a very important one and we will use it throughout the chapter.

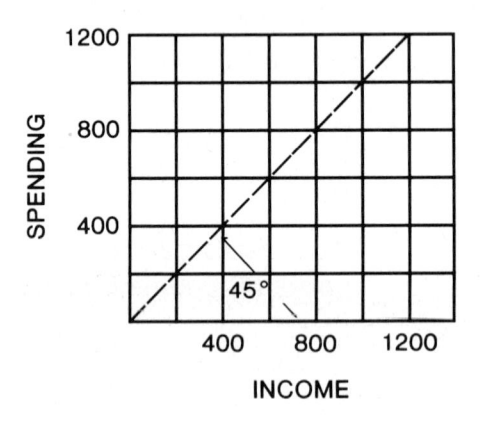

PART VII. 5
Select a point on the 45° line to test this for yourself. For example, at point B spending is $1000, and income is $1000.

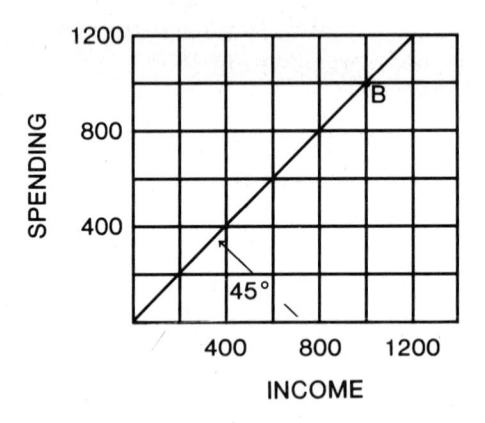

We will use this property of the 45° line to relate spending to income dollars in the economy. As you learned in the circular flow of income and product, the value of all goods and services being produced is equal to the total amount of dollars received as income.

PART VII. 6

Back to the graph. The axes are still labeled "Income" and "Spending." (All future labeling of this Income-Expenditures graph are just refinements of these labels.)

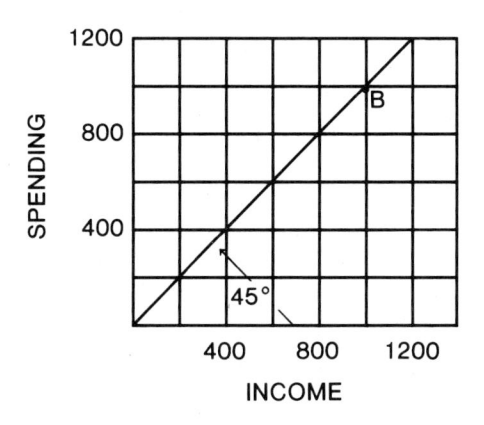

PART VII. 7

Remind yourself that at any point on the 45° line there is an equilibrium of spending and income, by picking any point *off* the 45 degree line—say, Point A. At A, "Spending" is only $400 while "Income" is $600. Since income is the same of all payments to product output, production is creating more spending ability than is used.

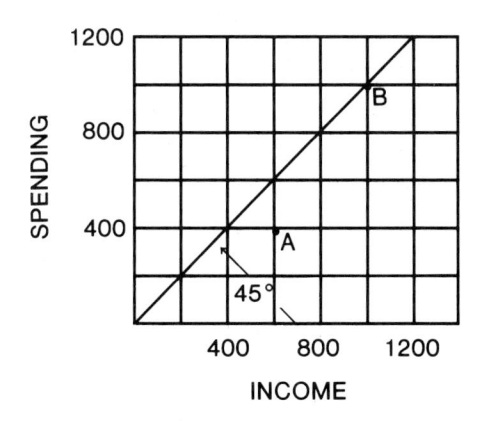

PART VII. 8

Now let's graph the relationship between consumption spending by households and income; the consumption function, labeled C.

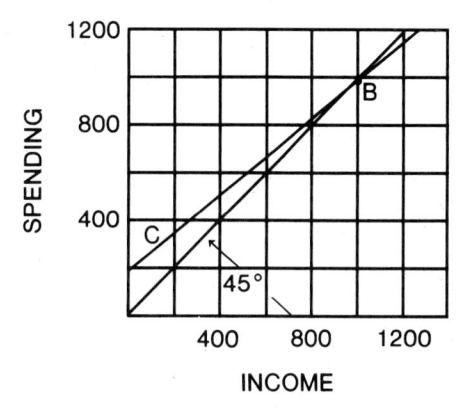

The above graph shows that consumption rises as income rises, but not at the same rate. All along the consumption function, the *change* in consumption equals $80 with a *change* in income of $100. For example, as income goes from $1000 to $1200, consumption goes from $1000 to $1160. (Note that autonomous consumption, which is spending *not* related to income level, is $200.)

The difference between the *consumption function* and each point on the 45° degree line at income levels to the right of B is the amount of income saved. The difference between consumption and the 45° line at income below point B is dissaving. That is, people are pulling their savings from the bank, or getting loans. They are currently being produced. As the economy moves faster in response to demand for consumption goods, production hurries up and more factors are hired. The income receivers spend most of what they are paid, so that production and income go up until . . . spending equals income at equilibrium.

III. THE AGGREGATE DEMAND-AGGREGATE SUPPLY METHOD OF FINDING THE EQUILIBRIUM LEVEL OF NATIONAL INCOME

  A. *Equilibrium:* A stable condition maintained unless disturbed by outside forces.

   1. At the equilibrium level of income, all income resulting from production is exactly spent for C or I. This means that aggregate demand equals aggregate supply. There is no general surplus of goods (excess aggregate supply) and no shortage.

   2. If aggregate demand is not equal to aggregate supply, income will change. (Notice here that income will change, not prices. This is a very important concept in this Income-Expenditures model.)

   3. If there is more spending than output (excess aggregate demand), national income will rise. With the excess aggregate demand, goods are bought faster than they are produced.

      a. Firms are forced to use up inventories because of expanded sales. *Inventory:* Goods kept on reserve by business to meet fluctuations in demand.

      b. Production increases to meet demand; more workers are hired.

      c. Output and employment increase, raising national income.

      d. The process continues until spending is equal to income or equilibrium.

CHAPTER 12 HIGHLIGHTS 235

    4. If there is less spending than output (excess aggregate supply), national income falls; all national income is not spent, causing sales of goods to be lower than planned.

        a. Firms accumulate inventories and, in effect, invest in their own goods.

        b. Producers cut back on production and fire workers.

        c. Output and employment falls, lowering national income.

        d. This procedure continues until equilibrium is reached where spending must equal income.

NOTE:

The following is an alternate method to find equilibrium level of national income.

IV. A SECOND METHOD OF FINDING THE EQUILIBRIUM LEVEL OF NATIONAL INCOME: THE SAVINGS LEAKAGES EQUAL TO INVESTMENT LEAKAGES METHOD

    A. Leakages-Injections method arrives at the same national income equilibrium as aggregate spending equals aggregate supply method. The differences in procedure are

        1. only part of total expenditures are analyzed.

        2. the stream of investment (I) and the stream of savings (S) are compared.

        3. equilibrium income is reached when households plan to save what businesses plan to invest.

    B. For income to stay the same, the flow of injections into the spending stream must equal the flow of leakages out of the stream.

1. *Leakage:* Draining away of income from the spending stream.

    a. Planned saving (S) is a leakage.

    b. Income earned in producing output that is not spent on output reduces the size of the circular flow. If this leakage out is greater than injections in, unemployment results and national income falls.

2. *Injection:* New spending of income into the spending stream.

    a. Planned investment (I) is an injection.

    b. Planned I offsets savings leakage; when investment increases, workers are hired and the national income rises.

3. The equilibrium level of income and product is that level at which people plan to save the same amount businesses plan to invest.

    a. (S) equals (I).

    b. The circular flow stays the same.

    c. The national income stays the same.

C. There is a constant movement toward a balance of investment-savings equilibrium.

   1. Investment in the simple model is assumed to be autonomous. *Autonomous Spending:* Spending not affected by the level of income. In your text, the horizontal I line represents the same amount of I at all national income levels (a simplified assumption).

   2. Saving (what is not spent out of income) is positively related to income; as income goes up, so does saving.

   3. Equilibrium income is that income where savings intersect investment; where the injections to the circular flow (investment) equals leakages (savings) out of the circular flow.

HINT

PART VII. 9

Stop to recall that you are working through a form of the Keynesian Income-Expenditures Model. It suggests why we don't stay at one level of national income and why we can have surges of unemployment and falling GNP, and its opposite. Keynesian theory began to gain acceptance during the depression of the early 1930s when we seemed stuck at a low level of output and a high level of unemployment.

Keynes might summarize his contribution as follows: "In spite of classical beliefs about the economy (that savings are automatically used up in investment) this is *not the way it works*. Savers save for their own reasons. Investors may feel differently about the economy; they may try to invest more than there are savings available or may not use up all the available savings. These different ways of acting, plus the fact that prices may not fall much in response to lowered demand, mean that there is no 'built-in,' natural tendency to stay at full employment. Or, if this natural tendency to full employment does operate, it may operate so slowly that considerable harm may be done to the economy before full employment equilibrium is reached. It may be desirable to have spending off set by another sector to stabilize the ups and downs of the economy."

V. How and Why Equilibrium Level of National Income Fluctuates: Introducing the Income Multiplier.

    A. Recall the difference (defined in Chapter 11) between a movement along a curve and a shift of the entire curve.

        1. A movement along a consumption line, for example, shows the change in C spending that results from a change in national income.

        2. A shift of the entire curve shows that at every income level a different amount is spent than before.

VI. THE EFFECT OF NEW SPENDING IS MAGNIFIED ACCORDING TO THE SIZE OF THE MULTIPLIER.

  A. The larger the MPC, the larger the multiplier. The more people spend of extra income, the greater the respending, resulting in a larger national effect of new spending.

  B. The larger the MPS, the lower the multiplier. The more extra income people save, the lower is the effect of spending.

  1. The paradox of thrift rests on the economic truth that what may be good for the individual may not be good for the nation.

  2. *Paradox of Thrift:* As many individuals try to save, they withdraw spending from the income stream: businesses pile up unplanned inventory and cancel orders; the economy slows down; national income falls; people cannot save as planned. Thus, the paradox of thrift: as individuals try to save more, incomes fall so they actually save less.

VII. CONTRACTIONARY AND EXPANSIONARY GAPS: DISTANCES ON EACH SIDE OF FULL EMPLOYMENT INCOME.

Full Employment: When only frictional or normal job changing results in unemployment. Aggregate demand equals aggregate supply at full employment.

  A. *Inflationary Gap:* When aggregate demand exceeds full employment aggregate supply, people try to buy more output than can be produced, with no unemployed resources in the economy. Thus, prices are pushed up and buying expands income without creating more output, and inflation results.

  B. *Recessionary Gap:* When aggregate spending is less than full employment aggregate supply. The entire output of the economy is not purchased; production slows down and workers are fired.

FILL-IN REVIEW

Select between the choices underlined or fill in the blank. Cover the answers until you have provided your own.

The concept of the consumption function is basic to the model being developed. Simply stated, this is the relationship between people's incomes and their _____. Consumption depends on _____. When the consumption function is graphed, it begins above income. This is the amount of spending people do regardless of their income level. It is termed _____

expenditures
income

autonomous consumption

To find how the economy's level of income and employment is determined, we examine the different components of total spending (called total spending aggregate demand). A total is an _____. Total planned spending in the economy is called _____ _____ (_____) or ___. This spending includes expenditures by households, called _____, and business spending, called _____. We also look at the production of goods and services that results from spending. We call the total of this production _____ _____. The value of goods and services will equal the value of the payment for those same goods and

aggregate

aggregate demand (spending)   *C + I*

consumption
investment

aggregate supply

demand	services. It follows that when spending is equal to income, aggregate _____ (C+I)
aggregate	will equal _____ supply. An aggregate
45 degree	supply line, when graphed, is a __ _____
aggregate demand (C+I)	line with _____ _____ (___) on the
income	vertical axis and aggregate _____ on the horizontal axis. When all income is spent on
equilibrium	output, we have _____ level of national income. At equilibrium there are no surpluses or shortages of total output. If national income is not exactly used up by either total
aggregate demand	spending or _____ _____, income will fall. If planned total spending is greater
rise	than national income, income will ___.
	Goods that are kept on hand for sales by
inventories	businesses are called _____. When there is more demand for goods than there are goods available, we say there is excess aggre-
demand	gate _____. The extra demand depletes stocks of inventories and creates demand for
more	*more*/*less* goods. The demand is translated into orders for products; workers must be hired to increase production. Greater employ-
national income	ment leads to higher _____ _____. This
equilibrium	process continues to _____, where
equal	spending (C+I) is exactly ____ to national income.

FILL-IN REVIEW

On the other hand, the reverse of this process takes place if total demand is lower than total _____. In this case, when all of national income is not used for spending, sales are _____ than planned. Firms have a build-up of planned _____ so that orders are cancelled, production is *increased/cut back*, and workers are _____. Income, output and employment fall until _____ is reached. This is the aggregate _____-aggregate _____ approach to the determination of national income.

income

lower

inventories

cut back

fired

equilibrium

demand

supply

The leakages and injections approach reached the same conclusions by only considering _____ and _____ in the economy. In this approach, leakages from the total spending stream are _____, and injections into the stream are _____. For equilibrium level of national income, the two must be _____.

savings   investment

savings

investments

equal

To identify the reasons for fluctuations in national income, we use the tendency for people to spend extra income, called their _____ _____ __ _____, or _____. When people have a high MPC, it means that they tend to spend a *large part of/ small part of* extra income. When people have

marginal propensity to consume
MPC

large part of

UNIT VII: PART TWO

small	a low marginal propensity to save (MPS), they have a tendency to save a *small/large* part of extra income.
	The tendency to spend or save extra income is important to the maintenance of the production and income in the economy.
5 1 4	The MPC is the basis for the multiplier effect on national income. To calculate the multiplier, take the reciprocal, or the "upside down" of the MPS. If the MPS is ⅕, the multiplier is __; people save __ dollar out of every extra 5 dollars of income and spend __ dollars out of every extra 5.
new *multiplier change* *more*	By using the multiplier concept, we can predict the effect on national income of ____ spending (new C, or new I). To find the change in national income of new spending, we use a simple formula: new I (or C) times the _____ equals the _____ in equilibrium level of national income. Note that income changes by *more/less* than the change in new I or new C.
	Let's use a small example of the multiplier effect that can be generalized to the whole economy. A new investment of $1,000 is undertaken. Someone receives a check for

FILL-IN REVIEW

$1,000. Let's also say the general MPC in the economy is .8. What effect does the .8 MPC have? (You know!) People spend ___ ___	*80 percent*
or .8 (either) of new income. $800 of the new $1,000 is spent and $200 saved. Of the $800 received, $640 is spent and $___ is saved.	*$160*
The person receiving the $640 spends $___	*$512*
and saves $___; the one receiving the $512	*$128*
spends $___ and saves $___, and on and on.	*$410* *$102*
Each receiver of extra income will spend ___%	*80*
of it and save ___%. When we add all the dollars spent on consumption from the initial new spending of $1,000, we reach an amount	*20*
much *larger/smaller* than $1,000. We now have a way of calculating how much national income will increase because of new spending. To find the change in income, multiply the new spending by the multiplier. The multiplier in the above example is ___; the amount of	*larger*
	5
new investment is $___. 5 times $1,000 equals $5,000; therefore, national income	*$1,000*
rises/falls by $5,000. The multiplier also serves to lower national income in the same	*rises*
way when investment ___. These examples	*falls*
emphasize how *unimportant/important* new investment is to the economy; every dollar invested has a *minimized/magnified* effect on	*important*
	magnified
___ ___.	*national income*

PROBLEMS, PROBLEMS, PROBLEMS...

Answers are at the end of this unit.

TRUE-FALSE

Circle either "T" or "F" for each statement.

(T) F 1. National Income is the total income received by individuals in the form of wages, profits, interest and rents.

T **(F)** 2. The economy cannot be in equilibrium when aggregate supply equals aggregate demand.

(T) F 3. When aggregate supply is greater than aggregate demand, national income will fall.

T **(F)** 4. Keynes said planned investment always equals planned saving.

(T) F 5. Inventory adjustment makes actual investment always equal to actual saving.

T **(F)** 6. The multiplier causes new I or new C to have an effect on national income that is less than itself.

(T) F 7. The multiplier is the amount by which a change in investment must be multiplied to reach the change in equilibrium level of income.

(T) F 8. A marginal propensity to save of ⅓ results in a multiplier of 3.

T **(F)** 9. If the MPC = ½ and the change in Investment = 100, the change in national income will be 100.

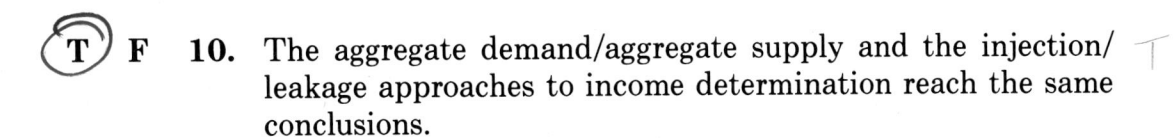

T F 10. The aggregate demand/aggregate supply and the injection/leakage approaches to income determination reach the same conclusions.

T F 11. The larger the marginal propensity to consume, the larger the multiplier.

T F 12. Either the marginal propensity to consume or the marginal propensity to save determines what the size of the multiplier will be.

MATCH-UP

Match each item in the first column with a term in the second column. Use no term more than once.

d 1. Long-run employment is impossible.

b 2. A condition that is maintained unless disturbed by outside forces

h 3. More output than spending so that national income falls

c 4. Total of all planned spending in the economy

j 5. Goods kept on reserve by businesses to meet fluctuations in demand

e 6. Aggregate spending equals aggregate supply method; leakages equal injections method

i 7. Investment that stays the same at all levels of national income

g 8. Total of all goods and services produced in the economy

f 9. Draining-away of income from the spending stream

a 10. Amount by which new I or C is multiplied to get the change in equilibrium national income

a. multiplier
b. equilibrium
c. aggregate spending (C + I)
d. classical economists belief
e. the two methods to determine national income
f. leakage
g. aggregate supply
h. excess aggregate supply
i. autonomous investment
j. inventory

MULTIPLE CHOICE

For each of the following statements, choose the one best alternative.

1. Of the following definitions, choose the best description of aggregate demand (or aggregate supply).

    a. The demand for agricultural products

    b. Relates quality of products to price

    c. Is the total of all planned expenditures

    d. All of the above are correct.

2. Aggregate supply

    a. is not synonymous with national product.

    b. can never be greater than aggregate demand.

    c. is the total value of all goods and services produced.

    d. is a wholesale firm owned by Mr. Aggregate.

3. All of the following are true about equilibrium in our simple model *except*

    a. Aggregate spending = aggregate supply.

    b. Inventory adjustment tends to pull the economy away from this point.

    c. Planned savings = planned investment.

    d. It can be obtained through either the aggregate spending/supply or the injection/leakages approaches.

4. If aggregate spending is greater than aggregate supply,

    a. income and output will fall.

    b. income and output will rise.

    c. output will fall while income rises.

    d. output will rise as income falls.

5. In the leakages/injections approach model,
   a. savings are a leakage and investment is an injection.
   b. savings are an injection and investment is a leakage.
   c. planned saving can never equal planned investment.
   d. All the above are true.

6. Each of the following is true of an increase in investment *except:*
   a. It shifts up aggregate demand.
   b. It shifts up the investment schedule.
   c. It has no effect on national income.
   d. It increases income by a multiplied amount.

7. The multiplier can be stated as
   a. = 1/MPC.
   b. = 1/MPC + MPS.
   c. = 1/MPS.
   d. = 1/1 − MPS.

8. Each of the following is true of the multiplier *except:*
   a. It causes new investment to change national income by an amount greater than the change in investment.
   b. It is based on people's tendency to spend extra income.
   c. If the MPC = .9, the multiplier would be 8.
   d. As the MPC gets larger, the multiplier gets smaller.

9. When a large number of people attempt to save more of their income, this causes a decrease in output and income which results in a lowering of savings for the entire economy. This is know as
   a. Benjamin Franklin's Revenge.
   b. Say's Law of Markets.
   c. Paradox of Thrift.
   d. Saver's Dilemma.

10. If the MPS = ⅕, and the change in investment = 100,000, the change in national income is

   a. 500,000.

   b. 1,000,000.

   c. 250,000.

   d. too small to notice.

11. What is it that a "multiplier" multiplies?

   a. It multiplies changes in investment or other new spending, which results in changes in income.

   b. It multiplies savings so that income increases.

   c. It multiples the marginal propensity to consume.

   d. It multiplies the interest rate.

12. Since money that is spent ends up as someone else's income, a change in investment spending yields a multiple of that change in income? The foregoing explains

   a. the action of interest rates.

   b. the action of the multiplier.

   c. the relation of savings and investment.

   d. why spending is not really important in the economy.

13. One of the following is *not* true at the equilibrium level of income. Choose that one.

   a. National income is stable.

   b. Desired savings equals desired investment.

   c. Spending equals national income.

   d. National income must fall.

14. In an economy with an MPC of 9/10, the multiplier is

   a. 1/10.

   b. 9/10.

   c. 1 2/8.

   d. 10.

15. In an economy with an MPS of 1/5, an increase in investment spending of $20 billion will increase the level of national income by

   a. $4 billion.

   b. $20 billion.

   c. $80 billion.

   d. $100 billion.

ANSWERS TO STUDY QUESTIONS

PART ONE

TRUE-FALSE
1. T 2. F 3. T 4. F 5. F 6. T 7. F 8. F

MATCH-UP

PART A *Classical or Keynesian*

1. C 2. C 3. K 4. K 5. C 6. K 7. C

PART B *Statements*

8. f 9. e 10. d 11. c 12. b 13. a

MULTIPLE CHOICE

1. d 2. b 3. c 4. b 5. a 6. d 7. b 8. d 9. c 10. c

11. PROPENSITY TO CONSUME IN ALPHA

DISPOSABLE INCOME	CONSUMPTION SPENDING	SAVING	APC	APS	MPC	MPS
$50	$54	−$4	108%	−8%	60%	40%
60	60	$0	100%	—	60%	40%
70	66	$4	94%	6%	60%	40%
80	72	$8	90%	10%	60%	40%

12. b 13. c

ECONOWORD PUZZLE

CLUES ACROSS

4. When everyone tries to save more, income falls so that people save as they plan: the _____ of thrift.
5. What makes the economy work? _____ does.
11. Savings are considered a _____ out of the circular flow.
15. A state of balance or rest
17. Marginal Propensity to Consume
18. Separation of a whole into its component parts
19. Businesses motivate to produce this.
20. Household income not used for consumption is set aside for _____.
21. The amount of expenditure households expect to make is _____ consumption.
23. Goods that a business has on hand for sale, or for use as inputs to production
24. Economists assume that if one is from a household, one is a _____.

CLUES DOWN

1. In economics, marginal means _____.
2. MPC is measured as the ratio of the _____ of C with a _____ of income.
3. Marginal Propensity to Save
6. New spending into the circular flow; or investment
7. A picture of economic relationships
8. Freely flexible prices that will guarantee a full employment equilibrium was the belief of the _____ economists.
9. Keynes said prices are not _____ downward.
10. The permanent income hypothesis is by _____.
12. John Maynard _____ concentrated on the sources of total spending.
13. An economic production unit
14. Business spending for capital equipment
16. The process by which an original increase in spending gives rise to the ultimate increase in national income
22. Consume

ECONOWORD PUZZLE

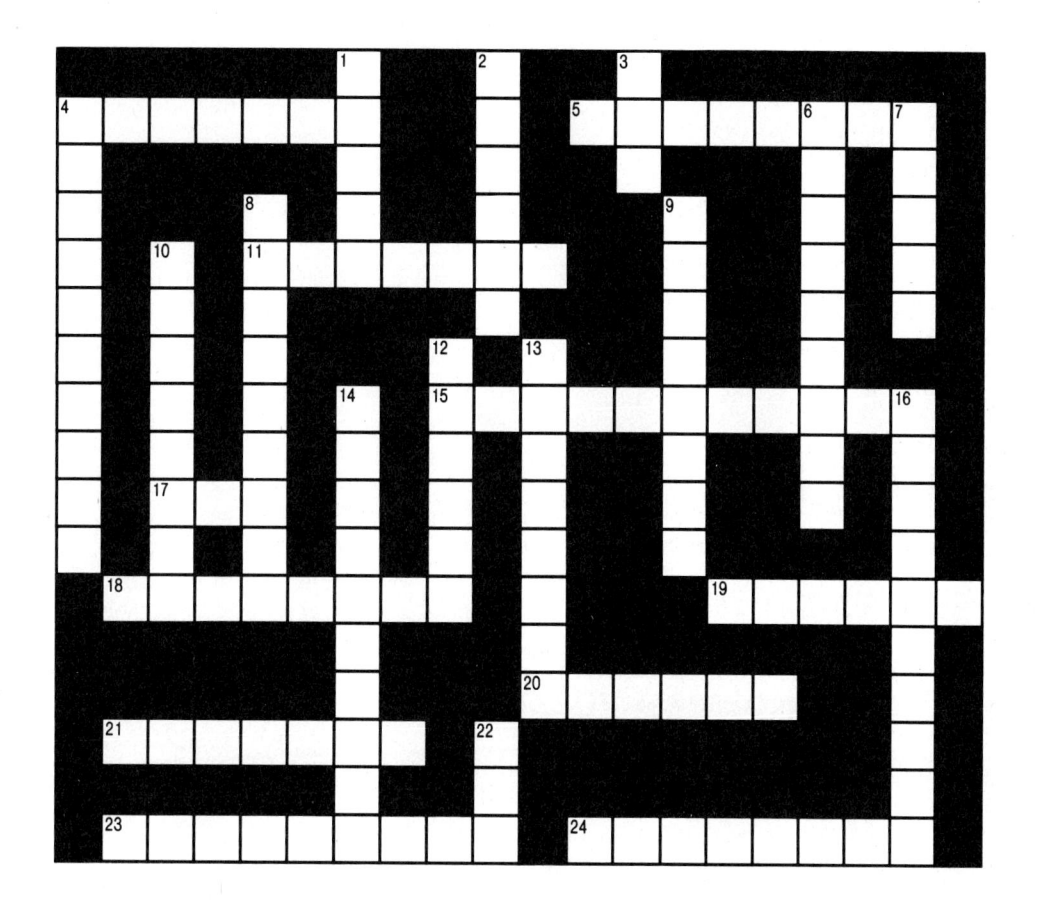

PART TWO

TRUE-FALSE

1. T 2. F 3. T 4. F 5. T 6. F 7. T 8. T 9. F 10. T
11. T 12. T

MATCH-UP

1. d 2. b 3. h 4. c 5. j 6. e 7. i 8. g 9. f 10. a

MULTIPLE CHOICE

1. c 2. c 3. b 4. b 5. a 6. c 7. c 8. d 9. c 10. a
11. a 12. b 13. d 14. d 15. d

COMPLETED ECONOWORD PUZZLE

INCOME AND EMPLOYMENT DETERMINATION

UNIT VIII

UNIT IN A NUTSHELL

PART ONE

Film: "Income, Go Forth and Multiply"

Text: Chapter 12

PART TWO

Film: "Balancing Act"

Text: Chapter 13

In the last Unit, we developed a beginning model of the economy that identified the effects of household and business sector spending in the flow of national income and product. Spending changes by either sector produce magnified, or "multiplier-effect" changes in national income.

Now, government enters the scene as a major participant, so that our model is a closer approximation of the real world. The unstable nature of the economy's macroequilibrium can be moderated by government policy. The government sector uses taxation and spending to stabilize the effects of private spending flows.

A major purpose of governmental tax and spending policy is to stabilize the economy and smooth out its booms and recessions. We will analyze how government raises or lowers taxes, increases or cuts back its expenditures in its use of fiscal policy to influence total spending in the economy.

UNIT OBJECTIVES

Objectives 1–3 can be met by reviewing Chapter 12 and viewing "Income, Go Forth and Multiply." After completing Part One, the student should be able to:

1. Define the average and marginal propensities to consume and be able to explain what each means.

2. Define the multiplier and explain the multiplier effect of new spending on national incomes.

3. Know how a change in investment (or consumption) causes a change in national income.

Objectives 4–6 can be met by studying Chapter 13 and viewing "Balancing Act." After completing Part Two, the student should be able to:

4. Know how changes in government spending and taxation affect the equilibrium level of national income.

5. Know the effect on the economy of balanced amounts of government spending and taxation.

6. Describe the effects of automatic fiscal policy.

PART ONE

UNIT VIII ASSIGNMENT: PART ONE

STUDY: Review Chapter 12, "Income and Employment Determination," *Economics Today* (*Note:* The study of Chapter 12 was included as part of the assignment for Unit VII, Part Two.)

STUDY: Film Summary, "Income, Go Forth and Multiply," *Study Guide*

VIEW: "Income, Go Forth and Multiply"

REVIEW: Chapter 12 Highlights, *Study Guide* (*Note:* These highlights are included in Unit VII, Part Two.)

FILM SUMMARY: "Income, Go Forth and Multiply"

The way in which increased spending multiplies to produce a higher level of national income, and reduced spending multiplies to lower national income is the subject of "Income, Go Forth and Multiply." In the film, Dynamics Corporation considers investing in new production, wanting to be part of a surge of new investment that Dynamics hopes will produce more income, jobs, and re-spending and which will provide (naturally) more company profits. The discussions surrounding these business opportunities serve to introduce the multiplier, which is closely linked to the MPC (the marginal propensity to consume) or the tendency to spend extra income.

Before dealing with the particulars of marginal propensity to consume, let's review propensity to consume as a general concept.

By now, it has been established that spending flows in the economy are the sources of employment and production. The market system works by providing goods and services in response to spending for them. In his analysis of the economy, John Maynard Keynes identified tendencies to spend, and then linked these tendencies (He called them "propensities to consume.") to people's expectations about what will be happening in the economy. He first referred to the tendency for people to spend and to save their *total* or *entire* income, and, then, their tendencies to spend and save their *extra* or *marginal* income. (In economics, marginal means extra: a very important concept.)

In Unit VII, the consumption function, which is the close relationship of consumption to national income, was discussed. It can be generally stated that consumption goes up as national income goes up, but by smaller and smaller amounts. Why? Keynes hypothesized that, for each level of national income, a certain percentage of the *entire* income received would be spent for consumption. He also maintained that when national income is low, the percentage of it that people tend to spend is high, and, conversely, when national income is high, the percentage of it that people tend to spend for consumption is low. Notice that we are talking about the *percentage* of income spent, not the total amount.

How can this be? Think about it a little: actually these spending patterns are familiar to us all. When people receive large incomes, they have a tendency to spend (propensity to consume) more dollars for consumer goods than if they receive low incomes. But even though people with high incomes spend more dollars, they spend a smaller *percentage* of their income than poorer people.

The other side of the relationship of spending to income is saving to income, and the tendency here is the same: the higher the income, the more that is saved. People with low incomes often do not save at all, while those with high incomes usually save part. Consider yourself as an example. If your own income is very low, it is difficult to save; but if your income doubled, or tripled, you would probably save part of it. Most of us would. These tendencies to spend and save out of *total* income were called, by Keynes, the average propensity to consume (APC), and the average propensity to save (APS). These APC and APS figures indicate the percentages that would be spent and saved, respectively, at various levels of national income.

Why bother identifying this large spending flow? Because APC, in effect, determines how much income received is returned by households as the basic consumption flow, and knowing APC allows economists to determine the size of the macroequilibrium level of income. In the film, Billings, a stockbroker, and Thomas discuss how the amount of income received that is turned back to the economy as spending determines the equilibrium level of national income. APS figures also allow us to determine how much new injection spending (investment) will be needed to bring income up to a full employment level.

We have already said that people either spend or save their *total* or *entire* income; so, too, they spend or save *extra* or *marginal* incomes. This propensity or the tendency for people to consume or save any extra income forms an important part of Keynesian analysis. It is now possible to discuss in more detail the concept of marginal propensity to consume (MPC) and marginal propensity to save (MPS).

Economists are especially interested in what people do with their extra, or marginal income. In Unit VII, Karen and Thomas received a gift from Uncle Halvor, and they spent 80 percent of it. Therefore, we identify their marginal propensity to consume as about .8. If this same MPC were applied when national income increases by $100 billion, $80 billion would be spent. MPC, then, is an indication of what percentage of extra (national) income will likely be spent in consumption.

If people don't spend, they save, and the corollary to MPC is marginal propensity to save or MPS. It was mentioned above that Karen and Thomas spent 80 percent of their extra income from Uncle Halvor. The remainder of it, 20 percent, they saved. Therefore, this simple example shows that MPC and MPS will always sum to 100 percent.

To use another example, let's say you receive a $1,000 bonus of extra income. You spend $500, half of it, therefore your MPC is ½ or .5, or 50%. How much do you save? Half of it. Your MPS is .5, or 50%. Now, consider the same $1,000 bonus. You spend $800, or 80%, or .8 of it: your MPC is .8. How much do you save? The amount that is left, or $200—20% of it, or .2. Again, MPC and MPS must always add up to 100%, or 1, of the extra income.

Let's stop to remember where we are in the Keynesian model of the economy. In order to show the effects of spending, we have identified the source of each part of the spending flow—consumption (C), and investment (I)—and we have described the type of spending done by each of these sectors. We have indicated the importance of the size and amount of consumption (C) in the economy and, further, have differentiated between what is spent out of total income and what is spent out of extra income. This careful breakdown of sources and kinds of spending has been introduced in preparation for showing exactly *how* changed spending changes national income. A multiplier effect of new spending on national income will be described. Once this is understood, it will be clear why the national government attempts to change the direction of spending to stabilize income.

The MPC multiplies changes in I and C and such new spending has a multiplied effect on income. Simply stated, the higher the MPC, the larger the effect of new spending on the national income, as new income gets "passed along" in the economy—expanding total spending more and more. And, the higher the MPS, the more the extra income is withdrawn from the spending flow—so that national income is raised by a smaller amount. In the film, Thomas, always the pessimist, complains that too many people are "salting money away" and, therefore, the upturn predicted by Jeremy Hosford would not be realized. In effect, Thomas thinks that the MPS will be too high for an economic recovery.

To elaborate on the re-spending effect, and to relate it more exactly to what happens to national income when there are changes in investment or consumption spending, it will be helpful to consult your textbook. Here, exhibits of changes in equilibrium national income are discussed. It is clearly shown that a shift in consumption or investment will cause the aggregate demand curve to shift too, resulting in a new equilibrium level of national income.

The multiplier process is the round-after-round of re-spending following a change in I or C. The practical results of the multiplier are dramatized in the film by the discussion about spending in the "White Elephant Sale," and the theoretical aspects of the multiplier are explained to Thomas by Billings. He uses the example of household consumption of 4/5 (.8) of additional income, and savings of 1/5 (.2). Based on the MPC and MPS example, the multiplier is 5, and the macroequilibrium level of income can change by an amount equal to five times a change in investment or in C. Thus, new expenditures (or investments) of, say, $100 billion can raise national income by $500 billion.

It is important to keep in mind that the multiplier process is set in motion by all *changes* in spending. This means that, when investment of consumption spending decreases, the amount of decrease is also multiplied to *lower* national income. Thus, the multiplier acts to raise as well as to lower national income when there are changes in spending.

The significance of the multiplier is indeed great. As we have often said, spending determines national income, and the importance of spending patterns in determining what will happen in the economy in response to new spending cannot be overemphasized. Thus, the Keynesian multiplier analysis gives us an important tool to forecast what effect new spending will have on the economy.

It should be understood that the graphs and calculations of the consumption function are not exact, but are tools which allow us to predict (with reasonable certainty) propensities to consume and save. We acknowledge that the consumption function is not completely stable or dependable. Predictions based on consumption spending are, however, more reliable than those based on investment spending, which reacts in a volatile way to both business and social events in the economy.

In earlier Units, you learned that consumption (spending) is responsive to the ways people feel about the state of the economy. When people worry about the future, or try to pay off debts instead of making new expenditures, the entire consumption function moves down, lowering national income: when people are confident, they spend and take out loans for more spending, and the consumption function shifts up, raising national income. Now, you are able to graphically demonstrate (by shifting the consumption function) how such responses affect national income. Therefore, our model of income and expenditures provides a framework for clearly identifying the sources and effects of spending, and Keynesian analysis proves to be a useful approach in analyzing the effects of withdrawals and injections into the income stream.

REMINDER

Go back to review and restudy text Chapter 12 and your *Study* *Guide* Section VII Part Two, before going on.

PART TWO

UNIT VIII ASSIGNMENT: PART TWO

STUDY: Chapter 13, "Fiscal Policy," *Economics Today*

STUDY: Film Summary: "Balancing Act," *Study Guide*

VIEW: "Balancing Act"

REVIEW: Chapter 13 Highlights, *Study Guide*

COMPLETE: Fill-in Review *and* Problems, Problems, Problems ..., *and* Econoword Puzzle *Study Guide*

FILM SUMMARY: "Balancing Act"

Herman Drew who works in a Washington D.C. government office visits Thomas and then becomes involved in a heated discussion with Thomas's boss, Larry Dutweiler, about the long-run economic value of government spending programs. At first, we hear mostly bias and peevishness from Dutweiler, whose understanding of the use of government spending is surprisingly naive for a successful businessman. Herman Drew, no less agreeable and tending toward boisterous overstatement when government spending is the theme of the discussion, is just as wrong headed as Dutweiler. Government spending and taxation policies are made by the Congress and since Herman Drew is neither a senator nor a representative, his comments merely represent strong points of view.

In this film program, the role of government as a national economic force is introduced. Together with the explanation of the roles and effects of household consumption and business investment already presented in our discussion of the aggregate demand model, we can now add government spending. The identification of government as the third major sector in the economy, able to affect national income by its policies, is a major theme of this program.

Equilibrium national income occurs where spending by all sectors is the same as income received. As we have said before, there is no guarantee that the equilibrium reached will be at a full employment level. Indeed, as we have seen, when consumers and businesses try to spend increasing amounts of their incomes, national income rises, and if they withdraw spending power from the economy into savings (and these savings are not returned to the economy as investment spending) national income falls.

Since the multiplier process is set in motion by changes in spending, lowered spending in one sector of the economy that is not offset by increased spending in another sector, has a downward multiplier effect on income. When consumers spend less (without a balancing increase in investment) or business investment falls (without an offsetting increase in consumption), the effect is to send waves of lowered spending through the economy. This should reinforce what you already know from the earlier text discussions about the unstable nature of macroequilibrium.

Keynes pointed out that when households and businesses are not buying-up the full employment output of the economy (causing income to stay below a full employment equilibrium) government spending or taxation can function as a stabilizer in the economy. Government can thus increase national income or slow down an inflated economy. But, remember that the classicists believed the economy would automatically set itself on a full employment course. They also believed that freely flexible prices would guarantee that the economy, given enough time to accommodate itself to changes in demand, would right itself if unsettled. Keynes replied, something to the effect, that the consequences of taking enough time to allow inflexible prices to fall, when there is insufficient demand, will be serious indeed for the economy. Long periods of high employment can, instead, be avoided by judicious use of government fiscal policy.

We could say that the level of national income is a little like the level of water in a bathtub: investment is the faucet; saving is the drain; and the former replenishes income while the latter reduces it. Keep the amount drained out equal to the amount coming in, and the water level will stabilize. So, too, by keeping saving and investment the same, equilibrium level of income will stay the same.

This simplified concept of the basic income flow equilibrium can provide a rationale for use of compensatory government spending and taxation or simply, fiscal policy. When spending in the private economy is too low to generate full employment or when spending is running too fast and inflation results, government can intervene. To attempt to raise national income or control inflation, government can use the fiscal policy tools of changes in taxation and changes in its own expenditures. Congressional decisions, therefore, form the policy that aims at overcoming both recessionary and inflationary gaps.

To review, we have seen how the multiplier process operates on new spending in the economy, producing repeated rounds of consumption and saving until, when all the new spending is added together, national income is increased by an amount greater than the new spending. Since the multiplier process is set in motion by any new spending, such as new C, and new I, it is also activated by new G. A change in either government spending or taxes (other things staying the same) will also lead to a greater than proportional change in national income. Conversely, when government spending is reduced, the multiplier is reduced accordingly and the demand function shifts downward.

Now that government, as the third sector in the economy is included in our model, the value of government expenditures and government taxation are added to aggregate demand: aggregate demand, therefore, is now the sum total of planned household consumption spending (C), business investment (I) and government expenditures (G). In terms of our model, aggregate supply (the total of all final goods produced and sold in the economy) has the same definition as discussed in Unit VII and to find equilibrium level of income, we still equate aggregate demand and aggregate supply. If we use the alternate method of determining equilibrium national income (the leakages/injections method), injections now include government expenditures as well as planned investment, and leakages are taxation and planned savings.

We can now consider specifically what can be done when equilibrium national income does not generate full employment. When total planned expenditures don't fully use up the productive ability of the economy, causing a fall in equilibrium income, government-lowered taxation and increased spending is used as fiscal policy. Conversely, when spending is greater than the productive capacity of the economy, government-increased taxation and lowered spending is appropriate fiscal policy.

When government spending is changed, it has the same effect on the economy as any other sector change in spending. However, when government spending is offset by government taxes (balanced budget spending) it changes national income only by the amount of the spending itself. This means that when government increases its spending and taxes by the same amount, the change in equilibrium national income will exactly equal the change in the spending.

The above statements regarding the outcomes of government fiscal policy are theoretically true. But in actual application of the policy, important conditions in the rest of the economy may not have been taken into consideration. The actual effects, therefore, may be quite different from what was intended by congressional policy makers. Remember that this is one of the bases for the heated discussions between Larry Dutweiler and Herman Drew. If the government expenditures crowd out private investment, then, instead of increasing national income, government may simply replace private investment with its own spending.

CHAPTER 13 HIGHLIGHTS

Defined words are underlined.

    I. CHAPTER OVERVIEW

        A. We now add government to our simple model.

            1. Aggregate spending will now include government (G) as a major source of spending.

            2. Since only its taxation and expenditures are relevant to the total economy, we will only include the federal government.

        B. Adding government to the model, allows us to consider fiscal policy.

            1. *Fiscal Policy:* Changes of government expenditures and/or taxes in order to change equilibrium level of national income.

2. *Discretionary Fiscal Policy:* Congressional changes in tax rates and expenditure programs are used as policy in attempts to eliminate recessionary and inflationary gaps.

3. *Automatic Fiscal Policy:* Taxation policy that does not require new legislation; it operates automatically.

C. We apply the multiplier analysis to calculate the effects of fiscal policy on equilibrium income. We will look at the effects of

1. changes in government spending,

2. changes in taxation.

II. ADDING GOVERNMENT PURCHASES TO AGGREGATE SPENDING (AGGREGATE DEMAND)

A. To Consumption (C) and Investment (I), we now add Government spending (G).

1. For simplicity, let's assume there is the same government spending (G) at all levels of national income.

2. The new aggregate spending (total spending) curve will now include Consumption, Investment and Government spending, C + I + G.

a. In graphing, we add G to C + I.

b. The addition of G is graphed as a shift of aggregate demand spending.

B. With the additional spending of G in the economy, equilibrium national income rises.

1. The increase of aggregate spending has the effect of increasing aggregate supply.

2. The new spending for output of goods and services increases production of those goods and services.

C. The effect of new spending on national income is determined by the amount of spending times the multiplier.

1. The MPS or MPC is the basis of the multiplier.

HINT

Recall from Chapter 12, the multiplier is found by taking the "upside down" (reciprocal) of MPS. For example, with MPC of ⅘, MPS is ⅕. The reciprocal of ⅕ is 5; the multiplier, therefore, is 5. The larger the MPS, the smaller the multiplier; the larger the MPC, the larger the multiplier.

2. To calculate the change in equilibrium level national income caused by additional spending, multiply the new spending times the multiplier.

   a. For example, with a multiplier of 5 and new G spending of $100 billion, the change in income is 100 times 5, or $500 billion.

   b. The new G spending affects equilibrium national income in the same way as new C or new I.

   c. We use the symbol Y for national income, Y = C + I + G (recall Chapter 9). The graph shows that the spending for national output (aggregate spending) shifts upward with the new G.

      1) The national income changes by the multiplier times the amount of new G.

      2) In other words, the national income rises by more than the new spending.

3) The size of the MPC determines how much income will rise. (If people spend a large proportion of their extra income, the effect is large.)

D. Another method for finding the equilibrium national income is the "injections-leakages" approach.

1. Government spending can be considered another injection of spending into the circular flow.

2. We add G to injection's side of the leakages-injection model:

   a. At equilibrium, S = I+ G.

   b. Leakages must equal injections.

3. The addition of G *graphically,* results in an upward shift of the "injections" schedule.

4. With the same new G, national income rises the same amount with the injections-leakages approach as with the aggregate demand approach.

III. TAXES AFFECT EQUILIBRIUM NATIONAL INCOME: TAXES CHANGE AGGREGATE DEMAND WHICH CHANGES INCOME.

A. Taxes are also used as tools to change national income—the aggregate demand method.

1. Taxes lower aggregate demand, causing the equilibrium level of national income to fall.

2. Consumption drops, saving drops.

   a. The amount consumption initially drops is the tax times the MPC.

   b. The amount saving drops is the tax times MPS.

3. Graphically, there is a downward shift of aggregate spending.

B. Taxes are used as a tool to change national income—leakages-injection method.

1. Taxes are a leakage out of the spending stream.

2. We can term taxes (T) and add taxes to the leakage side of the model.

    a. Leakages must equal injection at equilibrium.

    b. I + G = S + T.

C. The tax multiplier is used to show the change in national income that is produced by changes in taxation.

1. The tax multiplier is smaller than the spending multiplier.

    a. The change in planned saving reduces the national income effect of tax changes.

    b. The tax increase lowers consumption and also lowers planned saving.

2. Government expenditure (G) change has a more powerful effect on income than the tax change.

D. When government spends the same amount it takes away in taxes, the effect is called the "balanced-budget multiplier."

1. The increased government spending (G) expands income.

2. Increased taxes on the same amount contracts income, but does not balance (G).

3. The balanced-budget multiplier is one; this means national income increases by the amount of equal increases in government expenditure (G) and taxes (T).

IV. GOVERNMENT USE OF FISCAL POLICIES

    A. Increased government spending (G) can be used to fill the recessionary gap.

        1. *Recessionary Gap:* National income is less than it could be at full employment.

        2. The multiplier effect of government spending (G) raises income.

    B. Lowered government spending (G) can be used to reduce the inflationary gap.

        1. *Inflationary Gap:* National income is higher than it would be at full employment.

        2. To reduce inflation, cut government spending.

    C. A change in taxes can be used to close recessionary or inflationary gaps.

        1. Increase taxes to control an inflationary gap.

        2. Lower taxes to control a recessionary gap.

V. AUTOMATIC FISCAL POLICY (BUILT-IN STABILIZERS) DO NOT REQUIRE NEW LEGISLATION: THEY ARE ALREADY PART OF THE ECONOMY AND OPERATE AUTOMATICALLY.

    A. The progressive income tax has a stabilizing impact.

        1. It rises with high incomes and drops with low incomes.

        2. It moderates fluctuations.

    B. Unemployment compensation also moderates fluctuations.

CHAPTER 13 HIGHLIGHTS

C. Fiscal policy affects the government budget.

1. *Deficit:* Government spends more than tax revenues.

2. *Surplus:* Government takes in more taxes than it spends.

3. *Full-Employment Budget:* What government revenues would be at full employment.

VII. SEVERAL BUDGET PHILOSOPHIES MAY BE USED BY GOVERNMENT TO AFFECT NATIONAL INCOME.

A. *Annually Balanced Budget:* Government expenditures equal to tax revenues each year.

B. *Cyclically Balanced Budget:* Balancing surpluses in prosperous years with deficits in recessionary years.

C. *Functional Finance:* Use of fiscal policy for growth and/or full employment, without concern for a balanced budget, except as it may affect inflation.

FILL-IN REVIEW

Select between the choices underlined or fill in the blank. Cover the answers until you have provided your own.

income	In this chapter, government is brought into the model of the economy. To review the model up to this chapter: the equilibrium level of _____ in the economy is determined by
aggregate	the level of total spending, or _____
demand	_____. In earlier chapters, the two main components of aggregate demand,
consumption investment	_____ demand and _____ were analyzed. They were analyzed in words,
graphs	and by _____ in two different ways that
the same	each give *different/the same* result. These two approaches are two ways of analyzing the same process. The two ways of analyzing are
aggregate aggregate supply	the _____ demand-_____ _____
leakages-injections	method and the _____-_____ method.
income	Continuing to review: both consumption and investment fluctuate, especially investment, and when C and I change, national _____ changes. The relationship between a *change* of consumption or investment and a
national income	*change* in equilibrium _____ _____ is
multiplier	called the _____. You will recall that

equilibrium national income is not necessarily the full _____ national income. If equilibrium income is greater than the full employment income, there is an _____ gap; if equilibrium national income is less than the full employment national income, there is a _____ ___. This chapter deals with the fiscal policies that can be used by government to close those ___.

employment

inflationary

recessionary gap

gaps

In this chapter, spending by _____ is added as part of total spending, called aggregate _____ for the economy. Government finances its expenditures partly by tax revenues. Both government spending and taxation affect the level of _____ _____. Government spending and taxation undertaken in order to change equilibrium level of national income is called _____ _____. There are two kinds of fiscal policy, discretionary and automatic. Deliberate congressional changes in tax rates and expenditure programs to eliminate recessionary and inflationary gaps are called _____ _____ _____. Fiscal policy that does not require new legislation and which operates automatically to stabilize the economy is called _____ _____ _____.

government
demand

national income

fiscal policy

discretionary fiscal policies

automatic fiscal policy

276 UNIT VIII: PART TWO

progressive income

unemployment

Examples of automatic fiscal policy are the _____ _____ tax and _____ compensation.

All increases or decreases in aggregate demand change national income. National income changes by the change in spending times the _____. This is true of all the three parts of aggregate demand: _____ demand, _____ demand and _____ demand. The multiplier is based on MPC and MPS.

multiplier

consumption

investment

government

Changes in government taxation policy affect aggregate _____ and therefore affect national _____. To analyze the effect of tax changes, a *lower/higher* multiplier is used. The reason for a lower taxation multiplier is that some of the effect of a tax change is modified by the drop in planned _____, because of the lower after tax income. Because of this lower multiplier effect of a tax change, government expenditures (G) have a *more powerful/less powerful* effect on income tax than tax changes.

demand

income

lower

saving

less powerful

When government spends the same amount as it takes away in taxes, the effect on income is called the _____ _____ multiplier. When government changes both taxes

balanced budget

and expenditures by the same amount, the *change* produced in national income is exactly equal to the amount of _____ expenditure itself or (G). This balanced budget _____ effect can be generalized. There are important practical implications of the balanced budget multiplier process. In a full employment economy, an increase in government spending for any purpose will cause an inflationary ___ unless taxes are *increased/decreased* by _____ than enough to balance the budget. In an economy operating at less than full _____, a tax reduction will *increase/reduce* aggregate demand, raising national income. This tax reduction could have the effect of *expanding/reducing* the private business sector of the economy.

government

multiplier

*gap   increased
more*

*employment
increase*

expanding

Government spending and taxation thus have effects on national income. These policies used to raise or lower national income are called _____ policy. A recessionary gap may be closed by increased _____ spending or by lowered _____. The multiplier effect operates to raise _____ _____. An inflationary ___ may be closed by *lowered/increased* government spending or by _____ _____. The _____ effect operates to lower

*fiscal
government
taxes
national income
gap   lowered
higher
taxes   multiplier*

income	national _____ and reduce the amount of inflation.
deficit	When government spends more than it receives in tax revenues it runs a _____.
surplus	When government receives more than it spends in taxes it runs a _____. What government revenues and taxes would be at full
full	employment can be called a _____
employment budget	_____ _____.
	In its budget management, government may choose to follow three budgetary philosophies. If it chooses to keep annual expenditures equal to tax revenues each year, it will
annually	be following the philosophy of an _____
balanced	_____ budget. This philosophy may allow contractions and expansions of the business cycle to affect national income.
deficits	If government chooses to balance surpluses in prosperous years with *deficits/surpluses* in recessionary years, it will be following the
cyclically balanced	philosophy of a _____ _____
budget	_____.
	The use of non-inflationary fiscal policy for growth and full employment without concern for a balanced budget is the philosophy
functional finance	of _____ _____.

PROBLEMS, PROBLEMS, PROBLEMS...

Answers are at the end of this unit.

TRUE-FALSE

Circle either "T" or "F" for each statement.

T (F) 1. The effect of adding government expenditures to the model is to decrease aggregate demand.

(T) F 2. Government, through its spending and taxing policies, affects national income.

T (F) 3. New government spending, unlike new consumption and new investment spending, does not have a multiplied effect on national income.

(T) F 4. In the aggregate demand-aggregate supply method of determining national income, equilibrium income will occur where total planned spending equals total income received.

T (F) 5. In the leakages-injections approach to determining equilibrium national income, the results are completely different from the level found by aggregate demand-aggregate supply approach.

(T) F 6. Planned total income is equal to total spending at the equilibrium level of income.

(T) F 7. The equilibrium level is the level toward which income will naturally move.

T (F) 8. When investment increases, the equilibrium level of national income rises, but by a smaller amount.

280 UNIT VIII: PART TWO

(T) F 9. If marginal propensity to consume is 0.75, then the multiplier is 4.

T **(F)** 10. The larger the marginal propensity to consume, the smaller will be the multiplier.

(T) F 11. Graphically, an intersection between the 45 degree line and the total spending curve defines an equilibrium level of income on the income axis.

(T) F 12. Because of the multiplier effect, new C, new I or new G spending in the economy increases national income by a larger amount than the spending.

MATCH-UP

Match each item in the first column with a term in the second column. Use no term more than once.

_e_ 1. Symbol for government spending

_c_ 2. Symbol for taxation

_h_ 3. The change in equilibrium level of national income is equal to new spending times the _____.

_m_ 4. Marginal propensity to save

_k_ 5. New G spending affects equilibrium national income in the same way as _____.

_a_ 6. With additional government spending in the economy, equilibrium national income _____.

a. rises
b. an inflationary gap
c. T
d. discretionary fiscal policy
e. G
f. budget surplus
g. automatic stabilizers
h. multiplier
i. budget deficit
j. cyclically balanced budget

MATCH-UP

__n__ 7. When government increases spending by the same amount it increases taxes, the effect on national income is called _____.

__d__ 8. Deliberate congressional changes in tax rates and expenditure programs to eliminate recessionary and inflationary gaps

__b__ 9. When national income is higher than it would be at full employment, there is _____.

__f__ 10. When government collects more in taxes than it spends

__j__ 11. Balancing surpluses in prosperous years with deficits in recessionary years

__e__ 12. Progressive income taxes, unemployment compensation

__i__ 13. When government spends more than it collects in taxes

k. new I

l. consumption and investment and government (C+I+G)

m. MPS

n. balanced budget multiplier

MULTIPLE CHOICE

For each of the following statements, choose the one best alternative.

1. All of the following are automatic stabilizers *except* one. Choose that one.

    (a.) a one-time tax reduction

    b. unemployment compensation

    c. progressive income tax system

    d. corporate profits' tax

    e. social security payments

2. A decrease in the level of government spending would cause

    a. aggregate supply to increase.

    b. national income to increase.

    (c.) aggregate demand to decrease.

    d. aggregate demand to increase.

3. The full-employment budget states

    a. that taxes should be the sole method of raising revenues.

    (b.) what government revenues and spending would be during years of full employment.

    c. that budgets should be balanced every year.

    d. that the budget should be balanced over the business cycle.

4. Given an increase in government spending, the increase in output and income that results from a change in government spending will be greater

    a. the larger the MPS.

    b. the smaller the APC.

    c. the smaller the MPC.

    (d.) the smaller the MPS.

5. The proper fiscal policy during a period of inflation would be to
   a. lower G and/or lower tax.
   b. raise G and/or raise tax.
   c. raise G and/or lower tax.
   d. lower G and/or raise tax. ✓

6. If the MPC for our economy is ¾ or .75, and the economy is at equilibrium, and government spending rises by $25 billion, you could predict that
   a. equilibrium income will rise by $33.3 billion.
   b. equilibrium income will fall by $100 billion.
   c. equilibrium income will rise by $100 billion. ✓
   d. equilibrium income will rise by $25 billion.

7. Active fiscal policies to stimulate spending in the economy are associated with movement of the government budget toward a position of
   a. deficit. ✓
   b. surplus.
   c. balance.
   d. equilibrium.

8. Active fiscal policies designed to reduce inflation are associated with a movement of the government budget toward a position of
   a. deficit.
   b. surplus. ✓
   c. balance.
   d. equilibrium.

9. If government chooses to balance surpluses in prosperous years with deficits in recessionary years, it will be following the philosophy of

   a. an annually balanced budget.

   b. functional finance.

   c. a cyclically balanced budget.

   d. an annual budget deficit.

10. Automatic fiscal policy

    a. requires action by Congress for its use each year.

    b. is typified by job creation programs.

    c. does not require new legislation.

    d. operates to destabilize the economy (is countercyclical).

11. Government spending on public projects, job creation programs and changes in taxation rates are examples of the use of

    a. an annually balanced budget.

    b. automatic fiscal policy.

    c. discretionary fiscal policy.

    d. None of the above are correct.

12. The appropriate fiscal policy during a period of recession would be to

    a. lower G and/or lower tax.

    b. raise G and/or raise tax.

    c. raise G and/or lower tax.

    d. lower G and/or raise tax.

ANSWERS TO STUDY QUESTIONS

PART TWO

TRUE/FALSE

1. F 2. T 3. F 4. T 5. F 6. T 7. T 8. F 9. T 10. F
11. T 12. T

MATCH-UP

1. e 2. c 3. h 4. m 5. k 6. a 7. n 8. d 9. b 10. f
11. j 12. e 13. i

MULTIPLE-CHOICE

1. a 2. c 3. b 4. d 5. d 6. c 7. a 8. b 9. c 10. c
11. c 12. c

ECONOWORD PUZZLE

CLUES ACROSS

1. To stabilize is also to _____.
4. John Maynard Keynes developed an important _____ of the macroeconomy.
5. To calculate how much a given amount of new spending will affect
6. This Unit deals with _____ spending.
8. At equilibrium, national income _____ national spending.
9. To find aggregate demand, we add consumption ____ investment ____ government spending.
10. Government taxation and spending policy to influence aggregate demand
12. Aggregate demand is the _____ of all spending in the economy.
14. Taxes change aggregate demand which changes _____.
16. Fluctuations in the economies are characterized by alternate periods of boom and _____.
17. When government sells a bond it is receiving a _____ from the private sector.
18. The tendency for people to consume or save extra income is the marginal _____ to consume.
19. Most of us would agree that _____ income is better than less.
20. Net _____ product
21. What economists say households do.
22. Keynes talked about the _____ of income spent when national income is high or low.
25. Goods not sold are _____ goods.
27. Cyclical _____ is of serious concern to policy makers.
28. The _____ of the MPC determines how much income will rise.
29. Marginal propensity to consume
30. To determine underlying causes
33. Inflation is sometimes defined as a sustained level of _____ prices.
38. The _____ gap results when national income is less than it could be at full employment.
40. When it is time to pay a loan, we say it is _____.
41. In economics, marginal means _____.
44. When two quantities are equal, such as S and I, they are _____.
45. To moderate the ups and downs in the economy

CLUES DOWN

1. Tendency to consume extra income; _____ PC
2. An entire part of the economy, such as the private _____
3. Keynesians believe the economy is inherently _____.
7. Income that is received and turned back into the economy determines the _____ level of national income.
8. When you finish this course successfully, you will better understand the _____.
11. The total of all final goods produced and sold in the economy
13. A consumption unit in the economy—a whole sector
15. Spending by businesses for new productive capacity
19. A simplification of the economy: you are studying the Keynesian _____ of the economy.
23. The round-after-round process of respending following a change in investment or consumption
24. Marginal propensity to save
26. Aggregate _____ refers to all those goods and services produced by businesses.
31. The multiplied effect of government spending _____ income.
32. He first identified MPC, MPS, APC and APS.
34. Macroeconomics asks basic questions: what is produced; _____ is it produced; and for whom is it produced.
35. The unemployment _____ is used by government policy makers to decide whether or not to use fiscal policy measures.
36. This results when government spends more than its tax revenues.
37. The higher the MPC, the _____ the effect of new spending on the national income.
39. What households don't spend, they _____.
42. Government can raise revenues by means of a _____.
43. The multiplier acts on changes in spending, for example _____ C.

ECONOWORD PUZZLE

288 UNIT VIII: PART TWO

COMPLETED ECONOWORD PUZZLE

GOVERNMENT FISCAL POLICY

UNIT IX

UNIT IN A NUTSHELL

PART ONE

Film: "Thomas and the Fiscal Fighters"

Text: Chapter 13

PART TWO

Film: "The Inspectors"

Text: Chapter 13

This Unit continues your study of fiscal policy begun in Unit VIII. Household and business spending decisions are based on self interest; members of each of the private sectors decide for themselves what would be the best amount to spend. But in the aggregate, their decisions affect the whole economy, and an inflationary or recessionary gap in equilibrium national income can result. Government acts, instead, for the whole society, and can intervene to stabilize national income through its own spending and taxation decisions—that is, through its fiscal policy.

Expansionary fiscal policy has been considered a powerfully direct method of affecting national income, since government expenditures go directly into the spending stream creating additional spending through the action of the multiplier.

Does fiscal policy actually produce its intended effects? Does G add to real national income and employment? Or instead, does G alter incentives in the private economy; does it change relative prices, and thus expenditures; does its use lead to expectations of inflation? Further, does G lower private businesses' investment resulting in an increasingly dominant role in the economy for government?

UNIT OBJECTIVES

The following objectives can be met by reviewing Chapter 13 and viewing "Thomas the the Fiscal Fighters" and "The Inspectors." After completing this unit, the student should be able to:

1. Define fiscal policy, then distinguish between automatic and discretionary fiscal policy.

2. Know how government expenditures and taxes are used to change national income.

   a. Explain how fiscal policy can be used to overcome recessionary gaps.

   b. Explain how fiscal policy can be used to control inflationary gaps.

3. Explain how fiscal policy affects the government budget.

4. Define three budgetary philosophies: annually balanced budget, cyclically balanced budget and functional finance.

PART ONE AND PART TWO

UNIT IX ASSIGNMENT: PARTS ONE AND TWO

RESTUDY: Chapter 13, "Fiscal Policy," *Economics Today* (*Note:* This was originally assigned in Unit VIII.)

STUDY: Film Summary: "Thomas and the Fiscal Fighters," *Study Guide*

VIEW: "Thomas and the Fiscal Fighters"

STUDY: Film Summary: "The Inspectors," *Study Guide*

VIEW: "The Inspectors"

REVIEW: Chapter 13 Highlights, *Study Guide* (Note: These highlights are included in Unit VIII.)

REWORK AND REVIEW: Fill-in Review *and* Problems, Problems, Problems... for Chapter 13, *Study Guide*, Unit VIII.

COMPLETE: Econoword Puzzle, *Study Guide*, Unit IX

OPTIONAL STUDY: Chapter 13 Issues and Applications, *Study Guide*, Unit IX.

NOTE

This unit continues your study of government involvement in the economy through its fiscal policy. You will not study a new chapter but, instead, will review Chapter 13 from Part Two of Unit VIII.

Unit IX serves to complete our development of the Keynesian model of the economy. In completing this unit, you will consolidate your understanding in order to prepare for the next model—the monetarist way of viewing the macroeconomy.

FILM SUMMARY: "Thomas and the Fiscal Fighters"

Barbara and Herman Drew in our film, "Thomas and the Fiscal Fighters," take their differences of opinion about government fiscal policy so seriously that their disagreements lead to a debate that unintentionally spills over onto national TV. Seldom have personal points of view about fiscal policy been taken to such public extremes.

The angry debates between Barbara and Herman Drew on fiscal policy revolve around different budget philosophies. Barbara and Herman disagree on whether or not the federal budget should be unbalanced in pursuit of an activist fiscal policy. Since the 1940s, the federal government has pursued such policies and has been a stabilizer in the economy, attempting to change national income through changes in the public budget in order to reach full employment and keep prices stable. Theoretically, government attempts to counter changes in the business cycle with fiscal policy that moves the federal budget into a deficit during a recession and into a surplus during inflation.

Herman Drew is a staunch fiscal conservative and believes the federal government's budget should be balanced at all times. He means, simply, that government spending should not exceed its tax revenues. It follows that he cannot disagree more with all countercyclical fiscal policy, both automatic and discretionary.

A budget that is balanced annually cannot allow government spending to overcome recessions, or to increase taxation in order to dampen inflation. Herman is so sure of his point-of-view that government must be "fiscally responsible," that he has not considered how an annually balanced budget would intensify the ups and downs of the business cycle. To balance the budget during an inflation (as tax revenues increase because of higher incomes), government must increase its spending, or cut taxes, or both. Each of these fiscal policies will increase the rate of inflation. The reverse is true of balancing the budget during a recession. As incomes lower, tax revenues could then fall, and a balanced budget would require that government expenditures be cut. Such actions would deepen the recession. Far from the non-interventionist, neutral position Herman asks of government, a government which balances its budget annually will intensify the business cycle.

Herman is frustrated by what he considers government's failure to resist pressures to spend. The federal government's discretionary fiscal policies—deliberate changes by government in taxation and spending policies—have not been to his liking. He claims that discretionary fiscal policy for the last 20 years has been consistently expansionary. Rather than correctly functioning as a stabilizer in the economy, by lowering its own expenditures and raising taxes in periods of excess aggregate demand, government has, Herman believes, consistently entered the economy on the expansionary side. Increased expenditures have increased demand in the economy beyond production possibilities, and the resulting increased spending has put unending pressure on the economy. Serious inflation, Herman concludes, is the result.

Barbara Drew's opinion about the role of the government is, to put it politely, different from her husband's. Barbara is a believer in functional finance. True to her philosophy, she takes the position that the government should follow whatever steps are necessary to realize its twin goals of full employment and stable prices without inflation. Barbara Drew views government as a stabilizing force which can bring the economy to full employment through an increase in spending, lower taxes and job creation programs. She wants to balance the economy, not the budget, and she prefers deficits to unemployment.

Barbara believes that the government should intervene in the economy, as much as is needed. She points out that there are effective automatic stabilizers built into the system that moderate the effects of the business cycle. Automatic stabilizers such as personal and corporate income tax, welfare payments and unemployment compensation lessen the impact of a cycle in the following ways: personal and corporate income tax revenues go *up* when national income increases, taking away spending power at boom times; unemployment compensation and welfare payments rise during a recession increasing consumers' spending power. Thus, appropriate fiscal policy occurs automatically to lessen the impact of inflationary or recessionary changes without explicit actions by legislative policy makers.

Barbara, however, wants more government influence than automatic stabilizers can provide. She believes in the expanded use of discretionary fiscal policy. In her philosophy, government has accepted the role of moderator of the economy on a grand scale. She argues that the built-in stabilizers can only moderate the extremes of the business cycle, yet they cannot correct serious changes in equilibrium national income. She wants changes in expenditures, tax rates and tax structures enacted by Congress to redirect a recession or inflation. Therefore, she would quickly change tax rates as needed and require activist government spending programs.

Barbara, as a believer in functional finance, does not consider a balanced budget of major importance. She believes that the problems of an unbalanced budget are slim indeed next to the grave injustices of prolonged unemployment. She insists that the budget is a means of achieving economic stability—not an end in itself. For her, the "insignificant" debts incurred through government's fiscal policy stabilization efforts will be paid off when national income rises.

If Barbara and Herman were willing to step back from their uncompromising positions with regard to fiscal policy, there might be an area of possible agreement available to them: for example, a budget balanced over a lengthy period, usually the duration of a complete business cycle, might please them both. With a so-called "cyclically balanced budget" government can, in theory, create a budget deficit by spending during a recessionary period, and can accumulate a surplus when times improve. In this "best-of-both-worlds" solution, government could balance its budget while still using countercyclical influence. A cyclically balanced budget, thus, could curtail government spending in order to equalize deficits with surpluses. A cycle of expansion and recession could end with a balanced budget, if the size and length of each phase of a business cycle have been correctly predicted. Agreed, anticipating the length of periods of recession and recovery is no easy task.

Neither of our "fiscal fighters," Barbara nor Herman, has actually clarified whether or not government fiscal policies accomplish their intended goals of full employment and stable prices. Their arguments have been more warm than they have been brilliant.

Stop to remember where we are. In earlier units we outlined the Keynesian theory of income determination, which focuses on sources of spending in the economy. The Keynesian equation states that consumption (C), plus investment (I), plus government expenditure (G) equal national income (C+I+G=Y). At this point, we are concentrating on the G part of the simple equation. It should now be clear that G refers to fiscal policy. And further, we are putting fiscal policy in its appropriate context of Keynesian analysis of the economy, so that when we come to the other major model of the economy—monetarism—we will have established a frame of reference for understanding some of the monetarist's criticisms of Keynesian policy.

In the film, Barbara asserts that she does not advocate excessive spending by government. She tells her television audience that without government intervention to stabilize the economy, national income constantly changes. Herman, on the other hand, believes government policy itself has resulted in destabilization and believes that, left to itself, the economy will prosper. Thus, they become symbols of two ways of seeing the economy and speak not only for those who hold that the economy is inherently unstable and requires intervention, but also for those who believe that the economy is basically a self-righting mechanism which needs only minimal assistance by policy makers.

FILM SUMMARY: "The Inspectors"

There may be times in the lives of all of us when we welcome the help of family, friends, or even an agency of government to help us through a difficult time. Perhaps, as individuals, we have not used the support and direct assistance of government, but are aware of its use in certain programs. In its efforts to moderate the effects of the business cycle or the economy through discretionary fiscal policy, government spending or tax programs may indeed affect our own lives.

At this point in our story, we introduce a specific form of fiscal policy—job creation programs. The program can be viewed as discretionary fiscal policy, intended to create income for groups considered most in need of employment. As Thomas and Karen explain in the film, the aims of the public works program involve raising incomes and job skills of certain groups of workers, while increasing the aggregate demand of the entire economy.

Karen and Thomas themselves had first-hand experience in a public service program when they were employed by the federal government's forest service. The government-sponsored jobs came at a time for Karen and Thomas when jobs were scarce and hard to find; that is, during a cyclical downturn in the economy. The majority of government programs are directed towards alleviating cyclical unemployment, a major focus of government spending.

Job training programs are an attempt to deal with the problems of structural unemployment. This type of unemployment is partially the result of rapid technological development which outdates workers' skills, and actually occurs as a result of changes in society: those unemployed have outdated job skills or they have no skills at all.

Actually, government goals of retraining and skill development may not be helped by its various job programs. Studies have indicated that government employment is skill-intensive, and is not capable of absorbing unskilled workers. In the film, this is confirmed by the administrator of the federal employment program, created by the Public Employment Act. The program resulted in a low level of participation by disadvantaged workers, according to the PEP administrator; fewer than 20 percent of those unskilled workers hired under this job program learned new skills. Instead, government salaries, benefits and skill-intensive jobs attracted skilled and experienced workers, who filled most of the job openings. In the film, Gisela Fairfield is an example of someone with high job skills who is hired in a job training program.

There are other "flies in the ointment," as Thomas calls them, regarding the successful implementation of the federal government's job program. Often, when state and local governments receive federal funds for the creation of new jobs in their areas, officials use them on positions already identified and advertised, instead of for the creation of new jobs. Consequently, training for new skills is not provided, and as a result, the goal of the program has effectively been subverted.

Another of the disadvantages in the public employment program is the so-called displacement effect. When state and local funds have been displaced or substituted by federal monies, the effect has been to shift the burden of paying for existing jobs and services from the local to the federal taxpayer.

An important criticism of the limitations of the federal government discretionary fiscal policy concerns time lags in implementation of spending programs or tax changes. The processes of identifying problems, suggesting solutions and choosing appropriate policy measures all take time. Lags develop in the implementation of those programs finally agreed upon, so that by the time the program finally reaches the economy, the phase of the cycle, that the intended policy was to alter, may have changed. Thus, expansionary policy may be directed into an already inflated economy, or restrictive policy may act to further deepen a developing recession.

"The Fiscal Fighters" and "The Inspectors" play to strong prejudices regarding the role of government fiscal policy in the economy. Fiscal policy as a tool to change national income has fervent supporters and equally adamant critics, as does Keynesian economics. Fiscal policy is based on a model of the economy in which Keynes demonstrated something considered revolutionary in his time. He showed that it is possible to have equilibrium in the macroeconomy at the same time serious unemployment exists. His analysis further suggests that there is no mechanism in the economy that moves it toward full employment. Instead, the volatile nature of investment results in an unstable aggregate spending stream so that income in the economy is always moving up or down. (Notice that this implies an inherent instability of capitalism.)

Recall, again, that Keynes wrote during the depression of the 1930s, a period of prolonged large-scale unemployment. Keynes' proposals for fiscal policy adjustments were his solutions to the problems of the time.

Keynesian budget solutions are politically attractive, since politicians find it possible to spend without balancing taxation. In other words, implementation of fiscal policy through the political process may have biased the selection of programs to upward adjustments of total spending (expansionary policy), ignoring the use of contractionary policy, which may not win votes. But, remember earlier units where you learned of the limitations on aggregate demand. That is, the economy can only produce up to its production possibilities at any given time. We will now go on to another view of the economy which proposes a different model and suggests other solutions to problems of income and employment.

SPECIAL INSTRUCTIONS

Chapter Highlights for the Issues and Applications part of text Chapter 13 is included since it contains examples of recent discretionary fiscal policy. It is optional.

CHAPTER 13 ISSUES AND APPLICATIONS

I. SECTION OVERVIEW: DISCRETIONARY FISCAL POLICY: DIRECT FEDERAL GOVERNMENT INTERVENTION

   A. The application of direct fiscal policy by the federal government

   B. Public employment programs

II. TAXATION AND GOVERNMENT SPENDING

   A. Government policy makers are free to adjust taxes and government expenditures to change aggregate demand during national economic distress.

      1. Contractionary fiscal policy could cool down an inflated economy.

      2. Expansionary fiscal policy could raise equilibrium national income.

   B. Recent examples of fiscal policies:

      1. The Kennedy-Johnson tax cut of 1964 resulted in lower unemployment, and additional I and G.

      2. The Johnson 1968 tax surcharge did not slow inflation.

3. In 1971, Congress increased the allowable depreciation of machinary for businesses to lower tax liability.

4. In 1971, a job development credit lowered taxes to businesses which invested in new machinery.

5. In 1975, a series of tax reductions were affected and later extended.

6. Because of the 1974–1975 recession, fiscal policy was stimulative.

7. Fiscal proposals during 1975–1976 were for ranged tax cuts and lowered government spending; in 1977–1978, there were proposals to continue tax cuts but to increase government spending.

   a. By 1979, inflation was the primary concern.

   b. In 1980, inflation rate still rose and the size of the national debt brought concern.

III. PUBLIC EMPLOYMENT PROGRAMS: GOVERNMENT PROVIDES FUNDS FOR MORE JOBS TO RELIEVE UNEMPLOYMENT.

   A. U.S. public employment programs began during the Great Depression of the 1930s. Three major programs were:

      1. Public Works Administration (PWA),

      2. Works Progress Administration (WPA),

      3. Civilian Conservation Corps (CCC).

   B. More recent employment programs:

      1. Economic Opportunity Act of 1965 established Operation Mainstream.

      2. Emergency Employment Act of 1975 was used to fund the Public Employment Program (PEP).

3. Comprehensive Employment and Training Act (CETA) of 1973 has provided billions of dollars for public service jobs.

C. The objectives of the public jobs programs fulfill the aims of fiscal policy. They attempt to increase total spending and they stabilize the economy. The attempt, however, is aimed at particular groups in the economy. Job programs are intended to

1. raise the wage rates and increase potential earnings for those with low job skills.

2. increase state and local public services.

3. reduce the number of those who are considered structurally unemployed (those who don't have skills needed in the workforce).

4. reduce the number of those who are considered cyclically unemployed (those who have lost their jobs because of a slowdown in the economy).

IV. PITFALLS OF PUBLIC EMPLOYMENT PROGRAMS

A. The difficulty of monitoring federal funds disbursement may allow a displacement effect.

1. State and local government agencies may substitute federal funds for their own, thus shifting payment for work projects from state and local taxpayers to federal taxpayers.

2. Government spending can crowd out private spending, when it is financed by bond sales.

B. It is difficult to absorb the unskilled and disadvantaged workers into state and local government jobs.

1. Job program structure and criteria often work against those with low skills and little education.

a. Government-sector jobs often require higher levels of skill than the rest of the work force.

        b. Relatively higher government salaries attract the more-than-qualified workers who successfully compete against the disadvantaged.

    2. The income-earning potential of job program participants is often not improved.

  C. There is a time lag in providing jobs and getting money into the hands of those in need.

    1. It takes Congress time to recognize the problem, propose solutions and act on recommendations.

    2. By the time implementation takes place, the recession may have passed and the economy may now be in a period of fuller employment, or inflation.

V. JOB VOUCHERS: A FORM OF SUBSIDIZED EMPLOYMENT. A SUGGESTED ALTERNATIVE TO PUBLIC JOBS PROGRAMS

  A. Under this proposed scheme, the federal government would send unemployed individuals a voucher to take to the employer of their choice.

  B. The employer who hired the worker and collected the voucher

    1. would be reimbursed by government.

    2. Reimbursement could be used to pay the worker's salary.

  C. The voucher alternative to public jobs programs would return some decision-making to the private sector.

ECONOWORD PUZZLE

CLUES ACROSS

1. Payment levied by government
2. The economy can be divided into the public sector, government, and the _____ sector, households and businesses.
4. Exchanges of goods and services occur in the _____ market.
6. Unemployment rate measures the percentage of workers out of a _____.
9. According to simple economic theory, households can use income in two ways: they either spend it or _____ it.
10. _____ level of national income occurs where spending is equal to income received.
13. The relationship between deficits and surpluses in a cyclically balanced budget
15. Criticisms of the limitations of the government's discretionary fiscal policy involves _____ - _____.
16. Periodic fluctuation of business activity
17. Taxation and spending policy by government to influence national income
18. What the government must do in order to create a budget deficit with a "cyclically balanced budget."
20. Type of fiscal policy which calls for deliberate changes by government
23. The income multiplier acts on all _____ spending.
24. When aggregate demand is _____, unemployment rises.
25. When _____ are granted by a bank, they must be paid back by a certain date.
27. Government can _____ a deficit by issuing bonds in which it borrows from the private sector.
28. Personal and corporate income tax revenues increase as national income rises.
29. Average Propensity to Save
31. New productive equipment, such as building, machinery
32. The difference between full employment spending and actual spending at full employment is the inflationary _____.
33. The number by which a change in autonomous investment (consumption) is multiplied to get the change in equilibrium national income
35. Fiscal policy undertaken to raise national income

CLUES DOWN

1. Fiscal policy requires _____ to take effect.
2. When government issues bonds, it borrows from the _____ sector.
3. A consumption unit in the economy which supplies land, labor and capital to businesses
4. The rate of _____ of the minimum wage may contribute to unemployment.
5. When the burden of paying for existing jobs and services is shifted from the local to the federal taxpayer
7. When government spending programs are reduced, we speak of a _____ in G.
8. Keynesian policies of discretionary fiscal policy place government in an _____ role in the economy.
11. When government spending does not exceed government income
12. The C+I+G=Y equation relating the sources of spending to income in the economy is the _____ equation.
14. Fiscal policy is undertaken to moderate or _____ economic activity.
17. The relationship between spending and income is a _____ one.
18. This type of unemployment is partially the result of rapid technological developments which outdate workers' skills.
19. According to your text, the difference between the actual spending at full employment and the full employment level of spending is called the _____ gap.
21. The structurally unemployed worker may simply not have the _____ required for the jobs available.
22. A sustained rise in the average of all prices
25. There are three levels of government: federal, state and _____.
26. When government taxes, it _____ to remove some spending power from the private economy.
27. In the _____ "The Inspectors," job training programs are discussed.
30. Marginal Propensity to Consume
34. A macroeconomics course concentrates on the way different aggregates function _____ the economy.

ECONOWORD PUZZLE

305

UNIT IX: PART ONE AND PART TWO

INFLATION

UNIT X

UNIT IN A NUTSHELL

PART ONE
Film: "The Shrinking Dollar"

Text: Chapter 8

PART TWO
Film: "Fast Food Economics"

Text: Chapter 8

When spending increases, it triggers off even more spending and the economy builds up into an expansionary boom. As the economy turns around, investment spending slows, consumer spending drops, and unemployment rises.

The ups and downs of the economy are referred to as the business cycles; that is, the general level of economic activity measured by changes in rates of output and unemployment. The cycle is reflected in alternate periods of inflation and recession. Why does the economy experience phases of prosperity and then phases of slowdown? Why does the unemployment rate rise? What do unemployment figures actually tell us? What are the causes and consequences of inflation? Recently, instead of alternating periods of recession and inflation, we have observed a new phenomenon, simultaneous inflation and rising unemployment.

UNIT OBJECTIVES

The following objectives can be met by studying Chapter 8, "Business Fluctuations, Unemployment, and Inflation," the Film Summary: "The Economic Roller Coaster" from Unit V, and viewing "The Shrinking Dollar" and "Fast Food Economics." After completing this unit, the student should be able to:

1. Identify the different phases of the business cycle.

2. Know how to calculate the unemployment rate.

3. List and characterize the different types of unemployment.

4. Define inflation.

5. Characterize demand-pull and cost-push inflation.

6. Know how to calculate a simple price index.

7. Identify which groups are hurt and which are helped by inflation.

PART ONE AND PART TWO

UNIT X ASSIGNMENT: PARTS ONE AND TWO

RESTUDY: Film Summary: "The Economic Roller Coaster," *Study Guide,* Unit V.

STUDY: Chapter 8, "Business Fluctuations, Unemployment and Inflation," *Economics Today* (*Note:* Chapter 8 was initially read in Unit V.)

STUDY: Film Summary: "The Shrinking Dollar" and "Fast Food Economics," *Study Guide*

VIEW: "The Shrinking Dollar"

VIEW: "Fast Food Economics"

REVIEW: Chapter 8 Highlights, *Study Guide*

COMPLETE: Fill-in Review *and* Problems, Problems, Problems ... *and* Econoword Puzzle for Unit X, *Study Guide*

REVIEW: Fill-in Review *and* Problems, Problems, Problems ... for Unit V, *Study Guide*

FILM SUMMARY:
"The Shrinking Dollar" and "Fast Food Economics"

Mother Weldon is at it again—rushing forth in all directions now that she has decided she has a cure for inflation. Her energetic response is to insist that wage and price controls be imposed by government. Her simple, "common sense" answer to a complicated problem is common enough, since traditionally, when inflation has been sustained for a long time, support for controls grows.

Although your film programs, "The Shrinking Dollar" and "Fast Food Economics," concentrate mainly on the inflationary aspect of business fluctuations, we will consider all of the phases of the business cycle in this Unit.

The long-term economic trend in the U.S. has been one of growth, but progress has been unsteady, with business expansion and periods of recession each lasting for several years. The term business cycle refers to these periodic ups and downs of business activity. Since the "booms" and "busts" do not occur in a smooth, predictable pattern, the term, "fluctuation," which does not have the connotation of regularity, may be more descriptive.

What actually happens during a fluctuation, or cycle? At the end of a period of expansion, the national product is close to full employment and the economy is "booming" at or near capacity. This period is most likely to be accompanied by a sustained, general rise in prices. Then, business production begins to decline and a recessionary phase starts. During this phase, although output falls (and with it, employment) prices are likely to be inflexible, and only fall when the recession is especially long and deep. The recession continues through a low period when output and employment have "hit bottom" and then begin to recover. With the recovery phase, output increases (and with it, employment) and, as it picks up momentum, the price level may again begin to rise. (At this point, you should go back to Unit V to reread the film summary of "Economic Roller Coaster" in which business cycles are introduced.)

Wage and price controls are our "fast food" responses to inflation in the film "Fast Food Economics." The implication being that "fast food" cures provide a restricted menu of economic choices that can be quickly delivered. But these quick responses result in longer run problems so that controls are doomed to failure in their intent to hold down prices. Efforts to control inflation have been with us as long as inflation itself has been around. From the time of the ancient rulers of Babylonia, who tried to keep wages and prices in line—and threatened death to those who violated their decrees—to the present time, man has tried to set legal limits on certain prices and wages.

During a number of periods in our recent economic history, controls have been imposed by government in an attempt to control prices. Mother Weldon herself lived through the World War II administration of the Price Control Act which imposed rigidly controlled wages and prices. It was a period when rationing was ultimately used, instead of the free market price system, to allocate some goods in short supply. The success of the price controls resulted in the failure of the price mechanism to serve a rationing function.

President John Kennedy in the early 1960s tried to gain voluntary compliance from workers and businesses for limiting wage increases to no more than gains in productivity. The inflation of 1974–75 was aggravated by the price controls of 1971–73, which lowered incentives to produce some goods. Supply dried up and bottlenecks developed so that, when the controls were removed, the prices in many areas rose more quickly than they would have if controls had not distorted incentives.

Price controls result in shortages and are frequently accompanied by arbitrary allocations for the goods controlled. For example, regulations by the U.S. Department of Energy in 1979 required oil refiners to sell specified amounts of gas at a controlled price to certain dealers, while at the same time dealers were required to sell more gas to certain favored groups. This cumbersome system of controls and allocations hampered the operation of market forces which, if left to themselves, would have quickly simplified the problem. The price control policies made the problem worse. Thomas's example of controls being a black tape over an overheating boiler pressure gauge is an explosive one—but apropos.

Dr. Teal has no encouragement for Mother Weldon's efforts to find support for her price control cause. Dr. Teal, ever the analytic economist, recommends an inquiry into what actually causes the problem of inflation, and indeed it is in the pursuit of such an inquiry that much present day economic research is devoted.

Theories of inflation are part of the inquiry into the causes of economic instability. You have already studied the classical, and a simple Keynesian theory of cycles, and have encountered several more in Unit V.

Before 1930, economists believed that economic downturns and high unemployment were always temporary. These classical economists believed that complete flexibility of all prices (including wages and interest rates) would guarantee economic recovery. Their faith was challenged by the persistent high unemployment and stagnating economy of the 1930s when wages, prices and interest rates all dropped, but their fall did not provide a recovery.

John Maynard Keynes attacked the classical ideas saying that falling wages result in falling purchasing power, without which consumers could not demand goods and services. Without demand, producers fail to invest. Keynesians saw economic instability as caused by instability of private investment.

Your Unit V film summary of "Economic Roller Coaster" lists a number of theories that also attempt to explain business fluctuations. The causal agent in these theories range from sunspots, major inventions, and war activity, to the belief that fluctuations are caused entirely by the quantity of money in the economy. In explaining these cycles, recessions are associated with unemployment, while inflation generally characterizes periods of strong expansion.

All of the theories mentioned can be classified as demand-pull. Demand-pull inflation occurs when total demand in an economy is rising at the same time that the available supply of goods and services is in short supply. This can happen because the economy is at its full capacity already or because all factors of production are not being fully utilized.

However, not one of these theories can provide the complete analysis of the modern situation of unemployment accompanied by inflation. A cost-push classification has been recently introduced to attempt to explain how prices go up when aggregate demand and employment are low. According to this theory, inflation can be initiated by spontaneous wage, price or profit increases. An example is a rise in the price of an international commodity, such as oil.

A comprehensive theory which is able to explain simultaneous inflation and unemployment may involve drawing from a number of different explanations for underlying causes of the business cycle. In Unit XII, the monetarist model, which explains cycles through changes in the money supply, is contrasted with the Keynesian model which explains cycles in terms of volatile investment spending. In this Unit, we will briefly discuss newer areas of economic research, yielding analysis of unemployment, job search and expectations as they influence inflation.

Although economists differ on the cause of cycles, the level of aggregate demand is generally agreed to determine output and employment. In a market economy, businesses produce what can be sold at a profit. When demand is high, production (and employment) is high; when demand is low, production falls, together with employment. With spending changes, the force of the business cycle is felt throughout the entire economy and few can escape its effects. We live in a technologically advanced society and our jobs, incomes and survival needs are interwoven with those of everyone else.

Depending upon where we earn our livelihood in the economy, some are more affected by the business cycle than others. Employment in the construction industry, automotive and other consumer durable's production is especially vulnerable to business changes, as is employment in the capital goods industry. Output and employment in nondurable goods, however, is not as sensitive to recession.

There is a close relationship between the recessionary gap and unemployment in the economy. Whatever the causes of unemployment, a prolonged and deep recession leaves psychological and sociological costs to the society which are incalculable. Frictional unemployment (workers "between jobs"), structural unemployment (workers without salable skills) and cyclical unemployment (caused by the business cycle) together cost society dearly in foregone production. That is, as a society, we sacrifice more of the potential output we could have shared the farther we produce from our capacity.

In the film "Fast Food Economics," our economic actors do not fear recession as much as they feel the need to battle inflation—albeit, ineffectively and with little understanding of their enemy. We have defined inflation as a sustained rise of the average price level. What is wrong with higher prices? Every inflated price is perceived by others as income, so what is the problem? How does inflation affect us, anyhow? Are some helped while others are hurt?

The effects of inflation are not felt evenly in the economy. There are real income effects. Those living on fixed incomes are hurt, whereas those living on flexible incomes *may* benefit from inflation. Those who have savings in banks are harmed, since their savings represent lower buying power as inflation progresses. If those who loan don't anticipate inflation when they agree to a contract, they may be harmed. On the other hand, inflation benefits those who borrow since loans will be repaid in money that is worth less.

Another important effect of inflation that is not anticipated is the redistributional effect between age groups. Older people who have fixed savings and fixed bond holdings watch inflation cut into their purchasing power, whereas younger workers are able to use inflation to help them repay debts. Thus, inflation redistributes income from the old to the young. As a last and important kind of redistribution, inflation has actually accomplished a major redistribution of spending ability from the private sector to government.

Dr. Teal emphasizes that incidence of income redistribution effect depends on whether or not the inflation has been anticipated. We must recognize, however, that people are intelligent and good observers, and following a sustained period of inflation individuals eventually begin to adapt accordingly. If the inflation is anticipated, creditors will require higher interest rates, organized workers will insist on higher wages at contract renewal time, and before accepting new jobs, applicants will expect a higher salary—all to keep pace with inflation. A fully anticipated inflation may have little or no effect on relative prices or incomes.

CHAPTER 8 HIGHLIGHTS

Defined words are underlined.

I. THE UPS AND DOWNS IN ECONOMY-WIDE ECONOMIC ACTIVITY: BUSINESS FLUCTUATIONS

   A. Defining and dating business fluctuations

      1. *Recessions:* A period when business activity temporarily falls below its usual increase. An official definition of recession is two consecutive quarters of falling national output.

      2. *Expansion:* A recovery period when business activity moves with, or exceeds the usual increase. Expansion is defined as three consecutive quarters of increasing national output.

   B. *Business Indicators:* Measurements (statistics) which can be used to predict or identify what is going on in the economy.

      1. *Leading Indicators:* Change fairly reliably before overall economic changes. (Examples are average work week for production workers and changes in business inventories.)

      2. *Coincident Indicators:* Change at the same time that the overall economy changes. (Examples are the unemployment rate and consumer installment debt.)

      3. *Lagging Indicators:* Change after the economy has changed; these are useless for prediction. (An example is the unemployment rate.)

   C. Durable goods' industries have wider and deeper output changes than non-durable goods' industries.

      1. *Durable Goods:* Goods produced to last longer than one year.

         a. Consumer durables are refrigerators, cars, television sets.

         b. Producer durables are machines, heavy equipment.

2. Spending on durable goods can be postponed or speeded up; spending falls during recessions and rises during expansions.

3. *Non-durable Goods:* Goods not expected to last, such as food, clothing, etc.

II. UNEMPLOYMENT, AN IMPORTANT ELEMENT OF THE BUSINESS CYCLE

    A. *Rate of Unemployment:* Is obtained by dividing the number of persons unemployed by the number of persons in the civilian labor force. (Definitions of employment categories are complex, because of the need for exact survey methods.)

        1. *Unemployed:* Persons who are looking for and available for work.

        2. *Labor Force:* The number of people either working or looking for work.

        3. *Labor Force Participation Rate:* The percentage of available individuals of working age who are actually in the labor force.

    B. Business fluctuations and duration of unemployment

        1. The average duration of unemployment is closely tied to the business cycle.

        2. Official unemployment rates may understate or overstate the true rate.

            a. Discouraged workers may want jobs but may give up searching.

            b. Changes in average duration of employment affects employment statistics.

    C. The major types of unemployment are:

        1. *Frictional Unemployment:* The continuous flow of individuals voluntarily changing jobs (regarded as around 5 percent of the labor force).

a. Regarded as desirable and inevitable.

b. Workers are free to search for higher productivity positions.

c. *Full Employment:* Sometimes calculated as the amount of frictional unemployment subtracted from the full labor force: full employment actually may mean 5–6% unemployment.

2. *Cyclical Unemployment:* Associated with changes in business conditions, primarily recessions and depressions. Cyclical unemployment is the target of economic policy which attempts to stabilize the economy.

3. *Seasonal Unemployment:* Changes with seasonal demands for particular jobs.

4. *Structural Unemployment:* Associated with changes in technology and the kinds of goods and services consumers are willing to buy.

a. Structurally unemployed persons cannot find any job they can do.

b. Structural unemployment is associated with the displacement of workers by labor-saving machines.

III. *Inflation:* A SUSTAINED RISE IN THE AVERAGE OF ALL PRICES OVER A PERIOD OF TIME.

A. Inflation is measured by using a price index: GNP figures are adjusted for price changes.

1. The money GNP figures for several years may have overstated the real output increases.

a. The money measure of output does not accurately reflect real output.

b. Both increase in real output and price increases are reflected in GNP.

2. *Price Index:* A tool to compare prices between two different years. A price index converts the value of goods in current dollars (or nominal present-day dollars) to the value of the same output in constant dollars.

    a. *Current Dollars:* Dollars uncorrected for inflation.

    b. *Constant Dollars:* Dollars that have had a price index applied to remove the effects of inflation.

    c. *Base Year:* Beginning year, or reference point for measuring price changes.

3. A number of price indexes are in use.

    a. *Consumer Price Index (CPI):* An index of prices of several thousands of goods and services in general use among consumers.

    b. The CPI for Urban Consumers is a new index to include a large percentage of the civilian population.

    c. The Revised CPI for Urban Wage Earners and Clerical Workers is a modernization to better measure current spending patterns.

    d. The Wholesale Price Index measures changes in average prices of about 25,000 items purchased by business firms.

4. Price indexes are not completely accurate.

    a. Too much weight is given to goods whose prices have risen.

    b. Changes in quality are difficult to take into account.

B. Who is affected by inflation?

  1. Individuals on fixed income are hurt by inflation.

2. Creditors lose, debtors gain when inflation rates are unanticipated.

    a. *Anticipated Inflation:* A rate that is expected (one that loan rates may be set for).

    b. *Unanticipated Inflation:* A rate higher than expected.

3. Cash-holders lose part of the value of their money.

4. Long-term contracts may or may not take into account inflation.

5. Inflation can benefit the federal government.

    a. Government is a debtor and can repay its debts with inflated dollars.

    b. Inflation pushes taxpayer's nominal income into higher brackets; with the progressive income tax system the average tax rate rises.

C. Types of inflation.

    1. *Demand-Pull Inflation:* Demand for goods rises while available supply of goods does not.

    2. *Cost-Push Inflation:* According to some this is due to one or more of the following:

        a. the power of big unions,

        b. big business monopoly power,

        c. raw material price increases.

FILL-IN REVIEW

Select between the choices underlined or fill in the blank. Cover the answers until you have provided your own.

The periodic ups and downs of the economy are called business _____ or _____.	***fluctuations cycles***
These cycles are *regular/irregular* in their length and intensity. A period of three consecutive quarters of increasing business activity	***irregular***
is called an _____ (or recovery), while three consecutive quarters of falling national	***expansion***
output is called a _____. Statistical measurements which can be used to predict and identify the direction of overall economic	***recession***
activity are called _____. A good that is produced to last longer than a year is a	***indicators***
_____ good. Goods and services which are expected to wear out or to be used up quickly	***durable***
are termed ___-_____. Historically, the	***non-durable***
_____ goods' industries have experienced wider fluctuations in output and employment	***durable***
than ___-_____ _____ industries. Dura-	***non-durable goods'***
bility is related to business _____.	***fluctuations***
While purchases of non-durable goods stay relatively stable, durable goods' spending *falls/rises* during recessions, and *falls/rises* during expansions. This is not surprising since	***falls rises***

durable	_____ goods' purchases may be either
postponed	speeded up or _____ depending on pro-
does	duction needs. Full employment *means/does*
not mean	*not mean* that there is no unemployment in
	the economy. The rate of unemployment is
	obtained by dividing the number of
unemployed	_____ by the number of persons in
work force	the _____ _____. The average duration of un-
business	employment is closely linked to _____
fluctuations	_____. In our economy, unemployment
	is classified into several types depending on
	the cause. Unemployment which is a result of
	workers moving from one job to another is
frictional	called _____. A current estimate is that
	around 5 percent of our unemployment is of
	this type. Full employment can be defined as
frictional	the amount of _____ employment sub-
	tracted from the work force. The kind of un-
	employment associated with a general decline
cyclical	in business activity is _____ unemploy-
	ment. Unemployment rates are different for
	different groups within the economy: the
teenagers	highest rate is among _____, the lowest
heads of families	rate is among _____ __ _____.
Inflation	_____ is a sustained rise in the aver-
	age price level. An increase in the price of one
does not	good *does/does not* constitute inflation. In the

history of the U.S., inflation and ____ have occurred at the same time. The United States *shares/does not share* its history of rising prices with other countries. Inflation is a *U.S./worldwide* problem. The rate of inflation can be measured by using a ____ ____. This is a ratio of prices in ____ different time periods. A price index converts the value of current output to _____ dollars. A formal definition of a price index is: quantities of _____ in the current year valued at their ____ year _____. The Consumer _____ _____ measures the average price level of goods and services _____ buy. The average prices of goods purchased by businesses are measured by the _____ Price _____. Price indexes are *perfect/not perfect* measurements of inflation. Changes in *quality/quantity* are not included and since measurements are from a ____ year, there is an _____ bias. Some groups hurt by inflation are: _____, who have not _____ the inflation; holders of ____; those on _____ incomes; and those operating under contracts that *do/do not* take the rate of inflation into account. In some ways, inflation can be said to benefit the federal _____, because

war

shares

worldwide

price index

two

constant

outputs

base   prices   Price Index

consumers

Wholesale   Index

not perfect

quality

base

upward

creditors   anticipated

cash   fixed

do not

government

debtor	government is a _____ and because of the
tax	progressive personal income ___. When your
up	nominal income is pushed __ by inflation,
tax	you move into a higher ___ bracket. There are
	different classifications of inflation, named for
	the major explanation for the price rises.
	When total demand in the economy is rising
	while the total supply of goods is limited,
demand-pull	_____-____ inflation occurs. If the econo-
full employment	my is near the ___ _____ level of out-
	put, where little new output can be supplied,
demand prices	the increased _____ pulls up _____. For
	the type of inflation called cost-push inflation,
union	three explanations have been offered: _____
monopoly	power; _____ power; and raw-materials-
	push. In these explanations, the increased cost
pushes	of production _____ prices up.

PROBLEMS, PROBLEMS, PROBLEMS...

Answers are at the end of this unit.

TRUE-FALSE

Circle either "T" or "F" for each statement.

(T) F 1. During a recession, there are high levels of unemployment.

T (F) 2. When the economy is at full employment, everyone has a job.

(T) F 3. Durable goods' production fluctuates more than the non-durable goods' production.

T (F) 4. Total spending on durable goods rises during a recession and falls during prosperity periods.

T (F) 5. The ups and downs of business activity called business fluctuations (cycles) occur at regular, predictable intervals.

(T) F 6. Frictional unemployment results from a business cycle fluctuation.

(T) F 7. Downswings in business cycle (fluctuations) cause cyclical unemployment.

T (F) 8. A recession is defined to be when national output falls in six consecutive quarters.

(T) F 9. The existence of hidden unemployment may cause the unemployment rate to be understated.

T (F) 10. A coincidental indicator is one that tends to move ahead of the general level of business activity.

(T) F 11. Job mobility would be almost impossible if there were no frictional unemployment.

MATCH-UP

Match each item in the first column with a term in the second column. Use no term more than once.

__d__ 1. Mrs. Q. has quit her job and is looking for a management job in a hospital; her unemployment is _____.

__f__ 2. Workers are laid off because of changes in business conditions; their employment is _____.

__h__ 3. During the coldest part of winter, construction workers are laid off because of the difficulty of building during severe weather; their unemployment is _____.

__j__ 4. An indicator that moves with the general level of business activity

__a__ 5. A fall of national output for three consecutive quarters

__e__ 6. A periodic fluctuation in business activity over a period of years

__b__ 7. This production fluctuates widely over the business cycle.

__i__ 8. When everyone who wants to work is working, except those changing jobs

__c__ 9. A good that technically lasts less than one year

__g__ 10. That part of the business cycle characterized by rising output, income and unemployment

a. recession
b. durable
c. non-durable goods
d. frictional
e. business cycle
f. cyclical
g. recovery
h. seasonal
i. full employment
j. coincidental

MULTIPLE CHOICE

For each of the following statements, choose the one best alternative.

1. Unemployment of people who are in-between jobs for relatively short periods of time is known as

    a. seasonal.

    b. frictional. ✓

    c. cyclical.

    d. structural.

2. A large number of workers are laid off because of a fall in demand for the product they produced. This is an example of

    a. seasonal unemployment.

    b. frictional unemployment.

    c. cyclical unemployment.

    d. structural unemployment. ✓

3. Unemployment rates vary for different groups. Of the following which has the highest rate?

    a. female heads of households

    b. male heads of households

    c. all teenagers

    d. black teenagers ✓

4. Unemployment rates vary for different groups. Of the following which has the lowest rate?

    a. women heads of households

    b. male heads of households ✓

    c. all teenagers

    d. black teenagers

5. "We don't need to worry about unemployment because it affects only a small percentage of the population." This statement does not consider

   a. human suffering of unemployment.

   b. loss of dignity of unemployment.

   c. loss of savings from unemployment.

   d. loss of national output from unemployment.

   e. all of the above.

6. The economy is at "full employment" when

   a. there is only frictional unemployment.

   b. there is only structural unemployment.

   c. only a small percentage of women and teenagers are out of work.

   d. everyone in the economy has a job.

7. Which of the following workers would be classified as structurally unemployed?

   a. a bookkeeper laid off because of the purchase of a new computerized accounting system

   b. a worker who has re-entered the job market after her divorce and finds that her skills are outmoded

   c. a worker with little education and few skills

   d. All of the above are correct.

8. The unemployment rate is

   a. the percentage of the population over 16 years of age and not working.

   b. the percentage of people who are employed.

   c. the percentage of the civilian labor force that is unemployed.

   d. the percentage of the labor force that is collecting unemployment compensation.

9. In both Chapter 8 and the film summary, wage and price controls
    a. have historically always been effective in lowering inflation.
    b. have never been used in the U.S.
    c. reduce economic efficiency.
    d. never lead to black markets or rationing.

10. Groups that lose from unanticipated inflation include
    a. debtors.
    b. creditors.
    c. government.
    d. younger workers.

11. One of the following completions is *incorrect*. Choose that one. Inflation redistributes income from
    a. the private sector to government.
    b. older persons living off fixed assets to younger workers.
    c. creditors to debtors.
    d. those who had anticipated inflation.
    e. government to the private sector.

12. A leading indicator
    a. will turn up before a recovery.
    b. has no relationship to economic activity.
    c. turns up after a recovery occurs.
    d. turns up as a recover occurs.

13. If the rate of inflation is correctly anticipated by everyone, then
    a. inflation will redistribute purchasing power.
    b. GNP will rise.
    c. no distribution of purchasing power will occur.
    d. GNP will fall.

14. A definition of a price index is quantities of outputs in the current year value at their _____ values.

   a. base year *(circled)*

   b. current year

   c. average

   d. total

15. The durable goods' industries will

   a. never experience fluctuations.

   b. fluctuate more than the non-durable goods' industries. *(circled)*

   c. fluctuate less than the non-durable goods' industries.

   d. fluctuate the same as non-durable goods' industries.

16. The depression of the 1930s

   a. challenged the faith of the classical economists that fluctuations are temporary.

   b. saw both employment and prices fall.

   c. saw a rapid expansion of the money supply. *(circled)*

   d. saw unemployment rates of 25%.

17. Inflation can be defined as a situation in which

   a. some prices are rising.

   b. an average of all prices experiences a sustained rise. *(circled)*

   c. prices are changing.

   d. some prices fall when others rise.

ABOVE AND BEYOND

CALCULATE A SIMPLE PRICE INDEX.

1. Select a good you usually buy, such as bread, shoes, gasoline or whatever.

2. Write the price of that good: call it the present year cost.

3. Find out the price of that same good five years ago. That year will be your base year.

4. Write the base year price of your good.

5. Divide the present year price of the good by the base year price.

6. Multiply your result by 100.

7. You have a one-good price index, a percentage comparison of prices from the base year you selected. (The base year price index is always 100.)

ECONOWORD PUZZLE

CLUES ACROSS

1. Fiscal policy is directed toward correcting the _____ of the economy.
3. The duration of unemployment is related to the time devoted to a _____ for a job.
6. A fully _____ inflation may have little or no effect on relative prices or incomes.
9. Periodic ups and downs of business activity
11. A price _____ measures the changes in prices from a base year.
14. Work
15. The _____ period of simultaneous inflation and recession has challenged the simple Keynes theory of income determination.
16. Statistical measurement which can be used to predict and identify the direction of the overall economy
18. The product of the economy is also referred to as its _____.
20. Three consecutive quarters of increasing national output
22. Gross National Product
25. The effects of inflation are not felt evenly in the economy. The incidence of income _____ effects depend on whether or not inflation has been anticipated.
26. When the average level of all prices _____ and is sustained, we have inflation.

CLUES DOWN

1. According to Keynesian theory, spending depends on _____.
2. Unemployment _____ are used by Congress in deciding what fiscal policy will be applied to the economy.
4. To obtain aggregate demand, simply _____ C plus I plus G.
5. In a market economy, when income is below full employment and when aggregate demand rises, production increases to _____ levels.
7. Business fluctuations
8. Prices serve to _____ scarce goods.
10. Sustained rise in the average of all prices over a period of time
12. Dollars that have a price index applied to remove effects of inflation
13. Two consecutive quarters of falling national output
15. Business fluctuations proceed through a recessionary phase and ultimately into a _____ phase.
17. Inflation _____ those on fixed incomes.
19. Workers whose wages are _____ to the CPI are not as affected by inflation as those whose wages are not.
21. Land, labor and capital exchanged in factor markets _____ rent, wages and interest.
23. One early theory of the business cycle blamed storms on the _____.
24. Consumer Price Index

ECONOWORD PUZZLE

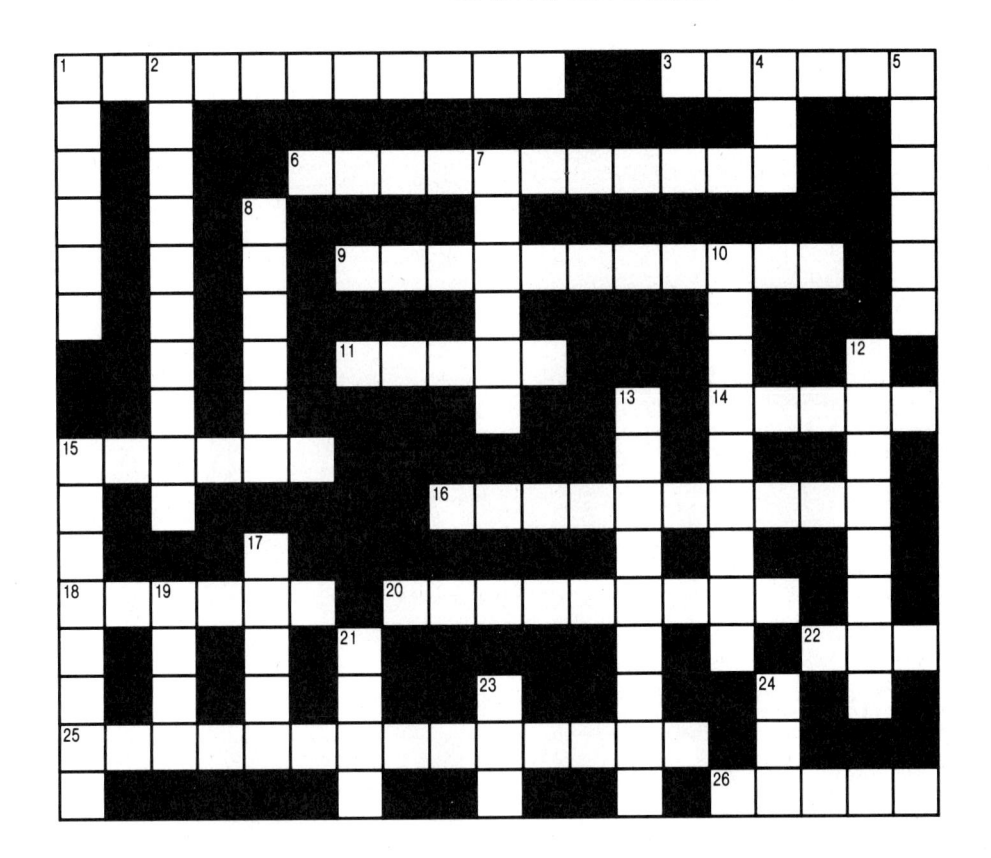

ANSWERS TO STUDY QUESTIONS

TRUE-FALSE

1. T   2. F   3. T   4. F   5. F   6. T   7. T   8. F   9. T   10. F
11. T   12. F   13. T

MATCH-UP

1. d   2. f   3. h   4. j   5. a   6. e   7. b   8. i   9. c   10. g

MULTIPLE CHOICE

1. b   2. d   3. d   4. b   5. e   6. a   7. d   8. c   9. c   10. b   11. e
12. a   13. c   14. a   15. b   16. c   17. b

COMPLETED ECONOWORD PUZZLE

	I	N	S	T	A	B	I	L	I	T	Y			S	E	A	R	C	H
	N		T												D				I
	C		A			A	N	T	I	C	I	P	A	T	E	D			G
	O		T		R				Y										H
	M		I		A		F	L	U	C	T	U	A	T	I	O	N		E
	E		S		T			L				N							R
			T		I		I	N	D	E	X		F			C			
			I		O			S			R		L	A	B	O	R		
R	E	C	E	N	T					E		A			N			
E			S				I	N	D	I	C	A	T	O	R	S			
C				H						E		I				T			
O	U	T	P	U	T		E	X	P	A	N	S	I	O	N		A		
V		I		R		E				S		N		G	N	P			
E		E		T		A			S			I		C		T			
R	E	D	I	S	T	R	I	B	U	T	I	O	N		P				
Y					N				N			N		R	I	S	E	S	

MONEY AND BANKING

UNIT XI

UNIT IN A NUTSHELL

PART ONE

Film: "All That Glitters is Gold"

Text: Chapter 14

PART TWO

Film: "A Run for Your Money"

Text: Chapter 15 and Chapter 16

What is money? Is gold money? Silver? Large rocks? Shells? Societies have used these and many other commodities as money. Money is what people believe is money. As long as people have confidence in what serves as their money, money will serve as a method of exchanging things, a convenient way to hold savings, and a way to compare the values of things. But when people's confidence in their money weakens, if money can no longer serve its functions in a market economy, money collapses.

The functions that money fulfills are vital to an advanced economy. Without money, complex modern economic systems cannot operate. In addition to simplifying exchanges of goods and services, money makes possible the many credit and savings transactions of advanced economies. Without money we would be forced to return to a cumbersome and costly barter system.

Does money need gold to "back it up"? And what creates money or destroys it? Money is created and destroyed through the normal functioning of the banking system itself. In addition, the central bank in the U.S., the Federal Reserve, has control of tools that affect the U.S. money supply.

NOTE

Material related to the gold standard is included in Chapter 22 in *Economics Today: The Macro View* (which is also Chapter 38 in the combined hardbound edition, *Economics Today*).

UNIT OBJECTIVES

Objectives 1-5 can be met by studying Chapter 14 and viewing "All That Glitters is Gold." After completing Part One, the student should be able to:

1. Define money.

2. List and explain three functions of money.

3. Define the money supply in the U.S.

4. Briefly state the relationship between the amount of money in circulation and the general price level.

5. Describe the structure of the U.S. banking system, including the U.S. central bank: the Federal Reserve System.

Objectives 6-11 can be met by studying Chapters 15 and 16 and viewing "A Run For Your Money." After completing Part Two, the student should be able to:

6. List the functions of the U.S. central bank: the Federal Reserve.

7. Explain what is meant by a fractional reserve banking system and understand how the required reserve ratio is related to money creation.

8. List the steps in the process of money expansion (contraction) following a Federal Reserve open-market committee purchase (sale) of government securities.

9. Explain how the Federal Reserve uses each of its tools to control the money supply in the economy.

10. Since total spending supports total economic activity, recognize the importance of a "credit expansion" or a "credit contraction" in the economy.

11. Explain why the prices of bonds and interest rates move in opposite directions.

PART ONE

UNIT XI ASSIGNMENT: PART ONE

STUDY: Chapter 14, "Money and the Banking System," *Economics Today*

STUDY: Film Summary: "All That Glitters is Gold," *Study Guide*

VIEW: "All That Glitters is Gold"

REVIEW: Chapter 14 Highlights, *Study Guide*

COMPLETE: Fill-in Review *and* Problems, Problems, Problems . . . , *Study Guide*

FILM SUMMARY: "All That Glitters is Gold"

The most basic function of money is as a medium of exchange. The alternative to money is exchange by barter, the direct exchange of goods without the use of money. Barter is cumbersome since it requires a "coincidence of wants." For each one who has goods to exchange, there must be another who has not only the goods the first person wants, but who wants what that individual has to exchange. It is an unwieldy and complex arrangement, and not used in any but the simplest of cultures.

In most societies, people sell goods or services for money, then use the money to buy wanted goods or services. It might seem, at first, as if using money is more complicated since it involves *more* transactions than barter.

But, the truth is, since few persons have the same coincidence of wants, money transactions are simpler.

Yes, money does simplify transactions and also simplifies economic life. But, extra money in itself will not make it possible for people to buy more than the economy can produce; and money complicates the economy (as we've seen earlier) by helping to cause both recession and inflation.

Banking and the use of paper money has evolved in all economies. The process goes something like this. Historically, a commodity regarded as beautiful, useful or valuable for any reason was accepted by all members of a society as a medium of exchange. Many goods have served this function—copper, diamonds, oil, beer, slaves, shells, rocks, cigarettes, tobacco, gold, wives. The valuable commodity fulfilled the functions (some far more easily than others) of money: as a medium of exchange, a store of value and a unit of account. The commodity represented the value of goods so that the goods themselves did not have to be exchanged (a medium of exchange); it could be stored away and brought out later to be used in financial transactions (a store of value); lastly, the commodity served as a measurement of how much things were worth (a unit of account), so that goods could be said to be worth this many shells or cattle. In this way, the commodity fulfilled the important functions of money.

Most commodity money was valued for its own sake, its intrinsic worth. But in all such cases, whatever is used as money comes to be valued for what it will buy—not solely for its own sake. Thus, money becomes a convention and is accepted *because it is acceptable* as money.

As money evolved in commercial economies, the commodity (usually precious metals) was stored for safe-keeping in banks. Eventually, paper, as evidence that the bearer really owned the valued commodity, was used as a simpler-to-handle replacement for the commodity. Paper money, compared to gold or silver, is light and easy to carry. It is also easy to store and can be divided into whatever size units are desired.

As a next step, the paper itself was kept in banks. Gradually, it became more convenient for holders of money deposited in banks to pay others by means of written authorizations (checks). The bank, then, subtracted the amount authorized from the holder's account and added the amount to the account of the bearer of the check. In this way, money was then finally transferred from one bank to another. Ultimately, the commodity backing of the paper money was removed.

It is obvious that the evolution of money has been an involved and long process. From a precious commodity whose stable value was trusted by those who used it, to slips of paper verifying ownership of the commodity, money in an economy now exists largely as entries in bank checking accounts.

The common denominator in each of these evolutionary steps is the society's trust in whatever is used as money. This applies to modern money in the same way as it applied to any of the commodity monies (gold, for example): the basis of the acceptability of money is trust in that money.

As the film commentator says, "Money is what people believe is money; it is whatever people will generally accept in payment for things." Acceptability of money, then, is based on confidence in its value to perform all the functions of money (to serve as a medium of exchange, a unit of account and a store of value). If all other things stay the same, increasing the money supply will very likely raise prices, since money itself does not increase production. Since scarcity determines the value of money, government monitors the supply of money to insure its stability.

A simple definition of the money supply is the total of all the coins, currency and demand deposit accounts in banks, with demand deposits being by far the largest component. Since it is true that money is bank book entries, we can have a clear way to understand how the money supply can be controlled. Anything that can cause these money entries in banks' books to become larger or smaller causes the money supply to change. A banking system under the control of a central bank, such as The Federal Reserve in the United States, can increase or decrease the amount of money in the economy, and hence, have an effect on spending in the economy.

Recall what we have emphasized before: spending is what determines national income. We have carefully identified sectors as sources of spending, analyzed the types of spending done by each sector, and then considered how the sectors interact. All through the earlier discussions, mention of money was minimized; instead, the term "spending" was used, not money. The two terms are related, similar but very different.

In the development of the Keynesian model, when we mentioned the importance of putting more spending into the economy, we meant more buying. More money in the economy does not mean the same thing as more spending. Added spending means that money is used to buy goods and services, inventory, capital equipment or other inputs to production. And, as you know, when there are unemployed resources, increased spending speeds up economic activity.

Now, since we have begun to bring money into our consideration of the macroeconomy, we need to examine the mechanisms of the banking system and monetary control. With regard to the system itself, your text explains that the network of privately owned banks is headed by our central bank, The Federal Reserve (the Fed). Consider, then, that the Fed is actually a bank for banks. It was created to be a source of money for our country's banking system and to hold the reserve deposits of member banks.

The Fed is charged with supplying currency for the economy, holding bank reserves, providing check clearing, acting as the federal government's banker, and supervising banks. However, its most important function is to regulate the money supply. It is in the discharge of this responsibility which brings the Federal Reserve under the most scrutiny, not only by the private economy but, as well, by the Congress. The Fed has a number of powerful tools of money control. (A description of the methods by which the Fed actually exercises its power to manipulate the money supply is reserved for the second part of this unit.)

In this film program, Mr. Aronsteil, is an advocate of the return to a gold standard. In his criticisms of the rising level of inflation, he shows little confidence in our own money. He refers again and again to its drop in value. He blames the policies of the central bank for the inflationary growth of the money supply. Aronsteil feels that, in the past, when Congress enacted fiscal policy by spending programs requiring deficit spending, the central bank "monetarized" the debt by allowing the money supply to increase, thereby helping to create inflation. Mr. Aronsteil does not agree that the U.S. central bank should have the power to control the expansion or contraction of money in the economy.

Mr. Aronsteil is a believer in a gold standard; he brings a mildly hysterical note to his insistence that the only safe commodity in an inflated economy is gold. He says the money supply in a gold-backed monetary system could not be manipulated to create the level of inflation experienced in the last few years. Therefore, he wants the physical limitation of gold to limit the amount of money that can be created.

He is concerned about the direct effect of an increased money supply on the price level. The quantity theory of money and prices states that the price level in the economy is directly proportional to the quantity of money in circulation. (Monetarists who hold this theory believe that control over the total quantity of money is the overriding factor in determining equilibrium national income.)

A surprising number of people are unaware that neither is gold money in the U.S., nor is our money backed by gold. People often express the belief that to really be of value, that is, to truly be money, any nation's currency must ultimately be replaceable by gold. They believe that gold has an inherent or intrinsic value that nothing else can have. Does money still need to be backed up by a precious commodity, such as gold? Does gold have the only "true" value, as the gold bugs in the film insist?

Consider, just what can gold do? Can gold feed, clothe, warm or provide a protective shelter? Not really. Gold is beautiful. It shines, is easily divided into small units, and is mailable, and can be formed into ornaments to hang on the body. It does not rust or corrode, and we find it in ancient graves still shiny and almost unchanged even after thousands of years. Mankind has had a fascination with gold because of these qualities, and it has often served as money partly because of these attributes.

There is another characteristic of gold, which is the most important one. It is severely limited in quantity. There are some who feel that only these physical limitations can prevent governments of men from overextending the supply of their money. This restraint, in turn, would serve as a check on the federal government in its attempt to accomplish programs beyond its own economy's production possibilities. Some do not agree that government should have a large role as stabilizer for the economy. These critics go further and insist that a form of discipline should be placed on policy makers to limit their ability to create spending programs. Therefore, these critics would place a commodity backing of gold to force a limitation of the amount of money created.

We are, however, getting far ahead of ourselves with criticisms of federal spending and the role of the Federal Reserve. Our job next is to see how the Federal Reserve operates to influence the money supply.

CHAPTER 14 HIGHLIGHTS

Defined words are underlined.

I. CHAPTER OVERVIEW: THIS CHAPTER DEALS MORE WITH DEFINITION THAN ANALYSIS. DEFINITIONS ARE GIVEN FOR

   A. money and the functions of money.

   B. the structure of the Federal Reserve System.

II. MONEY IS WHAT WE USE IN EXCHANGE FOR THE THINGS WE WANT TO BUY.

   A. Money has three functions. Money is a

   1. medium of exchange; sellers accept it as a means of payment.

      a. Without money, we would have to barter for goods.

      b. *Barter:* Direct exchange of goods for goods.

   2. unit of accounting; money serves as the standard for valuing things.

   3. store-of-value; money is a convenient form in which to hold savings, or stored-up value.

      a. Money is the most liquid of all assets.

      b. *Liquidity:* A measurement describing how easily an asset can be changed to money without losing its value.

   B. Money is not the same as credit.

   1. *Credit:* Funds or savings made available to borrowers. When credit is made available, debt is created.

   2. Credit can exist in a society without money.

C. There are many definitions of the money supply.

    1. The total of all currency (paper money and coins) and demand deposits held by the public in banks is called M-1.

        a. M-1 is the narrowest definition of the money supply.

        b. By far the largest component of the money supply is demand deposits. *Demand Deposits:* Checking account balances.

    2. A slightly wider definition included M-1, plus savings account deposits which can be automatically transferred to checkable deposits.

D. *Near Monies:* Highly liquid assets that are almost, but not quite money. Near monies are

    1. time deposits in banks,

    2. money market mutual fund shares.

E. Why do people accept money as payment? What "backs up" the money supply?

    1. U.S. money is not "backed up" by gold; money's value depends on the public confidence in the acceptability of money in exchange for goods and services.

    2. Currency has been designated by government as legal tender for all debts.

    3. Money's value depends on its predictability.

        a. Its value must not change abruptly or frequently.

        b. The value of the dollar varies inversely with average prices. If the price index goes up, the value of money goes down.

CHAPTER 14 HIGHLIGHTS

III. CLASSICAL ECONOMISTS SAW A CLOSE LINK BETWEEN THE MONEY SUPPLY AND THE PRICE LEVEL: THE QUANTITY THEORY OF MONEY AND PRICES.

    A. The relationship between the quantity of money and the price level is one of the oldest known in economic thought.

    B. The quantity of money theory can be crudely stated by MV=PQ, where M=money, V=velocity, P=prices, Q=quantity of goods produced.

    C. The concept of income velocity of money (V) refers to the number of times in a year each dollar is used to buy something; a synonymous definition of V is the number of times each dollar flows around the income stream of the economy.

        1. Money is a stock, an amount measured at one time.

        2. Income is a flow of money during a specified time period. (For example, national income is a measure of a flow of money spent and income received.)

        3. The quantity of money theory asserts that V is relatively stable, or constant.

    D. The quantity theory of money and prices states that the level of prices in the economy is directly proportional to the quantity of money in circulation.

    E. The implication of the quantity theory is that control over the total quantity of money is the most important element in trying to control the equilibrium level of national income.

    F. The long-run evidence for the quantity theory is favorable, but in the short run the quantity theory does not predict price changes well.

IV. THE FEDERAL RESERVE SYSTEM—"THE FED"—IS THE CENTRAL BANK. THE FED CONTROLS THE MONEY SUPPLY BY REGULATING THE BANKING SYSTEM.

A. The organization of the Federal Reserve consists of

1. a board of seven governors.

2. twelve Federal Reserve banks, one in each of the twelve Federal Reserve districts of the U.S., plus 25 branch FRBs.

3. The Federal Open Market Committee, composed of the Board of Governors plus five representatives of the Federal Reserve banks.

4. member banks. (The definition of Fed membership is changing under the provisions of the 1980 banking reform legislation.)

   a. Nationally chartered banks are required to be members of the Federal Reserve.

   b. State-chartered banks may choose to be members.

B. Formerly limited to member banks, the Fed is now phasing in a reserve requirement for all banking institutions.

1. *Reserve Requirement:* A certain fraction of a bank's assets that must be held as vault cash, or in non-interest-bearing deposits with the district Fed bank.

2. The 1980 banking reform legislation makes all of the Fed services available to all banking institutions for fees.

C. The Federal Reserve System functions to

1. supply the economy with currency.

2. provide a system of check-clearing operations.

3. hold bank reserves.

4. act as the federal government's banker.

5. supervise banks.

6. regulate the money supply.

FILL-IN REVIEW

Select between the choices underlined or fill in the blank. Cover the answers until you have provided your own.

Money is whatever performs the function of money. In exchange for the things we want to buy, we use _____. Money has three functions. Sellers accept money as a means of payment; in this way, money functions as a medium of _____. (Without money, we would have to directly exchange foods for goods, a method of exchange called _____.) Money serves as a standard for valuing things, both in keeping accounts and for comparing the value of different goods. In this way, money functions as a unit of _____. Money is a convenient form to hold value. This function of money is a store of _____. In sum, the three functions of money are a _____ __ _____, _ ___ __ _____ and a ___ __ _____.

money

exchange

barter

account

value

medium of exchange   a unit of account
store of value

Money consists of currency (paper money and coins) and demand deposit accounts (checking accounts) in banks. The narrowest definition of the money supply is ____ which is the sum of all the _____, and _____ _____ _____. The value of our money

M-1

currency   demand deposit accounts

depends on public _____ in its acceptability. A price index measures the buying power of money over a period of ____. As a price index rises, the value of a dollar goes *up/down.*

confidence

time

down

The quantity theory of money and prices states that the price _____ in an economy is directly proportional to the _____ __ _____ in circulation. In the quantity theory equation MV = PQ, M stands for _____, V stands for _____, P stands for _____ _____ and Q stands for _____ of goods _____. The number of times each dollar flows around the income stream of the economy is called income _____ (V) of _____ (M). By holding V the same and Q the same, the quantity of money (M) can be shown to directly influence the _____ _____ (P).

level

quantity of money

money

velocity price level

quantity

produced

velocity money

price level

The American banking structure is composed of thousands of *privately/publicly* owned commercial banks and the central bank, the _____ _____ _____ (called the Fed). Banks accept demand deposit accounts and make loans to _____ and _____. This ability of the banks to lend out _____ deposited with them is an important influence on the money supply. The Federal

privately

Federal Reserve System

households

firms

money

FILL-IN REVIEW

Reserve regulates how much of their total demand deposits banks may ____ ____. The fraction of the bank's assets which must be held on reserve and not loaned out is called the _____ _____.

loan out

reserve requirement

The organization of the Fed consists of a seven-member policy-making group called the _____ __ _____; twelve Federal Reserve _____ in each of the twelve _____ _____ districts of the U.S.; a Federal _____ _____ Committee; and the privately owned _____ banks.

board of governors
banks   Federal Reserve   Open Market
member

The Fed has numerous functions which include supplying the economy with currency when needed, and providing check-clearing operations. By far the most important function of the Fed is _____ _____ _____.

money supply regulation

PROBLEMS, PROBLEMS, PROBLEMS...

Answers are at the end of this unit.

TRUE-FALSE

Circle either "T" or "F" for each statement.

(T) F 1. Demand deposit accounts are considered money.

T (F) 2. The money supply consists entirely of currency in circulation.

T (F) 3. Barter is the exchange of goods for money.

(T) F 4. The narrowest definition of the money supply is M-1, the total of currency and demand deposits in banks.

T (F) 5. Money is the least liquid asset.

(T) F 6. When sellers accept money as a means of payment, money is being used as a medium of exchange.

(T) F 7. The U.S. money supply is "backed up" by confidence in its acceptability.

(T) F 8. If a price index goes up, the value of money goes down.

(T) F 9. Income velocity of money is the measurement of how many times each dollar is spent in a given year.

(T) F 10. The quantity theory of money states that the level of prices in the economy is directly proportional to the quantity of money in circulation.

T (F) 11. Commercial banks are publicly owned non-profit institutions.

T (F) 12. The Federal Reserve (the Fed) has little control over the banking system.

(T) F 13. The reserve requirement is a fraction of a bank's assets which must not be loaned out.

T (F) 14. Of the many functions of the Fed, the least important is regulation of the money supply.

MATCH-UP

Match each item in the first column with a term in the second column. Use no term more than once.

__g__ 1. A medium of exchange, a unit of account, a store of value

__b__ 2. Regulate the money supply, hold bank reserves, provide a system of check clearing

__j__ 3. The number of times a dollar is spent during a year

__c__ 4. The value of money is backed up by this.

__a__ 5. A direct exchange of goods for goods

__i__ 6. By far the largest component of the money supply

__k__ 7. The total of all currency and demand deposits held by the public

__e__ 8. Highly liquid assets that are almost money, but not quite

__f__ 9. The price level is directly proportional to the quantity of money in circulation.

__h__ 10. One is in each of the Federal Reserve districts.

__d__ 11. A fraction of a bank's assets which must be held as vault cash or in a non-interest-bearing account at the district Fed bank

a. barter
b. functions of the Federal Reserve
c. confidence
d. reserve requirement
e. near monies
f. quantity theory of money and prices
g. functions of money
h. Federal Reserve bank
i. demand deposits
j. income velocity of money
k. money supply M-1

MULTIPLE CHOICE

For each of the following statements, choose the one best alternative.

1. Of the following list of the functions of the Federal Reserve, by far the most important is to

    a. supervise banks.

    b. provide check-clearing operations.

    c. regulate the money supply.

    d. hold bank reserves.

2. The quantity theory of money and prices states that the level of prices in the economy is directly proportional to

    a. the amount of business investment.

    b. the quantity of money in circulation.

    c. the amount of government spending.

    d. the amount of aggregate demand.

3. All of the following are functions of money *except*

    a. medium of exchange.

    b. unit of accounting.

    c. store of value.

    d. regulate the Fed.

4. By far the largest component of the money supply is

    a. gold and silver.

    b. currency.

    c. demand deposits.

    d. coins.

5. The concept of velocity of money refers to
   a. the measurement of money income.
   b. the value of a dollar spent.
   c. the number of times a dollar is spent in a given time period.
   d. the value of money, which depends on predictability.

PART TWO

UNIT XI ASSIGNMENT: PART TWO

STUDY: Chapter 15, "The Process of Money Creation," *Economics Today*

STUDY: Chapter 16, "The Federal Reserve, Monetary Policy, and the Multiplier," *Economics Today*

STUDY: Film Summary: "A Run for Your Money," *Study Guide*

VIEW: "A Run for Your Money"

REVIEW: Chapter 15 Highlights, *Study Guide*

COMPLETE: Fill-in Review *and* Problems, Problems, Problems ... for Chapter 15, *Study Guide*

REVIEW: Chapter 16 Highlights, *Study Guide*

COMPLETE: Fill-in Review *and* Problems, Problems, Problems ... for Chapter 16, *and* Econoword Puzzle, *Study Guide*

FILM SUMMARY: "A Run for Your Money"

When Thomas worries that he is not the success he feels he should be at his advanced age, Karen decides that a new car for him would be just the ego boost he needs. She attempts to take out a loan and buy Thomas the car any "self-respecting executive should be driving." Not only is the car expensive, but credit is tight. The loan application is turned down.

In the interval between the car loan application and Karen finally being told that she will not receive the money, Karen and Thomas learn about the process of money creation. They also learn about the roles of both the banking system and the Federal Reserve in the control of the money supply. What is necessary now is to gain an understanding of the actual mechanism by which the money supply is manipulated by the Federal Reserve.

As we mentioned in the last unit, by far the largest and most important component of the money supply is demand deposit balances. When we discuss the contraction or expansion of the money supply, we do not mean that truckloads of money are being moved around the country or that money is being printed or burned. Instead, think of the process of money expansion as people having more money in their checking accounts and businesses having larger balances in their accounts. The process of money contraction is the opposite.

From your last chapter, you recall that the reserve requirement is the percentage of a bank's total deposits that must be held on reserve with the Fed and not loaned out. Before we trace through the process of money expansion, be aware that the reserve requirement is not imposed on the use of bank reserves to insure that banks will have enough money to pay off depositors who want to withdraw their money. Not at all. The reserve requirement has a different and extremely important purpose: it is to limit the possible expansion of the money supply. As Thomas says, if there were no reserve requirement there would be no limitation on the possible expansion of money. Thus, the reserve requirement fulfills the function some people still believe should be held by gold. That is, it limits the supply of money.

The most-used tool of the Fed is open market operations—the buying and selling of government securities. The Fed, by means of the reserve requirement, moves reserves in and out of the reserve accounts of banks by open market operations and, thereby, changes the money supply. The money supply can expand through the action of the Federal Reserve in its open-market buying of bonds. We will trace the process of how banks create money.

In the first step in the process, the Fed purchases a bond on the open market from a private business, which it pays for by check (drawn on itself). The check goes into the bank account of the person who has sold the Fed the bond. The deposit increases that bank's reserve account and expands the amount of reserves that the bank has available for loans. As new loans are granted, they are in turn deposited in other banks throughout the economy. These new monies increase the reserve position of each bank receiving deposits, so that even more loans may be granted.

Recall, again, that money is mostly the demand deposits on account books of banks and notice what is happening as loans are granted: the total demand deposits in the system increase. According to our definition of the money supply, what actually happens is that the total money supply is expanding. New money has been created through the process of granting loans, and with it, new potential buying power.

And what halts this process of expansion of the money supply? The reserve requirement does. Since a percentage of each new deposit must be kept in reserve with the Fed, the balance that moves through the banking system constantly diminishes until finally no new loans can be made until a new deposit enters the system.

The process of money contraction is accomplished in exactly the reverse of expansion. The Fed, through open-market operations, sells securities. In this way, reserves are pulled out of the system, lowering the quantity of loans banks are able to grant.

What kind of bank deposit has the effect of increasing the money supply? Remember that no new money can be created when Bank X receives a check deposited to it that is drawn on another bank in the banking system. In that case, an increase in the reserves of Bank X is exactly offset by a decrease in the other bank's reserves.

The deposit that affects the money supply is one that comes from outside the banking system; for example, from the expansionary open market operations of the Fed. Recall that, when the Fed buys a bond from an individual or institution, it adds to the bank reserves of the person or institution selling the Fed a bond. That bank can now increase the amounts of loans it makes by the amount of new reserves it now has (minus the reserve requirement, of course). This action allows the money supply to expand. And how far can the expansion extend? By the deposit expansion multiplier times the new deposit. Check your text and Chapter Highlights to be sure that the multiplier is directly based on the reserve requirement.

We are now ready to consider the relationship of money to spending. Recall from earlier units how businesses decide to invest, and also consider what helps households decide to make major purchases such as cars and homes. It is the level of income for households, of course, and for both household and businesses, it is the interest rate—the cost of borrowing the money with which to make the purchases. If the interest rate is low, wouldn't *you* consider a new purchase? Other households and businesses use a decision-making process much like yours. Yes, the interest rate is very important in determining the profitability of business investment spending.

You already know how spending changes national income. You know that the economy depends on spending and that the interest rate is related inversely to the quantity of money in circulation. At this point, you may be thinking about the ways that changes in the money supply can be used by the Fed to affect national income. Monetary policy, then, is the name given to changes in the money supply undertaken by the Fed to affect national income.

We can now consider how monetary policy can work to change aggregate demand in the economy. Let's assume that the Fed wants to encourage businesses to build new plants, new capital machinery and add to inventory. As we've said, the interest rate is one of the major determinants businesses use to decide whether or not to invest. Through making money easier to get, that is, by lowering the interest rate, businesses may be encouraged to do what is needed to create additional jobs. And with more jobs comes additional income. The additional income, as we know from earlier units, has a multiplier effect on re-spending which, in turn, raises national income still further. So, we have identified interest rates as a way a change in the money supply is transmitted into a change in national income.

Monetary policy becomes the other major method (along with fiscal policy) for the federal government to stabilize the economy by raising national income when there is a recessionary gap or, when there is one, by closing an inflationary gap. The Fed was created to monitor the nation's money, and through using its tools, the Fed carries out the monetary policy for the nation. Although the regulation of the money supply is a function of government, it is carried out by the Fed which is set up as an independent agency. Theoretically, it can be as free as it wishes to decide monetary policy and can, through the use of its tools, either make money easy to get, or put the economy into a credit crunch.

And how well have they done? How effective has the monetary policy been? It is not simple to judge. The use of monetary policy has been highly criticized and occasionally praised. In your next unit, you will look at another view of the role of money.

CHAPTER 15 HIGHLIGHTS

Defined words are underlined.

I. CHAPTER OVERVIEW: HOW THE FEDERAL RESERVE AND THE BANKING SYSTEM TOGETHER DETERMINE THE MONEY SUPPLY.

   A. The Fed changes the money supply by actions that have a multiplier effect.

   B. A money multiplier process expands or contracts the money supply by means of the fractional reserve banking system.

II. THE U.S. HAS A FRACTIONAL RESERVE BANKING SYSTEM: ONLY PART OF TOTAL DEPOSITS ARE KEPT ON HAND AS RESERVES, THE REST MAY BE LOANED OUT.

   A. The Federal Reserve requires banks to maintain a specific percentage of their customer deposits as reserves.

      1. By law, member banks can count only deposits held at the district Fed bank and vault cash as reserves.

2. *Required Reserves:* The dollar value of a bank's deposits it cannot lend or invest.

3. *Excess Reserves:* The difference between legal and required reserves. Banks make loans from their excess reserves.

B. A bank's balance sheet is a summary statement of its assets, liabilities and net worth. *Asset:* Anything of value that is owned. *Liability:* Anything that is owed.

1. Assets of banks are total reserves, loans and securities.

2. Liabilities of banks are demand deposits, time deposits and borrowings from the Federal Reserve.

3. Assets minus liabilities equals *net worth.*

III. THE ROLE OF BANKS, EXCESS RESERVES AND THE FEDERAL RESERVE IN DETERMINING THE SIZE OF THE MONEY SUPPLY

A. The Federal Open Market Committee buys and sells government securities (bonds) in the open market. This is done to increase or lower reserves in the banking system.

1. The Fed buys bonds to increase banking reserves in the system. Step by step, the money expansion process works as follows:

a. The Fed buys a bond from a business.

b. The Fed pays by a check drawn on itself.

c. The check is deposited in a bank by the business selling the bond.

d. The reserves of the bond-seller's bank increase.

e. The excess reserves of the bond-seller's bank increase.

f. The Bank can make loans from its excess reserves.

CHAPTER 15 HIGHLIGHTS

     g. The new loan recipients deposit the loan in a bank.

     h. This same process occurs in many, many banks, expanding the money supply.

 2. The Fed sells bonds to lower banking reserves in the system. Step by step, the process to lower the money supply works as follows.

     a. The Fed sells a bond to an individual or company.

     b. The purchaser pays by check drawn on its account in the bank.

     c. When the check clears, the reserves of the bond-buyer's bank are lowered by the amount of the check.

     d. The excess reserves of that bank fall.

     e. This same process occurs in many, many banks.

     f. The reserves of the entire banking system are lowered, automatically lowering excess reserves.

     g. Banks' abilities to make loans are curtailed, since banks grant loans from their excess reserves.

     h. The money supply falls.

 3. The Fed can buy or sell bonds as it wishes.

     a. When it buys bonds, it announces a price attractive enough to cause bond-holders to sell.

     b. When it sells bonds, it lowers the price until there are buyers.

B. The relationship between reserves and total deposits

 1. How can a single bank make loans?

- a. If one bank has excess reserves, it can make loans; if it does not have excess reserves, it cannot, since loaned money soon leaves the bank granting the loan.

- b. If there are no excess reserves in the banking system, a single bank cannot add to the money supply. A transfer of deposits from one bank to another does not increase the total amount of deposits in the system.

2. How are deposits in the entire banking system created?

- a. Total deposits in the system directly affect the amount of reserves which must be held.

- b. Deposits are simply number entries on the bank's records.

- c. When money from outside the banking system is added to a checking account of a bank, new deposits are created. (For example, a check from the Fed is made as payment for a bond).

- d. The new deposit increases reserves, and therefore increases excess reserves.

- e. With new excess reserves, the bank receiving the deposit is able to make loans.

- f. When loans are made from the bank's excess reserves, the loans soon leave the granting bank to be deposited in other banks in the system.

- g. The new deposits, created by the re-spending of each loan, spread throughout the banking system, creating additional deposits. (Recall that the largest part of the money supply is demand deposit accounts.)

- h. The money supply can expand automatically by this loan-granting process from an introduction of new reserves into the system.

C. The amount which the money supply can change with changes in reserves is determined by the required reserve ratio. *Required Reserve Ratio:* The percentage of a bank's total deposits which must be kept on reserve at the Fed.

1. For simplicity, assume that the Fed imposes a required reserve ratio of 20 percent, or ⅕ on all banks.

2. With new reserves coming into the system, only 80 percent, or 4 out of 5 dollars can be loaned out. One dollar out of 5 must be kept on reserve.

3. The reserve ratio must be obeyed by all banks, so that as deposits are created by new loan money moving through the system, ⅕ of each deposit created must stay behind in the bank and not be loaned out.

4. The ⅕ reserve that must not be loaned out, limits the expansion of the money supply.

5. The maximum potential change in the money supply due to a change in reserves is called the *Deposit Expansion Multiplier*.

6. The formula for the maximum deposit multiplier is $\left(\dfrac{1}{\text{required reserve ratio}}\right)$.

Example: Required reserve ratio of 20 percent equals ⅕, so that the maximum deposit multiplier $= \left(\dfrac{1}{1/5}\right)$ or 5.

1. With new reserves coming into the system, the maximum demand deposit money that can be created is the new reserves times 5.

D. The deposit expansion multiplier could be termed the deposit change multiplier, because, with loss of reserves from the system, bank deposits contract.

1. When the Fed sells bonds in the open market, reserves in banks are lowered.

2. With fewer excess reserves, banks cannot lend as much as before.

   a. Banks may be forced to call in loans; the rate of new loans will decline.

   b. Money becomes "hard to get."

3. Deposit expansion may become deposit contraction.

E. In the "real world," the deposit expansion is smaller than the maximum.

1. There are leakages out of the money stream.

   a. People may want to hold currency.

   b. Banks may choose not to loan out all their excess reserves.

2. The money multiplier is between 2½ and 3.

FILL-IN REVIEW

Select between the choices underlined or fill in the blank. Cover the answers until you have provided your own.

Note: *The term "banks" will be used to represent all depository institutions.*

fractional	The U.S. has a _____ reserve banking
Only part	system. *All/Only part* of total deposits are
reserves	kept on hand as _____, the rest may be
	loaned out. The fractional reserve banking
	system, together with the Federal Reserve, op-

FILL-IN REVIEW

erates to enlarge or contract the money supply through the granting or cancellations of loans. The Federal Reserve requires banks to maintain a specific percentage of their customer _____ as reserves. By law, member banks can claim only deposits held at the district _____ _____ (or ___) banks, as reserves. These are called actual _____. The dollar value of a bank's deposits that it cannot lend or invest is called _____ _____. Actual monies beyond required reserves are called _____ _____. Banks may make loans from their excess reserves.

deposits

Federal Reserve   Fed
reserves

required reserves

excess reserves

The Federal Reserve Open Market Committee buys and sells government _____, (_____) in the open market to influence the size of the _____ supply. (Recall that the largest part of our money supply is demand deposits in banks.) Through controlling the amount of _____ in the banking system, the Fed can allow changes in the money supply.

securities   bonds
money

reserves

When the Fed buys bonds, the Fed pays for the bond by a _____ drawn on itself. The check is then deposited in a _____ by the person or company selling the bond to the ___. With the new deposit, the bank's reserves in-

check
bank
Fed

excess	crease, raising the allowable deposits that banks may use to make loans from its _____ reserves. With the increase in excess reserves
loans	the bank now may grant more _____, creating demand deposits. When the Fed buys bonds, this process continues throughout the banking system enabling the money supply to *in-*
increase	*crease/decrease*.
lowers	When the Fed sells bonds, it *lowers/ raises* the reserves in the banking system. The
excess	lower reserves also cut down the _____ reserves, a process which reduces the banks' abilities to loan money, and in that way cuts
demand	down on their abilities to create _____
deposits no	_____. The Fed has *great/no* problems buying or selling bonds. It is able to raise or
price	lower the _____ of the bonds, whichever is the goal of the Fed, until they are sold or bought.
deposits	A single bank can create _____ only
lend (or loan)	when it has excess reserves to _____. A single bank cannot create deposits by granting
loans	_____ when it has no excess reserves. When money from outside the banking system is
created	added, new deposits are _____. A check
Fed	from the ___ in payment for a bond is an ex-
reserves	ample of new _____ flowing into the system.

FILL-IN REVIEW

The amount the money supply can change is determined by the _____ _____ ____. With a ratio of 20% or ⅕, one dollar out of every _ must be kept on reserve and *not loaned out*/*loaned out*. When a bank grants a loan it creates a _____ _____ account for the person who obtains the loan. When that person writes a _____ on the newly created demand deposit account, that check is deposited in another _____. In the new bank, more _____ have been created, and therefore, more _____ _____. Since banks lend from their excess reserves, that bank now has an increased ability to grant _____, creating _____ _____ _____. This process goes on, and on, through the economy, until the reserve requirement has finally limited the increase in deposit expansion to a maximum of $\left(\dfrac{1}{\text{required reserve ratio}}\right)$.

required
reserve ratio
5
not loaned out

demand
deposit

check

bank
reserves
excess reserves

loans *demand deposit*
accounts

PROBLEMS, PROBLEMS, PROBLEMS . . .

Answers are at the end of this unit.

TRUE-FALSE

Circle either "T" or "F" for each statement.

T (F) 1. Banks increase the money supply by lending their required reserves.

T (F) 2. The money supply is made up entirely of the cash you hold, and cash in bank vaults.

(T) F 3. Banks make income by loaning out part of their depositors' checking account deposits.

(T) F 4. A bank is not likely to make loans unless it has excess reserves.

T (F) 5. Through open market operations of buying and selling bonds, the Fed can destroy existing reserves, but cannot create new reserves.

(T) F 6. In order for the money supply to expand, there must be excess reserves, and people must be willing to borrow.

(T) F 7. The deposit expansion multiplier is equal to the reciprocal of the required reserve ratio.

(T) F 8. Banks are legally required to keep a certain fraction of their reserves; the rest they may either loan or invest.

(T) F 9. The deposits in the Federal Reserve Banks are the reserves which the member banks have deposited there.

(T) F 10. A change in reserves coming into or leaving the banking system can result in a change in the money supply.

T **(F)** 11. A Federal Reserve sale of bonds in an open-market operation increases the money supply.

T **(F)** 12. With a required ratio of 20 percent or ⅕, the deposit expansion multiplier will be 10.

(T) F 13. The deposit expansion multiplier is the reciprocal of the required reserve ratio.

T **(F)** 14. The money supply cannot be influenced by the level of reserves.

MATCH-UP

Match each item in the first column with a term in the second column. Use no term more than once.

__e__ 1. The Federal Reserve Open Market Committee buying or selling government securities (bonds) in the open market

__f__ 2. A summary statement of a bank's assets, liabilities and net worth

__c__ 3. A system in which only part of member banks' total deposits are kept on hand as reserves, and the rest permitted to be loaned out

__g__ 4. The maximum potential change in the money supply due to a change in reserves is this.

__h__ 5. The deposit expansion multiplier when the required reserve ratio is 20 percent or ⅕

__b__ 6. Reserves minus required reserves

__a__ 7. The percentage of a bank's total deposits which must be kept on reserve at the Fed

__d__ 8. The major purposes of the reserve requirement

a. required reserve ratio

b. excess reserves

c. the U.S. fractional reserve banking system

d. money supply control

e. open market operations

f. a bank's balance sheet

g. deposit expansion multiplier

h. 5

MULTIPLE CHOICE

For each of the following statements, choose the one best alternative.

1. Why do people accept paper dollars in payment?

    a. Dollars are backed by the promise of government to redeem them in gold.

    b. Dollars are backed by silver.

    c. Because they are confident they can use them to buy something.

    d. People are gullible and don't understand that paper money isn't really money.

2. The extent to which the money supply can change when the banking system's reserves are changed is given by

    a. the exchange in reserves.

    b. the Federal Reserve Open Market Committee.

    c. the deposit expansion multiplier.

    d. the 12 Federal Reserve District banks.

3. All of the following statements about the Fed and the money supply are correct *except* one. Choose that one.

    a. Decisions of the Open Market Committee can directly influence reserves in the banking system.

    b. The real world money multiplier is less than the given formula would indicate.

    c. A member bank is required to lend out all of its excess reserves.

    d. The multiple expansion process is the maximum potential change in the money supply due to a change in reserves.

4. A single bank must meet a 20 percent reserve requirement. Assuming a bank currently has no excess reserves and someone walks in with $8,000 in deposit money (a Fed check for example), the maximum amount of new loans that the banking system can create is

a. $6,400.

b. $32,000.

c. $40,000.

d. $1,600.

5. The impact of the process of the multiple expansion of money may be limited by

   a. the desire of the public to hold more currency.

   b. banks' concern with maintaining liquidity, keeping them from lending all their excess reserves.

   c. the reluctance of businesses to borrow.

   d. All of the above will limit the money expansion.

   e. None of the above, the multiple expansion process always continues to the maximum.

6. A single bank cannot lend out an amount greater than

   a. its value of securities.

   b. its current cash holdings.

   c. its required reserves.

   d. its excess reserves.

   e. its reserve ratio.

7. Suppose a bank has a 15 percent reserve requirement and you deposited $100 in your checking account. Which of the following statements is/are true?

   a. This bank could lend out a maximum of $850.

   b. Excess reserves increase by $15.

   c. Excess reserves increase by $85.

   d. Required reserves increase by $85.

   e. All of the above are true.

8. Suppose a commercial banking system has $200,000 of outstanding demand deposits and actual reserves of $40,000. If the reserve ratio is 10 percent, the banking system can expand the supply of money by the maximum amount of

   a. $160,000.
   (b.) $200,000.
   c. $40,000.
   d. $20,000.

9. A single bank with $5,000 in excess reserves, facing a reserve requirement of 25 percent, can safely extend loans by a maximum of

   a. $1,250.
   (b.) $5,000.
   c. $20,000.
   d. $25,000.

10. The Safeplace Commercial Bank has $2,000 in excess reserves and faces a reserve ratio of 10 percent. The bank must have

    a. $50,000 in demand deposit liabilities and $500 in actual reserves.
    b. $50,000 in demand deposit liabilities and $5,000 in actual reserves.
    c. $50,000 in demand deposit liabilities and $2,500 in actual reserves.
    (d.) $50,000 in demand deposit liabilities and $7,000 in actual reserves.

CHAPTER 16 HIGHLIGHTS

Defined words are underlined.

I. CHAPTER OVERVIEW

   A. Methods of controlling the money supply

   B. How changes in money supply influence other changes in the economy: a Keynesian interpretation.

1. A model of demand and supply for money

2. How changes in the money supply alter national income.

II. TOOLS OF MONETARY POLICY USED BY THE FEDERAL RESERVE ARE OPEN MARKET OPERATIONS, CHANGING THE RESERVE REQUIREMENT, AND CHANGING THE DISCOUNT RATE.

Monetary Policy: Influencing the economy through control of money and interest rates.

A. The Fed changes the money supply by changing reserves in the banking system through open market operations. *Open Market Operations:* The buying and selling of government securities to affect the money supply.

1. A sale of government securities results in a decrease in reserves and leads to a multiple contraction of the money supply. (See Chapter 15 Highlights.)

2. A purchase of government securities results in an increase in reserves and leads to a multiple expansion of the money supply. (See Chapter 15 Highlights.)

B. The Fed may change the money supply by changing the discount rate. *Discount Rate:* The interest rate the Fed charges member banks on loans of reserves.

1. When a bank must pay a high rate for borrowed reserves, it is less likely to borrow and will charge an even higher rate for loans.

2. If a bank may borrow reserves at a low rate, it may make loans at a low rate.

C. The Fed may change the money supply by changing the reserve requirement.

1. The deposit expansion multiplier is the reciprocal (the "upside down") of the reserve requirement. (See Chapter 15 Highlights.)

a. The maximum amount the money supply can change is the dollar amount of new reserves entering the system times the deposit expansion multiplier.

b. With a reserve requirement of 40 percent or $\frac{1}{5}$, the deposit expansion multiplier is 5 (the "upside down" of the reserve reqirement).

c. With a reserve requirement of 10 percent or $\frac{1}{10}$, the deposit expansion multiplier is 10.

2. To increase the money supply, the Fed can lower the reserve requirement.

a. Banks immediately have more excess reserves.

b. Loans may now be made from excess reserves, increasing demand deposits in the system.

c. With a lower reserve requirement, the deposit expansion multiplier increases, increasing still more the banking system's demand deposits.

3. To lower the money supply, the Fed can raise the reserve requirement. (Each step in the expansion process listed above is reversed.)

4. Changing the reserve requirement can result in large changes of the money supply, and is not used often by the Fed.

III. THE ROLE OF MONEY IN THE KEYNESIAN MODEL

A. According to Keynes, there are three reasons for holding money: transaction demand, precautionary demand and speculative demand. (The term "demand" here doesn't mean an intention to buy something. It only means the decision to hold money instead of some other asset.)

1. *Transaction Demand:* People hold money to use for buying products and assets. Since people spend more as incomes rise, this demand goes up with income.

2. *Precautionary Demand:* People hold money for use in emergencies.

3. *Speculative Demand:* Related to the price and the expected changes in prices of other assets.

   a. Speculation involves buying and selling assets (bonds, stocks) based on what the buyer expects will happen to these asset prices.

   b. If the asset price is expected to fall, potential buyers will hold money until the price of the asset rises.

   c. If the asset price is expected to rise, buyers use money to buy it before the rise.

B. The speculative demand for money is closely related to the interest rate.

   1. What we pay for holding money (the opportunity cost) is the interest we could have earned on it.

   2. The higher the interest rate the less money will be demanded but the more other financial assets will be demanded.

   3. The price of a bond is inversely related to the interest rate.

      a. Keynes believed that when people are holding more money than they want, they buy bonds to earn interest.

      b. This decrease in the quantity of money demanded leads to an increase in demand for bonds.

      c. The increase in demand for bonds causes their prices to rise.

      d. Bonds pay a fixed amount of interest (yield) on their "face value" no matter what is paid for them. (For example: A $1,000 bond that pays $100 dollars a year has an interest yield of 10 percent. If the price of the bond is forced up to $2,000, it still pays $100, but now its yield is 5 percent.)

      e. The same process goes on all over the economy, so that bond prices are inversely related to interest rates. As their prices go up, the interest yields go down; as their prices go down, the interest yields go up.

C. Adding monetary policy to the Keynesian model: changing the interest rate affects investment, which changes national income.

    1. Investment is undertaken by businesses in the hope of making a profit.

      a. The hoped-for profit must exceed the interest rate paid for loans to buy capital goods.

      b. The higher the interest rate (other things being equal) the lower the amount of investment.

    2. The Fed can use monetary policy to attempt to change national income by influencing the money supply and the interest rate. (See Chapter 15 Highlights.)

      a. Through open market operations, the size of the money supply is expanded (or contracted) by increases (or decreases) in loans.

      b. The Fed also can change the discount rate or change the reserve requirement, to affect the money supply and interest rates.

    3. Because the interest rate is the cost of borrowing, investment falls as interest rates rise and investment rises as interest rates fall.

FILL-IN REVIEW

Select between the choices underlined or fill in the blank. Cover your answers until you have provided your own.

	To develop the Keynesian role of money in the economy we begin with a discussion of the tools of monetary policy used by the Fed.
open-market operations reserve requirement discount rate	Three tools of monetary policy used by the Federal Reserve are: ____-_____ _____, changing the _____ _____, and changing the _____ ____.
reserves *securities (or bonds)* *contraction* *increase* *expansion*	Through open-market operations, the Fed changes _____ in the banking system. A sale of government _____ results in lowered reserves and leads to a multiple _____ of the money supply. On the other hand, a purchase of government securities leads to an _____ in reserves and a multiple _____ of the money supply.
discount *opposite*	The interest rate the Fed charges member banks on loans of reserves is called the _____ rate. An increase in the discount rate makes it harder for banks to borrow, therefore, making it harder to grant loans. For a decrease in the discount rate the <u>same</u>/

opposite is true. As you recall, the money supply changes through the amount of loans extended by banks.

A seldom used tool of the Fed is the change of the _____ _____. With a   *reserve requirement*
reserve requirement of 20%, or ⅕, the deposit expansion multiplier is __. With a reserve requirement of 10% or 1/10, the deposit expan-   *5*
sion multiplier is __. The deposit expansion   *10*
multiplier is the _____ of the reserve re-   *reciprocal*
quirement. When the reserve requirement is expressed as a fraction, ⅕ for example, flipping it "upside down" produces the deposit
_____ _____. The deposit expan-   *expansion multiplier*
sion multiplier goes down as the reserve requirement goes *down/up*. When the Fed   *up*
changes the reserve requirement, *very large/*   *very large*
small changes in the money supply can result.

Of the Fed's three tools for accomplishing
_____ policy, the one that is used the   *monetary*
most freely is ____-_____ _____.   *open-market operations*
The Fed buys or sells government _____   *securities (or bonds)*
almost continuously throughout the year to
regulate the _____ supply.   *money*

We are using Keynesian monetary economics to discuss how changes in the _____   *money* supply affect the economy. According to _____, there are three reasons for holding money.

The first is the desire to hold money for day-to-day use, or _____ demand for money. People also hold money for use in emergencies. This demand is called _____ demand for money. The third reason for holding money is related to prices and the expected changes in prices of alternative assets. This demand is called _____ demand for money. This speculative demand for money is closely related to the _____ rate. The higher the interest rate, the *less/more* money will be demanded. As interest rates go up, people will not want to hold as much money and instead will buy _____, since bonds yield _____ payments. The increase in the demand for bonds pushes bond prices *up/down*. Since bonds pay a *fixed/variable* amount of interest on their face value, when the price of the bonds is pushed up, the actual interest yield goes *up/down*. What is important to remember is that as the open market prices of bonds go up, the interest yields earned by the buyers of these bonds go down. All the money and _____ markets

FILL-IN REVIEW

are closely tied together, so that changes in _____ rates affect all bond markets. If interest rates rise, bond prices ___; if bond prices rise, interest rates ___.

interest
fall
fall

In the Keynesian model, the changes in interest rates are linked to changes in _____. Investment is undertaken in the hopes of increased _____. High interest rates diminish the chances of profit. If businesses can borrow money at low interest rates, investment *rises/falls*. If interest rates are high, investment *rises/falls*.

investment
profit

rises
falls

Recall from earlier chapters that the multiplier will enlarge the effect of new investment by a _____ amount to change national income. In this way, monetary policy affects investment through the _____ rate, and changes in investment have a _____ effect on national income and GNP.

multiplied

interest
multiplied

FILL-IN TABLE

Fill in the following table to show how each of the listed tools of the Fed can affect the money supply. Use either the word "expansion" or "contraction" to define what is happening to the money supply.

FED POLICY	ACTION	EFFECT ON MONEY SUPPLY
Reserve Requirement	Increase	1. contraction
Reserve Requirement	Decrease	2. expansion
Discount Rate	Increase	3. contraction
Discount Rate	Decrease	4. expansion
Open Market Operations	Buy bonds	5. expansion
Open Market Operations	Sell bonds	6. contraction

PROBLEMS, PROBLEMS, PROBLEMS...

Answers are at the end of this unit.

TRUE-FALSE

Circle either "T" of "F" for each statement.

T **(F)** 1. The Fed's most used tool of monetary policy is changing the reserve requirement.

(T) F 2. There is an inverse relationship between the price of bonds and interest rates.

T **(F)** 3. To expand the money supply, the Fed sells government securities in open market operations.

(T) F 4. To expand the money supply, the Fed sells government securities in open market operations.

(T) F 5. The Fed may change the money supply by changing the reserve requirement.

T **(F)** 6. With a reserve requirement of 20 percent, or $\frac{1}{5}$, the deposit expansion multiplier is 2.

(T) F 7. When the Fed increases the reserve requirement, the money supply will contract.

T **(F)** 8. According to Keynes, there is no reason for holding money.

T **(F)** 9. Changes in the money supply cannot affect interest rates.

(T) F 10. Monetary policy is used to attempt to close inflationary or recessionary gaps.

T **(F)** 11. Fixed-interest bonds rise in value when the interest rate rises.

(T) F 12. The amount of investment businessmen want to undertake is partly determined by the interest rate.

MATCH-UP

Match each item in the first column with a term in the second column. Use no term more than once.

__f__ 1. Influencing the economy through control of money and interest rates

__h__ 2. This monetary policy tool of the Fed can result in large changes in the money supply and is not used often.

__d__ 3. The desire to hold money for unforeseen future needs or emergencies

__c__ 4. The desire to hold money in order to take advantage of an expected drop in the price of a financial asset

__e__ 5. The interest rate the Fed charges member banks for loans of reserves

__b__ 6. The buying and selling of government bonds by the Federal Reserve System for the purpose of changing the money supply

__g__ 7. The desire to hold money for day-to-day expenses

__a__ 8. The price of bonds is inversely related to this.

__i__ 9. The agency of the federal government with the power to alter the money supply

a. the interest rate
b. open market operations
c. speculative demand for money
d. precautionary demand for money
e. discount rate
f. monetary policy
g. transaction demand for money
h. changing the reserve requirement
i. the Federal Reserve

MULTIPLE CHOICE

For each of the following statements, choose the one best alternative.

1. Which of the following is *not* a policy tool of the Federal Reserve?
   - **a.** fiscal policy ✓
   - **b.** open market operations
   - **c.** changing the discount rate
   - **d.** changing the reserve requirement

2. Which of the tools of the Fed is *not* used often because a small change in it can result in excessive changes of the money supply?
   - **a.** open market operations
   - **b.** reserve requirement ✓
   - **c.** discount rate
   - **d.** All of the above result in excessive changes.

3. A sale of government bonds results in
   - **a.** an increase in reserves and a multiple contraction of the money supply.
   - **b.** a decrease in reserves and a multiple expansion of the money supply.
   - **c.** a decrease in reserves and a multiple contraction of the money supply. ✓
   - **d.** none of the above

4. To lower the money supply, the Fed can
   - **a.** lower the reserve requirement.
   - **b.** lower the discount rate.
   - **c.** buy bonds in open market operations.
   - **d.** raise the reserve requirement. ✓

5. The entire banking system has an excess reserve of $800. After making new loans of $3,200, the system is just meeting its reserve requirement. This means the required reserve ratio is

   a. 10 percent.

   b. 20 percent.

   c. 25 percent.

   d. 40 percent.

6. A depositor puts $1,000 cash in a bank. The reserve ratio is 25 percent. The banks send the $1,000 to the Federal Reserve Bank. As a result, the reserves and excess reserves of the bank have increased respectively by

   a. $1,000 and $250.

   b. $1,000 and $750.

   c. $1,025 and $1,000.

   d. $750 and $1,000.

7. Which of the following is *not* one of the Keynesian demands for money?

   a. consumption demand

   b. transactions demand

   c. precautionary demand

   d. speculative demand

8. When monetary policy is added to the Keynesian model, the change in interest rate affects which of the following the most?

   a. consumption

   b. investment

   c. government spending

   d. exports abroad

ECONOWORD PUZZLE

CLUES ACROSS

3. Paper money and coins
4. If a bank may borrow reserves at a low rate, it may make loans at a _____ rate.
6. Initials for savings account
7. The Fed may change the money supply by changing _____ in the banking system.
9. He said there are three reasons for holding money: transactions, precautionary and speculative demands.
10. Raising reserve requirements will lead to a _____ of the money supply.
13. Unit XI is all about controlling its supply
14. The United States monetary unit
16. The buying and selling of government securities to affect the money supply is open _____ operations.
17. Initials for loan account
18. The discount rate is the _____ rate the Fed charges member banks on loans of reserves.
19. Gold or money's commodity backing was originally stored here, now we keep demand deposit accounts here.

CLUES DOWN

1. It's what an actor does on stage. A lowering of the reserve requirement will _____ to increase the money supply.
2. The majority of the money supply is demand _____ in banks.
4. A bank extends it to you after having secured your obligation to pay it back.
5. A certain fraction of deposits are kept as reserves in our _____ reserve system.
6. The central bank of the U.S., plus a network of private banks is the Federal Reserve _____.
8. Lowering the reserve requirement can result in an _____ of the money supply.
11. When the Fed buys or sells government bonds to regulate the money supply it is using open-market _____.
12. Economists and strikers are fond of this word. Keynes gave us three kinds of this as reasons for holding money.
15. The earnings on money is an interest _____.

ANSWERS TO STUDY QUESTIONS

PART ONE

TRUE-FALSE
1. T 2. F 3. F 4. T 5. F 6. T 7. T 8. T 9. T 10. T
11. F 12. F 13. T 14. F

MATCH-UP
1. g 2. b 3. j 4. c 5. a 6. i 7. k 8. e 9. f
10. h 11. d

MULTIPLE CHOICE
1. c 2. b 3. d 4. c 5. c

PART TWO: Text Chapter 15

TRUE-FALSE
1. F 2. F 3. T 4. T 5. F 6. T 7. T 8. T 9. T 10. T
11. F 12. F 13. T 14. F

MATCH-UP
1. e 2. f 3. c 4. g 5. h 6. b 7. a 8. d

MULTIPLE CHOICE
1. c 2. c 3. c 4. b 5. d 6. d 7. c 8. b 9. b 10. d

PART TWO: Text Chapter 16

TRUE-FALSE
1. F 2. T 3. F 4. T 5. T 6. F 7. T 8. F 9. F 10. T
11. F 12. T

MATCH-UP
1. f 2. h 3. d 4. c 5. e 6. b 7. g 8. a 9. i

MULTIPLE CHOICE
1. a 2. b 3. c 4. d 5. c 6. b 7. a 8. b

COMPLETED ECONOWORD PUZZLE

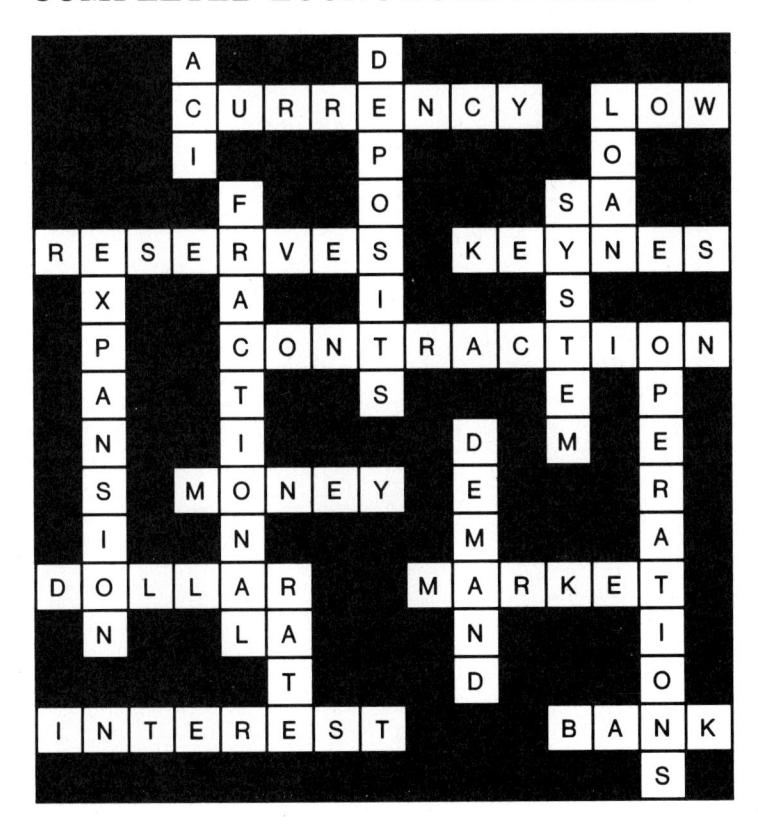

THE DILEMMA AND POLICIES OF STABILIZATION

UNIT XII

UNIT IN A NUTSHELL

PART ONE

Film: "Karen Goes Political"

Text: Chapter 17

PART TWO

Film: "All of the People, All of the Time"

Text: Chapter 18

There is another way of viewing money's role in the economy—the monetarist approach. Monetarists hold that it is fundamentally the money supply that determines the price level and the amount of economic activity in the economy. The monetarists disagree with the use of easy and tight money policies to change the "ups" and "downs" of the business cycle. That is, they disagree with the use of discretionary monetary policy.

Monetarists affirm that only a gradual increase of money, along with increased economic productivity, will assure stability. We can now contrast these two basic points-of-view about how the economy works and begin to consider whether or not either is adequate to fully explain the modern dilemma of inflationary recession.

Has the dynamic interaction between inflation and unemployment been a result of expansionary monetary and fiscal policy that attempts to hold unemployment below a "natural rate"? When inflation is persistent, don't workers and investors adapt their expectations and change their wage and price demands accordingly? Further, when people expect policy makers to alter monetary or fiscal policy, do they recall past experience and act according to their own rational expectations of what will happen in the economy?

UNIT OBJECTIVES

Objectives 1–5 can be met by studying Chapter 17 and viewing "Karen Goes Political." After completing Part One, the student should be able to:

1. Define monetarism and know what is meant by the term monetarist.

2. Know what determines the monetarist demand for money.

3. Contrast monetarism and Keynesian fiscal/monetary policy as alternate views of the stabilization of the economy.

4. Know how monetarism has emerged as a criticism of Keynesian policies.

5. List the issues in the fiscal-monetary policy debate between monetarists and Keynesians.

Objectives 6–11 can be met by studying Chapter 18 and viewing "All of the People, All of the Time." After completing Part Two, the student should be able to:

6. Understand the basic idea of the Phillips curve; discuss the so called trade-off relationship.

7. State the criticisms of the Phillips curve.

8. Define the recently-coined term "stagflation."

9. Explain why traditional monetary and fiscal policies are difficult to apply successfully in a period of "stagflation."

10. Understand what is meant by supply-side economics.

11. Discuss the role of expectations of inflation.

PART ONE

UNIT XII ASSIGNMENT: PART ONE

STUDY: Chapter 17, "Another View of Money's Role," *Economics Today*

STUDY: Film Summary: "Karen Goes Political," *Study Guide*

VIEW: "Karen Goes Political"

REVIEW: Chapter 17 Highlights, *Study Guide*

COMPLETE: Fill-In Review *and* Problems, Problems, Problems ..., *Study Guide*

FILM SUMMARY: "Karen Goes Political"

Karen and Thomas take their individual views on the economy so much to heart that they become economic adversaries. Thomas takes a strong government-intervention Keynesian stance in the ensuing marital battles, while Karen opposes him with an equally emphatic monetarist viewpoint. Their familiar loyalties to each other temporarily dissolve in favor of loyalties to economic models of the economy. Perhaps the debate is a little contrived, but it is intended to clarify some of the larger differences between the two ways of analyzing the economy.

Karen and Thomas disagree on the effects in the economy of "monetary rule" versus Keynesian fiscal/monetary policy. In the last unit, we looked at how a deliberate change in the growth of the money supply can be used to affect the economy. We saw how a change in monetary policy by the Fed changes the amount of excess reserves in the banking system, altering interest rates and thus the level of planned investment—to ultimately change equilibrium level of national income. It was partly through the effect of interest rate changes in investment that the simple Keynesian model established a new equilibrium national income level.

We will now consider a strongly opposing view of how the economy operates. The modern quantity theory of money is based on a different theory for the demand for money. While the simple Keynesian theory suggests that changes in interest rates are important, the monetarist believes, instead, that people hold a constant fraction of their income as cash and that, as income changes, so does the amount of money people want to hold.

In terms of behavior, it follows that people will get rid of excess money they don't want to hold for future use by spending it on goods and services. When this happens, aggregate demand in the economy will rise. If the economy is below full employment, output can expand, but, if it is already at full employment or if there are inflexible areas in the economy which do not respond to changes in demand, only prices will rise, producing inflation.

Karen is a protoge of economist Dr. Stephanie Teal, who represents monetarist thought when she emphasizes "money matters." Karen and Dr. Teal see changes in the money supply as the most important force in determining the level of output, employment and prices. They strongly disagree with any "tampering" of the quantity of money by the Fed above that allowed by following the simple rule that an annual increase of money must be proportional to the economy's annual increase in productivity.

Facing Karen across the kitchen debate table is Thomas, the Keynesian. He believes, as does his economics professor, Dr. Beck, that major attention must be paid to the sources of spending in the circular flow. Thomas says money has a secondary role to the total spending flow and that the sum of the spending of all sectors—household, business and government (C+I+G)—is the appropriate focus for understanding and directing the economy. Thomas says that, of course, Keynesians agree that the money supply is important, but they can't accept such a primary role for money as do the monetarists.

Where the Keynesians look to income level and profits expected by new investment to determine spending, monetarists point to the amount of money that people hold. To see the point of view of the monetarist, instead of viewing spending as a sum of Keynesian flows of C+I+G, consider expenditure as the monetarist do, as a flow of dollars moving through the economy. First, visualize the money in the economy and then add in the speed at which it moves through markets and through the entire circular flow. Then, visualize the product resulting from the expenditure of money and give a unit of each product an average price.

To give your mental picture symbols, use the monetarists' basic equation, $MV=PQ$, where M is the money supply, V is the velocity of money the number of times a year an average dollar is spent for new output (speed of the money flow), Q is the physical amount of goods and services produced, and P is the average price per unit of output.

The velocity can be of importance since, with a high velocity, a small amount of money could enable a large amount of spending. But if we consider velocity as stable, then for total spending to increase, the money supply must increase. Since $MV=PQ$, if V stays the same and Q doesn't change significantly, then, when M increases it follows that only prices will rise. You can see why the monetarist would increase M only by the small amount that Q rises each year.

The simple Keynesian equation, C+I+G= national output (and income) is, however, not totally different from the monetarist simple quantity theory, $MV=PQ$. They are two ways of looking at the same thing, each from a different vantage point. When spending is considered as a great moving flow of money through the economy, instead of as a sum of C+I+G, we are looking as monetarist do, at economic activity through "money lenses."

Monetarists see money V as stable since, for them, money functions mainly as a medium of exchange; they give less importance to money's function as a store-of-value. Keynesians see the velocity of money as unstable, challenging what monetarists say is the close dependable relationship between changes in the money supply and output. Keynesians believe the fluctuations of private investment cause the economy to be unstable, requiring active fiscal and monetary policy. The monetarists believe government policy harms the economy by limiting its ability to provide its own flexible response to changes. Monetarists criticize expansionary fiscal policy because of the so-called crowding-out effect on investment. They point out that if increased G leads to a budget deficit, then the U.S. Treasury will have to sell bonds to finance the deficit, raising interest rates, thus lowering or "crowding out" private investment.

To proceed one step further, monetarists state as long as money gradually increases along with the increase in productivity, interventionist policies are not needed. Fiscal/monetary policy harms the economy, acting to destabilize a naturally behaving market economy. Karen puts it this way: "The monetarist doesn't favor strong manipulation of the money supply ... [and] no sudden change in the money supply. Monetarists want a steady rate of increase ... instead of tightening up during booms and loosening in depressions."

Monetarists view cycles in the economy as results of money mismanagement, while Keynesians see an inherently unstable economy requiring management. The monetarists point to various time lags in the application of money management; that is, a change in M could change output within six months, or not have any effect for as long as two or more years. Since it is impossible to predict the time lag a given policy action will take, deliberate fiscal and monetary policy may destabilize the economy. Monetarists insist that interest rates should not be stabilized, but they favor, as does Karen, the stabilization of the rate of growth of the money supply. Milton Friedman, a leading monetarist, advocates a monetary rule that the money supply only expand at the same rate as the growth in real GNP.

The film gives a review of a simple Keynesian theory that you know by now, and, in addition, it gives you another view of money's role in the economy. You must recognize that the debate between Karen and Thomas and, also, between Dr. Beck and Dr. Teal, has overly simplified the two economic models.

The two points-of-view are far from being merely academic since national advocates of each bring to the debate their own understanding of how the economy works. Since Keynesians believe the economy cannot stabilize itself, the policy outcomes of their viewpoint contain a primary role for fiscal/monetary policy to moderate national income. The monetarists, on the other hand, who believe in an inherently self-regulating free economy, emphasize that what is required is the maintenance of a stable quantity of money.

Karen and Thomas may be a little like economists; it is when conditions really get serious that they begin to agree on what should be done and how. They temporarily resolve their differences by recognizing that each kind of policy has its areas of success. We will save for another day our consideration of whether either model of the economy has all the answers to modern problems.

CHAPTER 17 HIGHLIGHTS

Defined words are underlined.

I. CHAPTER OVERVIEW: A MONETARIST MODEL WHICH DISAGREES WITH THE KEYNESIAN MODEL ON THE DEMAND FOR MONEY.

   A. There are differences in monetarist and Keynesian beliefs about the demand for money.

   B. Changes in the money supply will work through different transmission mechanisms.

   1. Keynesians believe that money affects the economy indirectly, through interest rates.

   2. Monetarists believe that money affects the economy directly.

   C. The policy implications of the two different models of the economy differ.

II. A DIFFERENT DEMAND FOR MONEY, THE BASIS FOR THE SIMPLE MONETARIST MODEL OF THE ECONOMY.

Monetarist: An economist who believes that changes in the money supply have most important effects on spending, prices, production and employment.

   A. The monetarist demand for money is primarily dependent on nominal income and not on changes in interest rates as in Keynesian speculative money demand.

1. The Cambridge equation of the demand for money shows that the fraction of income held as money stays the same.

   a. According to the Cambridge equation, as income changes, the demand for money changes.

   b. Note the similarity to the Keynes transactions demand for money.

B. The effects of changing the money supply in the simple monetarist model:

   1. If the money supply is increased when people are holding the amount of money they wish, the excess money will be spent on goods and services, increasing aggregate demand. (Recall, the Keynes model indicates that people will buy bonds.)

   2. The increase in total spending resulting from the increased money supply drives income up.

   3. If the money supply is lowered when people are holding the amount of money they wish, people will lower their spending on goods and services.

   4. The lowered total spending will drive income down.

   5. Income eventually stabilizes where the quantity of money demanded equals the quantity of money supplied.

C. A basic assumption of the monetarist model is that people together must accept the total money supply offered by the Fed, although individually they can determine their own holdings.

   1. Extra money is spent on goods and services pushing up nominal income.

   2. If the economy is at less than full employment, output will expand, driving up real income.

   3. If the economy is at full employment, only prices will rise, output cannot.

III. MODERN MONETARIST THEORY INCLUDES A MORE COMPLETE DEMAND FOR MONEY.

    A. Demand for money is related to the interest rate on other assets and the expected inflation rate as well as to nominal income.

    B. When the Fed increases the quantity of money, the modern monetarist theory says that people will mainly buy goods and services, but also will buy many different kinds of assets.

    C. Historically, the money supply and nominal GNP have gone up together. Keynesians and monetarists disagree on the interpretation of this positive correlation.

        1. Some monetarists believe "money matters a lot" and that a change in the money supply leads directly to a change in consumption and investment.

        2. Some Keynesians look at the same historical data and suggest that an aggregate demand increase pushes up national income so that there is a greater demand for money. The greater demand may make an increase in the deposit expansion multiplier.

        3. The Keynesian-Monetarist debate is a current one.

IV. THE FISCAL POLICY DEBATE BETWEEN THE MONETARISTS AND THE KEYNESIANS

    A. Fiscal policy has been basic in Keynesian policy making.

    B. Some monetarists contend that government expenditures "crowd out" private spending.

    C. In the so-called "crowding-out" effect,

        1. government deficit spending can be financed by the sale of government bonds.

2. Higher demand for credit by the government drives up interest rates.

3. Higher interest rates result in lower private investment, "crowding-out" private investment.

4. The lower private investment, times the multiplier, lowers income.

5. The higher government spending, times the multiplier, raises income.

6. The net effect is to reduce the expansionary effect of government spending but to increase the role of government in the economy.

D. Critics of fiscal policies suggest that increased deficits resulting from expansionary fiscal policy lead to higher future taxes.

E. Modern monetarists do not usually support active government fiscal policy. They take the position that

1. government spending and taxation should only be used for pressing social matters,

2. the money supply should be increased at a constant rate.

F. The modern Keynesians' and monetarists' fiscal-monetary positions are not as extreme as often presented, since the presentations usually stress differences.

1. Modern-day Keynesians prefer fiscal policy but also suggest monetary policy.

2. Modern-day monetarists feel that neither monetary nor fiscal policy can be effective because of lags and controls.

FILL-IN REVIEW

Select between the choices underlined or fill in the blank. Cover the answers until you have provided your own.

monetarist	An economist who believes that changes in the money supply have important effects on spending, prices, production and employment is called a _____. The basis for the simple monetarist model of the economy is a demand for money that is determined by nominal _____. This is different from the Keynesian speculative demand which is based on changes in _____ rates. According to the simple Cambridge equation of the demand for money, the fraction of income held as money *stays the same*/*changes* as income changes. According to the monetarist school, when the money supply is changed (by the Fed's open-market operation for example), there are direct effects on the economy. In this model, if the money supply is increased when people are holding the amount of money they wish, excess money will be *used to buy bonds*/*spent on goods and services*. Increased expenditures *raise*/*lower* aggregate demand. The increased aggregate demand will *raise*/*lower* nominal income. If the economy is below full employment, output will *lower*/*expand* and real income will *go up*/*down*. If the
income	
interest	
stays the same	
spent on goods and services	
raise	
raise	
expand go up	

economy is already at full employment, output cannot increase and there will only be an increase in _____. — *prices*

The modern monetarist theory includes a more *complete*/*simple* demand for money, including a relationship to interest rates and to the expected rate of _____ as well as to nominal income. — *complete* / *inflation*

Historically, the money supply and nominal GNP have moved in *opposite*/*the same* directions. — *the same*

In the recent past, one of the major debates between the monetarists and the Keynesians has been over the effectiveness of _____ policy. In order to finance fiscal policy, government can finance deficit spending by the sale of government _____. Some monetarists contend that government expenditures drive up _____ rates by the bond sales, thereby "crowding-out" private _____, and increasing the role of government in the economy. — *fiscal* / *bonds* / *interest* / *investment*

Modern-day Keynesians prefer fiscal policy but also suggest _____ policy as stabilizers for the economy, while modern-day monetarists feel that *both*/*neither* type of policy can be effective. — *monetary* / *neither*

PROBLEMS, PROBLEMS, PROBLEMS...

Answers are at the end of this unit.

TRUE-FALSE

Circle either "T" or "F" for each of the following.

(T) F 1. According to the monetarists, when government deficit spending is financed by the sale of bonds, crowding-out results.

T (F) 2. The recent debates between the monetarists and the Keynesians centered around the usefulness of gold and silver money.

T (F) 3. A monetarist is an economist who believes that our money supply should be fully backed by gold.

(T) F 4. A monetarist is an economist who believes the money supply has important effects on prices, production and employment.

(T) F 5. The Cambridge equation of the demand for money shows that the fraction of income held as money stays the same.

T (F) 6. According to the Cambridge equation, as income changes the demand for money remains the same.

MATCH-UP

Match each item in the first column with a term in the second column. Use no item more than once.

__e__ 1. An economist who believes that changes in the money supply have very important effects on production prices and employment

__b__ 2. Government deficit spending, financed by the sale of bonds, forces up interest rates and lowers private investment.

__c__ 3. The simple monetarist model of the economy is that the demand for money is based on this.

__d__ 4. Historically, these have gone up together.

__a__ 5. Recent debates between monetarists and Keynesians were based on this.

a. fiscal policy
b. crowding-out
c. nominal income
d. money supply and nominal GNP
e. monetarist

MULTIPLE CHOICE

For each of the following statements, choose the one best alternative.

1. A monetarist is an economist who believes that changes in the money supply have primary effects on
    a. spending.
    b. prices.
    c. production.
    d. all of the above

2. The basis for the simple monetarist model of the economy is that demand for money is determined by
    a. interest rate.
    b. imports of gold.
    c. nominal income.
    d. government expenditures.

3. According to the monetarist theory, people wish to hold the amount of money that is
    a. always the same.
    b. a constant fraction of income.
    c. determined by government.
    d. independent of income.

4. The recent debate between the monetarists and the Keynesians centered around
    a. gold as a backing for the currency.
    b. effectiveness of fiscal policy.
    c. effectiveness of monetary policy.
    d. all of the above

5. In determining national income and prices, monetarists emphasize the central role of

   a. fiscal policy.
   b. **the money supply.** ✓
   c. transfer payments.
   d. government spending.

6. The "crowding-out" effect refers to

   a. **government spending replacing private investment when government runs a deficit.** ✓
   b. private investment replacing government spending.
   c. government surpluses replacing household expenditures.
   d. government surpluses resulting in recession.

7. Monetarist Milton Friedman favors a money growth rule that

   a. increases the money supply at twice the economic growth.
   b. **increases the money supply at the rate of economic growth.** ✓
   c. follows interest rates.
   d. stabilizes the economy through rapid responses to changes in national income.

8. Modern monetarists argue that tight money policy during booms and loose money policy during recessions is

   a. useful, and should be used along with fiscal policy.
   b. **ineffective and often harmful because of time lags.** ✓
   c. inferior to fiscal policy.
   d. effective in combatting inflation and recession.

PART TWO

UNIT XII ASSIGNMENT: PART TWO

STUDY: Chapter 18, "Stagflation, Supply-Side Economics, and Stabilization," *Economics Today*

STUDY: Film Summary: "All of the People, All of the Time," *Study Guide*

VIEW: "All of the People, All of the Time"

REVIEW: Chapter 18 Highlights, *Study Guide*

COMPLETE: Fill-In Review *and* Problems, Problems, Problems ... *and* Econoword Puzzle, *Study Guide*

FILM SUMMARY: "All of the People, All of the Time"

Thomas, Karen and their friends find themselves in the worst of both worlds, an inflationary recession. In the film program, Dynamics Corporation has shut down some of its departments, forcing Thomas out of a job. He is aware that he is only one of many and not only is there increasing cyclical unemployment, but inflation seems to be continuing unchecked.

The simplest Keynesian theory, which explains inflation as a result of excessive aggregate demand pushing against the overly stretched resources of a fully employed economy, does not provide a clear answer for Thomas as to why the economy experiences inflation at the same time unemployment rises. The Keynesian theory, which was formulated during the 1930s, and used to analyze a deflated, depressed economy, gave plausible explanations of inflation and unemployment in the U.S. from 1951–1969, but does not explain why high unemployment and inflation rates occur together.

The simple quantity theory of the monetarists, discussed in Part One of this Unit does not give Thomas a simple answer either. The quantity theory holds that the price level is proportional to the quantity of money in circulation and explains inflation as resulting from excessive aggregate demand caused by injections of new money into the economy. This theory predicts that, if the economy has experienced a sustained rapid increase in its money supply, the result will be sustained with very rapid inflation. (A rapid and sustained inflation is called a hyperinflation.)

Many historical examples bear out this relationship, and the quantity theory is entirely explanatory for this use. But for an analysis of short-run stabilization policy, the quantity theory is not as exact. The simplest forms of these two models do not explain the complex stagflation events of the 1970s and 1980s.

What is needed is a way to explain how a change in the level of nominal income and output is actually transferred into changes in prices, employment and real *output*. Both of the simplest versions of quantity theory and Keynesian theory are found lacking in clearly explaining how this happens. Thomas considers another crude version of a theory that seems to relate unemployment to inflation in an appealingly simple way. In this theory, unemployment and inflation are seen to be in an inverse, trade-off relationship: lower unemployment is traded for increased inflation and vice versa.

A. W. H. Phillips, in testing a hypothesis relating wage rates to unemployment, published data which has come to be seen as suggesting a stable relationship between inflation and unemployment. The graphical representation of this concept is what has come to be called the Phillips curve. The Phillips curve invites the misinterpretation that policy makers may choose a compromise level between levels of inflation and levels of unemployment. The problem with such an interpretation is that the so-called stable relationship of rates of unemployment to rates of inflation does not stay stable over time.

In the late 1960s, it was noticed that the actual tradeoffs between inflation and employment no longer fit the Phillips curve of the 1950s. The curve had drifted upward from the earlier curves, so that greater levels of inflation linked with higher levels of unemployment. Economists noted that, far from a stable tradeoff of unemployment and inflation, the upward drift of the curve may well have been *caused* by the very fiscal/monetary policies chosen to direct the economy along a supposedly stable curve. Policy makers are therefore unable to choose a particular level of inflation, where, for example, high level of unemployment could be "bought" by a low level of inflation. Why not? Policies that are chosen to place the economy on certain tradeoff positions on the curve can actually cause the Phillips curve to shift to a new position.

In their struggle to understand the present state of the economy, Thomas and Karen consider what kind of policy can be used to deal with "stagflation," simultaneous inflation and unemployment. They consider "supply-side" economics which aims at increasing productivity without increasing inflation. It involves lowering marginal tax rates so that incentives to do extra work are rewarded by higher extra incomes. Supply-side economists argue that with lower marginal rates, people will not have the incentive to search out tax loopholes to avoid taxes. Thus, they say that resources will be put to more productive uses.

There is no simple way to stabilize stagflation. Whichever policy tool is useful for lowering unemployment, such as increased government spending or increased money supply, it has the effect of increasing inflation; while the opposite policy tools used to control the inflation directly worsen unemployment. Thomas and Karen recall that the data, unemployment rates, against which the success of policies is measured may be misleading.

Unemployment statistics may misinform as to how many people actually have jobs. Since unemployment is measured as the percentage of the number of people in the labor force, and not the percentage of the entire working age population, unemployment statistics may be mis-stated. This is not to say that unemployment statistics can be ignored. What should be emphasized is that we need employment figures in a usable form to help us understand the relationship of inflation to unemployment.

The length of time that an average worker is unemployed, the *duration* of unemployment, is an important part of the unemployment picture. In the U.S., even in years of high unemployment, *short* periods of unemployment are the most characteristic. The average duration of unemployment is directly related to the unemployment rate, that is, anything that affects the amount of time spent by an unemployed worker for a job search has an influence on the rate, and vice versa.

Workers, searching for jobs, look until they find one that pays the wage they expect, and expectations are based on their adaptations to past experiences. The rate of inflation either fools the job searcher or does not, and the length of time the worker searches for a job depends on her/his expectations of inflation. If inflation is progressing at a faster rate than workers have expected, the new job they find is likely to pay a higher wage than they expected; therefore, the job search takes less time. However, the new job holders don't realize yet that they will need the higher wage to keep up with the inflation rate they hadn't expected.

The reverse is also possible. If inflation is slowing down more than the worker expects, the search for a job will take longer. Why? With inflation slowing down, the workers won't be able to find the wage expected. It will take time for him/her to recognize that what has actually happened is different than expectations.

When the inflation rate is one the worker has adapted to and is expecting, the rate of unemployment is termed the "natural rate." The so-called "natural rate" of unemployment is not identified as an "appropriate" or "good" rate. It has been defined as the long-run rate, or the rate when no one is fooled by the rate of inflation.

A number of government policy programs are aimed at lowering the "natural rate" of unemployment, which often is calculated at around 5–6 percent. Note that from earlier discussions in Unit X, unemployment was defined as the number of workers between jobs, and this rate is considered to be around 5 percent. When people quit jobs to look for new ones, the resulting unemployment is counted as part of the unemployment rate, but frictional unemployment is considered a sign of a vigorous, healthy economy.

One of the targets of recent government policy is to lower unemployment to 4 percent in 1983, along with a lowering of the rate of inflation to 3 percent. However, new entrants into job markets, teenagers and women, tend to enter and leave the labor force frequently—adding to the unemployment statistics and lowering unemployment rates below 5 percent. Attempts to help the poor with minimum wage laws and unemployment compensation have actually had the side-effect of keeping the "natural rate" of unemployment high. As we mentioned in Unit XI, job training programs and public jobs have aimed to lower the rate but have not been shown to be effective. Lowering the natural rate of unemployment may require difficult trade-offs.

CHAPTER 18 HIGHLIGHTS

Defined words are underlined.

I. UNEMPLOYMENT AND INFLATION: THE POSSIBILITY OF AN INVERSE RELATIONSHIP.

<u>Inverse</u>: Two variables are inversely related if an increase in one is consistent with a decrease in the other.

　A. The Phillips curve shows a trade-off between unemployment and inflation rates. As unemployment rates go down, the rate of inflation goes up.

　　1. The implication of the Phillips curve is that it isn't possible to have full employment and no inflation at the same time.

　　2. If the Phillips curve implication is accepted, it means policy makers must decide on a trade-off between "acceptable" unemployment and "tolerable" inflation.

　　3. The Phillips curve shifts with time, showing higher rates of inflation from lower unemployment. Reasons for the shift:

　　　a. Unemployment compensation and welfare payments may result in longer job-search periods.

　　　b. A greater percentage of the population is joining the labor force.

　　　c. There are more teenagers and women in the labor force.

　　　d. A high minimum wage results in greater unemployment of the unskilled.

　　　e. Area population shifts.

B. Simultaneous unemployment and inflation do not easily yield to traditional monetary and fiscal policies.

   1. *Stagflation:* A recent term used to describe simultaneous economic slowdown plus rising prices.

   2. Fiscal and monetary policy used to control inflation can increase unemployment.

   3. Monetary and fiscal policy used to lower unemployment may fuel inflation.

C. Critics of the Phillips curve trade-off say

   1. it ignores the fact that workers will eventually correctly anticipate the future inflation rate.

   2. in the short-run workers can be fooled into accepting lower real wages, resulting in lower unemployment.

   3. in the long run there will be no trade-off between unemployment and inflation.

   4. when inflation is correctly anticipated the unemployment rate will stabilize at its long-run "natural rate."

   Natural Rate of Unemployment: Unemployment rate which exists because of the imperfections in job markets, (which may be a lack of job information, licensing or union limitations). Another way of describing the "natural rate" is the average unemployment rate over a relatively long period of time.

   a. Each economy will have its own "natural rate."

   b. The functioning of the labor market will determine the "natural rate."

II. SUPPLY-SIDE ECONOMICS: STAGFLATION CURE?

   A. *Supply-Side Economics:* The study of ways to increase productivity in the U.S. economy to create growth without inflation. Policy recommendations are for a reduction in marginal tax rates to stimulate productivity.

   1. Changes in tax rates refer to a change in the percentage of a base, not to a change in total tax revenue.

   2. Income taxes in the U.S. are progressive, that is, the tax rate increases on marginal units of income.

      a. The assumption of supply-side economics is that workers, savers and investors respond to small changes.

      b. The above implies that an expected after-tax benefit is important to the worker, saver, or investor.

      c. The greater the marginal tax rate, the lower the after-tax benefit of investing, saving or working. To say the same thing, the greater the marginal tax rate the lower the opportunity cost of leisure.

   3. Ways individuals can respond to high marginal tax rates include longer vacations, fewer supplemental jobs, early retirement, greater absenteeism, and refusal of higher paying jobs that require more work.

   B. *The Laffer Curve:* A hypothesis that after some point an increase in the tax rates will actually reduce tax revenues.

   1. The policy implication is that, after a certain tax rate, a lowering of rates will increase tax revenues. The curve suggests that

      a. at higher and higher marginal tax rates people have an increased incentive to lower their tax base.

      b. tax revenues can be zero at both a zero tax rate and a very high tax rate.

2. Critics of the Laffer curve hypothesis argue that

   a. no one knows where our economy is located on the Laffer curve.

   b. a tax cut may stimulate the economy but few believe a tax cut could actually increase tax revenues.

   c. perhaps in the long run, tax cuts would increase productivity and produce economic growth, but it is unlikely in the short run.

3. Is supply-side economics here to stay? Many say

   a. yes, while the nation experiences slow or no economic growth.

   b. yes, as long as progressive taxation coupled with inflation affect incentives and productivity.

NOTE:

The "Issues and Applications" section of the text chapter is included in the Chapter Highlights because of the topical material it contains.

III. ISSUES AND APPLICATIONS. IS SHORT RUN STABILIZATION POSSIBLE? THE PROBLEMS OF SHORT-RUN POLICY MAKING

   A. The economic policy maker's tool kit consists of monetary and fiscal policies: the question is how is a choice of a particular policy made?

   1. Policy decisions are based on past and current data of economic conditions, using models of the economy.

2. *Econometrics:* The use of statistics and mathematics to make quantitative economic analysis. Econometricians work with economic models to explain and predict economic conditions.

B. The goals of economic modeling are to understand and predict how the economy works so that policy makers are able to rely on the model when considering possible fiscal or monetary policy. *Short-Term Macroeconomic Stabilization:* Fiscal and monetary policy to influence the economy in the next year.

1. The Employment Act of 1946 declared the federal government responsible for economic stabilization.

2. There is serious questioning by some economists about the long-run effect of stabilization policy.

C. The unemployment rate is used in deciding whether to use stabilization policy; but the definition of full employment is arbitrary and changes with time.

1. Several years ago "full-employment" was 4 percent frictional unemployment.

2. Today, "full-employment" may be defined with as much as 7½ percent frictional unemployment.

D. Government uses a mixture of data and models in deciding on policies. The complex problems involved are

1. deciding which model, using which variables, to use.

2. the availability of accurate current information on important variables.

3. time lags of gathering information.

4. time lags in forming policy.

5. time lags in the effects of applying policy.

E. The various lags in short-run stabilization policy convince some critics that no short-run stabilization attempts should even be made.

F. Policy making and the public: Does the public have rational expectations? *Rational Expectations:* A theory that individuals use their knowledge of the effects of past policy changes to judge the future effects of new policy.

   1. According to this theory, if the public knows what policy will be enacted, it will use that knowledge to neutralize or negate it according to self-interest.

   2. If the above is true, then government policy makers can only be successful when the public is fooled.

   3. Rational expectations theory makes the debate between monetary versus fiscal policy irrelevant.

FILL-IN REVIEW

Select between the choices underlined or fill in the blank. Cover the answers until you have provided your own.

decrease	Over twenty years ago, a British economist named Phillips noted an inverse relationship between unemployment rates. Two variables are inversely related if an increase in one is consistent with a/an *decrease/increase* in the other. The implication of the Phillips's relationship is that low unemployment and low
inflation	_____ cannot exist at the same time. In order to lower one of these rates we must ac-
higher	cept a *higher/lower* rate than the other. This
Phillips	trade-off is described by the *Phillips/Laffer* curve.
cannot	The criticism of the Phillips curve is that workers *cannot/can* be constantly fooled and will eventually build an expectation of
inflation	_____ into their demands for wages. Because of this the Phillips curve relationship is
shifts	not stable and the curve _____ with time. Unemployment rates then return to the so-
natural rate of unemployment	called _____ _____ __ _____ in which there is only the unemployment due to imperfect job markets.

The effects of taxation on aggregate supply is the concern of the new _____-____ economics. More specifically, these policy makers wish to lower _____ tax rates to increase _____. The assumption of supply-side economics is that workers, savers and investors respond to _____ changes in income, and will work harder, save more or invest more when they are able to retain a larger after-tax _____ income.

supply-side

marginal
productivity

marginal

marginal

An important part of supply-side economics is the so-called Laffer Curve. The _____ curve postulates that at higher and higher marginal ___ rates people have *less/more* inventive ways to reduce their tax base, to both avoid and evade taxes. The Laffer curve suggests that tax revenues can be zero at both a zero tax rate and a very ____ tax rate. Reduction of tax rates may allow greater long-run _____ of the economy, although few economists believe that in the short run, government tax _____ will rise with a lowering of the tax rates.

Laffer
tax
more

high

growth

revenues

ISSUES AND APPLICATION

monetary   fiscal

choose which to use

understand   predict

models

full

time

no

fiscal

rational expectations

past

The economic policy maker's tool kit consists of _____ policy and _____ policy. The problem of policy makers is to *apply all policies at once/choose which to use* in a particular case. To do this, they must rely on models of the economy. The goals of economic modeling are to _____ and _____ how the economy operates so that economic policy makers can rely on the model when considering possible policies to use. There are serious problems in the choice of _____. To complicate matters even further, the definition of ____-employment which is used in decisions on policy, change with time. A second major set of problems are the lags in _____ between the choice of policy and its application.

These problems have convinced some that *all/no* short-run stabilization attempts should be made. A new theory that disregards the debate between monetary and _____ policy is called _____ _____. This theory argues that no policy can be effective because people use their knowledge of the effects of ____ policy to judge what are the planned effects of new policy to subvert it for their own self-interest.

PROBLEMS, PROBLEMS, PROBLEMS...

Answers are at the end of this unit.

TRUE-FALSE

Circle either "T" or "F" for each statement.

T **(F)** 1. The trade-off between low unemployment rates and depression is called the Phillips curve.

T **(F)** 2. The Phillips curve relationship has been shown to be stable over time.

(T) F 3. The natural rate of unemployment exists because of imperfectly functioning job markets.

(T) F 4. The effect of lowered marginal taxation rates on aggregate supply is the concern of supply-side economics.

T **(F)** 5. The supply-side economists believe that with lower marginal tax rates workers and investors will lower their productivity.

T **(F)** 6. All economists agree that short-run macroeconomic stabilization policy is effective in attaining its goals.

(T) F 7. Supply-side economists study ways to increase productivity.

MATCH-UP

Match each item in the first column with a term in the second column. Use no term more than once.

<u>i</u> 1. A trade-off relationship between unemployment and inflation

<u>e</u> 2. The Phillips curve relationship shifts over time and doesn't provide a basis for prediction.

<u>a</u> 3. A period of high unemployment (economic low down) and rising prices

<u>d</u> 4. Due to imperfections in the job market

<u>g</u> 5. Reduction in marginal tax rates to stimulate productivity

<u>f</u> 6. After some point, an increase in tax rates actually reduces tax revenues.

<u>h</u> 7. Fiscal and monetary policy to influence the economy in the next year

<u>b</u> 8. The use of statistics and mathematics in economic model building to explain and predict economic conditions

<u>c</u> 9. A theory that individuals use their knowledge of the effects of past economic policy changes to judge the future effects of new policy

a. stagflation
b. econometrics
c. rational expectations
d. natural rate of unemployment
e. Phillips curve criticism
f. Laffer curve
g. supply-side economics
h. short-run macroeconomic stabilization
i. the Phillips curve

MULTIPLE CHOICE

For each of the following statements, choose the one best alternative.

1. Stagflation is a recently coined word which describes simultaneous

   a. low rates of economic growth and falling prices.

   b. low rates of economic growth and rising prices.

   c. rapid rates of economic growth and rising prices.

   d. rapid rates of economic growth and falling prices.

2. According to modern unemployment theory, in the short-run, an unanticipated cut in the rate of inflation would

   a. lower the natural rate of unemployment.

   b. raise the natural rate of unemployment.

   c. lower the unemployment rate.

   d. increase the unemployment rate.

3. Supply-side economics studies methods to

   a. increase the supply of unionized labor in the U.S. industry.

   b. standardize production methods in the U.S. industry.

   c. achieve the "stationary state" in the U.S. industry.

   d. increase productivity in the U.S. industry.

4. The Phillips curve shows

   a. a positive relationship between unemployment and inflation.

   b. an inverse relationship between unemployment and inflation.

   c. an inverse relationship between productivity and marginal tax rates.

   d. a positive relationship between income and tax rates.

5. The Phillips curve shifts over time. All of the following are explanations of the shift *except*

   a. longer job search periods allowed by unemployment compensations.

   b. a larger percentage of the population joining the labor force.

   (c.) a long-run absence of change in the inflation rate.

   d. a high minimum wage resulting in unemployment of the unskilled.

6. The natural rate of unemployment can be defined as

   a. one that is determined by biological survival; that is, the birth rate minus the death rate.

   (b.) one that occurs when the actual rate of inflation is the same as the expected rate of inflation.

   c. the average of unemployment rate over a long period of time.

   d. All the above are correct.

   e. Only b and c of the above are correct.

7. According to rational expectations theory, short-run stabilization policy

   (a.) is easily achieved through fiscal policy.

   b. should not be attempted.

   c. is easily achieved through monetary policy.

   d. can be achieved easily by using both monetary and fiscal policies.

8. Supply responses in the economy will be stimulated by tax cuts, according to supply-side economists, since taxpayers are responsive to

   a. marginal tax rates.

   b. average tax rates.

   c. government tax revenues.

   d. government deficits.

ECONOWORD PUZZLE

CLUES ACROSS

1. A curve that shows an inverse relationship between unemployment rates and inflation rates
6. Simultaneous economic slowdown plus inflation
7. Reduction in marginal tax rates to stimulate productivity is _____ - _____ economics.
9. Fiscal and monetary policy to influence equilibrium national income
10. When one is unemployed, they are _____ of work.
11. The work of human beings
12. & 13. A theory that individuals use their knowledge of past economic policy changes to judge the future affects of new policy is _____ _____ theory.
14. The opportunity cost of something can be called a _____ - _____ .

CLUES DOWN

2. Better _____, than never.
3. The unemployment rate which exists because of imperfect job market (2 words)
4. Payment levied by government
5. The Phillips curve shows a relationship between the rate of _____ and the rate of inflation.
8. This semester you are studying your first course in _____ .
11. These lapses of time between the choice of policy and its application cause serious problems in using monetary and fiscal policy.

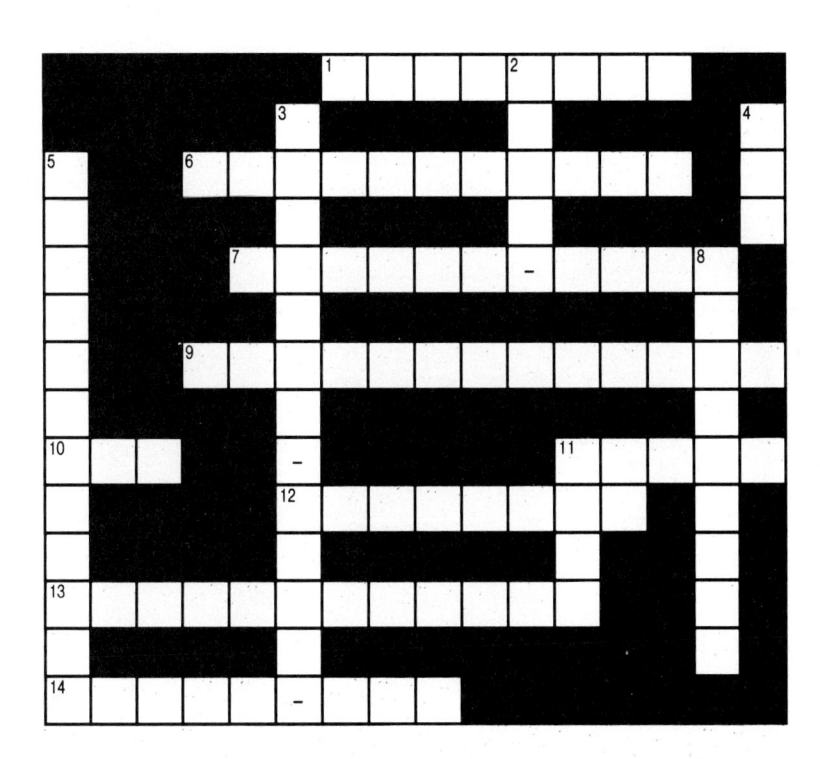

ANSWERS TO STUDY QUESTIONS

PART ONE

TRUE-FALSE

1. T 2. F 3. F 4. T 5. T 6. F

MATCH-UP

1. e 2. b 3. c 4. d 5. a

MULTIPLE CHOICE

1. a 2. c 3. b 4. b 5. b 6. a 7. b 8. b

COMPLETED ECONOWORD PUZZLE

PART TWO

TRUE-FALSE

1. F 2. F 3. T 4. T 5. F 6. F 7. T

MATCH-UP

1. i 2. e 3. a 4. d 5. g 6. f 7. h 8. b 9. c

MULTIPLE CHOICE

1. b 2. d 3. d 4. b 5. c 6. b 7. a

COMPLETED ECONOWORD PUZZLE

						P	H	I	L	L	I	P	S		
				N				A							T
U		S	T	A	G	F	L	A	T	I	O	N			A
N				T				E							X
E			S	U	P	P	L	Y	-	S	I	D	E		
M				R									C		
P			S	T	A	B	I	L	I	Z	A	T	I	O	N
L				A											N
O	U	T		L						L	A	B	O	R	
Y				-		R	A	T	I	O	N	A	L		M
M				A						G					I
E	X	P	E	C	T	A	T	I	O	N	S				C
N				E											S
T	R	A	D	E	-	O	F	F							

GROWTH AND DEVELOPMENT

UNIT XIII

UNIT IN A NUTSHELL

PART ONE

Film: "Slippin' Away"

Text: Chapter 19

PART TWO

Film: "A Steep and Thorny Path"

Text: Chapter 20

How can a country best develop so that its people are able to have more of the goods they choose to have? How can the capital, education, and advanced agriculture necessary to accelerate development be obtained? Should it be done from within a country's own economy, or should foreign aid be sought?

What is the trade-off between what might be ideal and what is possible? Is there always a trade-off between the natural environment and rapid economic development? Are politics involved when the choices regarding economic development are made?

Behind the dry and factual listing of circumstances that lead to economic growth are the emotional issues of human betterment or even survival. Economists leave the dramatic interpretation of the human condition to others; their task is to identify the possible outcomes from economic choices. In addition to the choices of how best to use the economy's resources, there are choices of how to increase resources—in short, of how to accomplish desired economic growth.

NOTE:

Before studying this section re-read Chapter 1 of your text to review the definitions of opportunity cost, production possibilities curve and comparative advantage.

UNIT OBJECTIVES

Objectives 1-5 can be met by studying Chapter 19 including the "Issues and Applications" section for that Chapter, and viewing "Slippin' Away." After completing Part One, the student should be able to:

1. Define economic growth and know how to calculate the rate of economic growth.

2. State some of the requirements for economic growth.

3. List arguments both for and against zero economic growth.

4. Graphically show economic growth as an outward shift in the production possibilities curve.

5. State the rule of 72.

Objectives 6-9 can be met by studying Chapter 20 and viewing "A Steep and Thorny Path." After completing Part Two, the student should be able to:

6. Define and identify the characteristics of less developed countries.

7. List several stages of development.

8. Understand the relationship between property rights' enforcement and the rate of capital accumulation by outside investment.

9. Explain why saving is difficult for LDCs.

PART ONE

UNIT XIII ASSIGNMENT: PART ONE

STUDY: Chapter 19, "Economic Growth," *Economics Today*

STUDY: Film Summary: "Slippin' Away," *Study Guide*

VIEW: "Slippin' Away"

REVIEW: Chapter 19 Highlights, *Study Guide*

COMPLETE: Fill-in Review *and* Problems, Problems, Problems . . . , *Study Guide*

FILM SUMMARY: "Slippin' Away"

With his flair for continual worrying, Thomas impulsively reacts to a TV speech about the decline in U.S. economic growth. Thomas is shaken by the idea of declining U.S. economic strength, and perpetuates this worry by indulging in fantasies of national and even world collapse from too much growth. Thomas's error in this case is to assume that the lowered productivity in the economy is a consequence of too much economic growth, specifically technological growth. Thomas's concerns actually conflict with each other.

In an attempt to clarify Thomas's dilemma, let's consider, in turn, the concept of the U.S. growth rate, and, then, Thomas's nightmare that the environment will be completely destroyed by modern technology.

Economic growth can be measured as a rate of increase in an economy's production; so that what increases productivity also contributes to growth: improved capital equipment, a more skilled labor force and technological progress.

The production possibilities curve shows various combinations of goods an economy could produce, given the factors of production it presently has, namely: the capital, technology, and trained labor. The curve illustrates not only that an economy chooses what combination of goods it will produce, but that production is limited by its present amount of factors. Economic growth can only be achieved by the increase of one or several of these given factors.

Economic growth can be shown graphically by the production possibilities curve; it shifts outward to show increased economic capacity resulting from additional capital accumulation or additional skilled labor. Recall that the production possibilities curve shows the maximum combination of goods obtainable from the full use of the economy's land, labor and capital. It is entirely possible, and in fact may frequently be the case, that the actual production in an economy is well inside the production possibility frontier.

The ways that production can increase are limited, especially by resource availability. It is unlikely that all resources can be increased in the same proportion. Since this is usually the case, the law of diminishing returns takes effect. It works in this way. As more and more of one resource is added to production while the others stay the same, eventually the resulting extra product will diminish. Thus, the law of diminishing returns puts important restrictions on profitable uses of resources. For example, if a nation has little capital equipment and a high population, it may attempt to increase production by larger and larger additions of labor. But, the extra product obtained in this way eventually diminishes. (More capital equipment would increase output; but without outside help, the economy may not be able to afford such expenditure.)

Economists identify growth-producing factors, but they don't agree on how to measure the individual effects of each factor. As the program suggests, the whole subject of economic growth is controversial.

One of the problems is the measurement of growth itself. If we want to measure growth we need to be clear on what we want to know from such a measurement. Are we interested in how well-off people are? "Well-being" can be measured by a comparison of GNP for two different time periods. To make such a comparison, a price index is used. Application of a price index will remove price changes, since we want to measure the increase the real goods and services people have, not the changes in prices. For example, what is the growth situation in the country whose GNP has gone up, but whose population has also risen? Are the people better off? To find out, divide each period's GNP by its population to arrive at a *per capita* (literally, per head) or per person figure.

The phenomenal growth rate in the U.S. has been the result of cumulative increases in productivity. If our productivity is presently declining, there are important consequences in terms of goods and services we have now and will have in the future. (No, the U.S. is not going to slip rapidly into being a "second or third-rate world power" as Thomas fears.) But the rate of capital investment has indeed lowered, the composition of the labor force has changed, and there is less business research and development. These changes result in higher production costs which reduce the ability of the U.S. to compete in international markets. These changes cannot help but alter the income and standard of living in the U.S.

Will growth ruin the environment? After listening to the doom-and-gloom speaker, Thomas broods about the environmental effects of growth because he fears its consequences. Thomas wants to stop economic growth, at the same time that he fears economic collapse. He argues that the faster our growth, the greater the resource depletion and environmental pollution. His anxious response is to accept the doomsday model of economic growth which prophesies nothing less than total collapse. For this model, salvation can be brought only by a drastic scaling-down of worldwide production by at least 75 percent. As you can see, Thomas shares the worries of both the growth-is-no-longer-possible and the anti-growth groups.

All growth produces a changed environment. It has been so from man's earliest recorded history up to the present. The ancient Greeks cut down their trees. The Romans cleared nearby forests to make room for the growth of their cities. The Chinese built dams to permanently flood areas behind the confining wall of dams. Medieval European farmers changed natural landscapes. And by-products created by 19th century industrial production were released into the air and water.

In producing more output, the growing economy can more fully realize its economic goals. For an underdeveloped economy, any increase in growth rate may lift people out of starvation. For such a population, any change in the environment would seem unimportant and would not be given consideration when production decisions are made. However, among the developed economies, concern for both environmental pollution and resource depletion has been serious enough to alter production methods. There is mounting controversy as to whether it is possible to continue to produce the benefits of growth while limiting some of the environmental costs.

The doomsday models assume that present production techniques will not change in the future. Such models may have underestimated the capacities of technological progress to change the combinations of inputs for the goods we produce, as resources become more limited and as new resources and production methods are discovered. The price system itself provides signals of changes in relative scarcity. As a good becomes scarce, its price rises, leading to searches for substitutes. In the book, *Scarcity and Growth*, Barnett and Morse remind us that the price system automatically adjusts. "The economy is not a mindless glutton that will devour the last morsel before it notices the plate is empty."

CHAPTER 19 HIGHLIGHTS

Defined words are underlined.

I. DEFINITIONS OF ECONOMIC GROWTH

Economic Growth: The increase in an economy's level of real output over time.

A. Growth is usually measured as a rate of change of GNP. As used for comparisons (between economies, or for the same economy between time periods), GNP must be corrected for

1. price changes by using a price index to obtain real GNP.

2. population growth by dividing GNP by the population to obtain *per capita* GNP.

B. The above definition of growth does not mention

1. the distribution of income. (Income may be concentrated in only a few groups.)

2. changes in leisure time available. (If more leisure is used, GNP understates growth.)

3. the quality of life or the happiness of satisfaction experienced.

C. Economic growth occurs continually over time.

1. Small changes in the present rate of growth lead to larger and larger changes in GNP over time.

2. The approximate time it takes any quantity to double is found by dividing the annual percentage growth rate into 72. This is the rule of 72.

II. U.S. Record of Growth

A. The U.S. has seen an almost constant improvement in its standard of living.

B. Economic growth can be shown by an outward shift in the production possibilities curve of a nation. <u>Production Possibilities Curve:</u> All different combinations of two goods that can be produced by an economy at full employment. (Go back to Chapter 1 if you need a review of this concept.)

1. The outward shift represents an increase in the productive capacities caused by increased capital, labor and other resources. (See text exhibit 19–4.)

2. Production possibilities curve represents maximum potential output.

3. Actual output can't be greater than potential output, but it can be smaller.

III. GROWTH REQUIRES THE EXPANSION OF MANY FACTORS.

   A. As a country develops, using more and more capital, equipment, and labor on a fixed quantity of land may make balanced growth difficult to obtain; the law of diminishing returns operates to lower marginal output.

      1. *Law of Diminishing Returns:* The principle stating that, inputs of any resource (factor) are increased while the quantities of other resources are fixed; the rate of increase in output eventually slows down.

      2. The fixed supply of one resource (factor) acts as a brake on the output. (In underdeveloped countries that fixed resource is often capital equipment.)

   B. Rich natural resources do not guarantee growth; they must be converted to a usable form.

   C. Accumulation of capital stock is important to development. *Capital Stock:* Machines and other durable goods used in the production of consumption goods.

      1. The sacrifice of present consumption is required to build capital for the future.

      2. The larger the capital stock for any given population, the higher the possible levels of real income.

   D. Technological progress allows a nation to produce greater output with a given amount of land, labor and capital. A nation's ability to sustain technological change depends on

      1. its scientific capabilities,

      2. the quality and size of its educational and training system,

      3. the percentage of income devoted to research and development.

IV. Is it Possible to Identify the Factor most Important to Development?

  A. The three determinants of economic growth are

   1. growth of capital stock,

   2. growth and improved skills of the labor force,

   3. technological progress.

  B. It is not hard to label the determinants of development, but how to measure each is not known.

   1. Technical progress has been considered a residual or unexplained part of growth after other measures have been taken.

   2. Measurement of capital and labor are imperfect. (How can the quality of capital or labor be measured?)

NOTE:

The "Issues and Applications" section of the text chapter is included in the Chapter Highlights because of the topical material it contains.

V. Issues and Applications: Issue I: The Mystery of Declining U.S. Growth.

  A. Productivity growth has been the strongest force underlying U.S. real GNP growth. Productivity is linked to

   1. the amount and quality of capital equipment,

   2. technology (work methods, for example),

   3. skill and education of the labor force.

B. The decline, since the early 1970s, in U.S. productivity is significant. In a search for reasons, we find that

1. investment has declined.

2. inflation has depressed the investment necessary to increase productivity. Inflation

    a. squeezes after-tax profits,

    b. lowers the ability to invest.

3. government regulation of business in the areas of pollution control, worker safety and health results in higher business costs.

4. high marginal tax rates may discourage new investment projects.

5. the quality of the labor force has changed.

    a. More unskilled laborers have entered the labor force, while some highly productive workers have retired.

    b. Educational attainment of the labor force has increased more slowly than in the past.

    c. Worker-alienation because of highly specialized jobs, or a decline in the "work ethic," can affect productivity.

6. improvements in the quality of capital goods as well as efficiency in their use may have declined. (Research and development may be lower because of economic instability and government regulations.)

C. Productivity declines contribute to higher labor costs, higher inflation and, therefore, to a loss of international markets.

VI. **Issue II: Should Growth Be Stopped?**

   A. Arguments that "growth is not desirable"

   1. Industrialized growth results in air, water and land pollution, noise pollution, ugliness and traffic congestion; growth causes spillover costs (externalities).

   2. Growth, in itself, does not erase poverty or guarantee a good life.

   B. "Limits-to-growth" (the doomsday models) say growth is not possible.

   1. Because of limited resources and the harm to the ecological system, population and growth will stop.

   2. The models project a collapse of the system by natural resource limits, pollution or famine.

   3. Zero-Economic-Growth (ZEG) is offered as a solution. A "stationary state" may be achieved by

      a. no population growth,

      b. no net capital investment,

      c. a dramatic reduction of resource use and pollution,

      d. a shift from industrial to food-and-services production.

VII. **Arguments Against the ZEG and Doomsday Models Say Human and Technological Progress Is Underestimated.**

   A. The price system in market economies provides signals of relative scarcities. (As resources become more scarce, their price will rise, leading to searches for substitutes.)

   B. New resources will be adapted and present resources will be used in new ways.

C. If we fully use our present knowledge and allow that knowledge to expand, a dramatic increase in food production is possible. (This can happen through increasing returns to large-scale production.)

D. Human behavior adapts to changing conditions.

FILL-IN REVIEW

Select between the choices underlined or fill in the blank. Cover the answers until you have provided your own.

The increase in an economy's level of real output over time is called economic _____.	*growth*
Economic growth is usually measured as a ____ of change of ____. There are problems with using GNP as the single measurement of economic growth. To be used for comparisons, GNP must be corrected for price changes by using a price _____ to obtain real GNP. GNP	*rate GNP*
	index
that expresses output of goods and services with the changes in prices removed is called ____ GNP. When a nation's GNP is divided	*real*
by that nation's population, ___ _____ GNP is obtained.	*per capita*
Also missing from the definition of GNP are indications of how equally or unequally income is divided-up among the population. This apportionment is called the _____ of income. GNP also does not	*distribution*

leisure	measure changes in _____ available, or the quality of life in a country.
production *possibilities* *an increase* *produce*	Economic growth can be shown graphically by an outward shift in the _____ _____ curve of a nation. This outward shift represents <u>*a decrease*</u>/<u>*an increase*</u> in capacity to _____, resulting from increased labor, capital and other resources. Growth requires expanding many factors that interact.
resources *capital* *technological*	These factors are natural _____, accumulation of _____ stock, and _____ progress. The larger the capital stock for any given population the <u>*lower*</u>/
higher	<u>*higher*</u> the possible levels of real income.
land labor capital	Technological progress allows a nation to produce greater output with a given amount of ____, _____, and _____.

ISSUES AND APPLICATIONS

Issue I: Declining U.S. Growth

Capital equipment, technology and education of the labor force are the major factors in determining _____. Productivity in the U.S. has *risen/declined* since 1971. One of the major reasons for lowered productivity is lowered business _____. Business may be unwilling to undertake investment because of _____, government _____ and high marginal ___ _____.

productivity
declined

investment

inflation   regulation
tax rates

Issue II: Should Growth Be Stopped?

The doomsday models state that within the next 100 years or so, growth will not be possible because of limited _____ and _____. These models predict a _____ of the system. The suggestion to avert global tragedy is to achieve the stationary state or ____ _____ _____ (ZEG). Arguments attempting to dispute the doomsday models remind us that in market economies, when resources become scarcer, their prices will *fall/rise*. This "rationing" effect of rising _____ will also lead to searches for _____ for the scarce goods.

resources
pollution   collapse

Zero Economic Growth

rise   prices
substitutes

PROBLEMS, PROBLEMS, PROBLEMS . . .

Answers are at the end of this unit.

TRUE-FALSE

Circle either "T" or "F" for each statement.

T **(F)** 1. Economic growth is the increase in an economy's level of money income.

(T) F 2. To obtain "real GNP," divide GNP by a price index.

(T) F 3. To obtain "per capita GNP," divide GNP by the population.

T **(F)** 4. Capital plays a relatively minor part in a country's economic growth.

T **(F)** 5. An inward shift of the production possibilities curve of a nation indicates economic growth.

(T) F 6. Technological progress allows a nation to produce more with a given amount of land, labor and capital.

(T) F 7. Economic growth has slowed down since the early 1970s in the U.S.

(T) F 8. The reduction in capital formation has been suggested as a cause for the slowing down of the U.S. growth rate.

T **(F)** 9. Government regulation of business results in increased productivity.

T **(F)** 10. The doomsday models say unlimited growth is possible but undesirable.

MATCH-UP

Match each item in the first column with a term in the second column. Use no term more than once.

_h_ 1. Inflation, governmental regulation, high marginal tax rates

_f_ 2. GNP divided by a price index to remove the effects of inflation

_c_ 3. GNP divided by population

_b_ 4. All the combinations of two goods that can be produced by an economy at full employment

_g_ 5. Growth of capital stock, improvement in the labor force, technological progress

_e_ 6. The increase in an economy's level of real output over time

_a_ 7. When inputs of any resource are increased while the quantity of another resource is fixed, the rate of increase in output eventually slows down.

_d_ 8. Lowered investment rates, slower technology advancement, a changed labor force

a. law of diminishing returns
b. production possibilities curve
c. per capita GNP
d. reasons for lowered U.S. growth rate
e. economic growth
f. real GNP
g. determinants of economic growth
h. reasons for lowered investment

MULTIPLE CHOICE

For each of the following statements, choose the one best alternative.

1. All of the following *except* one are determinants of economic growth. Choose that one.

    a. growth of the labor force

    b. growth of the capital stock

    c. growth in the price level

    d. growth in technological progress

2. Which of the following statements is true of the law of diminishing returns?

    a. It is not experienced in developed countries.

    b. It assumes at least one factor of production is fixed.

    c. It does not apply to inputs of capital.

    d. It assumes all resources are fixed in quantity.

3. According to the text chapter, all of the following statements are true *except* one. Choose that one.

    a. Economic growth can be shown by an outward shift in the production possibilities curve.

    b. Definitions of growth do not consider the distribution of income or quality of life.

    c. Economic growth measures money income change over time.

    d. Economic growth is the increase in per capita real output.

4. All of the following may account for the decline in U.S. productivity *except* one. Choose that one.

    a. Business research and development have declined.

    b. Government regulation has declined.

    c. The labor force has changed.

    d. Investment has declined.

5. With a growth rate of real GNP of 3 percent, approximately how long will it take for real GNP to grow and to double its present size?

   a. 9 years

   b. 17 years

   c. 20 years

   d. 24 years

PART TWO

UNIT XIII ASSIGNMENT: PART TWO

STUDY: Chapter 20, "The Economics of Developing Countries," *Economics Today*

STUDY: Film Summary: "A Steep and Thorny Path," *Study Guide*

VIEW: "A Steep and Thorny Path"

REVIEW: Chapter 20 Highlights, *Study Guide*

COMPLETE: Fill-in Review *and* Problems, Problems, Problems ..., *and* Econoword Puzzle, *Study Guide*

FILM SUMMARY: "A Steep and Thorny Path"

This is a program in which Thomas begins with one idea and ends with a very different one. (Throughout the drama of a kidnap to the mountains of Rio Lindo, be aware that Thomas is undergoing a learning experience.) The beautiful countryside Thomas sees and admires is part of a land where per capita income is very low, life expectancy is short, malnutrition is common, the mortality rate of babies is high, and few people can read (because only a small part of the nation's income is spent on education). Rio Lindo, however beautiful, fits the definition of a less-developed country (LDC). The per capita income of its people is less than $1500 per year. The film program includes an analysis of how Rio Lindo can be helped with economic development to improve its citizens' material welfare. More precisely, the film's theme involves a difference of opinion over whether industrial development should take place.

In this film program about the economics of developing countries, Thomas Weldon flies to Rio Lindo, a mythical Latin American country to investigate the investment possibilities for Dynamics Corporation there. They are joined during the flight by Julio Mendez, an economic advisor to Rio Lindo's President Correa and a representative of the Coalition for International Economic Development. Mendez, as a specialist in developmental economics, points out that, according to both socio-economic indicators of development, and the comparison of per capita income with other countries, Rio Lindo is an LDC. In order to plan what he considers to be the development necessary to lift the country from its poverty, crucial decisions regarding the building of new industrial capacity must be made.

Rio Lindo is in a simple stage of agriculture; that is, the vast majority of the population is employed producing food. It is a typical candidate to change from its present undeveloped economic state. First, it must go through the stages of manufacturing and then, ultimately develop a major service sector if it is to achieve developed economic status. There is, however, no certainty that these steps will be followed in the case of Rio Lindo, because development plans for any economy must be carefully analyzed, using specific targets and goals. Plans must be put into effect in a realistic and practical way; and such plans may require substantial foreign aid.

Although some production is presently taking place in Rio Lindo, much new investment must be undertaken, and the productivity of existing manufacturing improved in order to raise per capita incomes. Mendez is urging acceptance of foreign investment to bring in both expertise and technology.

There are profound problems in Rio Lindo of which Thomas has been unaware. Elyse Mercado was born in Rio Lindo; her parents left the country because "there was much poverty everywhere..." Poor people have little surplus to save. In LDCs, capital accumulation—machinery, factories—is low; therefore, the amount of goods produced is low. This is one of the crucial problems in LDCs: how to save enough out of the limited resources all share today to build more efficient machinery and productive capacities for the future. Building capital requires sacrifice of some of today's goods so that tomorrow will be better. In a poor society, this kind of saving is difficult indeed. When the impoverished people of LDCs have access to TVs and see programs which depict people in developed countries living on a rich scale, they may demand the same consumer goods and services from their governments. However, what is needed for economic development is investment in capital goods that will increase future production.

The charismatic head of the band of political exiles, Enrique Diaz, dreams of himself as leader of his country who will someday help extricate his people from their trap of poverty. Diaz is caught up in the notion that investment from abroad will enrich only foreigners, leave his people as poor or poorer than they now are, and, further, despoil the beautiful landscape.

A more realistic side of the question of development is raised when Diaz and Mendez debate. To answer Diaz's concerns regarding exploitation of the Rio Lindan people, Mendez points out that: 1) a stable government which can protect property rights of individuals and companies is vital to development, and 2) foreign investment may be one of the methods by which Rio Lindo can begin to develop its economy sufficiently to enable incomes to rise and the health and well-being of the people to improve. Mendez's questions to an idealistic Diaz are important ones. For example: Diaz does not say how he proposes to serve his people if he takes no steps to make them more prosperous. Further, Mendez wonders whether Diaz's concern with pollution is relevant when the economic development level is as low as it presently is.

Who really benefits from development? Who seriously believes that expanded production of goods and services is only for the rich? Where Diaz resists economic development on the grounds that his people will only be exploited by the presence of foreign investment in Rio Lindo, he is ignoring some of the facts he should know as a potential leader of his people. When the productive capacity of an economy increases, goods are produced that are available to people who could not formerly own them. The rich can always afford fine clothes and luxuries, whereas mass production makes more and cheaper goods available; and what had formerly been luxuries now become available to a wide range of people. In addition, through the process of economic development, medical-care facilities and safe water can become available, and family planning clinics and educational institutions can be established. (These are the services that can alter the mournful statistics that characterize the LDCs.)

Diaz's commitment to helping his people has caused him to be suspicious and critical regarding the motivations of outsiders when their help is preferred. Help from the United States to LDCs has been given in the form of: loans at low interest rates; grants of money that were, in turn, required to be spent for U.S.-made goods; gifts of food grown in the U.S. (food considered "surplus" since the government-subsidized U.S. price had been too high to clear the U.S. market); and military aid. Diaz's worries are shared by critics of foreign aid. Indeed, there are no guarantees that a specific form of aid will result in long-term benefit to the receiving country.

When its benefits and costs to both giver and recipient are fully taken into account, aid to LDCs has clearly not been an unqualified success. In a number of cases, it has increased the political problems of the recipient country (because of the power conferred to the group receiving large amounts of money). Grants of surplus food have served to distort the system of relative prices in the recipient country, and in so doing, have blurred the market signals necessary to encourage development of the receiving country's own agriculture. In the long run, regular shipments of surplus food to LDCs may serve to increase income of U.S. farmers, but at the same time, stunt the development of the farming sector in the recipient country.

From our point of view, foreign aid is often justified on grounds of U.S. security, developing stronger trading partners, lowering international political tensions, and exercising humanitarian concern for our fellow beings. Thomas and Elyse believe themselves to be humanitarians. But the humanitarian rationale may be best realized in the form of investments in industry, agriculture and education. It is this conclusion which not only Thomas, but Diaz himself, has reached at the end of the program.

NEW TERMS USED

Exploitation: Utilization of a natural resource; specifically in economics, exploitation may be defined as paying less for a resource than its market value.

Expropriation: Government takeover of property owned by citizens of other nations.

Nationalization: Transfer from private to public ownership, often without consent of the owners; sometimes with fair compensation, sometimes without.

Property Rights: Private property in market economies controlled and enforced through the legal framework of laws, courts and police.

CHAPTER 20 HIGHLIGHTS

Defined words are underlined.

I. LESS-DEVELOPED COUNTRIES (LDCs)

   A. LDCs are those countries with a per capita income of about $1,500 or less.

   B. Socio-economic indicators of development are

   1. life expectancy,

   2. infant mortality (death rate),

   3. literacy (ability to read and write),

   4. expenditures on education.

C. The large disparity between rich and poor countries is known throughout the world.

   1. Serious social unrest may result.

   2. Poor people of the world demand that their governments act to increase their standards of living.

II. THEORIES OF DEVELOPMENT

   A. A simplistic theory of little economic value

      1. "Geographical theory," also known as the north-south theory of economic development

         a. suggests that nations in colder climates will be more developed than nations in warmer climates.

         b. does not hold true for the past, and cannot be used to predict development.

   B. "Balanced growth," a more modern theory, claims that industry and agriculture must grow together in order for a nation to have economic growth.

      1. Modern industrialized nations have gone through stages of growth that are

         a. the agricultural stage when most of the population farms,

         b. the manufacturing stage when much of the population works in the industrialized sector,

         c. the service sector stage when the manufacturing sector declines in relative importance.

2. If it is assumed that currently developing countries must go through the above stages, important factors may be overlooked.

   a. A country's comparative advantage may be in agriculture not industrialization.

   b. Industrialization may be beneficial only if it comes about from market conditions that provide signals of profit in manufacturing.

C. "Social customs" theory contends that people's attitudes, customs and traditions are the most important elements in growth.

   1. Underdeveloped nations could invest in education and training of population—the development of human capital.

   2. As with all policy decisions, alternative costs and benefits of an investment program must be examined.

   3. Highly industrialized western nations subsidize their own agricultural sectors.

III. CAPITAL ACCUMULATION AND ECONOMIC DEVELOPMENT

A. To achieve domestic capital formation, saving is necessary. Resources must be released from consumer goods production in order to raise levels of productive capital.

B. Savings can occur in either rich or poor countries.

   1. In general, there is no pronounced relationship between the percentage of income saved and the level of income (over the long run).

   2. Saving takes place even in most poverty-stricken areas. (For example, storing dried onions is saving.)

3. The existence of religious monuments such as cathedrals or government monuments such as pyramids is evidence of past savings in poor countries.

4. Saving and individual capital accumulation will be greater, the more certain individuals are sure about the safety of their wealth/property; that is, with well-defined property rights.

5. Excess population may be the greatest deterrent to development and savings in LDCs.

C. Planning for development in the LDCs

1. Most of the governments of LDCs are establishing development plans with specific targets and goals for the growth of the economy.

2. Capital is usually earmarked for specific purposes to encourage development of priority sectors.

3. Some think that the long-run impact of higher oil prices on LDCs may be devastating; development will be slower, causing serious political instability. Others believe that oil price changes will change development of all countries.

D. Hope for LDCs

1. There is no guaranteed model of economic development for LDCs.

2. The importance and need for specific growth models can't be overstated.

FILL-IN REVIEW

Select between the choices underlined or fill in the blank. Cover the answer until you have provided your own.

less-developed countries LDCs *life expectancy, infant mortality, literacy education*	Those countries with a per capita income of about $1,500 or less are called ___-_____ _____ or _____. Socio-economic indicators of development are: _____, _____, _____ and expenditure on _____.
little *balanced growth* *agriculture manufacturing services*	A number of theories of economic development are simplistic and of *little/great* economic value. A simultaneous increase of both industry and agriculture required for a nation to have economic growth is the _____ _____ theory. It has been observed that developed countries have gone through stages of development. In sequence, these stages are (1) _____, (2) _____, (3) _____.
advantage *agriculture*	There is a problem with assuming that currently developing countries must go through the above stages. This problem is that a country's comparative _____ may be in _____ and not in industrialization. The theory contends that people's attitudes,

customs and traditions are the *least*/*most* important elements in growth is the _____ _____ theory.

most
social
customs

For any economy to produce its own capital it must ____. Resources must be *kept in*/*released from* consumer goods production to increase productive capital. Savings occur in both poor and rich countries. The more individuals are secure in the safety of their property rights the more savings and individual _____ accumulation can occur. Of the deterrents to development and savings in LDCs, the most important may be _____ _____.

save
released from

capital

excess
population

In planning for development in the LDCs, most governments establish plans with specific _____ for growth. Capital use is planned for development of priority _____. There is, however, *a guaranteed model*/*no guaranteed model* of economic development for LDCs.

goals
sectors
no guaranteed model

PROBLEMS, PROBLEMS, PROBLEMS...

Answers are at the end of this unit.

TRUE-FALSE

Circle either "T" or "F" for each statement.

- **(T)** F 1. Less-developed countries are classified as having per capita income of about $1,500 or less.

- T **(F)** 2. Expenditures on automobiles are an important socio-economic indicator of development.

- **(T)** F 3. Modern industrial nations have gone through stages of development. In order of sequence these are agriculture, manufacturing and services.

- **(T)** F 4. The more certain are the property rights, the more capital accumulation occurs.

- T **(F)** 5. There is a guaranteed model of economic development for most of the LDCs.

- T **(F)** 6. "Balanced growth" theory contends that people's attitudes, customs and traditions are the most important elements in economic growth.

- **(T)** F 7. To achieve capital formation an economy must save.

- T **(F)** 8. It is impossible for poor countries to save.

MATCH-UP

Match each item in the first column with a term in the second column. Use no term more than once.

e 1. Life expectancy, infant mortality, literacy, educational expenditures

f 2. Countries with per capita incomes of $1,500 or less

b 3. Industry and agriculture must grow simultaneously for a nation to have economic growth.

c 4. People's attitudes, customs and traditions are the most important elements in growth.

h 5. Reduce the incentive to save

d 6. A high degree of industrialization

g 7. Necessary to achieve capital formation

a 8. Stages of economic development

a. agriculture, manufacturing, services
b. "balanced growth" theory
c. "social customs" theory
d. developed countries
e. socio-economic development indicators
f. LDCs
g. saving
h. insecure property rights

MULTIPLE CHOICE

For each of the following statements, choose the one best alternative.

1. People in LDCs are not content with their economic lot today because
   a. of their bitter poverty.
   b. of the riches of the developed countries.
   c. of communication of the differences between developed countries and LDCs.
   d. all of the above

2. Savings occur in
   a. moderately developed countries.
   b. more developed countries.
   c. less developed countries.
   d. all of the above

3. Life expectancy, infant mortality, literacy and expenditures on education are all
   a. socio-economic indicators of aspiration level.
   b. socio-economic indicators of development.
   c. stages of economic development.
   d. stages of industrialization.

4. It has been observed that industrialized countries have gone through three stages of development. In sequence, these stages are
   a. agriculture, manufacturing, services.
   b. services, manufacturing, agriculture.
   c. manufacturing, agriculture, services.
   d. agriculture, services, manufacturing.

5. Which of the following refutes the theory that people in LDCs are too poor to save?

   a. the existence of excess population

   b. the existence of large amounts of leisure time

   c. the existence of religious and civic monuments

   d. the existence of an agricultural economy

6. In any economy, for capital formation to occur it is necessary to have

   a. profits.

   b. spending.

   c. savings.

   d. trade.

ECONOWORD PUZZLE

CLUES ACROSS

3. The second stage in the three stages of development
5. The more certain people are of a property _____, the more capital accumulation there will be (other things being equal).
9. The first stage in the three stages of development
11. The opposite of poorer
13. An economy where the per capita income is less than $1500 per year
18. The right to own and use your own_____ as you wish, is an important basis of a free enterprise system.
19. Economic _____ is the increase of an economy's real level of output over time.
21. Measured ratios between two things; many figures in economics are in terms of a certain quantity per some base, e.g. growth _____, mortality _____, literacy _____.
22. The proportion of deaths to population
23. The opposite of rich
24. Acronym for less-developed country
25. The theory that agriculture and manufacturing should develop simultaneously.

CLUES DOWN

1. The wealth that is accumulated through not spending
2. The end toward which effort is directed.
4. Total amount earned during the year
6. Spending for capital equipment
7. Education in developing countries is needed to _____ a more skilled work force.
8. Per-person, or literally "per-head"
10. If you are able to read and write, it can be said that you are _____.
12. The most important deterrent to economic development for the LDC is excess _____.
14. Agriculture, manufacturing and services are three _____ of development.
15. The _____ rate for infants is much higher in a LDC.
16. This chapter has been about _____ development of LDCs.
17. Machines, factories, tools
20. The economies of the entire _____ are increasingly interdependent.

ECONOWORD PUZZLE

ANSWERS TO STUDY QUESTIONS

PART ONE

TRUE-FALSE

1. F 2. T 3. T 4. F 5. F 6. T 7. T 8. T 9. F 10. F

MATCH-UP

1. h 2. f 3. c 4. b 5. g 6. e 7. a 8. d

MULTIPLE CHOICE

1. c 2. b 3. c 4. b 5. d

PART TWO

TRUE-FALSE

1. T 2. F 3. T 4. T 5. F 6. F 7. T 8. F

1. e 2. f 3. b 4. c 5. h 6. d 7. g 8 a

MULTIPLE CHOICE

1. d 2. d 3. b 4. a 5. c 6. c

COMPLETED ECONOWORD PUZZLE

	S																
G	M	A	N	U	F	A	C	T	U	R	I	N	G		R	I	G	H	T
O	V							N			P		N				R
A	G	R	I	C	U	L	T	U	R	E		C		E			V		A
L	N		I					O		R	I	C	H	E	R		I
	G		T			P		M				S				N
L	E	S	S	-	D	E	V	E	L	O	P	E	D	-	C	O	U	N	T	R	Y
	T		E		R		P		E		A		M			
C		A		C		A		U		A		P	R	O	P	E	R	T	Y
A		G	R	O	W	T	H		L		T		I		N
P	E	N		E		A		H		T		T			W
I	S		O			T			R	A	T	E	S				O
T		M	O	R	T	A	L	I	T	Y				P	O	O	R
A		I				O								L
L	D	C	C		B	A	L	A	N	C	E	D	-	G	R	O	W	T	H	D

INTERNATIONAL TRADE

UNIT XIV

UNIT IN A NUTSHELL

PART ONE

Film: "Don't Let Them Take My Job Away"

Text: Chapter 21

PART TWO

Film: "The Man Who Needed Nobody"

Text: Chapter 21

No country is completely self-sufficient. Just as each individual occupies a place in our national economy, and as each sector of the economy functions in the economy's circular flow, so do nations interact in the flow of the world's production of goods and services.

For each country, trade brings in vital raw materials and finished goods that are wanted. Trade sends out materials, products and services other nations want. Thus, other economies are able to produce some goods more cheaply than we can, or sell us cheaper raw materials that we need for our own production. We, in turn, sell some of our goods and raw materials abroad at prices established by international supply and demand. (No nation can continue to buy goods or services from abroad without selling its own goods and services in world markets.)

As we develop a theory of international trade, we will assume that for both partners trade is voluntary, carried on at prices established by international supply and demand, and is engaged in because the involved partners gain from the exchange. Trade is mutually advantageous; since it is based on the production gain of specialization and comparative advantage, it enables trading partners to have higher standards of living.

UNIT OBJECTIVES

The following objectives can be met by studying Chapter 21 and viewing "Don't Let Them Take My Job Away" and "The Man Who Needed Nobody." After completing this Unit, the student should be able to:

1. Explain why trade between countries takes place and the role of trade in our economic system.

2. Explain how to apply supply and demand analysis in international trade; use excess demand and excess supply schedules.

3. Define absolute advantage, comparative advantage and opportunity cost.

4. State the reasons countries specialize in the production of certain goods, and use your explanation to describe the potential benefits and costs of foreign trade to a nation.

5. Explain how import quotas and tariffs are the primary policy tools for trade restriction.

6. List the arguments against free trade, then link each argument with a corresponding pro-trade answer.

NOTE

Before studying this unit refresh your understanding of the concept of opportunity cost, supply, demand and equilibrium price of a good, by reviewing Units I and II.

PART ONE AND PART TWO

UNIT XIV ASSIGNMENT: PARTS ONE AND TWO

STUDY: Chapter 21, "Comparative Advantage and International Trade," *Economics Today: The Macro View* (This is Chapter 37 in the combined hardbound text, *Economics Today*.)

STUDY: Film Summary: "Don't Let Them Take My Job Away," *Study Guide*

VIEW: "Don't Let Them Take My Job Away"

STUDY: Film Summary: "The Man Who Needed Nobody," *Study Guide*

VIEW: "The Man Who Needed Nobody"

REVIEW: Chapter 21 Highlights, *Study Guide*

COMPLETE: Fill-in Review *and* Problems, Problems, Problems ... *and* Econoword Puzzle, *Study Guide*

FILM SUMMARY: "Don't Let Them Take My Job Away"

Thomas Weldon's emotional reaction to the closing of his boss's factory and his neighbor John Sights's job loss is a common one. Speaking for the men laid off because of the factory closing, Weldon argues for protection by the federal government from foreign imports. Unless the line is drawn, the men insist, "Foreign stuff is going to run everybody out of business." Their protests are understandable but their reasoning cannot stand-up. Their protectionist argument is echoed throughout the industrial world. Asian and European workers petition for tariffs against U.S. exports saying, "We must be protected against highest paid, efficient American workers who have equipment and skills superior to ours." The complicated issue of protectionism is explored in this film.

Economic concepts and principles can be applied throughout the world, and certainly this includes international trade and the restrictions that are put on it. Trade with the rest of the world is important to the U.S., and is even more important to other countries. Many of them would suffer serious hardships if deprived of their foreign trade. And how would the U.S. industries manage without tin, asbestos, chrome, aluminum, and oil? In economic terms, closing off trade would be expensive in terms of what we would be required to give up.

Do we want to be self-sufficient? Standards of living would fall, ours as well as those of other nations. Jobs for American workers depend on foreign markets. What is required is an understanding of the gains for trade and, following that, a realization of the need for international cooperation.

The concepts of comparative and absolute advantages are important to the understanding of the basis of trade. An individual or country that can do something better than another individual or country has an absolute advantage. An absolute advantage in production is not necessary, however, for trade to be beneficial to both trading partners. Trade can take place even though one country has an absolute advantage in *all* areas of production.

International trade is based on the differences between countries that result in each being able to produce some goods relatively more cheaply than others. Most countries specialize in production in which they have a comparative advantage. The key here is the word comparative—it implies all countries have an advantage in producing some things and a disadvantage in others. Even though two countries can produce the same goods, for each to specialize in production of some and trade for what the other produces most efficiently is of mutual benefit. Even though a country is rich and efficient it should specialize in production where the opportunity cost is the lowest. It should produce those goods for which it has a comparative advantage and import those for which it has a comparative disadvantage.

The workers in the film program lose their jobs when foreign-produced slippers become cheaper than American-made slippers, and Thomas goes to Washington to convince Congress to raise tariffs on the offending imports. A tariff is simply a tax on an imported good, and it can be set high or low. The higher the tariff the more restrictive its effect. Thomas can not make much of a case for protective tariffs although many before him have tried with considerable success.

Think about who pays the tariff—those who buy the imported goods pay it. Since the price of the imported good is higher, people must pay more and will buy less of the good. Notice how useful it is for a domestic producer if an imported good has a tariff placed on it. Domestic producers then can charge higher prices themselves. A little bit of tariff may provide a lot of protection from competition for a producer.

Import quotas are like tariffs, but they simply limit quantities of specific goods. Quotas create a shortage in the market, forcing prices up so that import license holders are able to make higher profits. Since there is less of the restricted good, domestic producers can sell more. Tariffs and quotas discourage imports and raise prices to the domestic consumer, destroying the international division of labor and protecting the more inefficient domestic manufacturer.

Our system is based on competition. Free trade generates a good bit of it. A competitive system forces the producer to keep costs down, be efficient and maintain high quality products. Customers, who have a choice, will buy from competitors. Competition helps consumers, but producers may not be as eager, since profits can be higher without the competition. Tariffs and protective quotas are often urged by congressmen and political representatives of particular areas, in order to protect or create jobs in their own districts. Many people have much to gain from specific tariffs.

It's hard to find those who argue for the incomes of all the consumers. Often people become convinced that tariffs actually do protect the nation.

And do tariffs protect the entire economy? There are arguments for tariffs that have limited validity. In his effort to convince legislators to place protective tariffs on slippers, Thomas Weldon cannot use the "infant industry" argument that struggling new industries should be afforded protection from imported goods until they more firmly establish their own industries. In this case, the U.S. shoe industry is well established; the infant grew up long ago.

Another argument for protection is that tariffs are simply excise taxes that are paid to the government by the buyers of the product. On the other hand, tariffs allow domestic producers to implicitly collect the tax on their products by charging a higher price.

Protectionists would have the buyers of a protected product subsidize its domestic production. This is usually not the way tariffs are justified; however, a tariff or quota is usually simpler to impose than an outright subsidy. Why? Because voters aren't hard to convince that "workers must be protected."

The national defense argument is often a convincing one when attempts are made to impose trade restrictions. How can industry vital to our defense be allowed to lose in international competition, the argument goes. Should an essential defense industry be allowed to decline? If trade restrictions are the only way to insure a strong defense industry, then perhaps they should be used—but they are not the only way. Economists suggest outright subsidies to such industries in order that the cost to the taxpayers is clear to all. In that way, all share in the cost of national defense, not just buyers of protected products.

Tariffs are sometimes used by a small country in order to diversify its economy by forcing the development of production in a good for which it does not have a comparative advantage. The local, protected producers gain at the expense of everyone else. When scarce resources are diverted to uneconomic production, everyone eventually loses.

Efficiency is what is important to production. The argument that we must protect American workers from low-wage, foreign competition is the poorest argument of all. American workers are highly productive. Consider which industries are the most successful in international markets—the high wage industries that are also highly productive. It is wages compared with productivity which makes an industry competitive in world markets. It is the ratio of product output to wages (worker efficiency) which makes the difference.

The short-run advantages of protecting Dutweiler's shoe workers may not be worth it for either the workers or consumers here in the United States. The long-run effects may not at first be obvious. The lack of competition in the U.S. market place can be used to drive prices up. U.S. goods have indeed become increasingly high priced in world markets. Not only do domestic markets suffer, but the high prices combined with high tariffs effectively cut U.S. goods from potential export markets. Unrestricted free trade enables people to live at a higher standard of living. Each nation is able to increase its own production possibilities so that the entire world's production possibilities are increased.

Effectively, we can neither raise our national living standards nor increase our workers' total wages by protecting domestic producers with high tariffs. These tariffs tend to increase the cost of living for all, and by more than any increase in money wages.

So, Thomas, and the out-of-work men he speaks for, can take little comfort in the hope that any piece of legislation will go far in solving national unemployment problems. Historically, protectionism has been shown to fail, ultimately, in protecting jobs. In a free trade economy, the gains from trade add far more than is lost by those who are hurt by trade. Tariffs cut down efficiency and, in the long run, nations lose their competitive position. Protectionism begets repercussions. A solution suggested at the end of the film, to produce a quality shoe product for the market abroad, may be a reasonable alternative. An expanded foreign market will, in the long run, provide the key to increased job opportunities for the American worker.

FILM SUMMARY: "The Man Who Needed Nobody"

Remember Robinson Crusoe? When he was shipwrecked, he was forced into solitary self-sufficiency on his tropical isle. Perhaps none of us has dreams, or nightmares, of being entirely self-sufficient; but what about the romantic notion of small group self-sufficiency or even national ability to go it alone?

Does anyone still believe that every nation's economy could be more solidly based and productive, and its citizens better off, if each nation was completely self-sufficient? Indeed, could each nation survive without the imported raw materials for the goods it manufactures? Are the farms of the world's countries able to feed all of each nation's inhabitants? Not at all likely.

The previous Film Summary discussed the gains available from trade. To sustain itself in technologically advanced economies, each nation requires some of the inputs and products that others provide. Complete self-sufficiency would prove to be gravely expensive in terms of opportunities lost. The same could be said for every community, family and individual. No one is an island; and with international trade there is both more total product and more income to share by nations who are trading partners.

In this film program, the original concept of H. B. Teal for the self-sufficient community named Celebration House is commendable, perhaps, from other than an economic standpoint. From an economic point of view, it is a bit of a bust. Each of the members, from the artist Ann Brinn, to the baker and Teal himself, participate in each of the community's enterprises. None of the members specialize; all spread themselves very thin. In a word, Celebration House uses its community's resources inefficiently. Celebration House does not use the members talents so that the entire group benefits by each member doing what he/she does best. By not specializing they lose their comparative advantages. Not only are individual members frustrated, but the entire group loses what they could have had.

Do countries continue with inefficient production, and sacrifice output? Through the force of political pressure (by some who individually stand to benefit by inefficient productive methods) or perhaps by not understanding the principle of comparative advantage, nations often make Teal's mistake. Each nation gains in trade by doing what it does best in comparison with other nations. The text uses the example of the French comparative advantage in wine production and a somewhat outdated example of the Japanese comparative advantage in silk production. (There are many examples of comparative advantage that describe Japan, particularly in the field of high technology.) Here, they specialize because they have human and material resources, as the French do in winemaking. Each of these nations has allocated its resources to achieve maximum production. Trade then shares the resulting extra productivity with both trading partners and is of substantial benefit to each one. There is no other economic reason for trade than mutual benefit.

As nations gains by doing what each does best, the Celebration House community would have done best had Teal allowed the members each to pursue comparative advantage. His desire for self-sufficiency proves costly. Teal's insistence that everybody, including himself, cooperate equally in doing all the chores actually lowers efficiency. Teal may have had an absolute advantage in the quarry, knocking rocks out of the hillside, but the hours there cost him the rest needed to supervise the community and the time to write his book. Ann Brinn may have been a good gardener, but she is a better artist and time to paint what would have been profitable pictures is not afforded her. The opportunity costs paid by Celebration House are high. The refusal to use members' talents denies the community the extra product that would have resulted from comparative advantage.

Instead, all the energies of uniquely talented people are used in tasks that could have been done at far lower opportunity costs. Had each followed a comparative advantage, the community could have had products to sell outside the House, bringing in extra income that could have improved the well being of the entire community. Such short-sighted use of valuable resources is not entirely uncommon.

With extra income, H. B. Teal could have considered importing energy into Celebration House. Purchasing the solar heater parts for his windmill is expensive. Teal's ideas about equating the lack of self-sufficiency with character weakness are, if nothing else, uneconomic. The result is that Teal's community and its members have lower real income levels. As Karen reminds him, the importation of plentiful and cheap raw materials allows us to save our resources for a more productive use.

For example, even though the U.S. is a major oil producing nation, oil-rich Middle East countries have lower opportunity costs in its production. Although national security and political considerations may have to be taken into account, we would find production of all of our own oil expensive indeed, in terms of the use of our scarce resources. Recall from the previous film, that in this interdependent world, no one is self-sufficient. As Karen reminds Teal, other nations buy our exports. For others to buy from us, we must in turn buy from them.

The world's nations benefit by specializing in what they do best and exporting their excess goods. Nations import the goods they want when the world market-clearing price is below their own cost of production. The more the price goes below national equilibrium price, the more likely the quantity demanded will increase and the greater the volume of imports. World trade follows market supply-and-demand forces, and the entire world of international trade is an efficient economic process. Basically, this process entails the efficient use of resources and labor and a specialization in what people do best. As a result, output is increased, opportunity costs are reduced and trade becomes profitable.

World trade exists because those engaging in it benefit by the trade. If importing or exporting proves costly then, simply, nations cease to trade. The greater the volume of world trade, the greater the incentives are for specialization, and as specialization increases world output does also.

CHAPTER 21 HIGHLIGHTS

Defined words are underlined.

I. PUTTING TRADE IN ITS PLACE

   A. World trade has increased from $1.3 billion in 1800 (measured in 1980 dollars) to $1 trillion today.

   B. International trade is more important for some countries than for others.

   1. For example, exports and imports represent 44 percent of GNP for the Netherlands, and 36 percent for Belgium and Luxembourg.

   2. Exports and imports represent only 9 percent of GNP for the United States.

   C. Examples of American consumer goods imports include oil, chocolate, cars, tea, coffee, wine and bananas. Examples of industrial raw materials imported are chrome, nickel, oil, tin, asbestos and aluminum.

D. Examples of American exports are grain, tobacco, cotton, coal, metal work and textile machinery and oil field equipment.

II. DEMAND AND SUPPLY OF IMPORTS AND EXPORTS

A. Trade must be beneficial to both parties, otherwise the transaction will not take place.

B. How much of any good will be imported? We can derive an excess demand schedule for that good. <u>*Excess Demand Schedule:*</u> The excess of quantity demanded over quantity supplied as prices fall below the equilibrium price in the domestic economy.

1. When domestic production cannot meet domestic demand, the difference is made up by imports.

2. The excess demand curve for a good is thus the same thing as the demand curve for imports of that good.

3. This curve is negatively sloped, since a fall in price would induce an increase in quantity demanded.

4. Example: the lower the world price of wine, the more wine we import.

C. How much of any good will be exported? We can derive an excess supply schedule for that good. <u>*Excess Supply Schedule:*</u> The excess of quantity supplied over quantity demanded as prices rise above equilibrium in the domestic market.

1. When domestic demand cannot match domestic production, the difference is made up by exports.

2. The excess supply is thus the same thing as the supply curve of exports.

3. This curve is positively sloped, since an increase in price induces firms to produce more for export.

4. Example: the higher the world price of grain, the more grain we choose to export.

D. Relation of exports and imports of any good

  1. If the world price of a good is exactly equal to the domestic price, both excess demand and supply are equal to zero.

   a. The country will neither export nor import.

   b. This is called the *zero trade point.*

  2. If the world price rises above the domestic equilibrium price, excess supply will be positive and the country will export the good.

  3. If the world price falls below the domestic equilibrium price, excess demand becomes positive and the country will import the good.

E. International equilibrium in a two-country world occurs where the quantity of exports supplied by one country just equals the quantity of imports demanded by the other.

  1. Graphically, this occurs where one country's excess supply curve intersects the other's excess demand schedule.

  2. In Exhibit 21-6 of your text, trade in wine between the U.S. and France is graphed.

   a. Equilibrium is at point E where the excess supply curve of France intersects the excess demand curve of the U.S.

   b. At equilibrium, the price is $1.50, while the amount of wine traded is 10 million liters per year.

III. COMPARATIVE AND ABSOLUTE ADVANTAGE

  A. *Absolute Advantage:* If a country can produce a good cheaper than another country, it is said to have an absolute advantage.

   1. Absolute advantage explains trade only when each country has an absolute advantage relative to the other.

2. One country can use better means of producing all goods but may still trade with other countries.

B. *Comparative Advantage:* Even if a country lacks an absolute advantage in the production of any good, it may still have a comparative advantage.

C. An example of absolute and comparative advantage: you are an executive, and can type faster and more efficiently than your secretary.

1. You have an absolute advantage over her in both managerial abilities and typing skills.

2. You have a comparative advantage in managerial skills; you can make more money by concentrating on being an executive and letting her type.

D. Countries specialize in the production of those goods for which they have a comparative advantage.

E. Comparative advantage and opportunity cost

1. *Opportunity Cost:* The highest-valued alternative that has to be sacrificed for the option that is chosen.

2. If an executive decides to do his own typing, his opportunity cost is the amount of money he could have made by pursuing his managerial function.

3. Comparative advantage merely says that traders try to minimize their opportunity costs.

F. Trade occurs because opportunity costs differ between countries.

G. Countries have different opportunity costs because of different resource mixes.

1. If a country has much land relative to its population, the opportunity cost of using land is low relative to that of labor. We would expect such a country to have a comparative advantage in land-intensive goods. Australia is an example of the above.

2. If a country has little land relative to its population, the opportunity cost of using labor is low relative to that of land. We would expect such a country to have a comparative advantage in labor-intensive goods.

H. There are costs of trade. Changing resource mixes cause comparative advantages to be constantly changing.

1. Changes involve costs of adjustment.

2. Countries losing a comparative advantage may face rising unemployment in the stricken industry.

3. Ultimately, workers can find employment elsewhere; but this may take a painfully long time.

4. Foreign trade raises average and total income in each country but some groups may suffer ups or downs in their own incomes.

I. The Japanese miracle: the comparative advantage at work

1. Real GNP in Japan has been growing at 10 percent a year.

a. Japan has a comparative advantage in manufacturing, leading to exports in cameras, cars, and steel which double every five years.

b. Because of its comparative advantage in manufacturing, Japan imports the raw materials for steel making, and exports the finished product.

IV. ECONOMIC GAINS FROM TRADE COME FROM SPECIALIZATION; ARGUMENTS AGAINST FREE TRADE POINT OUT COSTS OF TRADE.

A. Infant industry argument

1. New industries often face high costs which prevent successful competition against established foreign industry which has lower costs because of the economies of scale.

2. Proponents of the infant industry argument believe these industries should be protected from competition until they "mature" and are ready to compete.

   a. Methods of protection include tariffs and quotas.

   b. This argument is often abused. Some "infant industries" are decades old and the argument is used simply as a rationalization for preferential treatment.

B. National security argument

   1. According to this argument, reliance on other countries for certain raw materials imperils national security.

   2. An example is oil. President Eisenhower implemented quotas on oil imports to raise domestic oil prices and give oil companies incentives to find more domestic oil.

   3. Quotas have adverse distributional effects, raising consumer prices and giving windfall profits to oil companies.

C. Stability argument

   1. Foreign trade should be restricted because it introduces variations in our employment level.

   2. If this argument is followed to its logical conclusion, we would restrict trade among our own states.

D. Protecting American jobs argument

   1. Cheap foreign labor sometimes gives other countries a competitive edge over the United States.

   2. Import tariffs and quotas are one method of protection.

      a. Tariffs and quotas raise prices of goods.

      b. The institution of tariffs or quotas could start retaliatory tariffs by other countries, leading to a tariff war.

   3. The same argument can be used as a case against trade among our own states.

FILL-IN REVIEW

Select between the choices underlined or fill in the blank. Cover the answers until you have provided your own.

_____ _____ has grown enormously in the last two hundred years. For some countries, such as the Netherlands, international trade represents a substantial portion of ____. For the United States, the percentage is rather *large/small*, about 9%. But this figure is deceptive, for the impact of international trade on the domestic economy is qualitative as well as quantitative. American consumers *can get along without/have grown accustomed to* imported consumer goods.

Our industry *does not need/depends on* imported raw materials.

It is a common misapprehension that one country or another "gets the best" of others in international trade. We must remember, however, that ____ is voluntary; this means that a transaction must be _____ to both parties, or it would *always/never* take place. The excess of quantity demanded over quantity supplied as prices fall below the equilibrium price in the domestic economy is called an excess ____ ____.

	World trade
	GNP
	small
	have grown accustomed to
	depends on
	trade
	beneficial
	never
	demand schedule

negatively	This curve is _____ (or inversely)
import	sloped, and is synonymous with the _____ demand curve. On the other hand, the excess of quantity supplied over quantity demanded as prices rise above the equilibrium price in
supply	the domestic economy is an excess _____
schedule *positively*	_____. This curve is _____ sloped,
excess	and is synonymous with the _____ supply curve. When the world price is greater than the domestic price, there will be excess supply
export	and the country will *export/import* the good. When the world price is less than the domestic price, there will be excess demand and the
import	country will *export/import* the good. International equilibrium is obtained (in the two-country, two-good case) when the excess demand of each country equals the excess supply of the other, or when one country's
imports *exports*	_____ equal the other's _____. If the world price of a good is exactly equal to the domestic price, both excess demand and supply are equal to zero. This is called the ____
zero	
trade point	_____ _____.
	When a country can produce a good more cheaply than another country it has an
absolute	_____ advantage. The theory of absolute
trade	advantage explains international _____ only

when each country has an absolute advantage in some good. But if only one country has an absolute advantage for all goods, there is still a basis for trade. Whenever a country can produce one good cheaper than another good, it is said to have a _____ advantage, regardless of whether or not it has an _____ _____.

comparative
absolute
advantage

An example of comparative advantage is that of the executive who is also a champion typist. He has a/an *absolute*/*comparative* advantage over his secretary in both managerial and typing skills. Nonetheless, this executive will not do his own typing. Why? He can be more efficient being an executive than a typist; in more technical terms, the _____ cost of typing persuades him to specialize in being an executive. This is the law of comparative advantage. Traders will specialize in that function in which they have the greatest _____ _____ or lowest _____ cost.

absolute

opportunity

comparative advantage
opportunity

Trade results from differences in _____ costs between traders. One reason that opportunity costs differ is that factor endowments vary from place to place. When countries specialize in those industries in

opportunity

income

free trade

which they have a comparative advantage trade raises average and total _____ for each country. This is the powerful argument for ____ _____. Economic gains from free trade come from specialization of production. There are several arguments against free trade. It is argued that young industries face high costs which price them out of international markets. For these industries, protective tariffs or quotas are often used until the industries can become competitive. This is the

infant industry

competitive

_____ _____ argument. The problem is that under the protection of tariffs, many of these industries never become _____ at all.

national security

consumer

It is also argued that certain key raw materials should be protected in the case of possible war. This is the _____ _____ agreement, and oil is an example of this. Undesirable effects are high _____ prices and windfall profits to certain firms.

jobs

Many who oppose free trade argue that if we import low priced goods, we lose American ____. Following this argument to its logical conclusion, we would have to limit trade among our own states.

PROBLEMS, PROBLEMS, PROBLEMS...

Answers are at the end of this unit.

TRUE-FALSE

Circle either "T" or "F" for each statement.

(T) F 1. Trade must be beneficial to both parties, or it would not take place.

(T) F 2. The excess demand schedule is the same thing as the import demand curve.

T (F) 3. The export supply curve is the same thing as the import demand curve.

(T) F 4. In a two-country world equilibrium, each country's demand for imports equals the other's supply of exports.

(T) F 5. A country has an absolute advantage, if it can produce a good cheaper than another country can.

(T) F 6. A country can have a comparative advantage even when it suffers from an absolute disadvantage.

T (F) 7. Countries specialize in the production of those goods in which they have comparative disadvantages.

(T) F 8. One of the reasons opportunity costs vary between countries is they have different resource mixes.

(T) F 9. According to the infant industry argument, new industries which face high beginning costs should temporarily be protected from international competition by tariffs and quotas.

MATCH-UP

Match each item in the first column with a term in the second column. Use no term more than once.

__h__ 1. This is voluntary and must benefit both parties or it would not take place.

__j__ 2. A supply curve of exports

__e__ 3. Exports supplied by a country equal imports demanded by the other.

__d__ 4. Each country specializes in the production of that good in which it has a _____ _____.

__f__ 5. A country that can produce a good cheaper than another country has an _____ _____.

__b__ 6. Highest-valued alternative that has to be sacrificed for the option that is chosen

__c__ 7. Reason for different opportunity costs

__i__ 8. One of the costs of international trade

__a__ 9. Use of tariffs or quotas to enable young industries to begin domestic production

__g__ 10. Become self-reliant in strategic raw materials

__k__ 11. The world price of a good is exactly equal to the domestic price.

a. infant industry argument
b. opportunity cost
c. resource mixes
d. comparative advantage
e. international equilibrium in a two-country world
f. absolute advantage
g. national security argument
h. all trade
i. unemployment in some industries
j. excess supply schedule
k. zero trade point

MULTIPLE CHOICE

For each of the following statements, choose the one best alternative.

1. Trade is engaged in because it

    a. is never beneficial to both parties of the transaction.

    b. is occasionally beneficial to both parties of the transaction.

    c. is usually beneficial to both parties of the transaction.

    d. is always beneficial to both parties of the transaction.

2. The excess demand schedule for a good

    a. shows the excess of quantity supplied over quantity demanded as price falls below the equilibrium price.

    b. is exactly the same as the demand curve for imports of the good.

    c. is positively sloped.

    d. is exactly the same as the supply curve for exports of the good.

3. The excess supply schedule of a good

    a. shows the excess of quantity supplied over quantity demanded as price rises above the equilibrium price.

    b. is exactly the same as the demand curve for imports.

    c. is negatively sloped and follows the law of supply.

    d. shows the excess of quantity demanded over quantity supplied as price falls below the equilibrium price.

4. Trade provides advantages to trading partners. The most important economic advantage is

    a. prestige with foreign nations.

    b. obtaining goods that would otherwise not be available.

    c. lowered production of unnecessary goods.

    d. a more stable political system.

5. If the world price of a good is exactly equal to the domestic price
   a. the country will export the good.
   b. the country will import the good.
   c. excess demand is greater than excess supply.
   d. this is called the zero trade point.

6. When a country restricts the quantity of imports of a certain good it is using
   a. a quota system.
   b. an absolute advantage system.
   c. a tariff system.
   d. free trade.

7. When a country imposes a tax on each unit of a certain good it imports, it is using
   a. a quota system.
   b. an absolute advantage system.
   c. a tariff system.
   d. free trade.

8. International equilibrium in a two-country world exists when
   a. the exports supplied by one country just equal imports demanded by the other.
   b. the excess supply curves of the countries intersect.
   c. the excess demand curves of the countries intersect.
   d. the excess supply of one country does not equal excess demand of the other.

9. Both countries will gain from trade when they
   a. export what they have an absolute advantage in and import what they have a comparative advantage in.

b. import what they have an absolute advantage in and export what they have a comparative advantage in.

c. export what they have a comparative advantage in and import what they have an absolute disadvantage in.

d. export what they have a comparative advantage in and import what they have a comparative disadvantage in.

e. none of these

10. The following is a hypothetical table of person-hours required to produce coffee and pocket calculators in Brazil and the United States.

PRODUCT	UNITED STATES	BRAZIL
Coffee (lb.)	20 person-hours	2 person-hours
Pocket Calculators (unit)	4 person-hours	20 person-hours

Using the above information, what is the opportunity cost to the United States of one pound of coffee?

a. 24 person-hours

b. 5 units of pocket calculators

c. 4 units of pocket calculators

d. 20 units of pocket calculators

11. Which of the following is a true statement of the absolute and comparative advantages concerning coffee and pocket calculator production in the United States and Brazil?

a. Brazil has an absolute advantage in calculators and a comparative advantage in coffee.

b. The United States has an absolute advantage in both coffee and pocket calculators.

c. Brazil has both a comparative and an absolute advantage in coffee; the United States has both a comparative and an absolute advantage in pocket calculators.

d. Brazil has an absolute advantage in coffee, but a comparative advantage in pocket calculators.

ECONOWORD PUZZLE

CLUES ACROSS

1. Trade is based on _____ and comparative advantage.
6. Land of the free
7. Trade is _____ on comparative advantage.
8. Exchange
11. A tax on imports
12. A country which can produce more of something has an _____ advantage.
13. Trade is based on _____ advantage.
15. Supply and demand in international markets determine world _____ for goods.
17. There is more for the people of the _____ to share when there is free trade.
18. This is a common argument for the use of tariffs and quotas: the _____ industry argument.
20. By assumption, international trade is entered into freely; in other words is _____.
23. Trading partners share the _____ from trade.
25. Trade benefits _____ parties involved.
26. Even though specific groups of workers may, in the short run, be _____ by trade, in the aggregate the nation benefits.
27. Payment of labor

CLUES DOWN

1. The payment of public funds to private individuals
2. If goods are _____ to import, they will be imported unless there are trade restrictions.
3. Trade between countries is _____.
4. Arguments *for* free trade
5. The world exchange of goods and services takes place in the international _____.
9. The opposite of domestic
10. The requirement that only a certain number of a certain good can be imported
12. Comparative _____
15. American workers' rates of _____ reflect productivity.
16. Bringing in of foreign-made goods
21. Trade is _____ based on absolute advantage.
22. This *Study Guide* is for _____.
24. FRD's plan for economic recovery was called the _____ Deal.

ECONOWORD PUZZLE

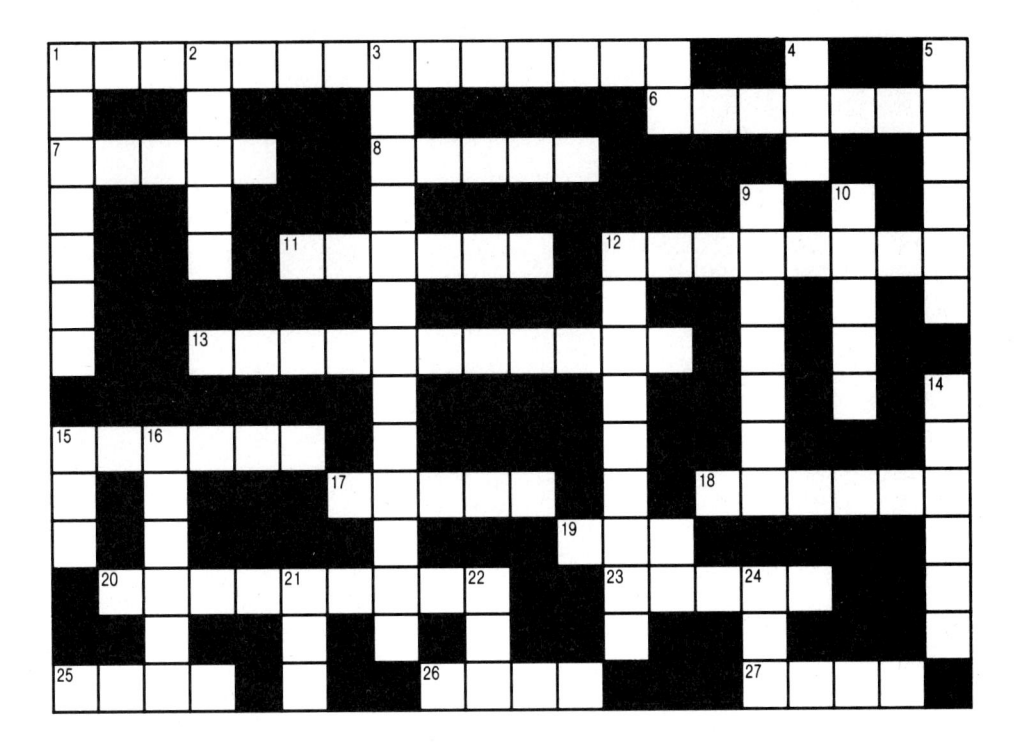

ANSWERS TO STUDY QUESTIONS

TRUE-FALSE

1. T 2. T 3. F 4. T 5. T 6. T 7. F 8. T 9. T

MATCH-UP

1. h 2. j 3. e 4. d 5. f 6. b 7. c 8. i 9. a 10. g 11. k

MULTIPLE CHOICE

1. d 2. b 3. a 4. b 5. d 6. a 7. c 8. a 9. d 10. b 11. c

COMPLETED ECONOWORD PUZZLE

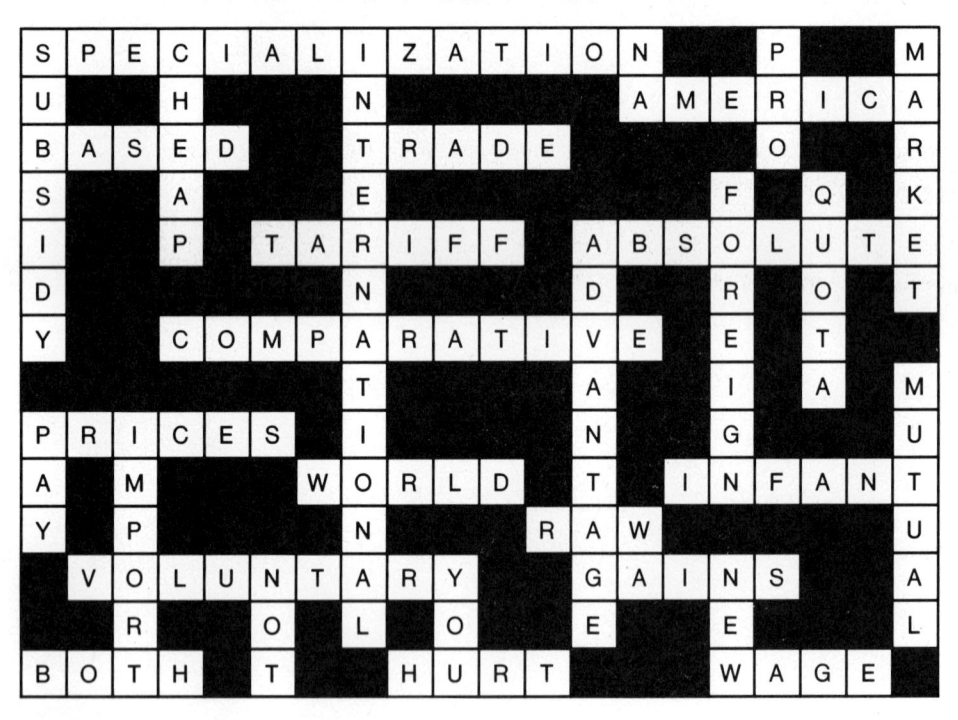

S	P	E	C	I	A	L	I	Z	A	T	I	O	N		P		M
U			H				N				A	M	E	R	I	C	A
B	A	S	E	D			T	R	A	D	E			O			R
S			A				E					F		Q			K
I			P		T	A	R	I	F	F		A	B	S	O	L	U	T	E
D							N			D		R		O			T
Y			C	O	M	P	A	R	A	T	I	V	E		T		
							T			A			I		A		M
P	R	I	C	E	S		I			N			G				U
A		M				W	O	R	L	D		T		I	N	F	A	N	T
Y		P					N			R	A	W					U
			V	O	L	U	N	T	A	R	Y		G	A	I	N	S		A
			R			O		L		O			E			E			L
B	O	T	H		T			H	U	R	T			W	A	G	E

INTERNATIONAL FINANCES

UNIT XV

UNIT IN A NUTSHELL

PART ONE	PART TWO	OPTIONAL
Film: "The Tightrope Walkers"	Film: "The Investors"	Text: Chapter 23
Text: Chapter 22	Text: Chapter 22	

In earlier Units, we discussed the economic development of less-developed countries (LDCs) which can result in their participation in international trade as manufacturers of finished goods. We have also talked about the gains from international trade, and its basis for comparative advantages. But we haven't yet discussed the actual mechanisms of international transactions.

From your study of money, our banking system and monetary policy, you are aware of the importance of money in an economy. There is no universal money used in international trade. International trade is not the same as domestic trade mostly because monetary units are different. Flows of money across national borders are vital to trade, but create problems for the countries involved. The ways that currencies are exchanged for each other (so that each country can be paid for its exports in its own money), and the ways that countries keep track of their balances of payments to other countries are the bases for international finance.

UNIT OBJECTIVES

Objectives 1–7 can be met by studying Chapter 22 and viewing "The Tightrope Walkers" and "The Investors." After completing this unit, the student should be able to:

1. Explain what determines the price of foreign currency to Americans.

2. Explain what determines the dollar's value in world currency markets.

3. Define balance of payments and distinguish it from balance of trade.

4. Be familiar with the effects on the U.S. money supply when the central bank buys dollars with foreign reserves.

5. Define currency crisis.

6. Know the difference between fixed and floating exchange systems.

7. Be familiar with the gold standard.

Objectives 8–13 can be met by studying Chapter 23. After reading this optional chapter, the student should be able to:

8. Know what net exports are and explain how they affect the equilibrium level of national income.

9. Understand the debates surrounding the creation of the IMF and know what changes have taken place in the international financial system since World War II.

10. Discuss the dollar shortage of the 50s and dollar surplus of the 60s.

11. Know what special drawing rights are.

12. Distinguish between "dirty" and "freely floating" exchange rates.

13. Discuss the effects of monetary policy under fixed and floating exchange rates.

SPECIAL INSTRUCTIONS

Both films of this unit relate to Chapter 22 "The Balance of Payments and Exchange Rates."

The Chapter Highlights, Fill-in Review and Problems, Problems, Problems . . . for "History and Problems of International Trade and Finance," Chapter 23, are included in this Unit, since some professors may choose to assign this chapter as a logical extension to the international trade section. For those students studying Chapter 23 the following objectives are included.

PART ONE AND PART TWO

UNIT XV ASSIGNMENT: PARTS ONE AND TWO

STUDY: Chapter 22, "The Balance of Payments and Exchange Rates," *Economics Today: The Macro View* (*Note:* This is Chapter 38 in the combined hardbound text, *Economics Today*.)

STUDY: Film Summary: "The Tightrope Walkers" and "The Investors," *Study Guide*

VIEW: "The Tightrope Walkers"

VIEW: "The Investors"

REVIEW: Chapter 22 Highlights, *Study Guide*

COMPLETE: Fill-in Review *and* Problems, Problems, Problems ..., *Study Guide*

NOTE

The film summaries for the programs in Unit XV are included in one Film Summary section.

FILM SUMMARY:
"The Tightrope Walkers" and "The Investors"

International finance is the subject of the two films of Unit XV. In "The Tightrope Walkers," Thomas, Karen and Larry Dutweiler fly to Rio Lindo to visit Enrique Diaz, who is now its president. In discussions with Diaz about Rio Lindo's purchases from Dynamics Corporation, the three recognize that Rio Lindo has experienced considerable economic development, some of it an outgrowth of American investments there. Rio Lindo now makes products that are in demand in international markets, strengthening the Rio Lindan peso. As it has industrialized, Rio Lindo has begun to manufacture some of the goods for itself that it formerly imported (some of them are from the Dynamics Corporation). The loss of this market distresses Thomas, who had expected Rio Lindo to trade with the U.S. out of loyal friendship because of the considerable amount of U.S. investment.

The realities of exchange rates, currency fluctuations and the international balance of payments are tough lessons for Thomas. He finds that prices of national currencies, as well as goods and services, are subject to supply and demand in international trade, and he gives up his notion that trade is based on something besides mutual benefits to the trading partners.

It is now time for a discussion of how international finance works to permit international trade. International trade differs from domestic trade in that different countries have different currencies that change in value relative to one another. With different currencies, however, each country is free to adopt the economic policies it considers most beneficial to itself. However, exchange of different currencies is necessary for trade between nations that use different money units. To understand how this is accomplished, we study how international currency markets operate and identify a balance of payments.

Let's begin by understanding that international trade is like any other kind of trade, except that first, one kind of money must be traded for another. People in foreign countries want to be paid in their own currencies. In order to buy goods from other countries, that country's currency must first be bought. All over the world, millions of American dollars are used daily to buy other currencies. With such money exchange we encounter the problems of balancing international payments and international finance.

We will proceed slowly through a subject which is complex but not actually that hard to understand. To use U.S. dollars to buy another currency, simply go to your bank. Whether or not your own bank carries deposits of many countries, it will have an arrangement with a large bank that allows it to buy foreign money. At your bank you will use your own dollars in exchange for a check drawn in the kind of foreign money needed. Your American bank owns the foreign currency (let's say German marks) which is deposited in its account in a German bank. The bank can write checks on its German account, just as you write checks on your own account.

So far so good, and not really very different from a domestic banking transaction. But what if the accounts get out of balance and American banks no longer have enough German marks in their accounts to cover what they want to withdraw? Next comes an agreement, by which German banks deposit more marks in our German accounts, while we, in turn, put more dollars in their U.S. accounts. Marks and dollars are exchanged constantly (at the same time we are exchanging currencies with all of our other trading partners). It often balances out, but when it does not, there are problems.

Let's consider what happens if the U.S. imports more than it sells abroad. In that case an imbalance is created, and foreign money we need for our purchases will soon be used up. In order to import more, we will either have to borrow or go into debt for our purchases. Every nation keeps an accounting record of international transactions, called its balance of payments. It is a record of the flows of goods, services and money between one country and all other countries. All the transactions between U.S. and foreign businesses, individuals and governments are added to show our international balance of payments of trade and financial dealings with the rest of the world.

Be sure not to confuse the balance of payments with the balance of trade. The balance of trade is concerned only with trade (goods and services), while the balance of payments includes flows of money, long-term investments and short-term capital movements, plus the balance of trade. Keep them separate in your mind by remembering that one is trade only and the other is payments as well as trade.

Now let's assume that from all the totals of international receipts and payments there is *not* an overall balance, but instead there is an overall deficit or surplus. How is it possible that international payments not be in balance? It cannot be out of balance. Payments for international transactions must be made up somehow. First, the overall deficit (or surplus) is calculated. Then, "official reserve transactions" are undertaken. These are accomplished by the central banks in each country in order to balance payments.

For example, if the U.S. balance of payments is in deficit, the people of the U.S. have been buying more from abroad than foreigners have been buying from the U.S. As a result, Americans will now supply more dollars in the foreign exchange market, and demand more of the foreign currency. The Fed will then correct this situation by using its reserves of foreign currency to buy up excess dollars. The currency purchase by the Fed is an official transaction, done in order to balance transaction totals. As your film narrator says, if one country imports more goods and services from another than it exports to that country, the imbalance must be compensated for by money flows. Therefore, the balance of payments always balance.

When currencies flow across national borders, they must be through exchange rate markets. A simple way of explaining the exchange rate is the amount of foreign money you can exchange for one unit of your own money. The need for exchanging one kind of money for another to participate in international trade complicates transactions; and as long as separate national economic systems exist it will be that way.

Exchange rates may be fixed or flexible, or countries may set their currencies to some type of gold standard. (A fixed exchange rate officially sets the price of a country's currency in terms of others.) Such a fixed exchange rate system for any currency must be maintained by the issuing government, since supply and demand do not establish its price. To prevent the exchange rate from depreciating (lowering in value) when, for example, there is a surplus of U.S. dollars in foreign exchange markets, the central bank must use foreign currency or gold to buy up the excess dollars to maintain the fixed rate. Since the Fed is putting in dollars, the effect is to lower the U.S. money supply. Recall from Unit XI, that lowering the money supply has important consequences for economic activity.

With a floating, or flexible exchange rate system, the world supply and demand for countries' currencies establish exchange rates. For example, when the supply of a country's currency in world markets increases, its supply curve shifts to the right, resulting in a lower exchange rate. When demand for a currency is high, the demand curve shifts, raising the price of the currency. There is a danger that speculation in a currency can actually destabilize a system. Because of this danger, floating exchange rate systems are managed by central banks which stabilize currencies because trade is out of equilibrium, or because inflation has changed the situation.

Under a gold standard, exchange rates are pegged to a specific quantity of gold, and currencies are convertible into gold. Increased gold in an economy thus raises prices and vice versa. An example here may help. Let's say country B has considerable inflation. It buys goods from country A. At any time, country A, which may hold large surpluses of nation B's money, may present it to B and demand it be converted to gold. Country B then experiences a foreign drain of gold. This outflow of gold lowers B's money supply and also its prices. Country A will experience a rise in its prices because of the increased money supply. (Notice how this process has "exported" country B's inflation abroad.)

As is mentioned in the film, "The Investors," the U.S. dollar was a troubled currency by 1968. So, in 1971, President Nixon suspended the convertibility of gold for dollars: the dollar balances held by foreign banks couldn't be exchanged for U.S. gold. Nixon also announced a wage-price freeze and, the U.S. dollar was revalued downward. The U.S. dollar was to float; exchange rates were to be loosened. (The dollar had been an overvalued currency, which helped to make U.S. goods more expensive in international trade.)

By now, you may agree that foreign trade is considerably complicated by the need to exchange one currency for another. The problems of financially equalizing the flows of goods and services among nations require a system that is flexible enough to change as economies change, yet stable enough to allow a smooth interchange of trade.

CHAPTER 22 HIGHLIGHTS

Defined words are underlined.

I. CHAPTER OVERVIEW: HOW IS INTERNATIONAL TRADE FINANCED?

International Trade: Movement of goods and services from one country to another.

  A. Three major international financial systems:

   1. Fixed exchange rates

   2. Floating (or flexible) exchange rates

   3. Gold standard

  B. How international flows of goods and payments for the goods are balanced:

   1. The balance of trade

   2. The balance of payments.

II. IN A FIXED EXCHANGE RATE SYSTEM, CENTRAL BANKS INTERVENE TO KEEP FOREIGN EXCHANGE RATES FIXED.

  A. Under this system, the price of the country's currency is fixed.

   1. Supply and demand no longer establish the currency's price.

   2. Government must maintain the fixed price.

  B. Since government does not allow the price to change by demand and supply, it must buy and sell currency on international exchange markets to maintain the fixed price. (We will use the U.S. dollar for a step-by-step example.)

1. If the fixed exchange rate for the U.S. dollar is higher than it would be with a floating system, there is an excess of dollars in foreign exchange markets.

2. Without government intervention, the exchange rate for the dollar would depreciate. *Depreciation:* Lowering of the value of a currency in foreign exchange markets.

3. To maintain its fixed rate, the central bank must use foreign currency or gold to buy up its own excess dollars.

4. When the central bank buys dollars with its foreign reserves, the exchange rate is stabilized, but the U.S. money supply is reduced.

   a. There is a contractionary effect on the U.S. money supply.

   b. Through expansionary open market operations, the central bank can increase the money supply to support the fixed exchange rate.

   c. Any country can eventually run out of the foreign currency needed to support the fixed price of its currency.

      1. *Currency Crisis:* Occurs when a country cannot support its currency in foreign exchange markets.

      2. Unilateral devaluation can follow a currency crisis.

      Devaluation: Official depreciation under fixed exchange rates. *Revaluation:* Official raising of a currency's value under fixed exchange rates.

C. Opponents of fixed exchange rates point out that many countries tried to keep the value of their currency from falling in the early 1970s by entering the exchange market and buying their currencies.

   1. Japan and European countries are examples.

   2. They offset the fall in their money supplies by expansionary open market operations, increasing their inflation rates.

III. Floating (or Flexible) Exchange Rates

Foreign Exchange Rate: The price of one currency in terms of another. (Example, if it takes $2.00 to buy one British pound, the exchange rate is $2.00.)

A. In a floating exchange rate system, foreign exchange rates are established by world supply and demand for countries' currencies.

1. The demand curve for a currency depends upon the demand for that country's goods, services and financial assets.

2. The demand curve for a country's currency is downward sloping: it follows the law of demand. (See Chapter Highlights for Chapter 4.)

3. The supply curve of a currency is upward sloping, since it follows the law of supply.

B. In general, a floating exchange rate system allows the laws of supply and demand for a country's currency to operate without interference.

1. When the demand for many of a country's products increases, the demand curve for that country's currency shifts to the right, raising the foreign exchange rate.

2. The supply of a country's currency is based on its expenditures abroad. When the supply of a country's currency increases on world exchange markets, its supply curve shifts to the right, lowering the foreign exchange rate.

C. The implementation of a floating system of exchange rates would, by definition, eliminate the country's balance of payments problems.

1. It would also reduce the incentive towards inflationary increases in the money supply.

2. There is historical evidence that floating exchange rates do reduce inflation rates.

CHAPTER 22 HIGHLIGHTS

IV. THE HYPOTHETICAL PURE GOLD STANDARD

    A. Exchange rates are fixed under the gold standard.

    B. Gold is the unit to which currencies are pegged.

        1. Gold is not necessarily the means of exchange, but money is convertible into gold.

        2. Nations agree to redeem their currency for a fixed amount of gold (upon request from any holder of that currency).

    C. An increase in a country's gold, and therefore the money supply, raises prices (in a full-employment economy); a decrease in gold lowers the money supply and lowers prices.

        1. A change in the money supply and prices within each country provides the adjustment mechanism.

        2. Adjustments are not made through the exchange rate.

        3. Each country absorbs the shocks of changes in international trade by adjusting its prices inside its own borders. This amounts to undergoing changes in real income through unemployment and price changes.

        4. No country's money supply can be protected from international balance-of-payments problems. (A country no longer has domestic control of its money supply.)

        5. No country would allow its internal economic affairs to be vulnerable to such internationally generated shocks.

V. THE REQUIREMENTS THAT THE PAYMENTS FOR INTERNATIONAL TRADE FLOWS BALANCE THE ACTUAL INTERNATIONAL FLOWS OF GOODS AND SERVICES

Balance of Trade: The difference between the value of exports and the value of imports.

Balance of Payments: All transactions both trade and financial between one nation and the rest of the world.

A. Under a flexible exchange rate system the balance of trade and the balance of payments are always in balance because of automatic adjustments in exchange rates. (The U.S. has not had a totally flexible exchange rate system.)

B. The balance of payments reflects the value of all international trade transactions.

   1. A deficit in the balance of payments means a country is buying more from abroad than it sells abroad.

   2. A deficit must be financed by flows of currency reserves abroad or by borrowing from abroad (by selling bonds, etc.)

If the fixed exchange rate for the U.S. dollar is higher than it would be with a floating system, there is *a shortage/an excess* of dollars in foreign exchange _____. In this situation, without government intervention the exchange rate for the dollar would lower in value or *depreciate/appreciate*. To maintain the fixed rate, the central bank must use foreign currency or ____ to buy up its own excess _____. The central bank stabilizes the exchange rate by this procedure. However, by buying up dollars the bank has affected the U.S. money supply. The purchase has *a contractionary/an expansionary* effect on the U.S. money supply. The central bank can offset this effect through expansionary, open market operations. Critics of fixed exchange rates point out that in so doing central banks have *increased/decreased* the inflation rate of their economies.

an excess

markets

depreciate

gold
dollars

a contractionary

increased

Foreign exchange rates are established by world supply and demand for currencies in a *floating (flexible)/fixed* rate system.

floating (flexible)

In a floating (flexible) rate system, foreign exchange rates are established by world _____ and _____ for countries' currencies. A floating exchange rate system would

supply   demand

eliminate	<u>*eliminate*</u>/<u>*create*</u> balance of payments problems. (Nations may avoid such a system because of other, international problems created.)
gold	Under a gold standard, exchange rates are fixed, or pegged to ____. Nations agree to redeem their currency for a fixed amount of gold. An increase in a country's gold raises the
supply	money ____ and therefore raises prices. A
lowers	decrease in gold *raises*/*lowers* prices. Each country absorbs the shocks of changes in in-
trade	ternational ____ by adjusting its prices inside its own borders. This will change real
income	____ through an adjustment process of
changes	price changes and employment ____.
exchange rates	Under a completely flexible exchange rate system, the balance of trade and the balance of payments are always balanced because of automatic adjustments in ____ ____. The difference between the value of exports and the value of imports is called the
balance of trade	____ __ ____. The total of all transactions between two nations for a period of a
balance of payments	year is called the ____ __ ____.

PROBLEMS, PROBLEMS, PROBLEMS . . .

Answers are at the end of this unit.

TRUE-FALSE

Circle either "T" or "F" for each statement.

T **(F)** 1. International supply and demand for its currency establish exchange rates for a country with a fixed exchange rate system.

(T) F 2. A currency crisis occurs when a country cannot support its currency in foreign exchange markets.

T **(F)** 3. There is no effect on the U.S. money supply when the central bank buys its own dollars with foreign reserves.

(T) F 4. Devaluation is an official depreciation under fixed exchange rates.

(T) F 5. A foreign exchange rate is the price of one currency in terms of the other.

T **(F)** 6. In a flexible (floating) exchange rate system, governments do not allow their exchange rates for their currencies to vary.

(T) F 7. Under a gold standard, exchange rates are fixed.

(T) F 8. Under a gold standard, when a country loses gold its money supply goes down.

T **(F)** 9. With a gold standard, all international money adjustments are made through the exchange rate.

MATCH-UP

Match each item in the first column with a term in the second column. Use no term more than one.

__f__ 1. The major international financial systems

__d__ 2. In this system, central banks intervene to maintain exchange rates.

__b__ 3. Gold is not necessarily the means of exchange, but money is convertible into gold.

__a__ 4. Allows the laws of supply and demand for a country's currency to operate without interference

__c__ 5. All transactions between one nation and all foreign nations for a period of a year

__e__ 6. The difference between the value of exports and the value of imports

a. flexible (floating) exchange rates
b. gold standard
c. balance of payments
d. fixed exchange rate system
e. balance of trade
f. fixed exchange rate, flexible exchange rate, gold standard

MULTIPLE CHOICE

For each of the following statements, choose the one best alternative.

1. If a country with a flexible exchange rate system has a balance of payments deficit, the international price of its currency will
   a. stay the same.
   b. rise.
   (c.) fall.
   d. either rise or fall.

MULTIPLE CHOICE

2. If prices for goods in other countries increased while country A's prices did not, demand for country A's currency would

    a. stay the same.

    b. rise.

    c. fall.

    d. either rise or fall.

3. If a country under a pure gold standard ran a balance-of-payments deficit, then

    a. the money supply would be reduced as gold leaves the country.

    b. the money supply would increase as gold enters the country.

    c. the price of gold would increase.

    d. the price of gold would fall.

4. Each of the following is a major international financial system discussed in your *Study Guide, except* one. Choose that one.

    a. the gold standard

    b. the silver standard

    c. fixed exchange rates

    d. flexible exchange rates

5. If you decide to buy a foreign car, your purchase will

    a. decrease the supply of foreign exchange.

    b. increase the supply of foreign exchange.

    c. increase the demand for foreign exchange.

    d. decrease the demand for foreign exchange.

6. With a flexible exchange rate system, the exchange rate (or the dollar price of a foreign currency) will be determined by

    a. the exporting country's governmental policies.

    b. the world banks' monetary policies.

    c. the U.S. government.

    d. international supply and demand.

7. Under a pure gold standard, in theory
   a. an imbalance in the balance of payments could never be corrected.
   b. a country's money supply is tied to the amount of its international transactions.
   c. imports must always equal exports.
   d. two countries which maintain fixed exchange rates could never change.

8. A U.S. demand for a foreign exchange is a derived demand. That is, it is derived from a
   a. demand for U.S. goods.
   b. demand for foreign goods.
   c. supply of U.S. goods.
   d. supply of foreign goods.

9. A country's balance of payments is a statement of its
   a. balance of all sales and purchases of goods and services with the rest of the world.
   b. balance of all purely financial transactions with the rest of the world.
   c. balance of all of its dollar surpluses held in foreign central banks.
   d. balance of all trade and financial transactions with the rest of the world.

OPTIONAL

UNIT XV OPTIONAL ASSIGNMENT

For those students whose professors have assigned text Chapter 23

STUDY: Chapter 23, "History and Problems of International Trade and Finance," *Economics Today: The Macro View* (*Note:* this is Chapter 39 in the combined hardbound text, *Economics Today.*)

REVIEW: Chapter 23 Highlights, *Study Guide*

COMPLETE: Fill-in Review *and* Problems, Problems, Problems ..., *Study Guide*

CHAPTER 23 HIGHLIGHTS

Defined words are underlined.

I. OUTPUT EFFECTS OF FOREIGN TRADE: ADDING THE FOREIGN SECTOR TO THE SIMPLE KEYNESIAN MODEL

   A. Net Exports

   1. <u>Exports</u>: an outflow of goods and services which generate an inflow of income.

   2. Exports, therefore, increase aggregate demand.

   3. <u>Imports</u>: an inflow of goods and services which generate an outflow of income.

4. Imports, therefore, reduce aggregate demand.

5. Net exports are the difference between exports and imports; *i.e.,* Net X = exports−imports.

   a. If Net X is positive, we export more than we import.

   b. If Net X is negative, we import more than we export.

B. Deriving the equilibrium level of national income

1. Aggregate demand is now equal to C+I+G+Net X.

2. Equilibrium income obtains where the new aggregate demand schedule intersects the aggregate supply schedule.

3. The new export multiplier

   a. Net exports are considered autonomous.

   b. An injection of foreign income (an increase in exports) leads to a multiplied increase in domestic income.

   Example: If the MPC is .8 and exports increase by $100, income will rise by $500.

   c. Policy implications:

      1. An increase in the trade deficit (a fall in net X) would lead to a fall in income (assuming no inflation).

      2. This would result in unemployment.

C. Sectoral effects:

1. Changes in the trade balance affect employment in export and import sectors of the economy.

2. For example, if Japan is able to reduce the prices of its automobiles, American auto makers will lose business, and auto workers may be laid off.

II. THE INTERNATIONAL MONETARY FUND (IMF)

   A. Historical background; reasons for its establishment:

      1. Collapse of gold standard in 1930s

      2. Devastation of European economies during World War II; greater need for imported capital

      3. European countries running large deficits to the United States

      4. In 1944, representatives of capitalist countries met at Bretton Woods, New Hampshire, to create an international payments system.

   B. Initial institutional arrangements of the International Monetary Fund (IMF)

      1. Fixed exchange rates

      2. Limited obligation to lend to deficit countries

         a. Lending obligation:

            1. Each country was required to provide the IMF with reserves.

            2. The size of the reserve obligation was set by a reserve quota, determined on the basis of the size of the economy, its trade volume, and other related factors.

         b. Reserve quotas to be paid either in domestic currency or gold

         c. The IMF to lend money from the reserves to countries in balance-of-payments difficulties

            1. Each country could borrow up to 25 percent of its reserve quota automatically.

2. To borrow more than 25 percent of its reserve quota, the country had to meet conditions set by the IMF, such as using monetary or fiscal policies to reduce the deficit.

3. The maximum a country could borrow is twice its reserve quota.

C. Modification of the institution's structure: The Adjustable Peg

1. *Par* or *pegged exchange rates:* Currency values set by the IMF and deemed "appropriate" to market conditions.

    a. Exchange rates were allowed to fluctuate a set percentage above or below the par value.

    b. From 1944 to 1971, exchange rates were allowed to fluctuate 1 percent or below par value; from 1971 until 1973, by 2.25 percent.

2. If the exchange rate showed signs of rising or falling beyond the allowed percentage, the government would be required to buy or sell its currency in the international market in order to keep the exchange rate within the prescribed levels.

3. If the exchange rate consistently tended to vary from the par value, the IMF could reassess its "appropriate" value and change the par value.

III. THE UNITED STATES DEVELOPS A DEFICIT.

A. Until the late 1950s, many countries ran deficits with the United States.

1. There was a "dollar shortage."

2. Everyone wanted dollars to pay their debts to the U.S.

B. Beginning in the late 1950s, several countries developed surplusses with the United States.

1. Now there was a "dollar surplus."

2. The surplus was especially great relative to Germany and Japan.

C. *Special Drawing Rights (SDRs)*:

1. SDRs are created by the IMF; they do not come from the reserve quotas.

2. They enable deficit countries to borrow from surplus countries.

3. An amendment has given the U.S. and European countries power over loans of SDRs, making SDR loans voluntary.

IV. DWINDLING GOLD STOCK

A. Under the IMF, the United States was required to redeem dollars for gold at the price of $35 an ounce, effectively pegging exchange rates to gold.

B. As the U.S. developed a deficit, more and more foreigners demanded payment in gold.

C. From 1945 to 1970, our gold stock fell from $22 billion to $11 billion.

D. In the 1960s, the United States tried to convince other countries to accept American securities instead of gold. Most countries went along with this, but some (such as France) did not.

E. The Two-Tiered Gold System:

1. In 1968, the United States finally announced it would not sell gold to private individuals.

2. We still were committed to selling gold to central banks, however; hence, the term "Two-Tiered System."

F. In the early 1970s, the U.S. changed its official price of gold from $35 an ounce to $42.42.

G. At the same time, countries began to abandon fixed exchange rates for floating exchange rates.

1. Countries still bought and sold currency to stabilize their exchange rates or to prevent "disorderly" adjustments on the exchange market.

2. Because of this intervention, the exchange rate system was described as "dirty" rather than "freely floating."

V. Exchange Rates and Monetary Policy

A. Under a system of fixed exchange rates, the central bank buys or sells currency to keep the exchange rate at par.

B. Example: The value of the dollar is falling.

1. The Fed buys dollars with its foreign reserves.

2. This stabilizes the exchange rate, but also reduces the money supply.

3. The contractionary effect of the fall in the money supply could be offset by expansionary, open-market operations.

C. Opponents of fixed exchange rates point out that many countries tried to keep the value of their currency from falling in the early 1970s by entering the exchange market and buying their currencies.

1. Japan and European countries are examples.

2. They offset the fall in their money supplies by expansionary, open-market operations, increasing their inflation rates.

D. Implementation of floating systems of exchange rates would eliminate these countries' balance-of-payments problems.

E. The United States experience:

1. The institution of floating exchange rates led to a depreciation of the dollar.

2. This meant that our exports had to increase to pay for the same quantity of imports.

F. Floating exchange rates and oil prices

1. Under a fixed exchange rate system, the sudden increase in the volume of imports caused by the increase in oil prices in 1973, would have led to a series of currency crises.

2. Proponents of floating exchange rates believe that floating exchange rates allowed the international monetary system to survive this shock.

FILL-IN REVIEW

Select between the choices underlined or fill in the blank. Cover the answers until you have provided your own.

_____ are an outflow of goods and services which generate an inflow of income; imports are an _____ of goods and services which generate an _____ of income. ____	*Exports* *inflow* *outflow* *Net*

exports	_____ are the difference between exports and imports. Aggregate demand in the open economy consists of consumption, investment, government, and ___ _____, (Y=C + I + G + NET X).
net exports	
Equilibrium income	_____ _____ still obtains where aggregate demand equals aggregate supply. Since we assume net exports are autonomous, there is a new export _____, which measures the multiplied effect on income of a change in net exports. For example, if the MPC = .75 and net exports fall by 200, income will ___ by ___. Notice that a fall in net exports has a _____ effect on the economy. If the government wished to offset this fall in income, it could _____ government expenditures, or decrease _____.
multiplier	
fall 800	
contractionary	
increase	
taxes	
1944	When representatives of the capitalist countries met at Bretton Woods in _____, they faced two great challenges: financing the reconstruction of war-torn _____, and rebuilding an international monetary order. __ ___ _____, the British representative, wanted the United States, with its trade surplus, to lend funds to the deficit countries of Europe. The American representative, Harry White, disagreed. He didn't want to commit the Unit-
Europe	
J.	
M. Keynes	

ed States to financing Europe for years to come. The upshot was a compromise. The _____ _____ _____ was created and a _____ exchange rate system was established, while the IMF allowed for limited financing of deficit countries by _____ countries. Each country supplied either currency or sold to the IMF according to its reserve _____. The IMF would lend these reserves out to countries with balance-of-payments difficulties. A country could borrow _____ of its reserve quota automatically; anything more than this percentage would be _____ on efforts by the country to reduce its deficit. The maximum a country could borrow was _____ its reserve quota.

International Monetary Fund
fixed

surplus

quota

25%

conditional

twice

The _____ ____ financed European reconstruction; it was precisely what _____ had advocated at Bretton Woods.

Marshall Plan
Keynes

Exchange rates were set by an "_____ ____" system under the IMF. This means that the IMF set (or pegged) the exchange rate at some level, but that the rate was allowed to _____ by some percentage around this value. If the exchange rate changed by more than this percentage, the government would have to enter the exchange

adjustable peg

fluctuate

exchange	market to buy or sell its currency with an eye to keeping the _____ rate within the acceptable range. If, however, market forces kept pushing the exchange rate out of the acceptable range, the IMF could _____ the rate.
readjust	
deficits	Through the 1950s, most countries had _____ with the United States; there was a "dollar shortage." By the late 1950s, however, roles were reversed and some countries had surpluses with the U.S.; there was a "dollar _____." At this time, the U.S. wanted surplus countries to _____ deficit countries. _____ _____ _____ (_____) were designed to provide just such financing. SDRs, however, did not come out of the reserve quotas, but were _____ by the IMF. SDRs can now be vetoed by the U.S. or by some European countries. This means they are purely _____, and not automatic.
surplus	
finance	
Special Drawing Rights (SDRs)	
created	
voluntary	
gold	Under the Bretton Woods system, the United States redeemed dollars for _____ at $35 dollars an ounce. As our _____ grew, many foreigners demanded to be paid in gold. This _____ our gold reserves dramatically. Finally, in 1968, we made a "two-tier" system. This meant we would no longer sell gold to
deficit	
reduced	

_____, but we would sell to central _____. | *individuals*
banks

In the early 1970s, most countries abandoned fixed exchange rates. The world shifted to a _____ exchange rate system. This was a _____ floating system, because governments intervened to protect their currencies from abrupt changes in value. | *floating*
dirty

Under a fixed exchange rate system, the _____ _____ buys and sells currency on the market to stabilize the _____ ____. This causes the money supply to fluctuate (with painful consequences) domestically. In particular, it is argued that after countries have bought currency to support their exchange rates, in order to prevent domestic contraction, central banks have pursued _____ monetary policies which have increased _____. Opponents of fixed exchange rates argue that, by removing the balance of payments constraint, _____ exchange rates diminish the incentive for central banks to make _____ increases in the money supply. | *central bank*
exchange rate

expansionary
inflation

floating

inflationary

PROBLEMS, PROBLEMS, PROBLEMS...

Answers are at the end of this unit.

TRUE-FALSE

Circle either "T" or "F" for each statement.

T F 1. Exports are an inflow of goods and services which generate an outflow of income.

T F 2. NET X = export−imports.

T F 3. In an open economy, aggregate demand (Y) is equal to C+I+G+NET X.

T F 4. If the MPC = ⅓, and NET X increases by $500, income will fall by $1,500.

T F 5. The British representative at Bretton Woods was J. M. Keynes.

T F 6. Under the IMF, each country supplied funds to the IMF in accordance with its reserve quota.

T F 7. Countries could borrow as much as they wanted automatically from the IMF.

T F 8. The U.S. lent money to Europe after WW II with the Marshall Plan.

T F 9. Exchange rates are not allowed to fluctuate around their par value.

T F 10. If a par value can not be maintained, the IMF could change it.

T F 11. In the 1960s, there was a dollar shortage as the U.S. deficit grew.

T F 12. Special Drawing Rights (SDRs) can be vetoed by the U.S. or by some European countries.

MATCH-UP

Match each item in the first column with a term in the second column. Use no term more than once.

____ 1. Difference between exports and imports

____ 2. An outflow of goods and services which generate an inflow of income

____ 3. The amount by which a change in net export changes income

____ 4. Created at Bretton Woods in 1944

____ 5. Components of reserve quota payments to IMF

____ 6. Exchange rates under IMF

____ 7. Caused by U.S. surpluses up to the late 1950s

____ 8. Voluntary loans by members of IMF

____ 9. U.S. will sell gold only to central banks, not to individuals.

a. adjustable peg
b. net export multiplier
c. net export
d. "two-tier" system
e. exports
f. dollar shortage
g. IMF
h. SDRs
i. currency and gold

MULTIPLE CHOICE

For each of the following statements, choose the one best alternative.

1. Exports are
    a. an inflow of goods and services that generates an inflow of income.
    b. an inflow of goods and services that generates an outflow of income.
    c. an outflow of goods and services that generates an outflow of income.
    d. an outflow of goods and services that generates an inflow of income.

2. Net exports equal
    a. imports minus exports.
    b. imports and exports plus tariffs.
    c. exports and imports.
    d. none of the above

3. If the MPC = .9 and net exports are autonomous, the net export multiplier is
    a. 10.
    b. 5.
    c. 4.
    d. 2.

4. Which of the following was *not* a major topic at the Bretton Woods Conference in 1944?
    a. financing post-war European construction
    b. the terms of peace to be offered Germany
    c. financing European deficits to the U.S.
    d. creating a new international monetary order

5. Which of the following was *not* true of the Bretton Woods Conference.

   a. It was held after the end of the first World War.

   b. J. M. Keynes was the British representative.

   c. Harry White was the U.S. representative.

   d. The IMF was created as a compromise solution.

6. Reserve quotas

   a. provided a means of financing post-war deficits.

   b. were the same size for all countries.

   c. were composed of only gold.

   d. had nothing to do with the size of the economy or its volume of trade.

7. Up to what percentage of its reserve quota could a country borrow automatically?

   a. 10 percent

   b. 25 percent

   c. 50 percent

   d. 75 percent

8. The Adjustable Peg System

   a. did not allow exchange rates to fluctuate at all.

   b. did not allow the par value to be changed for any reasons.

   c. allowed exchange rates to fluctuate by set percentages from the par value.

   d. forbade loans from the IMF to deficit countries.

9. Special Drawing Rights (SDRs)

   a. also provide a means of financing deficits with loans from surplus countries.

   b. were opposed by the U.S.

   c. were created by the world bank.

   d. are supplied by reserve quotas of member countries.

10. The U.S. gold stock

    a. increased while the U.S. ran a deficit in the 1960s.

    b. fell while the U.S. ran a deficit in the 1960s.

    c. increased from 1945 to 1970 by $20 billion.

    d. has remained constant since the war.

11. Today's floating exchange rate system is "dirty" because

    a. governments interfere with the operations of the market.

    b. it is a completely fixed system.

    c. members of the IMF disapprove of floating rates.

    d. governments cannot manage the floating rate.

ANSWERS TO STUDY QUESTIONS

PARTS ONE AND TWO

TRUE/FALSE
1. F 2. T 3. F 4. T 5. T 6. F 7. T 8. T 9. F

MATCH-UP
1. f 2. d 3. b 4. a 5. c 6. e

MULTIPLE CHOICE
1. c 2. b 3. a 4. b 5. c 6. d 7. b 8. b 9. d

OPTIONAL CHAPTER 23

TRUE/FALSE
1. F 2. T 3. T 4. F 5. T 6. T 7. F 8. T 9. F 10. T 11. F 12. T

MATCH-UP
1. c 2. e 3. b 4. g 5. i 6. a 7. f 8. h 9. d

MULTIPLE CHOICE
1. d 2. a 3. a 4. b 5. a 6. a 7. b 8. c 9. a 10. b 11. a

WHAT BUSINESSPERSONS READ

APPENDIX

The following is a sample list of popular newspapers and periodicals that are used by businesspersons and economists:

NEWSPAPERS

Most newspapers report selected economic news. Some that devote considerable depth to their coverage are: *The Wall Street Journal, The Washington Post, The New York Times,* and *The Christian Science Monitor.*

WEEKLY NEWS MAGAZINES

Time, Newsweek and *U.S. News & World Report*

BUSINESS PERIODICALS

Published weekly: *Business Week, The Economist, Barron's*

Published biweekly: *Forbes, Fortune*

Published monthly: *Nation's Business*

A brief general description of each source follows.

NEWSPAPERS

THE WALL STREET JOURNAL

The Wall Street Journal has become one of the leading national newspapers. Though a comprehensive business newspaper, its coverage is not limited to the business world. The "What's News" section on the front page offers a concise daily update on world affairs as well as developments in business and finance. (For more information see the WSJ's "Future Manager's Guide to *The Wall Street Journal*.")

Regular Economic Features

Weekly Special Reports:

"The Outlook" analyzes different aspects of the business environment (appears every Monday).

"Labor Letter" reviews and explains developments in the complicated world of labor relations (appears every Tuesday).

"Tax Report" clarifies some hazy aspects of the tax law (appears every Wednesday).

"Business Bulletin" features humorous facets of the business world (appears every Thursday).

"Washington Wire" keeps an eye on the politics, policies and legislation of the national capital (appears every Friday).

Feature Articles:

"Major Features" is a forum for points of view that differ from those of the editors.

"What's News" synopses of what are considered the most important business and financial events of the last 24 hours in the U.S. and the world.

THE WASHINGTON POST

The Washington Post is noted for its comprehensive coverage of the Washington governmental scene. The international section is thorough, although designed to be secondary to the coverage of domestic news. the editorials are well worth reading for their informed, clearly written commentary.

Regular Economic Features

"Business and Finance" is devoted entirely to business.

"Roundup" offers concise coverage of significant current business and economic developments.

"Wall Street Report" includes statistical summaries of the stock market with commentaries.

THE NEW YORK TIMES

The New York Times is a complete general newspaper with international as well as domestic coverage. A giant of a paper, *The Times* fully covers art, sports, theater, fashion and literature, as well as the business and political news.

Regular Economic Features

"Business Day" includes brief reports of topical business and economic news highlights.

"Currency Markets" features a daily update on exchange rates and gold prices.

"Foreign Stock Exchanges" reports on leading stocks in world markets.

THE CHRISTIAN SCIENCE MONITOR

The Monitor is a consistently objective newspaper. Coverage of international, domestic and business issues are broad, though not as detailed as in

The Times. The emphasis is more on appraisal and analysis of key issues. Economic news appears with other stories with the exception of a small financial section. There are no special business or economic sections.

MAGAZINES

TIME

Time gives particular emphasis to current political, social and economic issues. *Time* has the largest circulation of any news magazine in the U.S.— only *Newsweek* is a close rival.

Regular Economic Features

"Economy and Business" covers the major news in the U.S. and the rest of the world.

"World" covers the selected social and political events in the rest of the world.

NEWSWEEK

A major difference between *Newsweek* and *Time* is the style of writing.

Regular Economic Features

"Business" covers important current economic issues in the U.S.

"International" covers political and economic events around the world.

"National Affairs" emphasizes political and politically oriented economic news.

"The Columnists" is devoted to commentary on topical economic issues by well-known economists: Milton Friedman, Paul Samuelson and others.

U.S. NEWS & WORLD REPORT

U.S. News & World Report is an authoritative source of economics, politics and business news.

Regular Economic Features

"Finance Trends" reports on interest rates, treasury issues, Federal Reserve policy and credit controls.

"Managing Your Money" focuses on common problems of personal finance. These columns provide the student realistic exercises in applied economics.

"Newsletters" are messages from Washington and foreign capitals.

"News You Can Use In Your Personal Planning" features changes in items such as air fares, the price of silver, saving rates and veterans' benefits.

"Tax Rulings with Pocketbook Impact" features current developments in the individual income tax.

"U.S. Business" features business developments within the U.S. and includes a weekly index of business activity.

"What You Can And Cannot Do If You Own A Business" reviews recent court and government decisions that affect businesses.

"World Business" includes recent trends in business developments throughout the world.

THE ECONOMIST

Roughly the English equivalent of the United States' *U.S. News & World Report,* it concentrates on economic and political developments. The perspective is global, though special attention is centered on the Commonwealth nations and Europe.

Regular Economic Features

"Business This Week" summarizes the week's economic and business news from around the world.

"European Community" analyzes current political and economic news from the European economic community.

"Finance" provides a specialized review of developments in the international money markets, gold markets and eurodollar markets.

"World Business" discusses in-depth international investment opportunities, economic indicators and economic policy.

BUSINESS PERIODICALS

BUSINESS WEEK

Business Week contains concise, straight-forward, current articles; as well as graphs, charts and statistical tables that clarify the data covered.

Regular Economic Features

"Business Outlook" focuses on investment opportunities and trends affecting investment.

"Economic Diary" reports day-to-day fluctuations in economic activity and related economic indicators.

"Economics" deals with current economic problems and their affect on the economy.

"Finance" covers market trends, corporate finance, money and banking.

"Foreign Exchange Trader" updates the exchange rates of the leading industrial countries.

"Inside Wall Street" analyzes and reports on leading corporate stocks.

"In Business This Week" deals with major news events in economics, finance and marketing, using facts and figures extensively.

"International Business" surveys global business activity.

"Labor" reports and comments on labor wage rates and union activity.

BARRON'S

Barron's is a weekly review of business conditions which is widely read by stockbrokers and investment consultants. *Barron's* articles in investment opportunities are highly influential.

Regular Economic Features

"The International Trader" reviews currency market and trends in international trade and finance.

"Investment News and Views" covers investment opportunities by respected investment counselors.

"The Market Week" offers complete statistical coverage of the stock market over the past week.

"Monthly Scoreboard" is featured the first week of the month. This review of business activity over the previous four weeks includes statistics and commentary.

"The Week in Charts" is an easy-to-read set of graphs describing the economy's performance during the week.

FORBES

Forbes emphasizes business investment. It is intended for both the specialist as well as the lay reader interested in keeping pace with changing investment opportunities.

Regular Economic Features

"Companies" covers recent developments in the corporate sector, including personal profiles and candid business case histories.

"The Cover Story" includes issues chosen as cover features that touch a wide spectrum of current economic issues; this feature is the core of each issue.

"The Economy" supplies both theoretical and applied economics of inflation, unemployment, business cycles, and other dynamic elements of the economy.

"Statistical Spotlight" deals with economics, finance and the marketing data behind business news.

FORTUNE

Fortune features in-depth articles on business and general economic and investment topics. *Fortune* uses clear and colorful graphs, charts and illustrations.

Regular Economic Features

"Business Round-Up" emphasizes current business issues, suggesting possible outcomes.

"The Editor's Desk" analyzes and provides editorial comment on economic or economically oriented social or political issues.

"In The News" is a survey of predominantly economic news in the U.S. as well as the rest of the world.

NATION'S BUSINESS

Nation's Business is a monthly review of American business for executives.

Regular Economic Features

"Outlook" offers a comprehensive review of developments in different sectors of the economy.

"People in Business" features profiles of successful businesspersons.

"Washington Letter" is an update of political and legal developments from a business perspective.

82 83 84 85 86 9 8 7 6 5 4 3 2 1